The Ground Between

ANTHROPOLOGISTS ENGAGE PHILOSOPHY VEENA DAS,

MICHAEL JACKSON, ARTHUR KLEINMAN, BHRIGUPATI SINGH, EDITORS

Duke University Press ▪ *Durham and London* ▪ 2014

Typeset in Chaparral Pro by
Westchester Book Group

"Ethnography in the Way of Theory"
© João Biehl.

Library of Congress Cataloging-in-Publication Data
The ground between : anthropologists engage philosophy /
edited by Veena Das, Michael Jackson, Arthur Kleinman,
and Bhrigupati Singh.
pages cm
Includes bibliographical references and index.
ISBN 978-0-8223-5707-0 (cloth : alk. paper)
ISBN 978-0-8223-5718-6 (pbk. : alk. paper)
1. Anthropology—Philosophy. I. Das, Veena.
II. Jackson, Michael, 1940– III. Kleinman, Arthur.
IV. Singh, Bhrigupati.
GN33.G76 2014
301.01—dc23   2013042778

CONTENTS

■ This book is the result of collective energies and conversations that have remained ongoing over years, sometimes decades, between friends, colleagues, and collaborators. The idea for this book emerged in the course of animated conversations in Cambridge and Baltimore, and perhaps it bears the imprint of these two institutional locations, although our hope is that the kind of exploration we have undertaken here might extend much further.

Our first thanks go to the authors and contributors of this volume, for the enthusiasm with which they embraced this project and found it to express thoughts that they had been mulling over for years. The preparatory workshop for this volume was held as the W. H. R. Rivers Symposium at Harvard University and was made possible by the Michael Crichton Fund of the Department of Global Health and Social Medicine at Harvard Medical School. We want to express our gratitude to Marilyn Goodrich and Michele Albanese for their help in coordinating the Rivers Symposium, and to Melody Walker for helping with innumerable logistical issues throughout the production process. Two of the participants in our symposium, Naveeda Khan and Charlie Hallisey, were unable to submit their essays for this volume because of other deadlines and compulsions, and we keenly feel the loss that their thoughts would have brought to this endeavor. We are also grateful to Byron Good and Janet Gyatso for their participation in the workshop and for the thoughts they shared with us.

We would also like to thank our two anonymous reviewers at Duke University Press for their advice on revisions, particularly for the introduction to the volume; Elizabeth Ault and Jessica Ryan at Duke University Press for editorial help; and our editor, Ken Wissoker, for his valuable inputs. Last, we thank Andrew Brandel profusely for his efforts, spurred by his intellectual curiosity and sympathy for this project, in helping to bring this volume together at the final stages of its submission. We hope that this book will speak to students like him and to future interlocutors, many of whom we may never meet, who come to value anthropological and philosophical investigations as distinct but related ways of engaging the world.

Experiments between Anthropology and Philosophy:

Affinities and Antagonisms

Veena Das, Michael Jackson, Arthur Kleinman,

and Bhrigupati Singh

■ The guiding inspiration of this book is to explore the attraction and the distance that mark the relation between anthropology and philosophy. How are the dividing lines drawn between these modes of inquiry? Or, to pose the same question differently: What constitutes a philosophical undercurrent or moment in the practice of those who do not claim to be professional philosophers? In his influential "Questions in Geography," Michel Foucault (1980b: 66) wrote with a hint of impatience, "And for all that I might like to say that I am not a philosopher, nonetheless if my concern is with truth I am still a philosopher." For its part, anthropology, with its multiple origins and manifold subfields, has maintained a comparably uneasy relation of distance from and affinity with philosophy. In France Durkheim wanted to establish sociology as a discipline within philosophy, and in India the earliest departments of sociology grew out of social philosophy—yet an engagement between these two disciplines is neither easy nor assured. It is not that philosophers and anthropologists do not engage common issues. For instance, an abiding concern in both disciplines is an engagement with the limits of the human. In most cases, though, philosophers turn to thought experiments about these limits, and descriptions of actual human societies and their diversity are bracketed on the grounds that empirical data cannot solve conceptual questions. Anthropologists from different subfields and styles of thought would measure their distance from and affinity to philosophy very differently. Perhaps one should turn, then, not to philosophy and anthropology as two fully constituted disciplines but to their encounters in the singular and see if there is something to be learned from these encounters.[1]

With such a project in mind, in April 2011 the four editors of this volume invited twelve anthropologists to reflect on their own mode of engagement with philosophy. Our aims were modest. We were not trying to stage an interdisciplinary dialogue between anthropologists and philosophers, though this might emerge in an anthropologist's struggle with a specific problem. Our questions were simple and posed in specific terms: What kinds of questions or pressures have made you turn to a particular philosopher? What philosophical traditions (whether from West or East, North or South) do you find yourself responding to? We wanted to investigate specifically what anthropologists sought in these encounters, what concepts liberated thought, what wounded them, and how this engagement with a particular region of philosophy changed their own anthropological thinking. That said, to measure the different contours of this relationship in anything resembling its entirety would be an encyclopedic endeavor. Our aim was not to cover all or even most anthropological and philosophical traditions. Rather we asked a small number of scholars to reflect on their practice, in the hope that this would yield interesting ways of looking at the relation that anthropology bears to philosophy through singular encounters. Singularity does not, of course, exclude multiplicity; rather, as Lévi-Strauss (1971: 626) uses the term in connection with his study of myths, *singularity* is the nodal point of past, present, and possible events, the intersection where phenomena become manifest, originating from countless contexts, knowable and unknowable. In this sense, the particular scholars stand for themselves but are also treated as "intersection points," where the contested nature of anthropological knowledge becomes visible. Our relation to the particular scholar, then, is both personal and impersonal, as singular trajectories that also express genealogies of thought.

We want to emphasize that we were not looking to philosophy to provide "theory," as if anthropology were somehow lacking this impulse. We were asking these scholars what is specific in their anthropology that attracts them to some regions of philosophy within the context and course of concrete projects of research and thought. The results of this exercise were surprising, first, as to which philosophers were found to be most attractive as interlocutors and, second, for the passionate engagement with particular texts these anthropologists read in relationship to their ethnography. As such, it seems that for philosophy to have value in our world, it must learn to respond to the puzzles and pressures that an ethnographic engagement with the world brings to light. What we present in this chapter is a set of questions and puzzles that we hope will stimulate further reflections on what kind of place particular philosophers might have or have had in the making of anthropological knowledge.

As a starting point, we could perhaps accept that the philosopher's anthropology and the anthropologist's philosophy may mutually illuminate on some occasions but that it is also the friction between them that allows us to walk on our respective paths. A rush to theorize the relation between anthropology and philosophy in general terms has often led to vacuous generalizations that we want to avoid. Instead we suggest that this is a moment in which we might ask, What puzzles anthropologists and how does that relate to the puzzles in philosophy? Then the urgent issue is not to find solutions to our puzzles but to accept that to arrive at the right questions would be achievement enough.

The rest of this chapter is organized as follows. We first ask how anthropologists have rendered the problem of otherness not simply as a matter of cultural difference but as putting their own worlds into jeopardy. Is the matter of difference resolved by a strategy of overlooking the question of truth and reinterpreting what might be "true statements" in the world of one's respondents as "symbolic statements" in order to make them commensurate with our worlds? We then relate these questions to the many-worlds problem in philosophy and propose, as many of our contributors imply, that there can be no clear division between how one relates to the being of others and the modes through which we come to know the other.

Second, we take some pressing questions that have emerged anew in anthropology with regard to ethics and politics: Are there overarching transcendental concepts that anchor these fields, such as "obligation," "freedom," and "sovereignty"? In the case of ethics we propose that a closer look at habit as the site of both repetition and newness through an attunement to the world offers a different way to think of the relation between obligation and freedom than the stark opposition between these two modes that many recent works assume. Further, as the section on politics argues, rather than marking out a separate domain as that of "politics," the political frames many of the chapters that follow through the resonance of concepts of coercion and consent, belonging and falling out within collective habitation, as well as through an examination of myths and rituals of power and powerlessness.

Third, we ask, What is the image of thinking through the signal controversies on where thought is seen to reside? We focus on the figure of

Lévi-Strauss, whose debate with Sartre might be seen as an emblematic moment in which anthropology tried to wrest the claims of philosophical thinking on behalf of the "primitive" or "savage" mind. But has anthropology been able to learn from other forms of thought, such as that embodied in ritual or in the way that philosophers from other traditions, such as Islam, must render their philosophy as something other in the globalized world today?

Finally, we give a brief account of how these themes resonate in the following chapters, noting that the chapters cannot be neatly organized around one theme or another; rather it is the overlapping of these themes that makes up the rich tapestry of this book. Might it be that concerns common to philosophy and anthropology, such as those of asking what is it to be awakened to our existence within the context of life as it is lived, might be inhabited "differently" or inhabited "otherwise" in these two disciplines—much as how such terms as *confession, prophecy, world*, and *subject* were inherited from theology but made to mean otherwise in philosophy? We suggest that what is important in this book is the absence of settled positions with regard to the importance of "philosophical thinking" for anthropology or the perils of such thinking; rather it is in the course of our investigations or when we are in the grip of a situation that the questions we ask of philosophy arise.

WAYS OF WORLD MAKING

Is there one single neutral world that can serve as an arbitrator of difference so that the plurality of worlds can be rendered simply as different versions through which reality is represented? And if cultural differences are a matter not simply of different representations but of different assumptions about the being of, say, different kinds of humans or of gods and animals (Wittgenstein would call such differences noncriterial differences), then how is any communication across these worlds possible—a question that haunts Crapanzano's chapter. For many scholars (e.g., Descola 2006), these issues of difference cannot be uncoupled from questions about how we conceive nature as a universal category. They argue rightly that Western conceptions of "nature" as something that stands apart from culture provide only one model—but having made this very nice move, they make a quick jump from representations to ontologies. Descola, for example, argues through a thought experiment that because there are different kinds of bodies (e.g., human bodies, animal bodies) and different interiorities that can be subjected to different permutations and combinations, one ends up with different ontologies rather than simply different representations of the world. His basic premise is rooted in phenomenological understanding that uses the basic building blocks of bodies and intentionality. In this mode of thought the social is something added later to the mix—yet much of the analysis is based on such products of collective thinking (or imagination) as the repertoire of myths or shamanic practices. While all the authors of the chapters that follow are in implicit or explicit agreement that the social is not the ground of all being, the state of the human is seen as that of a "being-with," of a thrownness together; there is no originary moment or foundational contract from which human relationships (including those between the anthropologist and his or her respondents) emerge. It is striking that in a lot of anthropological writing within the so-called ontological turn, questions of skepticism within human life or of the sense of being fenced off from certain experiences that offer a horizon of possibility but cannot be fully grasped are simply made to disappear. While the step to critique the manner in which statements that are held to be true in one world and not in another are "domesticated" and made commensurate within anthropology by making them appear symbolic or metaphorical is an important step, we cannot assume that the "real" is transparent and available in collective forms of representations. One might argue instead that experience cannot be derived from collective representations and that vulnerability and fragility of context is built into human worlds, as is the experience of being fenced off from certain experiences of oneself and of another (see Biehl, Kleinman in this volume; Boeck 2005; Das 2007).

We take only one example here to illustrate what kinds of puzzles arise when we take the thought of there being a plurality of actual worlds seriously and not simply as an intellectual game. We might ask if ontologies are well made or badly made. We might ask which worlds are genuine and which are spurious. What happens when these worlds are brought within competing frames of reference? The philosopher Nelson Goodman famously argued that there are not many different versions of one real world but that there are different actual (as distinct from possible) worlds. In one reading of Goodman, one could say that he is pointing to the fact that any description of the world needs a frame of reference. For instance, within one frame of reference the sun never moves, while within another, the sun moves from the East to the West. But do the terms *sun* and *moves* mean the same thing in the two sentences? Goodman is not proposing a complete representational relativism but arguing that there is no neutral world with reference to which these claims can be adjudicated. Thus there is no way of aggregating pictures of the world described under different frames of reference to provide one composite picture. But neither is one entitled to say that no pressure is exerted among these different descriptions. But then, as he says, one never just stands outside as a judge would and asks, Which world is genuine and which is spurious? These questions arise because we are always thrown in the middle of worlds that are being made.

Goodman's contention that worlds are not so much found as made, and thus world making, as we know it, always starts from worlds that are *already at hand*, clearly has an appeal for anthropologists since he breaks from the usual oppositions between realism and constructivism without succumbing to any notion of a direct and unencumbered access to the real. We shall see that even when not directly addressed as a "many-worlds problem," the questions of how anthropological modes of knowing confront the issue of different presumptions under which worlds are made or remade, communication occurs or fails, and how people belong to a world or sometimes fall out of it give an urgency to the anthropologist's quest for making his or her experience of intimacy and alterity available for both anthropology and philosophy.

The difficulties of reality and the difficulties of philosophy inform each other within the anthropological text whether the scene is that of an ancient ritual (Puett in this volume) or the failure of care in modern medical and economic regimes (Biehl, Kleinman). Then the anthropologist's work may have in common with philosophy the task of bringing experience nearer to reality by generating concepts from life rather than taking them from abstract discussions and thought experiments and fitting them to the flow of experience. There is a very interesting tension that runs through the volume on whether philosophy answers or can answer to our needs of being responsive to the worlds we encounter. While no straightforward answer does or can emerge, the pressures put by the anthropologists gathered here on the specific philosophers they engage with shows which paths of engagement might remain open. We imagine that no anthropologist would be comfortable today with Husserl's (1970: 16) contention that "European humanity bears within itself an absolute idea, rather than being merely an empirical anthropological type like 'China' or 'India.'" And yet, as Fischer and Puett both note in their chapters, there is a great difficulty in inheriting the modes of thought from other philosophies unless what we define as philosophy is itself put under question.

Recently Didier Fassin (2012) proposed the term *moral anthropology* to explain how moral questions are embedded in the substance of the social. Fassin draws attention to the differences in the Kantian genealogy through Durkheim, where the emphasis is on social norms and obligation, and an Aristotelian legacy, with its emphasis on virtue ethics. (In addition to Fassin 2012, see also Faubion 2006; Jackson 2004; Kleinman 2006; Laidlaw 2002; Lambek 2010.) An interesting tension marks those who think that the biggest obstacle to the emergence of an anthropology of ethics was Durkheim's Kantian legacy that reduced the understanding of ethics to that of following the moral codes of a given society, resurrecting the difference between the moral and the ethical.[2] However, the view of obligation is somewhat simplistic in these discussions as they do not take into account the rich philosophical literature following Wittgenstein on the gap between the formulation of rules and how they are followed. We get a much more complex picture of the interplay between obligation, coercion, and desire in the following chapters, as in the way that Das contrasts the two poles of action and expression, linking it to Austin's (1962) formulation of the illocutionary force of words, which Das, following Stanley Cavell (1996, 2005a, 2005b, 2005c), links to the order of law and perlocutionary force, which is then linked to the disorders of desire or, in Hage's chapter, that deepens our understanding of habit and dispositions as forms of attunement to the world.

Instead of assuming that the opposite of freedom is a slavish obedience to custom, a more sustained philosophical and ethnographic reflection on *habit* takes this category not as mere residue of repetition but as an intermediary within which two poles of the human subject—activity and passivity—are put into play. The notion of habit actually loosens the contrast between morality seen as submission to social obligation and ethics seen as exercise of freedom. In different forms this concern appears in a number of essays in this volume in which the mechanical aspects of repetition are countered by reference to the fragility of the everyday (Das, Han, Jackson), on the one hand, and the experiments with language and ritual that generate concepts from within the everyday, on the other (Singh, Puett). In anthropology Bourdieu ([1980] 1990) is credited with bringing back concepts of habit and practice to counter the overemphasis on cognition alone. However, Bourdieu inherits a particular lineage of thought, as Hage's chapter shows with the wonderful metaphor of "overhearing"

Bourdieu's philosophers. Thus he interprets Bourdieu's *habitus* as the principle behind the accumulation of being in the form of social or practical efficacy. He asks how it is that human beings, by repetitively engaging in or mimicking the behavior of people, animals, and even certain objects around them, end up being more than just automatons and develop a creative "generative" capacity out of what Aristotle called the "sedimentation" of previous experiences. In effect what is being proposed is a refutation of the easy opposition between obligation and freedom, bringing to light the double nature of habit as what Ravaisson (2009) called grace and addiction.

CONCEPTS OF THE POLITICAL

Anthropologists have long contested teleological accounts of modernity and politics, and yet the history of the discipline itself is often narrated in teleological terms as, for instance, moving from the study of "stateless" societies to postcolonial "new states" and thereafter to a "globalizing" present. Parallel to changes in political formations appears the narrative of anthropology as a succession of "isms," which risk assuming an equation of the old with the outmoded and thus of suppressing the multiplicity of a thought through false unities. For instance, in his chapter Singh argues that the term *poststructuralism* brings together sharply divergent, even opposing philosophical genealogies into a seeming unity.

We suggest that considering the attractions to and repulsions from particular philosophical figures and concepts might provide a different, nonteleological rendering of how the category of the political has been formulated in anthropology, provided we eschew a "before" and "after." For instance, it would vastly oversimplify matters if we were to render Marx's influence on political anthropology in terms of a unified school called Marxist anthropology rather than in terms of a multiplicity of tensions (see, e.g., Roseberry 1997). Concepts or moral imperatives from a particular philosopher's oeuvre might take new forms, even after the historical moment of that philosopher is supposedly over.

Another way into these questions is to ask how and when specific ideas, such as the concept of sovereignty derived from political philosophy, implicitly leave their tracks within anthropological thought, even when philosophy is disavowed. Consider the example of an antagonism but also a subterranean affinity to philosophy in a classic anthropological text, *African Political Systems* by Fortes and Evans-Pritchard (1940), renowned for its sharp disavowal of Western political philosophy and the inauguration, in some ways, of political anthropology. Radcliffe-Brown (1940: xxiii) begins his preface to the volume by undermining the idea of Europe as the bearer of ideal political norms and criticizing the notion of a state as having a unified will, "over and above the human individuals who make up a society," which is, he argues, "a fiction of the philosophers."

Comparably, Fortes and Evans-Pritchard's (1940: 4) introduction to their work offers a sharp negation of philosophy: "We have not found that the theories of political philosophers have helped us to understand the societies we have studied and we consider them of little scientific value." Turning to the well-known distinction in moral philosophy between the *ought* and the *is*, Fortes and Evans-Pritchard further argue that "political philosophy has chiefly concerned itself with how men *ought* to live and what form of government they *ought* to have, rather than with what *are* their political habits and institutions" (emphasis in original).

Toward the end of his preface, however, Radcliffe-Brown (1940: xxiii) must set out his own positive definition of what constitutes politics, and the definition he offers implicitly rehabilitates the very concept of sovereignty that he had seemingly rejected: "The political organization of a society is that aspect of the total organization which is concerned with the control and regulation of the use of physical force." Similarly when Fortes and Evans-Pritchard (1940: 14) have to summarize the conceptual heart of the book, namely the difference between the two kinds of political systems they encountered—one in which order was maintained through a balance of power in "segmentary" systems of intersecting lineage and territorial units and one in which control is exercised through centralizing political institutions such as a ruling chief—they turn back to the language of philosophers: "In societies of Group B there is no association, class or segment which has a dominant place in the political structure through the command of greater organized force. . . . In the language of political philosophy, there is no individual or group in which sovereignty can be said to rest."

This is not to say that *African Political Systems* is "secretly" a book of philosophy or simply "applies" a pregiven concept. The richness of the book reveals that there are indeed facets of the world that anthropological inquiry illuminates that cannot be gained even by the most sophisticated philosophical speculation, for example, the dynamics of power in these two systems and the conceptual move to recognize them as systems and not simply as "prepolitical" entities at the doorstep of modernity, as well as the sharp critique of the ways these political systems were being reshaped by the coercive power of European colonial rule. In this sense it remains important to preserve the separateness of anthropology from philosophy, as Fortes and Evans-Pritchard contended, for no amount of philosophical gymnastics and thought experiments would have disclosed the deformation of these worlds.

At the same time, we sense the book's affinity to political philosophy. Even in its proclaimed disavowal of philosophy, *African Political Systems* inhabits, perhaps as its core issue, the constitution and reconstitution of sovereignty, which has returned as one of the central questions of political anthropology at present.[3] The promise of "the political" in anthropology, it seems to us, is that while there may be certain continuities in the questions that are asked (and the overlap of these questions with philosophy), such as an interest in the myriad forms that relations of authority and of cohabitation may take (whether through obligation, by physical or ideological force, through relations of kinship or territory, or through more deterritorialized forms of exchange), the specific shape that these ideas take is unpredictable, in the sense that the old may unexpectedly reappear as the new, for instance in rituals and symbols (Geertz 1980; Kertzer 1988), fetishes (Taussig 1997), and forms of illegibility (Das and Poole 2004) and theodicy (Herzfeld 1992) that anthropologists have variously found animating the modern state.

The political in the chapters that follow might not be signaled as such, but it provides the frame within which we can understand the particularity of the descriptions. Consider Puett's chapter, which takes up a ritual of the transfer of sovereignty performed by a son following the death of his father, the ruler, through a series of what appear to be role reversals. Anthropological analysis, Puett contends, has often taken a "distancing" stance from the ritual it describes. He then daringly suggests that ritual theory here is as self-aware as we take modern philosophy or anthropology to be. It operates by assuming the conditions of its own "ultimate failure" and of a tragic disjuncture between the ritual and the dangerous energies that traverse the world outside of the ritual. The ritual works, then, by understanding its finitude and the temporary interventions it makes within these conflicting energies. We might read Puett's essay as an invitation to translate this insight into other times and places, as a way of understanding the relation between ritual and politics and the play of life forces.

Moving from ritual to the political significance of myth, Singh rediscovers a seemingly arcane text by Georges Dumézil on Vedic and Roman mythology as suggesting a concept of sovereignty different from Agamben's (1998) and Schmitt's (1985). This concept, as Singh shows, names not simply an abstraction but specific forces of violence and welfare that an ethnographer may sense in everyday life, in the forms in which "power over life" is expressed. In a related but interestingly different mode, Das's essay illuminates a different region of the political within anthropology, taking up what she calls, citing Poe, "a series of mere household events" in the lives of the urban poor, such as getting a document or carrying gallons of water over hilly terrains perched precariously on a bicycle. It is through these events that the political is made to emerge.

In these senses, rather than offering a strict definition of "the political" within anthropology, the essays gesture toward a terrain that ranges from the explicitly philosophical to the implicit resonance of concepts of coercion and consent and collective habitation, to myths and rituals of power and powerlessness and the everyday as an uncanny and ordinary space of threats and possibilities.

WHAT IS THINKING? REVISITING LÉVI-STRAUSS

Among the chapters that follow we will find a lively debate on the conditions of possibility for a conversation between anthropology and philosophy, but the issue that was at the center of debate at one time—the difference between modern rational thought and primitive modes of thinking—does not arise here.[4] Instead what counts as thinking figures in many of the chapters that ask how ordinary life itself gives rise to puzzles we might call philosophical or how we might treat other forms in which thought is expressed as coeval with anthropological thinking. This is a different view of knowledge than the assumption that there are "theory moments" in anthropology that make it turn to philosophy. An earlier debate on a similar issue that came to a head in the three-cornered discussion between Lucien Lévy-Bruhl, Jean-Paul Sartre, and Claude Lévi-Strauss on the question of "primitive thought" is well worth revisiting here.

For Lévy-Bruhl ([1923] 1985: 93), primitive thinking, while "normal, complex and developed" in its own terms, departed from modern habits of thought by its blending of the actual world and the world beyond, for primitive experience of time, he thought, "resembled a subjective feeling of duration, not wholly unlike the durée described by Bergson." Bergson (1935) himself responded to this claim by providing instances of "primitive mentality" within our own modes of thought, especially with regard to the way we treat the relation between necessity and contingency with regard to illness, misfortune, and death.[5] Lévi-Strauss responded sharply to Lévy-Bruhl's ([1923] 1985) contention that whatever its complexity, primitive mentality cannot be said to possess "knowledge" or "thought" since it is only "felt and lived" and does not work with "ideas and concepts." This sharp distinction between cognition and affect had led Lévy-Bruhl to characterize primitive thought as "exclusively concrete." Beginning with this very starting point of the concrete, or sense perception, Lévi-Strauss claimed a science and a knowledge practice for the so-called savage mind, one that was not based on mystical or nonlogical causation. Such knowledge, Lévi-Strauss contended, is not only prompted by organic or economic needs but is cultivated as a mode of curiosity about the world. Is this mode of curiosity somehow lower that that of the scientist and the engineer?

In the second half of *The Savage Mind* Lévi-Strauss (1966) confronted Sartre's contention that the "highest" form of human reason is "dialectical historical consciousness." What was at stake here was the status of collective products of imagination such as myths as representations that are acceptable to multiple subjects simultaneously. As with savage thought, Lévi-Strauss (1966: 262) attempted to break down historical reasoning into some of its constituent elements, describing how, within this form of thought, principles of selection were arrived at in the nature of a chronological code and its accompanying principle of a "before" and an "after," classes of dates and periods standing in relations of differentiation to one another, and varying scales and levels such as national, biographical, or anecdotal history and so on. Having unpacked this form of reasoning, Lévi-Strauss asked a more "prelogical," affective question about historical consciousness: Why do we set such store by our archives, personal or public? Would the past disappear if we lost our archives? These are, after all, only objects or pieces of paper. In what ways are objects marked and valued and stored? Here Lévi-Strauss turned to a much discussed object in older anthropology, the Churinga and its sacred character. What impressed him was not only the formality of sacred ritual but also the affective tie between the participants in the ritual and the Churinga. He quotes an Australian ethnographer to stress this point: "The Northern Aranda clings to his native soil with every fibre of his being. . . . Today tears will come into his eyes when he mentions an ancestral home site which has been, sometimes unwittingly, desecrated by the white usurpers of his group territory. . . . Mountains and creeks and springs and water-holes are, to him, not merely interesting or beautiful scenic features. . . . they are the handiwork of ancestors. . . . The whole country-side is his living, age-old family tree" (Strethlow quoted in Lévi-Strauss 1966: 243).

Lévi-Strauss (1966: 244) understood these affects not as an expression of "prelogical" causation or a "lower" form of perception than historical reason but rather as telling us something about where historicity and modern archival practices themselves find their most genuine value: "Think of the value of Johann Sebastian Bach's signature to one who cannot hear a bar of his music without a quickening of his pulse . . . [or] . . . our conducted tours to Goethe's or Victor Hugo's house. . . . As in the case of the churinga, the main thing is not that the bed is the self-same one on which it is proved Van Gogh slept: all the visitor asks is to be shown it."

This affective relationship to knowledge practices and the claims made on behalf of primitive thought need to be understood in the context of the postwar period, when confidence in the superiority of European Enlightenment rationality had collapsed. The French philosopher Claude Imbert (2008, 2009) argues that Lévi-Strauss turns to anthropological knowledge as a mode of inhabitation in the world precisely in this scene of collapse. She considers three major constellations of ideas in Lévi-Strauss; first is the attempt to find a way out of the usual ideas of experience that assumed either transparency or an easy way to translate and make intelligible what one encounters in fieldwork. (See also Crapanzano and Caton in this volume.) Imbert points out that the two concepts of transformation and generativity in Lévi-Strauss were both mathematical concepts, aimed not so much to solve a mathematical puzzle as to go beyond the limits of a phenomenological first-order description of fact, form, and things.

The most important point Imbert makes, however, is on the undecipherable face paintings of the Caduveo women. In *The Ways of the Masks* Lévi-Strauss (1988) notes with astonishment that while generations of interpreters had been unable to decipher the face paintings of Caduveo women, the women themselves were able to render them graphically on the flat plane of the paper without the anatomical surface of the face. To Lévi-Strauss this meditation on the face as mask, with designs that are undecipherable to the anthropologist (as well as the missionaries who took these to be too beautiful to be anything other than the work of the devil), brings home the limit of anthropological knowledge. Imbert suggests that in the mutual acknowledgment of finitude, one might glimpse a relenting over the bitter observations on philosophy that he had made at the end of *The Naked Man* (1981).

Imbert invites us to go back to *Tristes Tropiques* and read it not as a reformist tract, as Geertz (1988) would have it, but as a meditation on survival. When, at the end of the book, in what might otherwise be an inscrutable statement, Lévi-Strauss ([1973] 1992) exclaims, "Yet, I exist," he declares his existence as a protest. For Imbert this "awakening" is not from the Cartesian dream of imagining whether I am alone in the world but from a nightmare, to henceforth honor the open credit of survival. One might still wonder at the infamous passages on the dirt and squalor of Asian towns in *Tristes Tropiques*, but at the end of the day, Imbert provides us with a powerful reformulation of the importance of the anthropological project to philosophy, when she states that Lévi-Strauss returned at the end of the European brutalities to revive not theoretical anthropology but the pursuit of a double place of experience and theory as an ongoing confrontation of fieldwork and its assumption of shared intelligibility. As Jocelyn Benoist (2003, 2008), the French philosopher of phenomenology, shows in several of his papers on Lévi-Strauss, although "explanation" in Lévi-Strauss always consists in showing an "arrangement," it constitutes finality without being finished. We can find freedom or *volonté*, says Benoist, at the level of the collective arrangement itself. Lévi-Strauss provides a very interesting figure through whom we can see several of the themes we have discussed: ethics as both adherence to collective codes and the exercise of freedom as well as a political critique of Enlightenment rationality in its denial of the rationality of other modes of thought.

THEMES AND VARIATIONS

It is not our intention to give a summary of each chapter; instead we offer some signposts by tracing how particular philosophers are addressed by the different authors and also what themes overlap in the chapters. First of all, let us ask: What is a particular essay's idea of itself, of its turn or return to philosophy? What image of writing and of reading animates these contributions? In an essay on Henry James's return to America, Cavell (2005a) invites us to think of James's image of writing as attesting to the possibility of the soil. But the divining of the secret of the garden that is not immediately visible can be made possible only by passing the lacerating hedge—as if, says Cavell, writing for James could not be done without touching blood. Or consider Emerson's (1844) extraordinary essay on experience in which the philosopher father's writing reveals itself as the grave in which the name of the dead son is buried and also the womb from which categories of a more diminutive stature (use, surface, dream) rather than the majestic ones of Kant (time, space) will emerge (Cavell 1995)—here philosophy is an attempt to bring experience nearer to reality.

A fascinatingly varied picture of when and why one would turn to philosophy emerges in the essays of this volume, as each author sustains a different kind of relation to philosophy. This relation seems to be shaped not by the kind of intellectual puzzles that might arise in a scholar's study as he reflects on how he (the masculine pronoun is deliberate) can prove that he is not alone in the world but rather through existential questions that arose in the course of fieldwork or in auto-ethnographic moments. The authors' ethnographic sensibilities might have been formed by a deep immersion in fieldwork (Das, Jackson, Caton, Han) or by events in their own lives; the labels we might put on them may be of auto-ethnography (Kleinman, Hage, Crapanzano), philosophical biography (Fischer, Puett), or attraction to a particular form of thought (Biehl, Singh, Fassin), but the tracks of texts that have been held in the hand, copied with great exactitude, and perhaps shut down in sudden moments of despair are all visible. For example, while reflecting on the opposite trajectories of two brothers in Sierra Leone, Jackson finds himself drifting into the philosophy of Sartre, thoughts coming unbidden to him and yet animated very specifically by the questions that the two brothers pose, to themselves and to Jackson, about success and failure, freedom and fate, life chances, and the different turns one may have taken. Kleinman opens long-forgotten exercise books in which, as a young man gripped with great uncertainty during a time of war, he used to copy edifying passages from the philosophical texts of Kant, Heidegger, Wittgenstein, and others. But he finds that none of these texts consoles or shows a path forward in the face of his massive loss in the death of his wife and longtime companion, Joan Kleinman. Caton returns to old ethnographic diaries and to questions of violence and mediation that have long interested him and experiments with rewriting part of his ethnography differently, spurred by Bergson's notion of duration but also in part because something in the events he described in *Yemen Chronicles* had remained resistant to his writing. Textures and tones in the writing of all the chapters are awash with pictures of what it is to do philosophy in relation to the work's idea of itself as, for instance, melancholic (Kleinman), pedagogic (Puett), containing the poisonous (Das, Han), the playful (Fischer, Singh), mutually constitutive (Biehl), re-membering (Caton, Jackson), abusive fidelity (Fassin, Hage), or as in the grip of a skeptical tempo (Crapanzano). Together the chapters give expression to certain conceptual puzzles but are also saturated with affects, which circulate in the mode of writing itself.

The originality of these essays lies not in a complete break from all earlier puzzles but rather in the deepening of some of the classic questions of anthropology and philosophy. For instance, a classic theme that explicitly emerges in many of the essays is the relation between concepts and life, or alternately, between experience and reflection, thought and being. Placed within a Kantian heritage of "philosophical anthropology," the issue might be stated as that of finding criteria for defining what it is to be fully human. As we know, discussions in contemporary philosophy and anthropology are wary of any recourse to foundational criteria, such as the appeal to transcendental reason, or criteria rooted in facts of biology or nature. Nonetheless most scholars, whether philosophers or anthropologists, are also wary of making the opposite error of assuming endless plasticity in the possibilities of the human body or human action. John McDowell (1994) made the important move of conceptually recasting our acquired habits as well as the larger work of culture as the acquisition of a "second nature" with some resonance with Durkheim's notion that society begins to appear as "sui generis" to the individual. McDowell's notion of the condition of the human as one of being in "second nature" that can even overcome "first nature" departs from Durkheim in that McDowell would include the capacity to reflect on and evaluate one's actions as part of this second nature.

From the anthropological perspective this formulation is important for the way it addresses the problem of "the myth of the given" in the construction of the human, but it is sparse on the work that needs to be done to understand how human beings move from "first nature" to "second nature." Nor does it take account of the work of scholars in the tradition of Canguilhem (1989, 1994), Foucault (2001) or Esposito (2008), who have problematized precisely the issue of how biology as first nature is to be accounted for in the making of the social. In that sense, many of the chapters in this volume do the hard work of showing in what manner biological norms and social relations are mutually constitutive, as also ways in which the natural and the social mutually absorb each other within a form of life. This is a major theme in Fassin's insightful essay as he delineates the distinction between "biopolitics" and "politics of life" in a gesture of what he calls abusive fidelity to Foucault. Exploring the trajectory of the relation between the biological and the social through the works of Canguilhem (1989, 1994) and Arendt ([1958] 1998, 1991), Fassin shows the opposite directions in which they take the problematic of the mutual inflection of biological and social norms. He then formulates the basic question underlying the politics of life as a tension between the abstract evaluation of life as sacred and the simultaneous indifference to the concrete inequalities that mark the conditions in which actual people live and the variable determinations of whose life is to be affirmed and who is allowed to "let die" (Foucault 2008) or even be killed.

Concern with biological norms enters in other chapters by other routes.[6] Kleinman discusses how a neurological disease such as Alzheimer's jeopardizes the security of relations that were taken for granted in states of health, creating a divided self in the caregiver. His essay is a profound meditation on what it is to acknowledge the claims made by the other, when one's own place in the world has become precarious. The essay is one of the best refutations of the notion that to be fully human is grounded in the concept of personhood, which, in turn, is seen to depend on the capacity to rationally evaluate one's first-order desires (Koo 2007). Instead Kleinman suggests that it is the ability to respond and to endure the baffling changes that a condition such as Alzheimer's brings about, and thus to treat the *other* as fully human, that marks the *human* in the caregiver. His definition of caregiving as a *practical* ritual of love aligns with William James's belief that a long acquaintance with particulars often makes us wiser than the possession of abstract formulas (cited in Kleinman).

Hage too offers a fascinating example of how a particular impairment might attune one to the world in a different way. Thus, when Hage lost his hearing, he lost what he called a "hearing reality," but on recovering his hearing through a transplant he did not simply recover this reality—he lost something too. What is this something that was lost? Here Hage makes an important point that goes even beyond Canguilhem's (1989) conception of disease as the capacity to set new norms for oneself more adequate to the loss one has borne. Instead Hage argues that when he regained some of his hearing back, his world gained the symbolic sharpness that had disappeared for him, but he lost the capacity to be immersed in the world in the mode of a certain "subliminal jouissance." Thus Hage offers us not only a fine-grained conceptual analysis of the genealogy of the concept of habitus and its relation to dispositions but also autographic reflections, which, like Kleinman's attention to his own divided self, become the ground for conceptual innovation. In this vein, we might read Biehl's ethnography as a different kind of investigation of impairment and the constitution and reconstitution of personhood as he attempts to recompose his main interlocuter, Catarina's words to constitute her person differently from the ways she is written and overwritten by abandonment and institutional regimes. We find a different form of Kleinman's divided self, what Biehl calls "the split of the I," in his conversations with Catarina. Even as he attempts to recompose this I Biehl asks how ethnographic writing may try to express incompleteness, a question for which he turns to Deleuze's concept of becoming, asking further what forms of *becoming* anthropology might express, in ways perhaps distinct from philosophy.

Das and Han too engage the question of the biological through its absorption in the social, but their ethnographic contexts differ from those of Kleinman, Hage, and Biehl, in that they are concerned not with individual impairment and its impact on the mode of being but with survival as a collectively addressed project of everyday life in lower-income urban neighborhoods. Thus both think of "need" as a call for ethical action, not charity or welfare (see also Han 2012). Both take up instances where the lines between ethics and politics begin to blur, as does the distinction between "self-interest" and an orientation toward others. Das and Han both privilege the quotidian as the place where ongoing political and ethical action takes place, and both show an insightful engagement with philosophical theories of performative action. Das finds that her ethnographic work offers one direction in which Austin's (1962) unfinished project on the perlocutionary force of words could be taken to see how action and expression are stitched together in performative utterances. She further discusses Cavell's (2005b) subtle critique of Austin through his formulation of "passionate utterances" and argues that ethnography reveals how we might see a better integration of action and expression in performative utterances.

Han's essay takes these themes further in pressuring philosophical reflection to bear on the seemingly habitual or mundane actions undertaken by the poor to attain or maintain a particular sense of dignity so as not to appear to be recipients of charity. While sympathetic to the critiques of humanitarianism and its underlying foundational assumptions about the sacredness of life, Han gives a beautiful reformulation of the problematic; as she puts it, it is not the common vulnerability of the human that is at stake but rather those points at which the vulnerability of the other becomes "mine to respond to." In offering her rich ethnography of how people devise ways of helping their neighbors so as to both acknowledge their state of precariousness and preserve their dignity, Han shows how philosophical theories of excuses and pretensions, as in Austin (1969a, 1969b), can be enriched much more through ethnography than Austin himself might have imagined, while also deepening and challenging classic anthropological ideas of the gift, and of giving and receiving, and contemporary debates on humanitarian aid.

Singh takes this discussion of giving and receiving in a different direction, asking if we may, on occasion, find the rigor of a philosophical concept in our ethnographic conversations. He encounters such a concept through the evocative ethnographic figure of Bansi Sahariya, a former bonded laborer, now a well-known ascetic in central India, known, among other things, for the large-scale village-level sacrificial potlatches that he organizes and oversees. In an extended ethnographic dialogue Singh draws out the conceptual depth of a crucial, albeit seemingly ordinary and habitual phrase in Bansi's lexicon, *lebo-debo* (give and take). Understanding this phrase in Bansi's terms requires a theory of sacrifice, sacrificial transactions, and ethical accounting and a discussion of how surplus capital is absorbed. Singh concludes, "Understanding Bansi's rise from a bonded laborer to a famous ascetic I realized that 'lebo-debo' was not just a throwaway phrase. It was a central concept in his lexicon, deeply attached to an understanding of life. Bonded and legitimate labor, power relations, marriage, sacrifice, kinship, intimacy, buying, selling, the very fabric of human relatedness depends on different understandings of the seemingly simple phrase 'give and take.'"

Putting these essays together, it seems that we could reformulate the issue of ethics as follows. A dominant mode of thinking of ethics is in terms of action that has public consequences and that stands apart from the habitual stream of practices. As we saw, for many philosophers, this capacity to evaluate and *reflect* is what defines personhood, which is then taken to be a fundamental premise of the claim to being fully human. An alternative genealogy of philosophical reflection (Wittgenstein [1958] 1973; Austin 1962; Cavell 1979; Laugier 2001; but other names could be evoked), on what it is to be human within practices that define one's participation in a form of life, contests such a view. Rather than a sharp contrast between moments of immersion in a lifeworld and moments of detachment at which practices are critiqued, philosophers within this lineage of thought consider agreement to be not agreements in opinions or deliberation but rather agreement in forms of *life*. It is not that philosophers in this lineage are assuming agreement or an automatic allegiance to one's culture as it stands; rather they understand that criticism is much more than an application of deliberative discourse or the capacity for detached reflection—for reason can turn demonic, or alternatively, the realm of everyday habits need not be unreflective or unresponsive to ethical impulses.

Some of the chapters in this volume (Das, Hage, Han) explicitly question the idea that habit is simple mechanical repetition, as discussed earlier. Others show how the world is critically constructed in moments of detachment, as in Biehl's example of Catarina's writing of words that might appear random or mundane unless one puts them in relation to her abandonment by her family and her experiences of the medical system, when they take on an uncanny critical force. Taking a different route, Jackson thinks of the relation between being and thought through the movements between immersion and detachment. He suggests that ethnography and philosophy might be rendered as corresponding to immersion and reflection, respectively. But Singh's chapter tries to unsettle what it is to think *critically* by emphasizing how habits of thought and reflection may themselves become ingrained into the flow of life, asking if we do not perhaps often confuse a particular mode of dialectical negation as thought itself. The richness of these tensions cannot move to an assured resolution, but in each case confronting these tensions creates more and better routes to understand anthropology's closeness and distance from philosophy.

In many of the other essays in this volume the theme of the relation between being and thinking, or the crafting of a world in which our moral aspirations can find expression and potential for action, is addressed in different registers. Following his thought on the double movement of immersion and detachment, Jackson continuously circles back to events that become deepened in his thought with each return. It is thus that he is able to think of the self not as a stable entity that endures through time but as the coming together of different potentialities—versions of the self that can be brought into being or discarded in the flow of life. Biehl too considers what it is to "return" to Catarina, as an anthropologist colleague challenges him to "put her to rest." He wonders if it would be acceptable (or what the objection might then become) if he thinks of his return to Catarina not as or not only as a return to an ethnographic interlocutor but also as a return to a conceptually generative presence, to whom one turns and returns, as one might, say, to Arendt or to Wittgenstein. Yet there is a subtle difference between Biehl's notion that "not letting go" is a gesture of fidelity and Das's, Crapanzano's, or Caton's idea that they, the anthropologists, were after all only fleeting presences in the lives of their interlocutors (despite almost lifelong engagements with them), whose separateness they accept as a condition of their being anthropologists.

We step back to the question we started with: How do philosophical concepts figure in the making of anthropological knowledge, and what constitutes philosophy for us nonphilosophers in this sense? And further: How might this question be tracked in the thinking and writing of particular anthropologists rather than in anthropology in general as a discipline? Here it is also important to pay close attention to the variation in tone and pitch of the essays in the volume. Consider Crapanzano's essay, which raises the famous philosophical question of the certainty and uncertainty regarding other minds and asks whether the social explanations we offer as part of fieldwork mask the opacity we feel about the other and about ourselves. Do the dialogues in the field, as in everyday life, have the character of shadow dialogues? At one point it looks as if Crapanzano is thinking not only of the situation of fieldwork but also of everyday life itself as a scene of trance and illusion, as a series of misreadings of the self and the other come to define the communicative milieu. However, he also thinks of social situations as consisting of other modes of knowing that come from being and working with each other. While Crapanzano cites Heidegger that it is in "concernful solicitude" that the other is proximally disclosed, he also faults Heidegger for sidestepping the subjectivity of the concrete other. It might be interesting to ask what pressures the desire for certainty exerts over our demand to know the other. What are the implications for anthropology of an open acknowledgment that the other (and by implication the self) is not transparent, and that even if the other were made of glass through and through we could not, or ought not, to be able to see into her? In different ways Caton and Das acknowledge that not only is their knowledge of the other incomplete but that this condition of fieldwork mirrors conditions of life in which, to use a phrase from Wittgenstein, "my spade is turned." As Crapanzano says, there is a difference between attitudinal knowledge and conceptual knowledge, between knowing about the other and knowing the other. In terms of a philosophical response to this impossibility of really knowing the other, Cavell's (1988) work, for instance, shows that it is not knowledge but *acknowledgment* that is often at stake in human relatedness, an acknowledgment that may itself remain uncertain.

A second theme that appears in many of the chapters is that of temporality and imagination. The defining question of Fischer's playful and provocative essay is how anthropology might be seen as a way of doing philosophy. Underlying his playful innovations, brought about by establishing a coevalness between different moments in time (his fieldwork in 1975 and 2004), different genres of writing (literary texts, anthropological dissertations, posters on walls), and the texture of different places, is the profound idea that a desire to find an uncontaminated or pure philosophical tradition (say, Islamic philosophy or Buddhist philosophy) is almost a denial of what time has done to these traditions. On the other hand, to read them in company with a constellation of other texts marshalling critical apparatuses of debate, placing them within pluralist civil politics, is closer to the picture of what it is to do philosophy with these traditions. Thus playing with what is distant and what is proximate, or with different constellations, Fischer offers us a different way in which philosophy might be inhabited across cultures. Theory for him is like a sudden ray of light, quite different from Jackson's idea of theory as returning to the same story in first, second, or third reflections, or Kleinman's and Das's notion of learning to occupy a space of devastation again. Fischer repeatedly evokes the notion of living in the fleeting and the fugitive and the aspiration for "actual life," and through such a lens he produces a picture of "doing anthropology" as a mode of "doing philosophy." His weaving of style and content into each other produces a stunning and original text. Yet a nagging question remains: Does the form of writing that Fischer employs allow us to master the apparatuses needed to address texts and forms of knowledge that have disappeared because they were not part of contemporary circulations? What other forms would fidelity to such texts within a framework that acknowledges their contemporary status and perhaps even their inevitable "modernity" entail? How could anthropology become a mode of doing philosophy such that it becomes the site on which these different philosophies might be enabled to converse, even as we acknowledge that their differences cannot be distilled into "pure" forms? Or is the desire for "actual life" an admission that the presence of such texts will inevitably become metaphorical for our intellectual concerns? What bearing does the idea of many worlds have for these issues?

Other chapters, especially Puett's, approach these issues from a different angle. Locating himself right within ritual theory from Chinese philosophy that offers a reflection on relations between fathers and sons, rulers and subjects, as well as the transience of time, Puett argues that anthropology has distilled ritual theory into its own categories (e.g., rituals of reversal), thus making theory emanating from other places into objects of study or philosophical speculation but not allowing it to challenge our own theories or taken-for-granted assumptions. In both anthropology and philosophy the import of non-European forms of thought is deflected by relegating them to a stable picture of tradition, broken up only by the destabilizing pressures of "modernity."

Thus premodern Chinese philosophy is routinely represented as an ontology of "harmonious monism," whereas Puett argues that the ritual he discusses takes for granted that the world is full of negative and conflicting energies and that ritual works to bring about small shifts through its own pedagogy. Similar conclusions can be drawn from Singh's remarkable analysis of the movement of deities and spirits that allows him to treat events in fieldwork as coeval with fragments of myth in the Sanskrit epics and with the concept of sovereignty in Dumézil (1988). Marshalling the Deleuzian concepts of thresholds, potencies, and intensities, Singh contends that these concepts are helpful inasmuch as they signal potential routes of ethnographic attentiveness but not as "theory moments" that can be applied to ethnography. Or, as Hage puts it in his incisive manner, a critical anthropology does not simply receive its questions from philosophy; nor does it take reality as already philosophically questioned.

We have left a discussion of Caton's essay to the last because it raises a deep question that goes to the heart of anthropological knowledge. In its most stark form the question might be posed as asking: Are anthropologists reliable narrators? After all, anthropological knowledge, as are all other forms of knowledge, is not only contained in the final book or chapter that is written; there are other things one writes—ethnographic diaries, letters from the field, personal memos. These are not, perhaps for any anthropologist, simply old "data" to be discarded. What relation do these writings have with what we end up producing as a book or a paper? Already in *Yemen Chronicle* (2005), Caton had experimented with time and memory. Now he asks: What impact does his recent engagement with Bergson ([1889] 1927, [1908] 1991, 2001) have on the kind of analysis and writing he did? Bergson's ideas of our being as immersed in multiple durations, that the past is not a succession of nows but that the whole of the past is virtually given at once, and that the real involves a complex relation between the potential, the actual, and the virtual, challenge the rendering of an event in terms of chronological time and orderly succession. Yet as Caton tries to imagine what it would be to write field notes not only in the mode of a recording of events as *told* by those who were eyewitnesses but also keeping in mind the multiple durations in which the actors are themselves immersed, doubts besiege him. He gives us an example of two rewritten (or reimagined) paragraphs that were taken from his ethnographic diary and reproduced in the book *Yemen Chronicle*. In these rewritten paragraphs he gives us an imaginative rendering of what supposedly went on in the mind of the sheikh who challenged the guardian of the boy with whom two girls from his family were alleged to have eloped. While earlier Caton had given us the meaning of the *gestures* that the sheikh produced, now he also gives us the rush of thoughts that might have been swirling in his mind. He then asks, Can such ethnography be written? What entitles the ethnographer to treat this other as if his thoughts were transparent to her? The issue circles back to the problematic of other minds.[7] Yet we think there is a subtle difference when this reading of other minds happens from some universalistic assumptions about how human beings think and feel and when it happens when the grammar of interactions within a lifeworld has been internalized by participation in everyday life. At its heart this can be read as a difference between ethnographic and philosophically speculative forms of knowing. After all, Caton produces these readings not from somewhere outside that lifeworld but from the impressions and potentia that circulate within it. Then we may say that Caton's argument hinges on the very important idea that it is consciousness that provides the ground of subjectivity and not specific psychological states at moments of action in the world. One might also add that the dilemma of other minds is not limited to the question of ethnographic knowing, but in many instances it is no different from the doubts that besiege us in everyday life. But we do manage to continue to live with possibilities of trust and betrayal, flashes of understanding and misunderstanding, not simply because we are pragmatic beings but because in navigating the many layered relations between the sheets of time, as Bergson would say, we accept our fallibility and the possibility of error. Caton's work is an important demonstration of how a philosophical thought might be absorbed in anthropology not as confirmation of our methods through which we read experience and subjectivity but as an interrogation of our mode of thought that goes far beyond issues of reflexivity and ethnographic authority.

This book, then, is about individual anthropologists wrestling with particular philosophers: we argue that to understand their puzzles is the best route to understanding anthropology's philosophy; it is not about a canonical tradition or "classics." There is no single tradition in philosophy that the anthropologists in our book are engaging. We are sure that another group of anthropologists would engage different philosophers and distinctive themes. It is the radical fragmentation that restrains us from attempting any synoptic or authoritative statement of the kind that assimilates all other experiences and traditions of knowing within a single magisterial "we" making the parochial appear as the universal. For us, it is our own era's human condition of multiplicity, diversity, and pluralism that shapes our own distinctive statement of a relationship between anthropology and philosophy that differs for each of us and invites our readers to experiment with their own engagement with particular philosophers and philosophical themes.

This is why this introduction to the book and the book itself are conceptualized as modest offerings on our part. It remains an open question for us as to what constitutes philosophy or a philosophical moment even within a practice that does not explicitly claim to be doing philosophy, whether in scholarly (or artistic or literary) domains or within the realm of everyday life. Even within a specific domain such as anthropology, we could name philosophical strands, affinities, and antagonisms that are underrepresented or absent from this volume. Perhaps it is a cause for hope rather than dismay that the potential for further discussion far exceeds what we actually offer here. We can only hope that others, within anthropology and perhaps in other disciplines, will continue and enrich the conversation that we have tried to initiate.

NOTES

1. We explicitly exclude from consideration the field of "philosophical anthropology" as it appears in German philosophers such as Kant and Heidegger since anthropology was for them a term for reflections on the question of the essence of man rather than an empirical inquiry into the differences among human societies. Similarly the examples of imaginary tribes in Wittgenstein were a device for allowing the voice of temptation to come into the text in order to show where the source of our confusion lay and had nothing to do with actually existing tribes.

2. The difference between the moral as located in the codes of the community and the ethical as constituted through social recognition has a complex history, but see especially Hegel (1952) and Habermas (1990).

3. For a useful summary of the "return" to sovereignty, see Hansen and Stepputat (2006).

4. The claim for the superiority of European thinking over other modes of thinking reappears, as in Levinas's (2001) comment that for all the claims made for primitive thinking it was left to a European to discover it.

5. Caton's chapter engages Bergson explicitly on the importance of his idea that the whole of consciousness is present at the moment of action rather than a single psychological state and its implication for ethnography.

6. Though a concern with life, nature, and biology occurs in most chapters, it would be misleading to place them within a "subfield" such as that of medical

anthropology, as if these concerns could be restricted to one or other subfield of anthropology.

7. Consider in this context Henry James's (1902) brilliant preface to *The Wings of the Dove*, in which he says that what he finds at the center of his work is the indirect representation of the main image—letting us get to know the central character by the ripples or storms it causes in others around her.

CHAPTER 1

Ajàlá's Heads: Reflections on Anthropology and Philosophy in a West African Setting

Michael Jackson

Dunia toge ma dunia; a toge le a dununia.
—Kuranko adage

■ In *Available Light: Anthropological Reflections on Philosophical Topics*, Clifford Geertz (2000: ix) observes that anthropology and philosophy share "an ambition to connect just about everything with everything else," leaving both disciplines unsure of their identity and constantly besieged by more specialized sciences that achieve better results by defining their focus and purviews more parsimoniously. Geertz's way of "narrowing the gap" between excessive generalization and overspecialization is to follow Wittgenstein's ([1958] 1973: 46e) exhortation to get ourselves off the "slippery ice where there is no friction and so in a certain sense the conditions are ideal, but also, just because of that, we are unable to walk," and to get back "to the rough ground" where our feet, and our thoughts, can gain some purchase. In brief, Geertz sees ethnographic fieldwork as a way of steering a course between the Scylla of empty theorizing and the Charybdis of not being able to see the woods for the trees. But what both Wittgenstein and Geertz seem to overlook is the *natural* tendency of human consciousness to oscillate between moments of complete absorption in an immediate situation and moments of detachment—when we stand back and take stock of what we are doing, how we are doing it, and why. This dialectic between engagement and disengagement is native to how we experience our being-in-the-world *before* it is consciously transformed into a scientific method of subjecting a hypothesis to empirical testing, or into the kind of disciplined and systematic reflection (the *vita contemplativa*) that characterizes the Western philosophical tradition. Scientific methods of induction and deduction also have pedestrian origins. People typically experience themselves as beings to whom life simply happens or feel that the world impresses itself upon their consciousness, disclosing hitherto invisible or underlying causes, motives, rules, or ordering principles. Just as typically, they experience themselves as viewing their lives from afar, as if their very existence could be made an object of contemplation. But neither of these modes of experience *necessarily* entails scientific methods or philosophical truths. They are simply alternating forms of consciousness, either of which may provide a fleeting and consoling sense that we may comprehend our relationship to the world. They echo a distinction that precedes the development of modern science and is recognized in all human societies: that we are creatures who suffer an existence we have not chosen, fated to exercise patience in the hope that we may, in the fullness of time or by the grace of God, be indemnified for our pains *and* that we are creators of our own lives, responsible for our actions, and capable of knowing and controlling with increasingly higher degrees of certainty the world in which we move.

Accordingly I construe philosophy not as a method for forming concepts but as a strategy for distancing ourselves from the world of immediate experience—social as well as sensory—in order to gain some kind of perspective or purchase on it. By contrast, ethnography is a strategy for close encounters and intersubjective engagements. Whereas ethnography demands immersion in a world of others or otherness, philosophy saves us from drowning by providing us with means of regaining our sense of comprehension, composure, and command in a world of confusing and confounding experience. As such, the turn to philosophy may be compared with the turn to analogy, whereby we grasp the familiar by way of the strange, or with narrative conventions of framing an account of reality by invoking a place and time distant from our own.

IN NORTHERN SIERRA LEONE

Translated literally, *Dunia toge ma dunia; a toge le a dununia* means "The name of the world is not world; its name is load." The Kuranko adage exploits oxymoron and pun (*dunia*, "world," and *dununia*, "load," are near homophones) to imply that the world is like a head-load, the weight of which depends *both* on the nature of the load *and* on the way one chooses to carry it. Such an attitude is suggestive of an existential view that human beings are never identical with the conditions that bear upon them; existence is a vital *relationship* with such conditions, and it is the character of this *relationship* that it is our task to fathom.[1] This view is also implied by the Kuranko word that most closely translates our words *custom* and *tradition*: *namui*. The word is from *na* (mother) and the verb *ka mui* (to give birth), as in the term *muinyorgoye*, literally "birth partnership," that is, close agnatic kinship, or "the bond between children of the same father and mother." *Namui* suggests that a person is born into a world of established customs in the same way he or she is born into the father's kin group. While one's social status and name are given through descent, one's temperament and destiny are shaped by one's mother's *influence*, hence the adage *Ke l dan sia; musi don den; ke l dan wo bolo* (A man has many children; a woman nurtures them; his children are in her hands) and the frequent attribution in Kuranko life of a person's fortunes to his mother's influence. Because it is the dynamic interplay of formal determinants and informal influences that decides a person's destiny, Kuranko would readily assent to Merleau-Ponty's (1962: 453) view that "to be born is both to be born to the world and to be born into the world. The world is already constituted, but also never completely constituted; in the first case we are acted upon, in the second we are open to an infinite number of possibilities."

From this arise many of the existential dilemmas of everyday Kuranko life: reconciling one's duty to uphold custom with the equally strong imperative to realize one's own capacity to make or replicate the world in which one lives; adjusting external constraints to inner desires; negotiating relations with others in ways that balance competing viewpoints and needs.

First Reflection

Following a well-established convention in anthropological essay writing, I have begun not in media res with an ethnographic description but with a set of somewhat summary, quasi-philosophical assertions that give little indication of what intersubjective events, conversations, or actions occasioned them. I have, moreover, rendered invisible the *connections* between my fieldwork and the general conclusions that my empirical research supposedly entailed. In effect I have left unexplored and unanswered several questions that pertain to the discursive relationship between ethnography and philosophy—a relationship between our experiences of a particular lifeworld and our retrospective analysis of that experience. Why, for instance, should any fieldwork experience invite, inspire, or require the kind of conceptual thinking we associate with philosophy? What is it about our empirical work that moves us periodically to distance ourselves from it, to have recourse to concepts? And having moved from participation to reflection, what compels the reciprocal and possibly redemptive movement back into the world of immediate experience?

Let me now begin with a specific ethnographic moment, before attempting to retrace the steps that led me to the generalizations with which I began this essay.

AN ETHNOGRAPHIC MOMENT

One afternoon in January 2002, as I was walking down a steep road in Freetown, Sierra Leone, a heavy truck, belching black smoke, lumbered up the hill toward me. Painted in large letters above the windshield were the words *Hard Work*. No sooner had the truck passed than a red *poda poda* appeared. Its logo spelled *Blessings*.

Second Reflection

No sooner had the truck and the poda poda passed than I spontaneously translated the words *hard work* and *blessings* into Kuranko. It then occurred to me that I might draw an analogy between the two vehicles and two Kuranko friends of mine who happened to be brothers. The elder was always extolling the virtues of hard work; the younger placed far more emphasis on blessings. Pausing on the roadside, I scribbled a note to myself, thinking that this incident (it would be an exaggeration to call it an epiphany) on the road to Lumley Beach might serve to introduce an essay on the complementary relationship between work and blessings in Kuranko thought and experience.

Third Reflection

One's duty (*wale*) is "that which you have to do"—the actions, obligations, and demeanor that come with one's role as a chief, a praise-singer, a wife, a farmer, or whatever. This is why *wale* is also work—the work one does in order to enact one's role, uphold custom, and play one's part in the order of things. A common phrase used in greeting a person, acknowledging a gift, approving words well spoken or behavior that conforms to the ideal is *i n wale* (lit. "you and work," meaning you are doing the right thing by your forebears, you are doing the right thing by your wife, husband, brothers, subjects, etc.). But while *wale* emphasizes a person's agency—his savoir-faire, his social nous, his personal conduct—the notion of *duwe* denotes the *outcome* of working well, which is *baraka*,[2] the state of being blessed. Thus the exemplary conduct of a paternal ancestor bestows good fortune, or blessings, on his descendants. *However, these blessings come to a person through his or her mother.* If she is a hard-working, faithful, and dutiful wife to her husband, then her children will receive the blessings of their patrilineal forebears, who become *duwe dannu* (blessed children). If she fails in her duty by being lazy, unfaithful, or disobedient, the path along which the patrilineal blessings flow will become blocked, and her children will be cursed. This is why Kuranko say "One's destiny is in one's mother's hands" and cite several adages in support of this idea: *Ke l dan sia; muse don den; ke l den wo bolo* (A man has many children; a woman raises them; his children are in her hands), and *I na l kedi sebene, i wole karantine kedi* (The book your mother wrote is what you are reading now)—which is to say that one's actions and disposition are direct reflections of one's mother's actions and disposition.

Ideally there is a reciprocal relationship between work and blessings. A person who is blessed is disposed to work hard and do his or her duty. A person who works hard and does his or her duty brings blessings to his or her family. But in practice people may give very different existential *emphases* to these ontological dispositions.

Consider the relationship between what is pregiven, culturally or genetically, and what emerges in the course of a relationship over time. There is a Kuranko adage: *Dan soron ma gbele, koni a ma kole* (Bearing a child is not hard; raising a child is). The irony here is that nothing would seem to be more difficult (*gbele* means "hard," "difficult," or "problematic") than bringing a child into the world, especially when infant mortality is high and many women die in childbirth. But the fact remains that the labor of nursing a child through its earliest years, caring for a child through times of famine and illness, protecting a child from the pitfalls of a politically unstable world, and working hard for a hard-hearted or indifferent husband so that one's child is blessed by its patrilineal ancestors amounts to greater hardship than the labor of giving birth. At the same time, this adage implies that although the bond between mother and child *begins* with birth, it is actually born of the intimate interactions and critical events that characterize primary intersubjectivity. In other words, it is the intense protolinguistic relationship between mother and infant, mediated by synchronous movement and affect attunement, including smell, touch, gaze, sympathetic laughter and tears, cradling, lulling embraces, interactive play, and the rhythmic interchanges of motherese, that creates the primary bond.[3] To speak of kinship as a "natural" bond or to invoke images of shared substances—blood (consanguinity), breast milk, semen, placenta, genes—or of common parentage, names, place, and ancestry *seems* to explain the strength of kinship ties. But such figurative language is a way of *retrospectively* and *selectively* acknowledging those experiences of a relationship that have confirmed a moral ideal. This is what William James (1978: 97) meant when he wrote, "Truth *happens* to an idea. It *becomes* true, is *made* true by events. Its verity *is* in fact an event, a process; the process of verifying itself."

Fourth Reflection

For the second time in this essay I have drifted from ethnography to philosophy, as if I were incapable of sticking to the facts or simply describing an event and allowing it to speak for itself—as if, indeed, every particular contained, suggested, or even compelled consideration of something more general. This tendency to stray beyond what is empirically given may reflect the intercultural character of my relationship with Kuranko. It is surely inevitable that I should not only be attentive to Kuranko thought but that I should, through a kind of countertransference, project my "foreign" preunderstandings onto theirs. In other words, an impulse to compare and contrast arises from my strangeness to what, for Kuranko, is familiar and taken for granted. My mind searches its memory banks for analogues that will close the gap between what I find bewilderingly new and what I already take for granted. Theodor Adorno provides a slightly different way of understanding this intersubjective interplay between "myself" and "the Kuranko" by arguing that any notion of an individual subject—self or other—entails a more abstract, categorical notion of subject, as in the phrases *the subject of anthropological inquiry* or *I am a Canadian subject*. "Neither one can exist without the other, the particular only as determined and thus universal, the universal only as the determination of a particular and thus itself particular. Both of them are and are not. This is one of the strongest motives of a non-idealist dialectics" (Adorno 1998: 257).[4]

Despite its focus on the local and particular, ethnography inevitably entails a set of *anthropological* questions concerning the relationship between individual and sociocultural modes of being, as well as a set of *philosophical* questions concerning the grounds on which we can claim a general understanding of others.

Before turning to the philosophical questions, let me address the anthropological ones by invoking what Michael Herzfeld (1997) calls "ethnographic biography" and exploring the interplay between *what* is determined by birth, *how* a life is shaped by circumstance, and *who* a person actually comes to be. This requires moving from a cultural account of the concepts of *wale* and *duwe* to a biographical sketch of two particular lives.

Fifth Reflection

Noah Marah was my field assistant during my first fieldwork in northern Sierra Leone between 1969 and 1972. His elder brother, Sewa Marah, had been an MP in the first postindependence government, though at the time I met Noah he was managing the Alitalia agency in Freetown. Although I became close friends with both men, they were never, themselves, at all close, and I was always disconcerted by the way Noah would diligently keep his distance from his elder brother, circumspect, deferential, and taciturn, or how Sewa, despite being aware of how fond I was of his younger brother, would deride him as an idler and wastrel, always looking to others to rescue him from difficulties rather than assume responsibility for himself.

During the war years Noah had lost his sight in one eye and had only limited vision in the other; in January 2002 he was out of work and demoralized. By contrast, Sewa was a powerful figure in the ruling Sierra Leone People's Party and President Tejan Kabbah's right-hand man.

"You are what you make of yourself" was Sewa's constant refrain when upbraiding the young men who fetched his bath water in the mornings, washed and ironed his clothes, helped him dress, carried his bags, and attended him. "If you don't work hard you'll get nothing in this world. You must be honest and straightforward. Young people today want something for nothing. They are not serious. Even my own children," Sewa confided. "I often think about them all night long. I don't sleep for thinking of them." He told me how much he wanted his sons to "do well," to be men of substance, status, and influence. That they were waiters in London filled him with shame. "Would I want people to know my sons are servants?" he asked. "These useless jobs. Living underground because they do not have residence visas." When I pointed out to him that Abu and Chelmanseh were taking courses in hotel management in London and were not simply waiters, Sewa said he wanted to be proud of them, he didn't want his sons to disappoint him. "These things weigh on my mind," he said. "After I am dead, what will happen? I wish Rose [Sewa's wife] would speak to them, urge them, tell them these things."

One evening, as we drove past the amputee camp in Murraytown, where I had been spending some of my time, Sewa made a strange comment. "They sell everything they are given," he said, as if to suggest that I should not pity the amputees since they were very capable of fending for themselves.

Noah, like me, found such opinions difficult to accept. "It's painful," he said, "when people tell you that you are not serious. Because often there is no work; often people have nothing, and they have no connections. I bear S.B. no grudge, but it pains me when he makes these remarks about my not being serious, for if I were not serious I would not have gone all out to support him in his campaigns in 1957 and 1962, and when he contested the paramount chieftaincy in Nieni in 1964."

Where Sewa invoked the Kuranko notion of *wale*—"What you have to do," as he put it; "doing your duty by others"—Noah spoke of the overriding importance of *duwe*, or blessings. But for Noah, the emphasis was not on the blessings he might earn through his own hard work or his dutiful acceptance of his role as younger brother but on the blessings that simply came to one, by virtue of being the child of blessed parents or through one's association with a benefactor. "You might be wealthy, well-educated, or well-born," Noah explained, "but if you lack blessings, nothing will work out well for you in life. In the old days, it wasn't easy to command respect, to have people heed your words at a public gathering. If you were not blessed, you would not be able to impose your will on people, to speak with authority, or command respect, and you would be called *danka dan* [accursed child]. But if you were blessed, this would make up for what you lacked in wealth, education or social standing. Thus," Noah added, "I tell my children that though I am not educated and am poor, I have blessings, and this is why people listen to me, heed my advice, and respect my opinions."

When I asked Noah if education, wealth, and hard work could compensate for not having blessings, he said no and cited the Kuranko adage *Lat-ege saraka saa* (No sacrifice can cut fate; nothing a person does can alter his destiny).

Noah's fatalism undoubtedly explained his formidable patience. Paradoxically it also explained his tendency to place his hope in others, to look for rescuers, benefactors, and saviors. And it underlay his habit of complaining bitterly about the people who had disappointed him in life or shut him out. Indeed his entire life had been a search for a mentor, a benefactor, a lucky break that would change the odds that seemed so stacked against him.

During my visit to Sierra Leone in early 2003, revising my first draft of Sewa's life story (Jackson 2004) and listening to Noah recount his experiences during the war, I became increasingly fascinated with the struggle for power and presence in these men's lives. Both had been born into a chiefly lineage and from an early age had imagined themselves to be worthy successors to their powerful forebears. Indeed when I first met Noah, his interest was in secular, not occult, power, and his ambition was to follow his elder brother into national politics. But instead of striking out on his own, he found himself at his brother's beck and call. In his own account of his early life, a series of entwined critical events defined his destiny. As a small boy, he was pledged to a Mende trader in the south by his elder brother, presumably in lieu of payment of a debt. Of these years of exile, Noah would recall bitterly that Sewa had "sold [him] into slavery." In 1957, only a few years after finding his way home, Noah's father died.

"Since my father's death I have been paddling my own canoe," he once told me, and went on to recount what it had been like in the years after his father died, when he went to live with his married sisters in Kabala and attend school: "It was not an easy time I had then. I remember one time my sister Mantene remarked that my father had petted me; now that my father was dead I would have to look after myself. So I was there, struggling—going to find food, laundering, doing everything in the morning before going to school. I had to take care of myself." But if Noah felt hard done by, there was always rescue at hand: "I remember one Lebanese, Mr. Hassan Mansour, who took pity on me at one time and told me I could always go to him when I needed help. As a small boy I often went to Hassan Mansour."

In 1959 Noah passed his selective entrance exam and went to high school in Magburaka. But in 1962, in the run-up to the first general elections after Independence, he was obliged to travel the length and breadth of *ferensola* (Kuranko country), canvassing votes for his elder brother. When he returned to school, the principal warned him that further absenteeism would not be tolerated. So when Sewa summoned him in 1964 to help with another political campaign, Noah's school career came to an end.

I couldn't go on because of hardship. I had to leave school and return to Kabala. I was there in Kabala for some time, struggling. One day I went to Lansana Kamara's shop to buy kerosene, and met Wing Commander Macdonald, the then district officer. We talked for a while and he asked me whether I would like to work. I told him I would, but there were no jobs. He asked me to find him in his office the next morning. I went to the office and found him. He offered me work as a native administration court clerk. But I had nothing of my own. He had to give me twenty leones to buy some soap and clothes.

After I had been there for some time, he posted me to Musaia in the Fula Saba Dembelia chiefdom. I was there doing the work. Then I decided to leave the native administration work because I felt I was deteriorating educationally. I then decided to pick up teaching. I was given an appointment in the district council school, the same school I had earlier attended as a pupil. So I was there fighting hard. At this time, while my contemporaries were still at school, I was struggling hard to earn my living.

Then I came into contact with Dr. Michael Jackson, who had come from Cambridge to do his research.

Of his earlier life in Kabala, Noah spoke of being under his brother's thumb, describing this period as one of domestic servitude. Despite the possibilities of being rescued from his situation by benefactors, his life was reduced to "sweeping, cleaning, fetching wood and water. Virtual slavery."

A turning point seemed to arrive with the general election of 1967, when Noah decided to run as a candidate for the opposition All People's Congress (APC). His ambition was quickly frustrated. Not only did Sir Albert Margai, the leader of the Sierra Leone People's Party (SLPP) and prime minister, ask him not to run, but his mother refused to countenance any public competitiveness between her two sons. "She began to pester me, crying to me all the time that she would be blamed, and people would mock us if I ran against my brother. She said, 'People will laugh at us and say, Oh, these two brothers fighting each other!' You see. So, mindful of all this, I dropped out."

It so happened that the SLPP lost the 1967 elections, and the APC came to power. "From this moment on," Noah said,

my life became very difficult. I was harassed. At one time I was detained. I had met a man called Babande in the village of Koba, who asked if I could help him find a cure for his sickness. My cousin Dr. Osayon Kamara was then at the Kabala hospital. So I told Babande to come to

Kabala and promised I would take him to my cousin. What I did not know was that Babande was a juju man. The APC people in Kabala knew this, and when they found out that I had sponsored Babande's trip from Koba to Kabala they had him arrested and accused me of hiring him to kill the prime minister, who was then Siaka Stevens, as well as Dr. Forna [minister of finance] and S. I. Koroma [the deputy prime minister]. The police came to my house that same night and arrested me. I was charged with sorcery. But the case against me failed, and I was discharged. But District Officer Gorvie, and the then paramount chief Baruwa Mansaray, decided I should be tried in the Native Court. This time I was fined fifty leones. I immediately came to Freetown to hire a lawyer and file an appeal against my conviction. Cyrus Rogers-Wright was willing to help me, but when I told S.B. what I planned to do he ordered me to drop the case.

Let me try to spell out the implications of this critical moment in Noah's life, when he was forced to renounce his political ambitions and was accused of sorcery. To do so it is useful to recall Winnicott's notion of culture as a kind of potential space in which certain elements are foregrounded and others backgrounded at any one moment in time. Transposed to the field of individual consciousness, this contrast is one between focal and peripheral frames of awareness. "Lived experience," observes Sartre (1983: 42), "is always simultaneously present to itself and absent from itself." Although, at any given moment, we have a fair idea as to who we are and what we might become, we tend to be blind to who we are for others and to the many unknown forces that may bear upon our fate. In Noah's case, he knows himself solely in terms of his desire to become a man of substance and influence. His consciousness is fixed on a specific objective and set on a specific course: the assumption of political office. He recognizes no other possible form of being for himself. But when thwarted in his desire to realize himself politically, his ambition fastens on an image that has, until that moment, lain dormant in his mind: the image of occult power.

Such transformations seldom occur painlessly; they are the outcomes of crisis. Accused of sorcery, this alternative form of power suddenly presents itself to Noah as another way of seeing himself—as an *analogue*, as Sartre (1940) calls it, because this new identity is initially mere potentiality, an object that is still absent and irreal. In an act of what Sartre (1987: 174) refers to as "provocative impotence," Noah now imagines himself not as someone who will simply follow in his brother's footsteps but as someone potentially capable of accessing higher powers and possessing great influence. Moreover he now becomes free, for in beginning to imagine he might actively become the person that he has been accused of being, he turns a stigmatizing identification to his own advantage, liberates himself from the humiliating position of existing in his brother's shadow, and acquires powers that, while marginal, nonetheless have a legitimate place in the social order.

The youngest in a family of eight, Noah has an acute sense of being "shut out," as he put it; this was, I suppose, a factor in drawing him toward the world of the occult. Thwarted in his youthful ambition to enter politics and become a man of means, Noah became increasingly attracted to what James Fernandez (1982: 215) calls "the occult search for capacity." In a country where the gap between expectations and opportunity is so great, "wild" powers such as witchcraft, sorcery, banditry, and religious zealotry have become increasingly alluring as avenues to recognition, ways of symbolically compensating for one's sense of exclusion and insignificance. During our last conversation, sitting together in the downstairs parlor at Sewa's house in Freetown, the daylight fading, Noah spoke to me of his occult gifts.

There was a certain Dr. Kawa, Noah said, a senior consultant surgeon at the Connaught hospital. Kawa's sister had borne a grudge against her brother from early childhood, jealous of his successes in life and his prestigious social position. So she bewitched him. He began to suffer dizzy spells and blackouts, sometimes during surgery. When several patients died, Kawa was suspended. He became known as Killer Kawa. Noah, who had acquired the powers of an alpha or mori-man, "cleansed" the doctor. The sister died not long afterward, punished, according to Noah, for her evildoing. Kawa was reinstated, and Noah submitted to an appendectomy and hernia operation under him, confident in the surgeon's skill now that he was free from his sister's baleful influence.

Earlier in this essay, an ethnographic digression led me to philosophy; now a biographical digression has seemingly taken me in the same direction. It is as if Sartre entered my thinking without any conscious prompting—a means of articulating, underscoring, or perhaps authorizing an interpretation that the empirical account alone seemed incapable of yielding. But before exploring this particular train of thought, let us consider whether Kuranko hermeneutics—or, more generally, West African hermeneutics—might offer the kind of interpretive insights I have drawn from philosophers like James, Merleau-Ponty, and Sartre and the psychoanalyst D. W. Winnicott.

The question for Kuranko of what relative weight to assign duty and blessings in explaining a person's fate and fortune echoes the question that has vexed so many Western philosophers concerning the relative weight of freedom and determinism in human life. But this is an existential issue before it is a philosophical one, and it should not surprise us to find that West African worldviews are also preoccupied by the dilemma of reconciling a sense of personal freedom with an equally strong sense of being conditioned and contingent.

Among the Tallensi, the tension between being an actor and being acted upon finds expression in the dialectic between chosen and preordained destinies. "Life—symbolized for the Tallensi in the breath (*novor*)—is only the raw material for living," writes Meyer Fortes (1983: 15). "What one makes of it depends on other spiritual agencies." These "other spiritual agencies" include the influences of one's mother, father, or other kin (strictly speaking "the Prenatal Destiny" of such significant others) and the influence of the Prenatal Destiny that one chooses for oneself before being born. This prenatal decision may be made against having a spouse, bearing children, or being a farmer—in effect, rejecting a normal moral life. Fortes refers to this as "Oedipal fate," contrasting it with the "Jobian fulfillment" that comes from recognizing the superior powers of the ancestors and seeking redemption through them. But just as a bad prenatal choice can be revoked by setting up a shrine and making sacrifices to one's ancestors—ritually submitting to and complying with "the norms and customs instituted by them" (23)—a person's positive dispositions may be undermined should he or she neglect or ignore the lineage ancestors.

According to the Yoruba of Nigeria, each person is said to make a choice about his or her preferred destiny before he or she is born. A divinity called Ajàlá, "the potter who makes heads," molds heads from clay, fires them, and places them in a storehouse. Because Ajàlá is an incorrigible debtor whose mind is seldom on his work, many of his heads are badly thrown or over-fired. *Ori*, the word for the physical head, also connotes the "internal head" (*ori-inú*), the inner personality "that rules, controls, and guides the life and activities of the person" (Idowu 1962: 170). The act of selecting one's *ori* is regarded as one of free will. But because of Ajàlá's irresponsible workmanship, many heads turn out to be defective. Nevertheless as soon as the choice of a head has been made, one is free to travel to earth, where one's success or failure in life will depend largely on the *ori* one picked up in Àjàlá's storehouse.

Ori is, however, only one aspect of human being. *Emi*, which means both the physical heart and the "active life principle," is the imperishable aspect of the person that continues to be reincarnated (Gbadegesin 1991: 41). *Emi* is given by Olodumare, the supreme being, after Orinsanla, the creator god, has formed the physical body of a person out of clay. The third aspect of a person is called *ese* (leg). Wande Abimbola (1973: 85) notes that while a person's destiny derives from his *ori*, the realization of that destiny depends on *ese*, the legs. A Yoruba tale nicely illustrates this complementarity of *ori* and *ese*.

All the *ori* meet together to deliberate on a project they want to bring to fruition. But they fail to invite *ese*. Having made their resolutions, the heads find that without legs they do not have the means to carry out their designs. As Abimbola (1973: 86) puts it, "The point of the story is that even if one is predestined to success by the choice of a good *ori*, one cannot actually achieve success without the use of one's *ese*, which is a symbol of power and activity." This "two-sided conception" of human destiny "is accepted by the Yoruba without question. It . . . means that in an inexplicable way, what happens to a person may be simultaneously the result of *Bi ó ti gbà a*—'As he received it (was destined),' and *A-f'-owo-fà*—'that which he brings upon himself'" (Idowu 1962: 183).

The Igbo also see destiny as a struggle for being. *Chi* is the incorporeal aspect of a person that presides over the prenatal choice of destiny. One's lot or portion on earth reflects a primordial bargain with one's *chi*. However, once a person is thrown into the world, he and his *chi* may find themselves at odds. Thus a person may fall victim to the demands of an intransigent *chi* or become locked into a struggle to revoke his prenatal choice (Achebe 1975).

How can such opposed imperatives and competing dispositions be reconciled?

In answering this question from a West African point of view one must consider in more detail the kinds of complementary forces that may offset or countermand one's prenatal destiny, providing room for intelligent purpose and conscious control in the actual working out of one's social destiny on earth. Edo ideas on this subject are particularly illuminating.

It is believed that before birth each individual predestines himself (*hi*) by making a declaration before Osanobua, the creator, setting out a life program and asking for everything needed to carry it through successfully. One's *ehi* (destiny) acts as a kind of prompt at this time and will remain in the spirit world as a guide and intermediary with Osanobua. Misfortune in life is explained as a failure to keep to the chosen life program, a result of having a "bad *ehi*," and a person may implore his *ehi* to intervene and improve his lot. R. E. Bradbury (1973: 263) notes that *ehi* "represents the innate potentialities for social achievement with which each individual is believed to be endowed." But while *ehi* implies the absence of personal control over one's fortunes, the head (*uhumwu*) "admits a greater degree of responsibility." The head is the seat of thought, judgment, will, or character, of hearing, seeing, and speaking. It therefore complements *ehi* and, in the past, was the focus of a cult concerned with the headship of families and the rule of the state. The second force that complements *ehi* is the hand (*ikegobo*), which connotes manual skill and successful enterprise. Also the focus of a cult, the hand symbolizes a person's vigor and industry in farming, trading, craftwork, and other undertakings. "It implies personal responsibility and self-reliance in a highly competitive and relatively individualistic society" (265). The English saying "Your fate is in your own hands" translates readily into Edo.

Among the Kalabari Ijo of Nigeria, one finds a similar conflict or division between a side of the personality that is decided before birth and a side of the personality that emerges in the course of a person's social existence. Rather than use Forte's allusions to Oedipus and Job to describe the tension between the dual aspects of the personality that Kalabari call *biomgbo* and *teme*, Robin Horton (1961) prefers the Freudian concepts of conscious and unconscious. While the *teme* refers to prenatal choices, and innate dispositions of which the *biomgbo* is unaware, it is possible for divination to bring to light the unconscious forces governing a person's fate and suggest a ritual action whereby the wishes of the *teme* may be resisted.

But why not place Sophocles' drama of Oedipus, Freud's model of the psyche, and Kalabari or Tallensi myths on a par? Why should we translate "their" idioms into "ours" unless we feel that "they" are epistemologically inferior, in the same way that myth is often alleged to be an infantile attempt to create history?[5] Why not see myth, as Ricoeur suggests, as "always-already-there" in what we call history or the human condition, in the same way that stories of beginnings are haunted by a sense of the origin—the precursive reality that makes the very idea of beginnings possible and that calls into question the discursive cuts we customarily make between religion and reason, myth and science, orality and literacy, tradition and modernity?

Seventh Reflection

I contend that the reason we turn to cosmology, theory, or philosophy in making sense of our lived experience has more to do with the existential imperative of distancing ourselves from the confusing immediacies of life as lived than it has to do with explaining and interpreting—though these are often the terms we invoke in rationalizing these distancing strategies. Objectivity is therefore to be understood not in the positivist sense of neutralizing one's influence on the social field one is seeking to understand but in the existential sense of needing to stand back, take stock, and gain some purchase over events that one was too involved in to see clearly or that one was simply overwhelmed by. If I have not had recourse to West African worldviews in elucidating Kuranko struggles to reconcile a sense of being bound or obliged and a sense of being free to defy tradition and define one's own destiny, it is *not* because those worldviews are intrinsically unphilosophical, unsystematic, or unedifying. It is because they are too close to the empirical field I am trying to think through and write about. Thought requires some distance from the object of one's thought. *But one must be careful not to see this distancing strategy as a sign of a superior intellectual skill nor to claim that the understanding acquired thereby has a superior epistemological truth-value.*

It was Sartre's *Search for a Method* that helped me articulate the inchoate understandings I reached in the course of my first fieldwork among the Kuranko. While Sartre's observations resonated with the West African views I have described, it was ironically his remoteness from the subject of my ethnographic work that helped me write about it. It wasn't that Sartre's existentialism "explained" Kuranko social processes and lived experiences. Rather in *juxtaposing* his concepts with my Kuranko materials I began to find a way of writing about those materials. Arthur Koestler (1975: 113) speaks of this process as bisociation.[6] It would inform my notion of critique, not as a technique for revealing what is not evident to others but as a technique for seeing what is taken as self-evident in a radically new way. In other words, critique and comparison do not allow the one who performs the critique or makes the comparison to lay claim to privileged powers of reason, intuition, or expression.

Fortunately there are several philosophers whose intellectual orientations and sensibilities make them obvious conversation partners for anthropologists. One of the earliest was Montaigne (2004), who cautioned that a philosophizing that presumes a view from afar risks estranging us from the very experiences to which we are trying to do justice. This is what Montaigne meant when he observed that "study and contemplation draw our souls somewhat outside ourselves . . . a state which both resembles death and which forms a kind of apprenticeship for it" (17). Montaigne goes on to say that "the labour of reason must be to make us live well"—to create pleasure rather than pain. Accordingly one might argue that the question of the relationship between anthropology and philosophy must be couched in such a way as to encompass the less obvious question as to how these academic disciplines may be made more experience-near and less experience-distant—edifying and enjoyable rather than dull and deadening. In other words, the question of writing ethnography comes to the fore—the question of how we can do anthropology or philosophy in ways that enable us to see ourselves and the world from new vantage points, transforming our understanding without promulgating yet another theory of knowledge. As Montaigne puts it, "There is no way of life which is more feeble and stupid than one which is guided by prescriptions and instilled habit (disciplina)" (386).

Final Reflections

The tension between life as thought and life as lived may be considered in terms of the Kuranko contrast between the domain of established order (the town) and the domain of wild powers (the bush). This distinction, which corresponds roughly to our distinction between culture and nature, or structure and agency, is understood in several ways. *Politically* town and bush imply different notions of power: the power of chieftaincy versus the powers of witchcraft, sorcery, and the djinn. This contrast between secular governance and spiritual influence also calls to mind the contrast between the power of men and the power of women. While the first is associated with a politico-jural structuration of the lifeworld, the second is associated with the capacity to generate and regenerate *organic* life. *Dialectically* the relation between town and bush implies that these domains of bound and wild energies "flow into each other like waves in the never-resting stream of the life process" (Arendt [1958] 1998: 33). Indeed the social order falls into entropy unless periodically revitalized by the powers of the bush. *Ethically* the town-bush contrast suggests a set of vexed issues that follow from this struggle to bring the "wild" energies and potentially destructive forces that belong to the bush safely into the space of the village, since the power to combat witchcraft is itself a kind of witchcraft, the power to ward off sorcery is acquired through training as a sorcerer, the initiation of children into adulthood requires sojourns in the bush, and the vitality and viability of the village depend on making farms in the bush, where capricious spirits must be appeased and the dangers of the unknown must be negotiated. Finally, the relationship between town and bush must be understood *existentially*, for though the social order of the town connotes all that predetermines one's life on earth—one's birthright, role, and status, as well as the rules and regulations governing what one may know, do, and say—the bush denotes a potentially antinomian world of choice, negotiation, and self-determination that transgresses the given and may bolster or destroy the established order of things.

As noted already, Sartre's existential Marxism echoes this West African leitmotif. The crux of Sartre's argument is that while our lives are shaped by conditions we do not entirely determine and can never entirely grasp, we nonetheless struggle within these limits to make our lives our own. The sense that the world I inhabit is mine or ours, and that my existence matters and makes a difference to others, may be illusory, but without such "illusions" I am nothing. For Sartre, we really *do* go beyond the situations in which we are thrown, both in practice and in our imaginations, so that any human life must be understood from the double perspective of what makes us and what we make of what we are made. We are, as it were, both creatures and creators of our circumstances. A mystery remains, however, of deciding whether the manifestly unpredictable and surprising ways in which a life unfolds is evidence of conscious decisions or mere contingency (retrospectively glossed as motivated, willed, or intended). In my view, this is a false antinomy. Seldom do we stand at some metaphorical crossroads, contemplating which direction to take, rationally appraising the situation, making a choice and acting on it. Equally rarely are we blindly and haplessly moved through life by forces utterly outside our ken and control, mere puppets or playthings of fate. Fatalistic submission, the influence or advice of others, and careful calculation all enter, to some degree and in constantly varying ways, into our responses to critical situations. But however we construe these moments in retrospect, recounting stories in which we were victims or heroes, passive or active, we are always strategists in a game where winning is judged according to how successfully we find ways of responding to the situations we encounter and of enduring them. Sartre's notion of praxis as a purposeful surpassing of what is given does not mean embracing the Enlightenment myth of the rational actor or possessive individualist like Robinson Crusoe who, from his own resources, creates a world from scratch. Nor does it imply a Romantic view of human agency and responsibility, exercised in a world no longer governed by gods, fates, or furies, since acceptance, anonymity, and abnegation are no less life choices than heroic projects of self-making or revolt. To speak of an existential imperative that transcends specific cultural values or worldviews is simply to testify to the extent to which being is never simply given or guaranteed, in genetic or cultural codes, by democracy or tyranny, by poverty or wealth, but must be struggled for and salvaged continually. And though the source of our well-being may be variously said to lie in the hands of God, depend on capital accumulation, or reside in physical, intellectual, or spiritual talents, it remains a potential that can be realized only through activity, through praxis. This is why, as Sartre notes, our analytic method must be progressive-regressive—fully recognizing that while every event, every experience, is in one sense a new departure, a rebirth, it conserves the ancient, inert, and inescapable conditions that make each one of us a being who carries within ourselves "the project of all possible being" (Merleau-Ponty 1962: 358).

If Sartre became for me a "natural" conversation partner in my anthropological work, it was not only because his philosophy engaged directly with the existential question of how we may live as actors in a world where our possibilities of action are delimited by circumstance and by the actions of others; it was because his focus on the conditions under which a human life becomes viable and enjoyable implied a critique of metaphysical and systematizing philosophies whose abstract character allied them with the forms of instrumental rationality in which the establishment, administration, and perpetuation of the modern state finds its intellectual warrant.

In comparable critiques of the bourgeois social imaginary, Norbert Elias (1994) and Herbert Marcuse (1968) have explored how, from the middle of the eighteenth century, human well-being came to be associated with refined manners, spiritualized ideals, abstracted rationality, and aestheticized values. Insofar as these etherealized forms of life masked the labor-intensive, emotionally demoralizing, physically exhausting, and life-destructive processes of industrial production and mercantile exchange, the bourgeoisie remained blind to the very conditions of the possibility of their privileged existence. Even money became ethereal, Simmel (2004: 443–48) argued, since in the capitalist imagination it possesses a metaphysical character, mediating social relations, introducing a calculative bias to intellectual life, and displacing the power of the gods in determining human identities and destinies. As money becomes an absolute subject—beyond the capacity of mere mortals to fully control or comprehend—people are reduced to objects, and this division between an ethereal realm of transcendent reason and an earthly realm of irrational thought, volatile emotions, changing moods, and brute physicality comes to underwrite *social* demarcations between men and women, parents and children, civilized elites and lumpen proletarians, rural peasants and savages. Toward the end of the nineteenth century this social imaginary finds expression in the anthropological conception of "culture" as superorganic and in psychoanalytical models of mind that imply that libido is to primitivity as superego is to modernity, or that hunting and gathering economies are "archaic" while neolithic economies based on the domestication of animals, the cultivation of grains, and the control of water through irrigation are synonymous with civilization.

Paradoxically the lifeworlds that the European bourgeoisie disparaged as primitive, feminine, infantile, archaic, or irrational are not necessarily inimical to cultivated or civilized life *but vital to it*—an insight exemplified by the African ethnography I have alluded to.

Even Freudian psychoanalysis never entirely overcame its ambivalence toward what Merleau-Ponty refers to as a *logos endiathetos* or "wild logos" of carnality, emotion, and sensation. It is as though a preoccupation with the domestication of desire could never fully accommodate or approve the consummation of desire. For Róheim (1971: 105), it is "in the nature of our species to master reality on a libidinal basis," deferring immediate gratifications and discharging instinctual energies in noninstinctual activities and objects. For Freud (1961: 44), civilization is "built up upon the renunciation of instinct," which "presupposes precisely the non-satisfaction (by suppression, repression or some other means) of powerful instincts." "This 'cultural frustration,'" Freud observes, "dominates the large field of social relationships between human beings . . . [and] is the cause of hostility against which all civilizations have to struggle." But Freud's dictum "Where id is, let ego be" fails to acknowledge the extent to which our inner nature is not only a set of instincts to be repressed *but a source of vitality to be channeled and liberated* (Marcuse 1966). In existential terms, this implies that human beings can never find complete fulfillment in slavish conformity to socially constructed, external patterns of behavior, for there must be for every individual some sense that he or she is not merely thrown into a world that has been made by others at other times but enters into it actively and vitally as someone for whom the given world is also a means whereby his or her own particular destiny is realized. In other words, the "bush" or the "wild,"—though commonly regarded as antithetical to social order, psychological health, or political stability, is the very source of the energies and power without which society falls into entropy and life ceases to be worth living. It is therefore ambivalence that is the issue—the dual sense that we are born into a world that circumscribes the possibilities of who or what we can become, yet in the course of our lives we realize possibilities that could not have been predicted or plotted. We live therefore *between* the poles of what is already constituted for us and what we constitute for ourselves; "in the first case we are acted upon, in the second we are open to an infinite number of possibilities" (Merleau-Ponty 1965: 453).

No one has more perceptively critiqued psychoanalytical perspectives from the standpoint of African ethnography than René Devisch, who has carried out fieldwork among the Yaka of southwest Congo since 1971. Devisch shows that rather than draw hard and fast distinctions between spaces within and outside domestication, Yaka deploy ritual techniques for mobilizing their imaginations, emotions, bodies, speech, and energies in ways that produce an "interweaving" of the intrapsychic and social, the paternal and maternal, the town and the bush. Instead of repressing libidinal forces, Yaka seek to express these in ways that interanimate individual, social, and cosmic bodies. And where Freud's psychoanalysis echoed a patriarchal ethos centered on "order, separation, deprivation . . . and restoration," Yaka therapeutic cults create a maternal or matrixial space, "a uterus-like environment where diverse forms of contact and sensation are re-elaborated" (Devisch 1999: 17). At the same time, Devisch echoes Devereux's call for anthropologists to reflect more profoundly on the ethnocentrist assumptions of omniscience that continue to perpetuate colonial delusions of superiority and the white man's burden (18). The notion that a Western scholar's observational skills and analytical powers may enable him or her to become conscious of what lies in the so-called unconscious of the other is but one expression of this view that Africans are incapable of fully knowing or effectively governing themselves.

Sartre (2004: 30) sees human intentionality as a vital if "undifferentiated" disposition of consciousness toward an external world that always remains to some degree separate from the objects at which it "aims," the persons with whom it forms attachments, or the cultural projects whereby it strives to "realise itself."[7] It is because the relationship between the thinking subject and the object of his or her thoughts is restive, indeterminate, and unstable that we find ourselves craving things even when satisfied with what we have, conjuring objects that, strictly speaking, do not exist, desiring to do things that are not socially acceptable, while denying the reality of certain objects and experiencing the reality of others in many different ways. The space of religion and the spaces outside domestication may be compared to the space of dreams, a penumbral domain where consciousness is loosed from the objects, routines, and environs to which it is conventionally tied and freed to entertain or succumb to other modes of objectification. It is a space as haunted by established models and extant memories as it is filled with the aura of imaginary possibilities. Of these possibilities, perhaps the most compelling are the most commonplace: our human capacity for making light of a situation, for transforming work into play, for making music, for finding in laughter, ebullience, and satire a freedom to defy the power of external circumstances to crush, oppress, and overrule us.

NOTES

1. *Existence* is from the Latin *ex-sistere*, "to stand out, to emerge." Existentialism thus emphasizes the human being "not as a collection of static substances or mechanisms or patterns, but rather as emerging and becoming. . . . World is never something static, something merely given which the person then 'accepts' or 'adjusts to' or 'fights.' It is a dynamic pattern which, so long as I possess self-consciousness, I am in the process of forming and designing" (May 1958: 12, 60).

2. *Baraka*, from the Arabic, is often used as a synonym for *duwe*, but the conventional way of accepting a gift is to say either *I n wale* or *N ko baraka* (I say blessedness), in order to approve or bless the person or party who has symbolically affirmed the value of your life.

3. See Stern (1985: 74–75). Ed Tronick's more recent summary of ongoing research on primary intersubjectivity emphasizes the *collaboration* of infant and parent in regulating interaction and laying down the neurobehavioral foundations of a "dyadic consciousness," incorporating complex information, experience, and mutual mappings into a relatively coherent whole that functions as a self-regulating system, effectively expanding the consciousness of one person into the consciousness of another. Dyadic consciousness begins in the stage of primary intersubjectivity, and should an infant be "deprived of the experience of expanding his or her states of consciousness in collaboration with the other . . . this limits the infant's experience and forces the infant into self-regulatory patterns that eventually compromise the child's development" (Tronick 2003: 37–41; cf. Schore 2003).

4. Adorno's comments are reminiscent of Sartre's (1987: 7–8) notion of the singular universal: "A man is never an individual. It would be better to call him a

singular universal: totalized and thereby universalized by his period, he retotalizes it by reproducing himself in it as a singularity. Universal by the singular universality of human history, singular by the universalizing singularity of his projects, he demands to be studied from both sides."

5. Horton (1961: 115) even suggests that West African cosmologies "probably represent attempts by other people to conceptualize motivational conflicts in an essentially Freudian way," as if Freud's analysis is analytically more sophisticated and therapeutically more useful than these primitive precursors.

6. Bisociation refers to the juxtaposition of concepts or images from two or more contexts ordinarily considered intrinsically different and incompatible. In contrast to associative thinking that works on a single plane, bisociation operates on more than one plane, bringing together "unrelated, often conflicting, information in a new way" (Koestler 1975: 113).

7. I find Georg Groddeck's (1977: 132–57) notion of the "it" helpful here—the nebulous, pre-objective, and amorphous life force that precedes specific symbolic or cultural expressions of identity, so that we may say not only "I live" but "I am being lived" and, methodologically, set greater store by abstaining from immediate interpretation than by rushing to judgment.

CHAPTER 2

The Parallel Lives of

Philosophy and Anthropology

Didier Fassin

Une "bonne" traduction doit toujours abuser.
—Jacques Derrida

■ "The question *what is philosophy?* can perhaps be posed only late in life, with the arrival of old age and the time for speaking concretely," wrote Gilles Deleuze and Félix Guattari (1994: 1–7) in 1991. The latter died the following year at the age of sixty-two. The former outlived him by three years, dying as he turned seventy. With this sentiment of urgency, their response reached a perfect combination of ambition and concision: "Philosophy is the discipline that involves creating concepts." Therefore, according to them, "it is not contemplation, reflection or communication," no more than it is "to know oneself, to learn to think, to act as if nothing were self-evident," as many professors of philosophy would have it. Now, what if we posed the same daring question with regard to anthropology and similarly risked a definition?

To this interrogation, Clifford Geertz's (2000: 89) answer is well known: "One of the advantages of anthropology as a scholarly enterprise is that no one, including its practitioners, quite knows exactly what it is." The elusion is certainly elegant and the humorous expression grasps the hesitations of the discipline as much as its diversity: "People who watch baboons copulate, people who rewrite myths in algebraic formulas, people who dig up Pleistocene skeletons, people who work out decimal point correlations between toilet training practices and theories of disease, people who decode Maya hieroglyphics, and people who classify kinship systems into typologies in which our own comes out as 'Eskimo,' all call themselves anthropologists." The observation is accurate. Yet if instead of describing the chaotic situation of the field ironically, we decided to take the question *what is anthropology?* seriously, how would we possibly answer?

Coming from a disciplinary tradition in which anthropology is qualified as social rather than cultural and is not part of a four-field approach with physical anthropology, archaeology, and linguistics but is viewed instead as one of the pillars of a unified social science, which includes sociology, history, and sometimes economics, law, and political science, I may be exposed to less heterogeneous practices than those to which Geertz refers. However, one could argue that he was himself a dissident in the American field and that his project of a "school of social science" had much in common with the structuring of the domain on the other side of the pond; it was definitely more Maussian than Boasian.

From this perspective, anthropology is not merely concerned with characterizing the permanent traits of mankind or describing the specific features of various cultures; it is not about resolving the tension between relativism and universalism; it is not about articulating the biological and the social—although all these dimensions are indeed parts of its realm. In a more condensed way, which attempts to apprehend its core signification, I suggest that anthropology consists in making sense of the world via a scientific inquiry into society. This definition is certainly a little less concise than that of philosophy, but probably no less ambitious. In any case, it may help us to circumscribe our domain in broad terms. Interpreting the world is the general objective of the discipline (in dialogue with sociology, history, and other social sciences). It implements this goal through a scientific investigation (as opposed to religious, ideological, or literary versions of this endeavor), which is oriented toward the understanding of society (thus differentiating it from the natural sciences, which share the same extensive intention of comprehending the world). One should rightly argue that the line is not so easy to draw as I suggest with literature and art, on the one hand, and natural sciences and their cognitive branch, on the other. Yet this initial delineation can be helpful. Indeed, I suppose that a majority of anthropologists would recognize themselves in this definition, which might even be obvious to most readers, just as defining philosophy as the creation of concepts seems evident to everyone—once it is formulated.

The reason I echo Deleuze and Guattari's ultimate effort to reflect on their intellectual life is that the confrontation of the two definitions can be a good starting point for a dialogue between our disciplines. Clearly delimiting the differences should avoid some of the confusion often observed in their mutual borrowing of words and objects. When it comes to engaging an interdisciplinary exchange, I contend that it is preferable to harden the lines rather than to blur them. There will always be time to remember that things are actually more complicated. So let us begin by taking the risk of being provisionally too simple.

What are the implications of the two definitions for our conversation between these disciplines? Philosophy is interested in concepts, whereas anthropology is concerned with the world. Philosophy creates and may be regarded as speculative. Anthropology interprets and does so by using a scientific method that moves back and forth between the theoretical and the empirical. Consequently, when they appropriate each other's language and tools, they probably ought to proceed with some caution. Philosophers should explore anthropology beyond the customary illustrations of differences in moral values or political principles among cultures, which will allow them to make their point about relativism, whereas anthropologists should resort to philosophy beyond the mere transposition of ideas into keywords that serve to interpret their material. Borrowing leads to redundancy in the first case and reification in the second one.

Logically, philosophers complain about the misunderstanding of their theories by those who mechanically adopt them, while anthropologists deplore the oversimplification of their interpretations by those who reduce them to culturalist exempla. I would like, however, to propose a different critique. Rather than reproach inaccuracy to these supposedly disloyal borrowers on both sides, I want to stand out precisely for it—as long as it proves to be heuristic. *Traduttore, traditore:* so goes the Italian proverb. This descriptive observation is reformulated into a prescriptive assertion by Derrida in the sentence that serves as an epigraph to the present text: a good translation should always abuse, he writes, a phrase that has become a sort of leitmotiv of contemporary theories of translation, with authors such as Philip Lewis (1985) calling for an "abusive fidelity." Shifting from the literary to the cognitive, from poems to ideas, I suggest that a form of respectful and loyal treason is justified every time it produces something interestingly new in the process of translation from one discipline to the other. This is what I will try to argue here, focusing more specifically on a concept that is crucial for both philosophy and anthropology, although from distinct perspectives: life.

Let me briefly evoke two personal anecdotes that may help illustrate my point about the heuristic of translation. I hope they will not be considered too trivial but will be viewed as what has been for me rather illuminating experiences.

The first episode concerns a research proposal I received not long ago from a Latin American student applying for graduate studies. It dealt with the issue of homicides of sex workers, drug addicts, and street children in his country. Here are the first lines of his abstract: "The thanatopolitical function of power operates in a biopolitical era in which the problem of sovereignty appears inadequate to explain how biopolitics anonymizes death through diffused and decentralized networks. My hypothesis is that the production of bare life does not belong exclusively to sovereignty and is completely compatible with the modern technology of power that intends to optimize and control life." One will have recognized the lexicon of Foucault (biopolitics, power, technology) and Agamben (thanatopolitical, sovereignty, bare life), or perhaps more exactly of Agamben reading Foucault. The condensation of these philosophical keywords renders the project, although apparently interesting in its intention, almost unreadable. This excerpt, which I quote in a somewhat uncharitable manner, is just one example among several proposals sent to me in recent years by social science students, mostly in anthropology, who attempt to problematize their research using this philosophical jargon. Their faithful but mimetic use of this vocabulary led them to what seemed to be a scientific impasse in which words, rather than concepts, were imposed on the ethnographical material, thus ossifying it. I chose this easy prey—a student's project that no one will identify—but consider it a sign of broader trends in the anthropological production, even if it often takes more subtle forms.

The second story involves me more directly. At the end of a lecture I delivered to a North American anthropology department under the title "The Biopolitics of Humanitarianism," a colleague and friend of mine, who is an authority in Foucauldian exegesis, leaped off his chair, vehemently affirming that what I had presented had little to do with biopolitics as defined by his intellectual master and that my use of the concept was actually an abuse. In fact, rather than studying the technologies deployed by humanitarian workers to regulate populations (camp settings, malnutrition programs, immunization campaigns, etc.), which would have corresponded to the definition of biopolitics by Foucault, I had analyzed what I realized to be the matter and meaning of their actions: how lives were concretely engaged in it and which idea of life was defended through it. My colleague was perfectly correct in his criticism, and his comment made me aware that I was indeed exploring something that Foucault had paradoxically ignored in spite of what the etymology of his concept of biopolitics seems to imply: life. Acknowledging my lexical error—and conceptual fallacy—therefore allowed me to express more adequately my problematic as to what, from then on, I began to regard as a missing link in the theory of biopower. Instead of talking of biopolitics, I suggested speaking of the politics of life to clearly delineate what I viewed as an entirely distinct research program in which the question would no longer be that of the norms through which populations are governed but of the value granted to life and the actual worth of lives, the discrepancy between the two opening new perspectives on inequality—a theme and even a word that is alien to Foucault's writings.

To summarize, in the first example, fidelity seemed antiheuristic; in the second one, infidelity appeared to be heuristic. In reference to the same philosophical corpus, the analytical payoff for anthropology was much greater when theories were freely distorted than mimetically reproduced. It is not my intention to fault the zealous student or extol my own example; actually I am not certain one could not find, in my own work, passages where I fall into the traps I criticize. It is to invite a deferential distancing, if not liberation, from a philosophical hold that often withers the originality of thought and the richness of ethnography. The paradox is that this apparent treason might be the best expression of loyalty to the spirit rather than to the letter of philosophical work.

The two anecdotes just mentioned have in common that they both concern the idea of life. It is this idea that I would like to discuss in light of the ongoing conversation between philosophy and anthropology. Life is a remarkably relevant object for the understanding of misunderstandings between the two disciplines. Indeed it has been a central question for moral philosophers from the origins of their discipline: *What is a good life?* has been a leitmotiv for two thousand years. And it could be argued that, although within a shorter temporality, it has also been the matter of the empirical work conducted by anthropologists: a minimalist definition of their activity is that they study the lives of people. Yet until several decades ago, there were few encounters between philosophers and anthropologists on the question of life. Actually the division of labor between the two domains was based on a grammatical difference in number: philosophers thought in singular (life) and anthropologists in plural (lives). The former embraced Aristotle's *bios* as their foundational concept, with its variants: intellectual life, political life, perfect life. The latter would have more easily recognized themselves in Plutarch's *bioi*, the parallel lives of noble men from mythical as well as historical times—not so different from the biographies they collected in the field.

Things recently changed, however, when philosophers rediscovered life not only as what had to be oriented to become ethical but as what defined Western modernity as such: it was not merely the existence, the course of which could be made moral, but the very substance on which human activity was being deployed through science and politics. It is generally assumed that Foucault was the main architect of this resurgence and reformulation. This is largely true, and certainly the last chapter of *The Will to Knowledge* (1989), which seems to emerge from nowhere, being in complete rupture with the rest of the volume of what is supposed to be a history of sexuality, has probably been one of the most influential dozen pages in contemporary philosophy, via what Foucault famously coined as "the entry of life in history," characterized by this often quoted excerpt: "What might be called a society's 'threshold of modernity' has been reached when the life of the species is wagered on its own political strategies. For millennia, man remained what he was for Aristotle: a living animal with the additional capacity for a political existence; modern man is an animal whose politics places his existence as a living being in question." This discovery of what Foucault momentarily called biopower, associating anatomopolitics and biopolitics, had a profound influence on the development of the social sciences, from historians of the colonies to historians of welfare, from anthropologists of science to medical anthropologists.

Paradoxically, however, in spite of this brilliant insight, Foucault did not pursue his exploration of the question of life (Fassin 2009). His lectures at the Collège de France keep the trace of this hesitation: in the last course of "Society Must Be Defended," in 1977, he briefly introduces the concept of biopower; the following year he begins the cycle "Security, Territory, Population," announcing that he will develop it but immediately abandons it for the study of governmentality, police, and *raison d'État*; one year later, the title "The Birth of Biopolitics" seems to indicate his will to address the theme eventually, but he turns to the analysis of liberalism and *homo oeconomicus*, declaring in his last course that what should be examined henceforth is the way the specific problems of life have been posed through technologies of government; finally, in 1980, in spite of the promising title "The Government of the Living," he develops his investigation of truth and truth-telling in early Christian writings, initiating what has sometimes been described as his "ethical turn." In other words, Foucault seems to have systematically eluded the confrontation with what had been one of his most remarkable intuitions: the place occupied by life in contemporary societies.

Making Foucault the initiator of the expanding interest of the social sciences for life certainly does justice to the exceptional imprint of this seminal text on biopower. However, the theoretical ground had been prepared by two other philosophers, one about whom he wrote a remarkable homage a few months before he died, the other whom he superbly ignored in his whole work: respectively, Georges Canguilhem and Hannah Arendt. Both belonged to the same generation that preceded that of Foucault, but whereas the former was an admired professor and his thesis advisor, he never met the latter and seemed to have a superficial apprehension of her thinking. It is likely that Canguilhem's teaching and books have influenced Foucault more than any other major figure of the intellectual life at the École Normale Supérieure in those years, particularly in his early exploration of the archaeology of knowledge and the genealogy of the clinic, a form of continuation of the program in the philosophy of science and medicine initiated by his teacher. Yet it is remarkable that his intuition about the centrality of life in the modern political project has such striking affinities with the ideas developed by Arendt in her study of the modern condition and her interpretation of the French Revolution. This paradox may shed light on what I suggest calling the politics of life.

In his essay "Le Concept et la vie," Canguilhem ([1966] 1994: 335) writes, "To interrogate the relations between concept and life is to deal with two questions, depending on whether, referring to life, one means the universal organization of matter or the experience of a singular living being, man, the consciousness of life." In other words, "by life, one can signify the present participle or the past participle of the verb to live: the living and the lived." He clearly indicates his hierarchy between the two: "The second sense is, for me, commanded by the first one, which is more fundamental." The rest of this essay as well as his whole philosophical work are indeed dedicated to life as the organization of matter, which is the object of the life sciences, but without entirely ignoring the singular experience of man. A few years before, in *The Human Condition*, Arendt ([1958] 1998: 97) proposed a parallel distinction: "The birth and death of human beings are not simple natural occurrences, but are related to a world into which single individuals, unique, unexchangeable, and unrepeatable entities, appear and from which they depart." She adds, "The chief characteristic of this specifically human life, whose appearance and disappearance constitute worldly events, is that it itself can be told as a story. For action and speech, which belonged close together in the Greek understanding of politics, are indeed the two activities whose end result will always be a story with enough coherence to be told, no matter how accidental or haphazard the single events and their causation may appear to be." Much of her work does focus on politics, understood as the way in which human beings treat other human beings, without eluding the living.

Both authors thus establish a distinction between two dimensions of life: one, natural, shared by all living beings and explored by the life sciences; the other, social, restricted to human beings and studied by social sciences and the humanities—biology and biography. Humanitarianism is at the heart of this tension between the biological and the biographical (Fassin 2011), as it was initiated by the Red Cross at the end of the nineteenth century to preserve the former via saving lives on battlefields and was reinvented a hundred years later by Doctors Without Borders to defend the latter through testimony about endangered lives due to military operations and natural disasters. Contradictions result from this dual mission, not only between the two objectives, for instance when bearing witness may expose the population supposed to be protected to grave peril, but also within each of them: the biological, when humanitarian workers have to make tragic choices and decide whom they will save, especially when human or material resources are scarce; the biographical, when they become the spokespersons of those they assist, therefore depriving them of their voice.

This apparent division of intellectual labor between the two philosophers—the living and science for Canguilhem, the lived and politics for Arendt—undergoes an interesting twist at some point in their writing, when the former imports politics into the living and the latter symmetrically analyzes the role of the living in politics. In *The Normal and the Pathological*, Canguilhem ([1966] 1989: 161) formulates this striking remark, drawing on Maurice Halbwachs: "Everything happens as if a society had 'the mortality that suits it,' the number of the dead and their distribution into different age groups expressing the importance which the society does or does not give to the protraction of life." More precisely: "The techniques of collective hygiene which tend to prolong human life, or the habits of negligence which result in shortening it, depending on the value attached to life in a given society, are in the end a value judgment expressed in the abstract number which is the average human life span. The average life span is not the biologically normal, but in a sense the socially normative, life span." Thus the matter of life is a product of political choices explicitly (through medical expenses or health prevention) or implicitly (via market regulation or social justice policies) made by society. The quantitative measure of life expectancy is an indication of the qualitative action toward human beings. In a symmetrical move, in *On Revolution*, Arendt ([1963] 1991: 112) affirms the specific logic and superior strength of the uprising of the poor against the rich, as opposed to that of the oppressed against the oppressor: "This raging force may well nigh appear irresistible because it lives from and is nourished by the necessity of biological life itself." She accuses Marx of having legitimized this logic via his materialist theory: "He finally strengthened more than anybody else the politically most pernicious doctrine of the modern age, namely that life is the highest good, and that the life process of society is the very centre of human endeavor." Of this introduction of the biological into the political and of this valorization of life as a supreme good, our societies would still have the legacy.

In sum, Canguilhem poses the question of the inequality of lives (plural), whereas Arendt raises the issue of the sacralization of life (singular). The latter emphasizes the extreme value our societies grant to life as a principle to defend, while the former reminds us that not all lives are worth the same from a social perspective. This contrast between the absolute value of abstract life and the relative worth of real lives is a major moral contradiction of the contemporary world. It is illustrated by the recent history of AIDS in South Africa (Fassin 2007). In the confrontation between, on the one hand, President Thabo Mbeki and his supporters and, on the other hand, the Treatment Action Campaign and most physicians, the former constantly referred to the social determination of the disease, invoking health disparities and putting social justice first, whereas the latter systematically focused on the biological dimension of the epidemic, promoting antiretroviral drugs in the name of the lives they would spare. Although it seemed possible to reconcile these positions, this is not what happened, thus revealing the apparently impassable conflict between the two standpoints—the social and the biological, the inequality of lives and the legitimacy of life.

It is remarkable that both of these essential traits of contemporary societies would have been missed by Foucault. This absence is revealing of how little his biopolitics was concerned with what I have proposed calling the politics of life, at the heart of which lies this tension between the affirmation of the sanctity of life and the perpetuation of the disparities of lives. It is this gap that Agamben ([1995] 1998) attempted to fill with *Homo Sacer*. By returning to the Aristotelian distinction—or more accurately, by reinventing a distinction Arendt had intuitively drawn from Aristotle—between *zoé*, the biological, natural life, and *bios*, the qualified, social life, he allows himself and his followers to be aware of the sacredness of life as an ambiguous legal foundation of the political exemplified by a figure of exception, that of the homo sacer, who, according to Roman law, was banned from the city and could be killed by anyone. However, this theory of the political as exception, grounding the social contract on the confusion of the *bios* and the *zoé*, does not account for the other side of this confusion, that is, the inequalities of lives, both qualitatively and quantitatively, as the most obvious and yet less visible—or perhaps most tolerated—fact undermining the contemporary world. His fascination with the theory of sovereignty probably prevents him from seriously thinking the question of social justice: to the ordinary of disparities he prefers the extraordinary of the exception.

Shifting the focus from the extraordinary to the ordinary, as Veena Das (2007) suggests, has been a major recent contribution of anthropology to the understanding of the politics of life. To do so, one has to renounce a distinction that was once heuristic but has become antiheuristic, between *zoé* and *bios*, bare life and political life. Actually Agamben ([2008] 2009: 32) himself cautions his readers against the temptation of taking what he called "paradigms," in reference to the Kuhnian concept, which he considers an influence of Canguilhem, for a mere representation of reality: they are "plans de clivage" in the human archive "that alone make it legible." The social sciences, when they adopt philosophical concepts, should not forget that these concepts are generally such paradigms, which have an epistemological function but cannot directly serve in an ethnographic work.

This is what I will attempt to show by making a paradoxical detour through cinema. Using a film for my demonstration may seem to contradict the scientific claim of my earlier definition of anthropology, which implied a dialogue between the empirical and the theoretical. This objection can be answered in two ways. First, the line between anthropology and literature—or art—is often blurred, in particular when one deals with life stories, not only, as a textualist approach would have it, because there is a literary dimension in the anthropological writing but also because the ethnologist and the novelist share the same search for "existential truths," even when they do it via diverse means. Second, the documentary, which corresponds to the cinematographic format used here for discussion, has much in common with ethnography, not only because they both depict "the real life of real people" but also because they imply a fabrication that is often forgotten by the viewer or the reader but needs to be remembered.

PRECIOUS LIFE AND UNEQUAL LIVES

Presented in the official selection of the International Film Festival of Toronto, winner of Best Documentary at the Israeli Academy Awards, and shortlisted by the Academy Awards in the United States in 2011, Shlomi Eldar's *Precious Life* has moved audiences worldwide with its enthralling and humane evocation of a Palestinian mother attempting to save the life of her baby with the help of an Israeli pediatrician. It was released in North America as a DVD, on its cover a remarkable photomontage showing a baby viewed from behind, sitting on a bed in his pajamas, an IV drip hanging over his head and a belt of explosives around his waist.

■ The movie tells the story of Mohammad, a boy from Gaza born with a severe autoimmune deficiency who will not survive beyond his first birthday if he does not receive the bone marrow transplant that a physician proposes his parents undertake in a Tel Aviv hospital. Two of his sisters have already died from the same disease, whereas three other siblings do not have the genetic anomaly. The intervention is expensive—$55,000, a sum impossible to raise for this poor family—and complicated: good immunological matches must be identified among relatives who live in a territory completely blocked by the army. The physician calls the film director, who is a renowned reporter, to help. Affected by the plight of the mother, Raida, Eldar decides to "join the race against the clock to save Mohammad's life" and makes a plea on television to raise the money needed. "His life depends on us alone and our intense desire to save him," he exclaims. On the screen that the mother is watching as she gently takes care of the little boy in the sterile room, waiting for donors to respond to the call, the image of Mohammad appears, while the presenter emotionally concludes, "This baby stole the heart of everyone." Later, the news announces the death of a Palestinian mother and her four children killed by the Israeli forces in Gaza. "Musa, the one-year-old baby, was named after his uncle Mus'ab who was killed by the army last year," explains the reporter. The camera follows Raida's eyes watching the news story as the cries of the desperate husband and father of the victims are heard. Soon after, Raida learns that a single donor has agreed to pay for her son's treatment, on the condition that the donor will remain anonymous. "I don't know his name, but he's an Israeli, a Jew. He has a son who was killed in the army," says Eldar, who later explains, "Since his son died in the army, he sanctifies life." Raida comments thoughtfully, "We are grateful to him." She pauses for several seconds, visibly trying to make sense of contradictory feelings. "He donated to a Palestinian boy even though his son was killed? The Israelis do strange things for us." She recalls how frightened she used to be, as a child, at the mere sight of "IDF soldiers" in the streets of Gaza, and she evokes the fear she felt, bringing Mohammad to the hospital in Tel Aviv, that she might never see him again.

Although the promise of the gift allows the medical procedure to be planned, the identification of a match for the marrow transplant is more difficult than anticipated because none of the three siblings is compatible with their young brother. The search within the larger family turns into a real odyssey with the sudden closing of checkpoints in Israel. "Because of the blockade, our hands are tied," says the doctor. "It's impractical to bring twenty-five cousins here to be tested." Yet thanks to Eldar's endeavors, the samples are taken in Gaza and the tests performed in Tel Aviv. A cousin who appears to be a perfect match is eventually found and, after a demanding journey, is brought to the medical center. As she walks up to the hospital with Mohammad's father, Fauzi, the young woman seems fascinated by the luxury of the environment. He notices her amazement and enthusiastically engages in a dialogue: "There is life here.—People know how to live here.—It's a modern country.—I've never seen anything like that before.—Do you know what you're walking on?—No.—On plants.—On plants?—It's grass! You haven't seen anything yet.—I've got ten days to see things.—These will be the happiest ten days of your life."

A week later, as the operation is about to start, the pediatrician explains to Mohammad's parents what they should expect: "After the transplant, the graft usually reacts adversely to the patient, and at the same time, the body also tries to reject the graft. So there is a struggle between two components, which must live side by side, each with its own desires and aspirations. But only if they coexist will they survive"—by which he obviously implies that on this survival depends the child's life.

A long period of suspense therefore begins. As the father has returned to his family in Gaza, leaving his wife alone in the hospital to await the outcome of the transplant, discussions take place between Eldar behind the camera and Raida, facing it. We learn that the family is confronted with rumors from other Palestinians, who wonder why Mohammad is receiving such special attention from the Israelis and suspect his parents of having betrayed their compatriots. In this tense context, the reporter initiates a curious dialogue, which provides a clue to the film's title and the DVD's cover illustration. He evokes the observance of Tisha B'Av, the annual fast day that "commemorates the destruction of the Temple, the day the Jewish Temple was destroyed two thousand years ago, in Jerusalem." Perplexed, Raida remains silent and then replies with a gentle but embarrassed smile, "Let's not discuss the Temple. It's the source of our problems. We claim it was ours. You claim it was yours. It's better not to talk about these things." Comparing his freedom to go to Jerusalem and her impossibility of getting there, she asks, "Isn't that deprivation?" But the journalist pursues, quoting Yasser Arafat's phrase about "a million shahids for Jerusalem," in reference to the Arab word for witness and martyr. She responds with conviction, "More than a million. All of us are for Jerusalem. All of our people." When she asks him whether he is angry, he provokingly retorts, "No, no, I just think the whole concept of shahid is silly." The young woman reacts strongly: "Death is a natural thing for us. We're not afraid to die. From the smallest infant, even younger than Mohammad, to the oldest person, we'd all sacrifice ourselves for Jerusalem. We feel we have the right to." Vexed and intrigued by this proclamation, Eldar expresses his incomprehension: "How come you're fighting over Mohammad's life, if you say death is a normal thing for you?" As this seems to be a barely disguised accusation of heartless fanaticism, she movingly describes the trying experience of the death of her two daughters and of their mourning, adding, however, "Allah gave them to me and Allah took them away from me. I can't object to death. Every soul is destined to die." Suddenly she asks him with a smile, "You don't believe in death?—No, to us, life is precious.—Life is precious, but not to us. We feel that life is nothing. Life isn't worth a thing. That's why we have suicide bombers. They're not afraid to die. It's natural. None of us fear death. Even our children (a silence).—I asked you before: after Mohammad recovers, would you let him become a shahid?—Absolutely.—Why?—If it is for the sake of Jerusalem, it's nothing to me." Later, the discussion resumes as she explains, "I know it's hard for you to understand. Our people die. You kill people in Gaza by the dozens, right?

Our people get killed dozens at a time. When one of yours dies, it shakes your entire world. For us, it's normal. We cry out in joy and celebrate when someone becomes a shahid." As he questions her a last time about the value of life, she softly but firmly replies, "No, life isn't precious." Interrupting the dialogue, she requests that he stop filming and asks, "Are you going to show this too?" But it is not clear at this point whether she wants it or fears it.

On his way home, Eldar expresses via voice-over his "disappointment and despair," confiding his intention to never go back to the hospital: "I had lost compassion for a baby whose mother is fighting for his life only to raise him to be a shahid." Yet after the father apologizes for his wife, attributing her statements to the anxiety she has gone through, Eldar finally returns to the hospital and tells Raida about his doubts after their discussion. In the presence of her husband, who is obviously distressed by the turn of the conversation, she attempts to explain: "I don't plan on him becoming a suicide bomber. It makes no sense for me to want my son to die like that. True, I hoped he'd be a shahid but in a peaceful march. . . . The Qur'an and the Prophet said that in the End of Times, war would break out between us. That's why I told you Mohammad would be a shahid. It's not that he'd be a . . ." (with her hands she forms the shape of a belt around her waist, in reference to terrorists' explosives, and bursts out laughing). But Eldar recounts a private conversation his cameraman had about her statements with the son of the Hamas prime minister, who reacted by telling him she was crazy. "When we say something to please them, they say we're crazy," Raida bitterly comments. "Why do they do suicide bombings if he thinks I'm crazy? I said what I said in order to defend myself, to appease the Arabs and all my brothers there." She explains that, after the announcement of the gift for her son, she had publicly commented that "the Jews are better than the Arabs." Consequently her remarks about the shahids in front of the camera were a tentative response to the hate messages she had then received from Palestinians: "I wanted to prove to the Arabs that I'm still a good Arab and that I have kept my Arab identity and principles—that I'm still one of them." She describes herself as "caught between a rock and a hard place," between her desire to express her gratitude to those who had helped her and her will to demonstrate her fidelity to her people who suffered like her. "Why didn't I notice the impossible realities that she faced?" Eldar lucidly regrets in voice-over. "Why did I push her into a corner?" As Mohammad's medical condition continues to improve, Raida is finally allowed to take him back to Gaza, where her family celebrates their return.

Three months later, on December 27, 2008, the war begins, called Operation Cast Lead by the Israelis, and the Gaza Massacre by the Palestinians. After intense bombing of the densely populated urban areas, the Israeli army invades the Gaza Strip. In a conversation on the phone, the pediatrician, who has been drafted into a medical unit, tells his journalist friend what the chief of his brigade commanded them: "Show the other side that the landlord is crazy," which he interprets as an open invitation to put "no limit to the amount of force to be used." When the Israeli forces withdraw two weeks later, the death count will be approximately 1,300 Palestinians and 13 Israelis. The film shows lines of corpses of Gaza inhabitants lying on the ground. During one of his broadcasts on Israeli television, Eldar receives a call from the first Palestinian physician to have a professional position in an Israeli hospital and whose house has been hit by Israeli tank fire, causing the death of three of his daughters; his tearing cries and racking voice, live on the air, provoke profound emotion worldwide, substantially contributing to the global discredit of the military operation. A little later, the reporter, after having tried for days, finally manages to talk to Mohammad's parents, who tell him that bombs are falling all around their house.

Two weeks after this conversation, when the war is over, the medical condition of the little boy deteriorates, but the blockade of the border prevents him from receiving treatment. When the authorization is finally provided, he is brought to Tel Aviv in a late stage of reaction to his graft, with severe cardiac complications. In the corridor of the hospital, Raida, who is pregnant again, fortuitously encounters the Palestinian doctor whose three daughters have been killed in the bombing of his house by the Israelis. Turning toward the camera, he comments sadly, "How long have you been working on your film? Just to save one child. The entire staff will spend years to save the life of a single person. But in just one second, you can ruin people's lives, not just for one person, but for as many as you can." In the following weeks Mohammad's medical condition improves and Raida gives birth to a healthy child warmly greeted by the Israeli pediatrician.

In the epilogue of the film, Eldar fulfills Raida's dream: he obtains the authorization to bring her to the Great Mosque in Jerusalem. Before departing, he speaks to her: "I have one last question to ask. Is Mohammad's life precious?" She replies with a smile, "His life is very precious to me," as a tracking shot across the Israeli night progressively unveils, in the background, the lights of the Holy City claimed by the three Abrahamic religions.

The story of Mohammad and Raida, of the Israeli pediatrician and the Palestinian physician, told by a journalist who is also a major protagonist of the narrative, since he makes it possible not only via his camera and voice but also in the real world by calling for the gift that saves the child from certain death, is almost too obviously an invitation to think about the politics of life in the sense that I have proposed. Based on the discussion of Canguilhem and Arendt, partially reframed by Foucault and Agamben, one can identify two lines of differentiation and interpretation of the story.

The first line distinguishes the living and the lived, the biological and the biographical. On the one hand, the film is about life as living matter. It deals with the medical intervention that will allow the little boy to recover from a lethal condition, which renders him vulnerable to any living organism due to the failure of the immune system. The description of the marrow transplant by the doctor makes this quite clear: it is the struggle between two living matters, the body and the graft, the self and the other, and on the survival of both depends the survival of the child. On the other hand, the documentary is about life as lived experience. It deals with the suffering of the mother, who has already had her two daughters die in her arms and sees her son exposed to a similar fate; the benevolence of the pediatrician and the generosity of the anonymous donor; the compassion and indignation of the journalist. As a backdrop, it is a narrative of the oppression of a population, confined within a small territory, reduced to misery and submitted to repression, as symbolized by the numerous crossings of checkpoints in the movie. This neat separation of the living and the lived is permanently troubled, however, in particular on two occasions, one poignantly tragic, the other almost insignificant. The first concerns the physician whose three daughters are killed by the bombing of his house: he is a figure of peace and hope, the first Palestinian doctor working in an Israeli hospital, suddenly crushed by the pain of the death of his children; the biological and the biographical are conflated, highlighting the obvious fact that the latter supposes the former. The second happens when the cousin who appears to be the perfect match comes to the hospital to donate her marrow to the little boy: what fills her with wonder, causing the delight of the husband, is the presence of grass. Coming from a place where vegetation is almost nonexistent as a result of the climate, intense urbanization, and military destruction, she marvels at the discovery of the verdure that is not only preserved but cultivated. The dialogue has an obvious political signification, reminding us that in the past two decades the Israeli army and colonists have systematically chosen, as a mode of repression and humiliation, to uproot olive trees in the Palestinian territories, thus mutilating what was for Palestinians the matter and symbol of life.

The second line articulates the sacredness of life and the inequality of lives. It is the interpretive thread that runs through the whole film. The quasi-simultaneity, on the television screen, of the call for Israeli donors to save Mohammad's life and of the killing of Musa with his mother and three brothers and sisters by the Israeli army opens the documentary. Closing the film are images of Operation Cast Lead with the order of the chief of the brigade where the pediatrician has been drafted unleashing deliberate violence and the alignment of the dead bodies of Gaza inhabitants, which contrast with the successful endeavor to save the little boy and halt the rejection of his graft. The indignant comments of the Palestinian physician in the hospital make the contradiction explicit: How many resources and efforts do you deploy to save one life while at the same time you kill innocents, suppressing dozens of lives and disrupting many more? he asks. The death count from the Israeli intervention in Gaza does not leave any doubt about the evaluation of lives on each side of the conflict: the war has provoked one hundred times more casualties among Palestinians than among Israelis, and, whereas the latter are exclusively soldiers engaged in the battle, the former are mostly civilians, many of them women and children. The film director does not say whether the saving of one baby can redeem the massacre of more than a thousand individuals, but he leaves his viewers with the sense of this profound contradiction at the heart of his society: the value of life, posed as a superior good, which gratifies the generous donor, the benevolent doctor, and the compassionate journalist, on the one hand, and on the other, the unworthiness of lives, expressed via the abstract numbers of the unavoidable casualties of a retributive and exemplary justice against the enemy.

Yet the vexing question that seems to trouble Eldar even more—and is illustrated by the provoking photomontage of the baby terrorist—is Raida's statement that she would be happy to have her cherished son sacrificing himself as a suicide bomber for the sake of their holy land. For Eldar, more than the external contradiction of one life saved and hundreds of others destroyed (which can be regarded as independent realities), it is the internal contradiction of the mother who accepts the gift to preserve the life of her child but declares that it is not precious (which seems to defeat the collective endeavor to help him live). The disappointment and despair of the journalist when he hears the young woman make this affirmation can be viewed, of course, as the sudden realization that the gesture of peace, in which he is personally involved as an Israeli helping a Palestinian and she is personally engaged as a Palestinian accepting the assistance of Israelis, may be in vain, as the saved child could in turn become an enemy responsible for the death of Eldar's own people. It also implies, more intimately, a sense of betrayal, since this revelation annihilates, by anticipation, Eldar's attempt to reconcile, if not the two people in the conflict, at least a few men and women of goodwill on each side and seems to show that his dedication to this humanitarian cause is not recognized. However, it is more than that. It is the radical incomprehension that something could be more important than life, or, to be more precise, that political life could overtake bare life: the sacrifice of one's life—and of the life of others—radically challenges the sacredness of life as the foundation of a common ethics.

In 1961, as the Algerian war of liberation—officially designated in France as "les événements d'Algérie," the events in Algeria—was at its height, Sartre ([1961] 2004: lv) wrote his famous preface to Frantz Fanon's *The Wretched of the Earth*, which includes the following assertion: "For the first phase of the revolt killing is a necessity: killing a European is killing two birds with one stone, eliminating in one go oppressor and oppressed: leaving one man dead and the other man free; for the first time the survivor feels a national soil under his feet." Such a declaration, which does not concern the killing of soldiers but implicitly justifies that of civilians, if it were delivered in the contemporary academic realm and adapted to the Israeli occupation of Palestinian territories, would certainly lead to the discredit and possible prosecution of its author, but it would also appear incomprehensible and inaudible, that is, cognitively and morally dissonant. Ghassan Hage (2003) thus evokes the discomfort and sometimes hostility of his students and colleagues at the simple idea that one could try to understand the gesture or even the context of Palestinian attacks in Israel.

Indeed in the case of suicide bombing, this dissonance is not simply the murder of innocent enemies; it is the sacrifice of oneself for the cause. In his reflection *On Suicide Bombing*, Talal Asad (2007: 65) wonders about the horror provoked by this act which has been subsumed under the qualification of terrorism: "Why do people in the West react to verbal and visual representations of suicide bombing with professions of horror? Unimaginable cruelties perpetrated in secret or openly, by dictatorships and democracies, criminals and prison systems, racially oriented immigration policies and ethnic cleansing, torture and imperial wars are all evident in the world today. What leads liberal moralists to react to suicide bombings with such horror?" Of course, one key element of interpretation is not that innocent victims are killed, since warfare produces many more casualties among civilians, so that, for instance, in the case of the Israeli occupation of Palestine, as in the case of the U.S. invasion of Iraq, the ratio of death between the two sides is around one to one hundred and concerns mostly nonbelligerent populations. It is that the individual (generally a man) who kills voluntarily kills himself. Not only does he not respect the sacredness of the life of others, but he does not respect the sacredness of his own life. The perceived violence of his act against the value of life can thus be regarded as tragically "balancing"—and probably eclipsing—the actual disparity of the worthiness of lives. In the contemporary world, disregarding the sacredness of life is definitely more consensually and emotionally compelling than disregarding the inequality of lives (Fassin 2005b). In fact the former is often presented in opposition to the latter, which it even serves to elude.

At the end of the dialogue between Eldar and Raida about the preciousness of life, a detail, which is a sort of cinematographic scoria, casts doubt in the mind of the viewer: "Are you going to show this too?" asks the young woman as she insists he stop filming. Why would she inquire about the fate of this sequence? And why would the director leave this phrase, which one could have expected to be cut? It is only later in the documentary that one understands the meaning of the question. After having experienced the generosity of the Israelis—the physician, the journalist, and the donor—the mother had publicly praised her benefactors, thus increasing the suspicion already raised among Palestinians regarding the reason for the favors she received from their enemy. By affirming that she was ready to see her son sacrificing himself for Jerusalem, she wanted to prove to her community that she was still "one of them" and "a good Arab." Her argumentative rhetoric was in fact a performative gesture. But can one be sure that, when she explained that she had been pretending to be indifferent regarding the sacrifice of her child for the Palestinian cause, she was not simply trying to convince the Israeli public this time? One element suggests that is the case: far from being spontaneous, both assertions—that she is ready to have her son die and that she said it to regain the trust of her community—result from a provocation by her interlocutor, who qualifies shahids as "silly" in the first scene and repeats the comment of the Hamas prime minister's son about her being "crazy" in the second scene. So where is Raida's "true" conviction? Does she believe Mohammad's life is sacred, or would she accept its being sacrificed? But is not the alternative an illusion? What kind of truth does one get from a discourse, and in addition, a discourse artificially triggered by a provocation and theatrically expressed in front of a camera? Affirming that one does not know Raida's theory of life is not to be radically skeptical. It is to acknowledge that social agents are never transparent to the observer.

This acknowledgment is an epistemological and ethical foundation of ethnography. It may be that here one is closer to Wittgenstein's "forms of life" than to Canguilhem's "living matter," Arendt's "life itself," Foucault's "biopolitics," or Agamben's "bare life." The expression—rather than the concept—of "forms of life," which is mentioned only five times in the *Philosophical Investigations* ([1958] 1973), has given birth to an important literature with quite distinct and even sometimes contradictory interpretations (Baker 2008). As I understand them, forms of life allow a compromise between the premise that meaning remains opaque to others and even to oneself and the observation that communication among human beings exists and works—in other words, that life is possible. This is how Stanley Cavell (1962) reads the later Wittgenstein: "We learn and teach words in certain contexts, and then we are expected, and expect others, to be able to project them into further contexts. Nothing insures that this projection will take place, just as nothing insures that we will make, and understand, the same projections. That on the whole what we do is a matter of our sharing routes of interest and feeling, modes of response, senses of humor and of significance and of fulfillment, of what is outrageous, of what is similar to what else, what a rebuke, what forgiveness, of when an utterance is an assertion, when an appeal, when an explanation—all the whirl of organism Wittgenstein calls 'forms of life.' Human speech and activity, sanity and community, rest upon nothing more, but nothing less, than this." In the film Raida's intention or desire seems accessible neither to the journalist nor to the viewer nor probably even to herself. Yet she is able to communicate it to her audience. The fact that she does so in different and almost opposite terms, depending on whether she addresses her community or the rest of the world, reveals her capacity to transform her discourse accordingly. In other words, it attests to her agency rather than unveiling her subjectivity. And even though she exposes little of her experience of living through the various ordeals she faces, she delivers a strong and profound message about the politics of life. Her intimate "truth" remains inaccessible, but her public truth is made evident.

If philosophy and anthropology consist in creating concepts and making sense of the world, respectively, I have attempted to show that their paths are parallel rather than convergent. Their mutual enrichment depends on the liberty they can manifest in their borrowing and adapting. From the perspective of the social scientist, which is the only one I can claim, this stance means a rigorous engagement with philosophers and their philosophy as well as a free translation rather than mere importation, the combination of the two being the condition for the process to be potentially heuristic. Life, it seems to me, is an interesting theme with which to explore the cross-fertilization of anthropology by philosophy, since in plural it is the matter of the former and in singular it is an object of the latter.

Whereas life has long been the exclusive arena of moral philosophers, it has become, over the past century, a new domain in philosophy for the study of science and the approach of politics. Using Canguilhem and Arendt more than Foucault and Agamben, who are usually convened on these issues, I have suggested that the realm of life articulated the living and the lived, the biological and the biographical, and that the politics of life put in tension the sacredness of life and the inequality of lives, which is a major characteristic of contemporary societies. The documentary I have discussed illustrates this polysemy and dialectics of life in the context of the conflict between Palestinians and Israelis. As the film proceeds, the biologically threatened life of the young boy becomes the politically threatening life of a future suicide bomber, whereas the efforts to save one child's precious life are contradicted by the killing of numerous other children's disregarded lives. The ambiguity of the mother, and her probable ambivalence as well, unveils this confusion in the politics of life. Yet in spite of the forced optimism of the last scene, she remains definitely opaque to the viewer, as their subjects always are, in the last instance, to the ethnographers. Ultimately one is left with this hypothetical proposition: Life may be what resists philosophical reduction as well as anthropological interpretation.

CHAPTER 3

The Difficulty of Kindness:

Boundaries, Time, and the Ordinary

Clara Han

█ In this essay I am concerned with kindness and the difficulties that it raises in both everyday life and anthropology, particularly with respect to the urban poor. Throughout my ethnographic engagement and writing, I have found sociological *explanations* of kindness rather unsatisfactory, that attempts to explain kindness in terms of a play of social interests or in terms of moral economies may evade certain problems that kindness may pose. Here I seek to elaborate this sense further by engaging how moments of hardship are acknowledged in everyday life. I consider how kindness—as both affect and likeness—in everyday life is implicated with the self's attentiveness and forgetfulness in relationships. Drawing from my work in La Pincoya, a *población* or poor urban neighborhood on the northern periphery of Santiago, Chile, where I have worked since 1999, I consider the boundaries that inform a living with dignity in this world and how the acknowledgment of need both emerges within them and engages them.

But this essay is also a response to the editors of this volume, who asked us to consider our engagements—affinities and antagonisms—with philosophy. They asked us how we might engage philosophy that does not do violence to everyday life and might appreciate the everyday as an achievement. I respond by considering how a sharpened perception of the ordinary in philosophy might be linked to my own perceptiveness in my relationship to ethnography. Thus, throughout this essay I hope to evoke the lived link between attentiveness and forgetfulness in everyday life and anthropological thinking.

In recent years a growing body of anthropological work on humanitarianism has critically engaged how sentiments such as compassion, mercy, and pity provide the impetus for intervention as well as obscure the structural inequalities that such intervention is premised upon (Bornstein and Redfield 2010; Fassin 2011; Ticktin 2011). Charting these sentiments through Christian valorizations of suffering and redemption, Didier Fassin (2012: 4–6) has argued that "a politics of precarious lives" has entailed a "translation of social reality into [a] new language of compassion," in which "inequality is replaced by exclusion, domination is transformed into misfortune, injustice is articulated as suffering, violence is expressed in terms of trauma."

Humanitarian reason, Fassin argues, not only informs the politics and practices of humanitarian organizations and state institutions but also presents a certain difficulty for criticism in the social sciences. As he remarks, "It is thus particularly difficult to apply critical reflection to these questions which tend to be placed beyond debate. Humanitarian reason is morally untouchable" (2012: 244). This difficulty is centered on its claims to respond to the suffering and pain of others and the moral categories of that response, a compassion that today is "self-evident." While humanitarian reason advances the equality of all lives, "echoing the ideas of Christian brotherly love" (Redfield and Bornstein 2011: 12), it reconstitutes Christian notions of charity that assert asymmetric relationships between givers and receivers: gifts of aid cannot be reciprocated. And, in asserting an ahistorical solidarity, understood here as an equivalence of lives, it not only rests upon structural inequalities but also propagates them by denying that structural, or sociological, difference. Revealing this difference and its denial is thus the task of criticism, which carries the risk of virulent reactions by "those who possess a legitimate truth and whose authority . . . may be shaken by such revelations" (Fassin 2011: 51).

Engaging the decision making and discourses of compassion within governmental or nongovernmental organizations, Fassin shows how different figures of vulnerability—including "the poor," "the child," and "the immigrant"—are morally valued in relation to their suffering. In turn, those who are seeking access to aid or benefits must draw on a lexicon of moral sentiments, appealing to charity and compassion for suffering, along with furnishing proof of their predicament, to best promote their case. While the critical work on humanitarianism seeks to reveal the moral order of *the* present, in which compassion has become a framework for politics, my concerns with kindness respond to the problem of acknowledging *another's present*, a problem that belongs at once to everyday life and to anthropological thought. This is not a problem that can be known by revealing the fact of sociological difference; rather, it is a problem that is repeatedly lived and is intertwined with the self.

La Pincoya was formed by *tomas*, or organized land seizures, by the urban poor in 1969 and 1970. As the demands for housing went unmet by President Frei Montalva's housing policy, Operación Sitio, the poor of the city organized *tomas de terreno* in which they occupied the land on the peripheries of the city and then negotiated with the state for housing and titles. The formation of La Pincoya took place in relation to both the limits of Operación Sitio and tomas. Under the Allende government (1970–73), families who participated in the tomas that emerged in response to the limited housing sites provided by the Frei government were given titles to property. In a process called *auto-construcción*, these families not only built their houses over time but also worked to build the neighborhood street by street, up to the ring of green hills that forms its northern border.

Today close kin relations may reside within houses, which are divided into multiple *piezas* (rooms where a relative lives with his or her children and/or partner) and across houses. These relations are marked by conditions of indebtedness from the growth of consumer credit toward poor populations, enormous efforts to "get to the end of the month," and precarious forms of labor that generate punctual moments of scarcity, often called "critical moments." In this world, pervasive feelings of resentment toward poverty programs invite further attention not only to the subtle ways critical moments are contended with in everyday life among kin and neighbors but also to the ways this moment of need poses the question of one's own responsiveness to others. When expressing anger and frustration with poverty programs, for example, women often remark, "No estoy limosneando" (I am not asking for alms). The fact that the word *limosna* is used to express these feelings signals the deep discomfort with seeing oneself as a recipient of charity.[1] However, this discomfort involves more than being placed in an asymmetric relationship with respect to the wealthy or the state.

Such a repugnance toward seeing oneself as a recipient of alms requires closer attention to how ideas of charity, poverty, and dignity have evolved in relation to each other. The historian María Angélica Illanes (2007) elaborates how, in the late 1800s, the Catholic Church sought to reaffirm its place within political life by reasserting its vision of an "unequal-complementary" ordering of society, which, it argued, modernity had put into crisis.[2] Particularly striking in Illanes's account are the anxieties that surrounded this vision and the way those anxieties were expressed: as a "*forgetting* of evangelical legal norms, based in the mutual obligations that the two classes—in which society was naturally and necessarily divided—owed to each other" (81, emphasis in original). It was the forgetting of this vision of society— that the rich and the poor lived in unequal but mutually sustaining relationship to each other—that implied a forgetting of the Church and God. In this scene of forgetfulness, however, "the poor" had a special place. The mother of the Church, Mary, implored the rich to share with the poor, who needed charity to secure themselves again in the fold of social life. A growing popular-sector literature, however, rejected charity, instead advancing a model of society premised on citizenship and claims to rights. Thus workers claimed their right to demand the government's protection of national industry, as a widely circulated popular text, *El Pueblo*, tersely stated: "We neither ask for alms nor implore for charity, rather we demand what we think we have the right to demand and the Government and Congress has the obligation to provide: work made possible through the protection of national industry. . . . WE ARE WORKERS NOT BEGGARS" (quoted in Illanes 2007: 67).

Complicating a picture that takes the Church as a monolithic entity with unified preoccupations, the historian Sol Serrano (2008) elaborates how brotherhoods of charity slowly morphed into a host of societies of mutual aid and charitable associations in the wake of the Chilean Civil Code's establishment of property rights and in response to ecclesiastical centralization. Tenuously articulated with the ecclesiastical government, brotherhoods performed mortuary rites to ensure a good death and eternal life, sustaining themselves by collecting alms. But now having to account for the correct use of funds, ecclesiastical authorities became quite ambivalent about them. While brotherhoods drew both the elite and the popular to worship, they were "disorganized, unruly, and even worse, a flank for regal and liberal criticisms because of their excessive festivity and financial abuses" (107). Charitable associations, on the other hand, focused not on assistance in a good death and in remembering the dead but rather in the incorporation of the poor into society through material assistance as well as work. Largely comprised of elite women who were responding to the "new poverty" of massive urban migration and who declared dependence on the ecclesiastical authorities to perform their work, these associations sought out those *pobres vergonzantes* (ashamed poor) "whose dignity did not permit them to ask for alms and whose modesty did not permit themselves to present at the hospital" (144). Such seeking out of those poor occurred amid suspicions over who was a *pobre verdadero* (truly poor) and who was "betraying public charity" with "the mask of indigence" (147).

Shame over being poor, suspicions of the poor, and the value of work, however, were sensibilities that came not only to inflect the categories of the "truly poor." They were also inflected in living life, in the stakes in claiming oneself as poor. In a compelling essay, the historian of late antiquity, Peter Brown, shifts the ground of historical studies of charity from the problem of who counts as poor to ask how an "aesthetic of society" shaped why the poor should matter in the first place: "Why remember the poor?" These are questions that are not confined to status but rather cut across a world. As Brown (2005: 519) remarks, "Paul's injunction to 'remember the poor' (Galatians 2:10) and its equivalents in Jewish and Muslim societies warned far more than a lapse of memory. It pointed to a brutal act of social excision the reverberations of which would not be confined to the narrow corridors where rich and poor met through the working of charitable institutions. . . . Put bluntly, the heart of the problem was that the poor were eminently forgettable persons. In many different ways, they had lost access to networks that had lodged them in the memory of their fellows. Lacking the support of family and neighbors, the poor were on their own, floating in a vast world of the unremembered." Forgetting "the poor" was articulated in medieval and early modern societies with a host of other forgettable persons, including the dead (whom, in the three religions, were "both shameful and inhuman to forget") as well as the clergy and God ("the one most liable to be forgotten by comfortable and confident worldings" [520]). Thus "the poor challenged memory like God" (520). More than a problem of compassion and generosity, charity "to the easily forgotten poor was locked into an entire social pedagogy that supported the memory of a God who, also, was all-too-easily forgotten" (520).

Today elements of this notion of the poor requiring charity to be remembered may now be animated in resentments that women express in relation to poverty programs. When social workers cast the poor as a "burden" to the state or when women must sign a "family contract" promising to improve themselves and their economic condition—through birth control and courses in family dynamics—in order to gain entrance into a program for extreme poverty, not only are the poor seen as needing reform to inte-grate back into society, but they are also seen as simultaneously being for-gotten by and needing to remember relationships that made them persons in the first place. Resentments emerge from the *assertion*, not the occlusion, of difference between humans. They grow from a world in which achieving dignity occurs through the work of intimate relationships in concealing the events—those critical moments—that threaten to make that difference an actuality.

As I elaborate below, the shame over being heard and seen to receive alms—to beg—is intimately related to the failure of relationships to help endure those critical moments. The deeper threat of this failure is one's forgetfulness in those relationships themselves. *Vivir con dignidad*, living with dignity, then, not only draws from a discourse of equality but is per-haps more deeply articulated to remembering and being remembered, or what today my friends call being *atento* (attentive) or *presente* (present): attentiveness to one's relationships in the ever so close reality of forgetful-ness. It is to be attentive to those quiet endurances amid critical moments and to act kindly with respect to the boundaries of the self.

These concerns with remembering and forgetting, or attentiveness and forgetfulness, offer a different orientation to acts of kindness—or giving—in everyday life. In contrast to a critique of humanitarian reason that renders the problem of charity and compassion within a logic of gift and countergift, revealing a sociological asymmetry in the ability to recip-rocate, my concern with everyday life focuses on the self's attentiveness and forgetfulness in relationships. Thus rather than place acts of kindness between neighbors within a successive time of the gift and countergift, I consider these acts in relation to "vertical time": *co-occurring or contempora-neous* acts, moments, and circumstances involved in these acts of kind-ness.[3] This vertical time can be imagined as a slice of time or a drop of time, like a slice of *mil hojas* (thousand leaves) cake in which each leaf is uniquely textured, or a drop of stream water carrying layers of dirt and organisms. My hope is that dwelling in that slice of time might help us appreciate a this-worldly generosity and kindness to others and to take seriously the stakes in that kindness for the achieving of everyday life.

SHAME, RECIPROCITY, BOUNDARIES

Let us now turn to life in La Pincoya and get acquainted with the boundar-ies that are crucial to living with dignity. In neighborhood life, critical moments are often mitigated by friends and kin who constitute domestic re-lationships. Asking for a loan to get to the end of the month, to borrow a credit card, or for tea, sugar, or bread, however, are not simple or unprob-lematic acts. Rather there is a deep sense that women should *aguantar* (en-dure) hardship, contending with it quietly and persistently: "Lo arreglo piola" (I fix it quietly), "Rebusco y rebusco por una luca" (I scrounge and scrounge for a thousand pesos). "Shame" (*vergüenza*) often shadows such acts of asking and ties into the vulnerability of a boundary between the two senses of *pedir*, asking and begging. To avoid a slip from asking to begging, "asking" is taken up into reciprocity, temporally tied into domestic relations of friendship and kinship.

For example, as I was standing with a few women in a neighbor's *alma-cén* (a storefront that is built into the house), they gossiped about a woman, Rosita, who was rumored to have asked for money from several neighbors. One woman remarked, "Qué vergüenza, andando llorando, pidiendo la lás-tima" (What shame, walking around crying, asking/begging for pity). The conversation spiraled outward to other women who cry and "beg for pity." Another woman remarked, "It's that . . . ayyy, that they need to understand, we are human beings. We do not walk begging in the street, like little dogs. We have dignity. One devalues oneself." The exclamation of "shame" here is a remark on the woman's voice, a woman whose "crying" is not heard as a human cry for help but verges dangerously into a whine. It is an exclama-tion of the shame generated by conditions that produce that voice, a failure of both family and domestic relations, tied into where that voice is heard and by whom—in neighborhood life and by neighbors (see Han 2011).

An asking that crosses the boundary between neighbor and friend or kin makes more vulnerable the boundary between asking and begging. We could think of shame as an affect that shadows boundaries, in which bound-aries are not sociologically defined sets of actual people but rather, as Mari-lyn Strathern (1981: 82) discusses, ideas in relation to which there are "boundary-effects." Such boundaries can be understood as crossing the self, meaning that the self inhabits multiple relational modes simultaneously. Through acts of reciprocity that constantly stabilize a woman's enduring, critical moments are quietly contended with and contained among kin and friends, shoring up moral boundaries when faced with hardship's cor-rosive potential.

In this relational mode, a time of "shared intimacies" makes possible an explicit recognition of critical moments through acts of reciprocity that sustain mutual obligation. That is, unlike neighbors, friends and kin have an evolving knowledge of the intimate personal difficulties of another and develop a sense of a life story through such knowledge. It is through such sharing of intimacies that Susana spoke about her friendship with Paloma, her "catching" or comprehending the moments when Paloma is going through hardship and the way she acknowledged such hardship:

> Paloma will never say that she is doing badly. . . . I will hear the little girl [Paloma's daughter] crying because she does not have milk, and *cacho* [catch] that she is in bad shape. I offer her a cup of rice, she takes it and eats it. . . . Her husband is a vagabond. He works for two months and vagabonds the rest of the year. And really, it gives me pain, conversing with Paloma. *Me caga la onda* [It shits on the mood]. Antonio says to me sometimes, "You have to stop listening to Paloma because it gives you pain, it makes you sick." But I feel that she needs to speak to me, I listen to her intimacies.

Later, when I asked Paloma who her "friends" were in the población, she responded, "Friends? I don't have many friends. Susana is my friend. We share our intimacies. Friends are few, neighbors are many." Indeed only upon meditation over the boundary between neighbors and friends did I begin to realize that the crucial difference between inhabiting friendship and neighborliness lay not in the perceptive activity of "catching" those signs of critical moments, such as the cry from Paloma's hungry child, but rather in *how* that catching would be or could be addressed. In friendship, asking and giving occur in the modality of reciprocity—of mutual obligations that carry a relation forward in time and in which personal intimacies are shared. I might venture to say that such sharing of intimacies and mutual obligations entails the work of sustaining and remembering that life story, a biography in which the place of friends is secured. But how would these critical moments be acknowledged by neighbors, if neighbors are expressly not supposed to know of these critical moments, and if explicitly acknowledging them might jeopardize the delicate work in enduring and containing those critical moments? What might be the place of neighbors in "remembering" that life story?

PRETENDING AND SILENT KINDNESS

As a relational mode that works through gossip, dissimulation, and pretending, the neighbor helps us consider a silent kindness that occurs in relation to and despite the rancors, disappointments, and jealousies that are pervasive in everyday life. In La Pincoya, gossip effects a pervasive uncertainty about neighbors' feelings toward each other, casting those relations with both ambivalence and artifice. Consider gossip about being a "bad pay," a *mala paga*, a person who takes advantage of others by delaying or avoiding paying back a loan from a friend or to local stores. To describe the effects of such gossip to me, Paloma recounted the story of Sra. Isabel. Sra. Isabel had taken money from several *pollas* (local rotating credit associations), but when her turn came she did not pay her share. Gossip (*pelambre*) spread that she was a mala paga. "Neighbors talked, 'She took advantage of others; she doesn't realize we're all facing the same needs; she's selfish, a swindler.'" Paloma described how neighbors stopped helping her, saying, "No fue solidaria con nosotras" (She wasn't solidary with us). Almacén owners made up excuses so she could not make purchases *al fiado* ("on trust"; payment at the end of the month). Unable to depend on others, Sra. Isabel and her family had to leave La Pincoya. "Where did she go?" I asked. "Don't get me wrong," Paloma replied. "I never knew her; I just heard the story."

Gossip has the potential to threaten the fabric of domestic relations between those accused and those circulating the gossip. Women engage in delicate work to avoid acknowledging those feelings of rancor, jealousy, and indignation in neighborhood life. The resulting avoidances and evasions combined with face-to-face courtesies are expressed in what many called the *doble sentido* (double sense/meaning) of everyday life. "Todo tiene un doble sentido" (Everything has a double sense): the necessary illusion that sustains a life subject to precariousness.

Anthropologists have explored the jealousies and hateful feelings manifest in this "double sense" of everyday life (Ashforth 2005; see Das 1998; Evans-Pritchard 1976). Perhaps less explored is how kindness could be possible next to and indeed intimate with such seething feelings. The kindness I explore below is distinct from those face-to-face courtesies and excuses that achieve that "double sense." Working through the subtle and indirect ways in which women perceive and acknowledge the "critical moments" of their neighbors is one way to consider the kindness that, along with the rancors, is concealed by this illusion of everyday life.

Despite one's desire to *aguantar* (endure), signs of hardship still seep out. A child's cry from hunger, the visit from a debt collector, the electricity cut, a domestic fight over bills spills out into the street, all signaling to others that despite oneself, one is in need and needs the help of another.

For neighbors, how to respond to this seepage or to the gossip about another's "critical moment" involves subtle performances that conceal both the critical moment and the act of giving.

Such performances occur in a manner that is barely noticeable. Here are a few scenes. One afternoon Ruby asks me if I can pick up her next-door neighbor's children from school, since I was already going to pick up Ruby's son for a few weeks. Maca's husband was a salesperson for NutraLife, a company that sells health supplements in middle- and upper-class neighborhoods. I had met him once when he stopped by Ruby's house during the coldest months of the winter of 2005 to learn how to rig the electricity meter from her husband, Héctor. At the time he had just started working for the company. He had impeccably cut chestnut brown hair and was wearing a yellow fleece sport jacket embroidered with the NutraLife logo. He asked me where I was from. I answered, "The United States." "No, I mean what city?" he insisted, indicating a kind of cosmopolitanism that moved beyond identifying nationality. "Oh, Boston," I said. "Good, good," he said approvingly. "We have offices in Los Angeles."

In the course of the next few months, neighbors said that Maca's husband had become *arribista* (a social climber) doing this work, that he got used to talking to the *chicas cuicas* (upper-class ladies). Then rumors circulated that he was beating Maca and had stopped paying the bills. "He's so well-dressed, and gives Maca *una miseria* [a pittance, a miserable amount of money] for the house." A few months later Ruby mentioned that she had heard that Maca's husband had left her for some woman in the *barrio alto*. Maca, she said, was now left with two small children. "I heard they are going to repossess the house," Ruby said. "She's going to have to look for work *afuera*" (outside the house). The next day, when we saw Maca cleaning her patio, Ruby went out to tell her that I could pick up her children from school for the week. "Don't worry about it. Clara's picking up Héctor *chico*" (her son). Afterward Ruby remarked to me, "I hope she finds her *príncipe azul*" (prince charming).

On another occasion Anita, a neighbor who was married to a distant cousin of Ruby's, stops by while Ruby was doing piecework sewing in her home. Ruby said, "Come in, come in, but I can't stop to talk. We'll talk while I work." Anita rarely stopped by Ruby's house. Yet this time she stayed for a couple of hours, first mentioning that she was starting a bicycle club for youth and asking if Ruby's sons might be interested. Ruby answered vaguely that one of her sons might be interested. Then they gossiped about others. Anita brought up having heard that Centro Restaurant, a company that subcontracts food preparation workers to restaurants and schools, was looking for workers. Meanwhile she started to help out with the sewing, using a knife to pull out small stitches in blouses that Ruby had not done well. A few days later a shopkeeper, Sra. Maria, stopped me as I was buying some sliced cheese for evening tea with Ruby. She asked me how Ruby was doing. I answered without exposing Ruby's acute financial problems: "I think she's okay. Busy as usual, why?" Sra. Maria said that she had heard rumors that Ruby and her family were on the verge of losing their house. "She's a hard worker. It's a pity."

A final scene: As Susana and I were walking up the street, we heard a heated argument coming from a neighbor's house. We only caught a couple of phrases. "And we don't even have a peso for bread," Jorge yelled! "Shut up! Shut up! You, you passing the days in the street, yelling cuss words like an idiot *flaite* [*tirando garabato como huevon flaite*]," Sara yelled. Two days later I ran into Susana on the street as she came home from an early workday. When we passed by the neighbor's house, she called for Sara through the patio gate. When Sara arrived, Susana asked her if she had made lunch yet. She hadn't, she said. Susana said that she had made too much food. She could send the kids over. "I have some things to do, but send them over in a bit." But when I arrived at Susana's house with her, she had not yet prepared any lunch, and she set herself and me to making a large pot of spaghetti noodles, with a sauce of tomatoes and pieces of hot dog.

Throughout these scenes, concealed acts of kindness—providing lunch, helping with sewing, passing a work contact, picking children up from school—acknowledge these critical moments without explicit recognition.[4] Such hidden or concealed gifts might be understood as a symptom of what Jonathan Parry (1985: 468) calls an "ideology of the free gift" that is particularly acute in "market societies," but more importantly Christian ones. Thus "free gifts" are "ideally given in secrecy without expectation of worldly return" since such acts are determinative of individual salvation: "The notion of salvation itself devalues this profane world of suffering. The unreciprocated gift becomes a liberation from bondage to it, a denial of the profane self, an atonement for sin, and hence means to salvation."

In an insightful engagement with Parry's analysis, Fenella Cannell (2004: 341) discusses how anthropology has to a great extent relied on a Christian theology that is "only ascetic in character." Further, she notes that anthropology in its claims to be a "secular" discipline has "incorporated a version of ascetic and Augustinian thinking in its own theoretical apparatus" (341).[5] Here I am concerned with what happens to kindness in accounts that see in Christian traditions only the renunciation of self and a denial of worldliness. This renunciation has implications for what is cast aside in investigating the gift: kindness is cast aside as that sentimentality or artifice that sweetens an action, geared to getting *real* results, namely, salvation or climbing the social ladder. In such accounts, kindness is considered in terms of representation, pointing beyond itself to what is hidden and invisible.

Turning to the Parable of the Good Samaritan in the New Testament's Gospel of Luke, for example, yields other possibilities for kindness within Christianity itself. Luke sets up the parable with the lawyer's question to Jesus: "Master, what must I do to inherit eternal life?" Jesus says to him, "What is written in the Law? What is your reading of it?" (Luke 10:25–28). The lawyer answers, but then asks Jesus, "Who is my neighbor?" Jesus offers the parable as his own reading of the commandment "Love thy neighbor as thyself," but interprets that commandment by throwing into question not only who is a neighbor but also to whom that question would be directed.

While there is a considerable theological literature on this parable, I will limit my discussion to Jesus' act of asking the counterquestion "Which of these three, do you think, was a neighbor to the man who fell into the hands of the robbers?" The theologian Ian McFarland (2001: 60) suggests that Jesus' question "redirects attention from the status of others to that of the lawyer himself. . . . 'Neighbor' is not a category that the lawyer is authorized to apply to others; instead . . . it *recoils back upon him* as a moral agent capable either of being or failing to be a neighbor to someone else" (my emphasis). In responding to Jesus, the lawyer then must respond to himself: "The one who showed him mercy." To further analyze the word *mercy* in relation to the neighbor, I turn to the Latin etymology of the Spanish word used, *misericordia*. *Misericordia* is derived from *miserēre* (to have piety), which itself derives from *misero* (wretched, deplorable), which is a transliteration of the Greek *mîsos*, "hate," in relation to *cordis*, "heart" (Barcia 1889: 372).

An intriguing insight that comes from this etymology is that the "love for the neighbor" might be inseparable from hate. We might consider such ambivalence in relation to Jesus' questioning "Which was neighbor?," which involves answering to oneself, or the possibility that one might fail oneself in relation to others. "Loving kindness" or loving a neighbor would be neither "sentimentality nor nostalgia." Rather, as Adam Phillips and Barbara Taylor (2009: 88) assert, "Kindness split from hatred breeds a fundamental loss of contact with oneself and others that leads to a prevailing feeling of unreality, or being unrecognized. There could be no intimacy without hatred, and no enduring pleasurable contact between people without surviving the hatred that always exists in relationships."

The delicate concealment of kindness in these ethnographic descriptions, however, make us turn from statements about kindness in general to a consideration of the specific threats that critical moments pose in this world and to the ways these concealments might be responding to them. To further elaborate, I draw from J. L. Austin's (1958) essay "Pretending." Austin's discussion of pretending helps me shift my attention on the gift in three crucial ways. First, it focuses attention to the co-occurrence of acts, that "vertical time," rather than expectation or futurity. In pretending, Austin remarks, "I must be trying to make others believe, or to give them the impression, by means of personal performance in their presence that I am (really, only, etc.) *abc* in order to disguise the fact that I am really *xyz.*" Thus "contemporary behavior misleads as to contemporary fact" (276).

Pretending requires the pretender to be "present and active in person to effect the deception by dint of his current behavior," but also, as Austin seems to assume by addressing his reader, that I, the pretender, must be present to another—or another must be in my present—to effect this deception. Pretending therefore has us reorient ourselves from the temporality of the gift and countergift to consider that "vertical time" in which a performance (an act) conceals another act (the giving) and in which both pretender and audience are in each other's present continuous.

Second, attending to the performance of concealing "something else" helps us consider what concealing might allow and protect in everyday life. As Austin remarks, "If there is no sort of urgency to hide what we elect to hide, we may prefer to speak of a leg-pull or of an affectation or a pose" (1958: 276). For example, in pretending to wash windows, I am "really up to something other than cleaning the windows," like casing the valuables in your house. Or children who are "pretending to play chess" are really "up to some mischief." In La Pincoya what is concealed is not only the giving but also the neighbor's "catching" of the critical moment. Concealing allows for the enduring to endure. It protects a living with dignity by explicitly recognizing neither that "critical moment" nor one's act of kindness, since as a neighbor, one should not have personal knowledge of such critical moments.

Such concealing differs from Bourdieu's discussion of gift and misrecognition. For Bourdieu, in precapitalist societies, acts of kindness are cast as "collective misrecognition" of the "objective truth of the game" of social interests: "the moral obligations and emotional attachments created and maintained by the generous gift, in short, overt violence or symbolic violence, censored, euphemized, that is, misrecognizable, recognized violence" ([1980] 1990: 126). In seeking to explain that "lasting hold over someone," kindness is quickly taken up into the player's interest. It is an obligation that, through the fact of time, accumulates symbolic capital and is wielded by the dominant over the dominated. As Bourdieu (2000: 237) moves to capitalist economies, domination is perpetuated by objective social institutions, and the poor, who have no symbolic capital, "are obliged to wait for everything to come from others, from the holders of power over the game." Taking pretending seriously, however, requires moving away from thinking of (and for) the poor struggling for recognition in a world of hierarchical identities. Instead, responding to the articulations of remembering and living with dignity in this world, we might consider this concealment as a sort of "mischief," an act of impersonal kindness outside of the boundaries of this domestic scene and right at the margins of this biography.

A third and related point: pretending reveals the moral energy in remaining silent about how and when one cares for others. Thus the animated silence here to make it occur as if nothing is happening at all suggests investigating the moral along the "threshold of perception" (Deleuze and Guattari 1987: 279). As Austin (1958: 274) writes, "A pretence must be not merely like but *distinctively* like the genuine article simulated." Thus if one is pretending to pass by, one passes by. One would not pretend to be "just chit-chatting" by greeting someone and running off. This engagement with the moral might be considered alongside anthropological work that focuses on the formalism of acts of reciprocity, which distinguishes them as "reciprocity" rather than "exchange" (Keane 2010), or that advances criteria for the ethical as those acts that have *public consequences* and that "*stand out* from the stream of practice" (see also Lambek 2010, 2011: 3).

Staying at that register of the "stream of practice" and considering those stream's layers—that vertical time—elucidates how words have the potential to destroy the delicate concealment crucial to enduring the critical moment, an essential aspect of "living with dignity." Such silence to achieve a living with dignity recalls Das's (2007: 92) attending to men's and women's "obstinate turn towards the ordinary" in relation to the violations of life itself: that ethnography might attend to the "extreme hesitation" of putting that which violated the "whole principle of life . . . back into words" and thus the "deep moral energy" not to speak of that which so violated life itself. Considering the gift in everyday life likewise helps us attend to the deep moral energy in silence, but within the ordinary itself. Thus pretending helps us attend to a quiet moral striving that happens every day but is almost imperceptible—an achieving of illusion.

Pretending brings into focus again the boundaries between the relational modes of friendship and neighborliness, specifically with regard to the personal and the impersonal. As we heard from Susana and Paloma, friendship involves sharing intimacies, a knowledge of those personal dramas that are occurring within the boundaries of a domestic scene, which includes intimate kin and friends. Keeping critical moments within such bounds is crucial to shoring up the boundary between asking and begging, a boundary that is constantly in danger of being corroded by economic precariousness. Within such a domestic scene, giving occurs through personal knowledge not only of the critical moment but also of the ways this critical moment emerges from and enters into a biography. Giving, then, occurs as an act of reciprocity in a relation of mutual obligation. It occurs as an explicit recognition of this moment, but only within the bounds of this domestic scene and to keep such moments within it.

In the relational mode of neighborliness, however, acts of kindness that acknowledge that critical moment cannot rest on that past and future of shared intimacies. Rather such acts of kindness seem to rest on a different kind of sharing. While gossip and seeping signs might betray the critical moment despite one's desire to endure, they also bring into focus a lived mutual vulnerability informed by the forces of economic precariousness. Giving in this relational mode is premised not on sharing personal intimacies but on a vulnerability that is a shared condition. In contrast to friendship, giving in this mode involves an impersonal "catching" and responsiveness—through gossip, seepage, and pretending—that helps that enduring to endure, concealing that vulnerability.

RESEMBLANCE AND RESPONSIVENESS

At the end of Austin's (1958: 271) essay "Pretending" he asks, "What, finally, is the importance of all this about pretending?" He responds, "I will answer this shortly, although I am not sure importance is important: truth is." Pretending has a "humble" place, he remarks, "in the long-term project of classifying and clarifying all possible ways of *not exactly doing things*, which has to be carried through if we are ever to understand properly what doing things is" (271, emphasis in original). Austin's discussion of pretending helps me sharpen my perception in this world, to "properly understand" how dignity is lived in this world, what counts. In this way, Austin's concern with real distinctions and resemblances helped awaken me to my own preoccupations that were not "proper" to this world. In other words, he asks us to consider the fit between words and world by awakening to, rather than fleeing, the ordinary.

I want to explore implications of this awakening for my own affinities and difficulties with philosophy, specifically with respect to our perception of and connection to others. To put it rather bluntly, the "catching" of those small and subtle seeping signs may *prove a point* about the self's inherence in the world; such perceptive activity shows us that the world is always already lining the self. But amid this ethnographic description, making this point has a strange ring to it. My relationship with this world is not asking me to prove a general self's inherence in the world based on examples drawn from their lives. It is asking me to respond to the problem of the self's *task* in making this world her own. Within this problem, the "truth" of perception is not as proof of inherence in *the* world but rather as the *attentiveness* with which one lives in *a* world.

To further elaborate, I turn to part 2 of Cavell's essay "The Avoidance of Love." In several moving pages, Cavell (2002: 337) asks how the expression of acknowledgment in theater might show us what acknowledgment in actuality is: "We are not in and cannot put ourselves in the presence of characters; but we are in, or can put ourselves in their present. It is in making their present ours, their moments as they occur, that we complete our acknowledgment of them. But this requires making their present *theirs*. And that requires us to face not only the porousness of our knowledge (of, for example the motives of their actions and the consequences they care about) but the repudiation of our perception altogether." Acknowledging separateness is necessary in making the other present to me: "In failing to find the character's present we fail to make him present. Then, he is indeed a fictitious creature, a figment of my imagination, like all the other people in my life whom I find I have failed to know, have known wrong" (337).

Let us consider the facing of this "repudiation of our perception altogether" alongside Merleau-Ponty's elaboration of perception in the world. I turn to his "Dialogue and the Perception of the Other": "Thus the other is not to be found in the things, he is not in his body, and he is not I. . . . There is no place for him except in my field, but that place at least was ready for him ever since I began to perceive. From the first time I relied on my body to explore the world, I knew that this corporeal relation to the world could be generalized" (1973: 136). Merleau-Ponty is not claiming to generalize his *particular* bodily experience to others. On the contrary, writing against any abstraction of the body from its environment, he claims that the body has "*a general capacity for measurement*" (Adamson 2005: 176, emphasis in original), and this general capacity is the body's perceiving and being perceived.[6]

In "The Intertwining—The Chiasm," Merleau-Ponty goes further in elaborating "that strange adhesion of seer and the visible," which he calls "the Flesh" (Merleau-Ponty and Lefort 1968: 139). Unlike the Christian notion of "the flesh" as both decaying and holy matter, Merleau-Ponty's notion of the Flesh is not substance or matter, nor is it a representation of mind. Like water, air, and fire, it is an "'element' of Being" an "incarnate principle" of genesis and growth which is inexhaustible. A "pregnancy of possibles" (250), it is that which *is* difference—the hidden hinge between experiences—making possible new and renewed forms of expression.

Rather than posit a subject who possesses or appropriates objects, Merleau-Ponty therefore insists on the implication of the seer with the visible: "We do not possess the musical or sensible ideas, precisely because they are negativity or absence circumscribed; they possess us." He offers the example of the performer who plays a violin sonata, in which the performer is no longer "producing or reproducing the sonata: he feels himself, and others feel him to be at the service of the sonata" (Merleau-Ponty and Lefort 1968: 151).

In an earlier draft I passed all too quickly over the dense prose on the Flesh, and thus too quickly denied a question that could be asked once we orient ourselves to the philosopher's desires rather than what he seeks to prove. Is the ontology of the flesh an expression of a desire for what could be shared? Let me return to other passages of Merleau-Ponty's essay in which he draws out the implication of ourselves with others:

> It is said that the colors, the tactile reliefs given to the other, are for me an absolute mystery, forever inaccessible. This is not completely true; for me to have not an idea, an image, nor a representation, but as it were the immanent experience of them, it suffices that I look at a landscape, that I speak of it with someone. . . . What I see passes into him, this individual green of the meadow under my eyes invades his vision without quitting my own, I recognize in my green his green. . . . There is here no problem of the alter ego because it is not *I* who sees, not *he*

who sees, because an anonymous visibility inhabits both of us, a vision in general. . . . But, what is proper to the visible is, we said, to be the surface of an inexhaustible depth: this is what makes it able to be open to visions other than our own. In being realized, they therefore bring out the limits of our factual vision, they betray the solipsist illusion that consists in thinking that every going beyond is a surpassing accomplished by oneself. (Merleau-Ponty and Lefort 1968: 143)

Reading these passages, I experience both attraction and hesitation. The attraction is to that desire for an inexhaustible relational and temporal capacity within human beings: the "inexhaustible depth" that "makes it able to be open to visions other than our own."[7] In her book *The Flesh of My Flesh*, Kaja Silverman (2009) also elaborates a similar desire for an infinite capacity or "oceanic feeling" that primordially connects all beings and things, what she calls "the Whole." Drawing on a range of writers and artists who have eschewed the "Christian narrative" of eternal life and have instead worked through likeness or resemblance, Silverman asks us to consider how the acknowledgment of human finitude permits a "radical openness" to resemblance, to analogies between things that are as different as the sky, my body, and a blade of grass and as similar as two blades of grass (2009: 146).[8] She elaborates this human finitude in terms of our mortality. Mortality here is not understood only in terms of biological life and death; it is the mortality of our unique identity.[9]

In the evocative chapter "Twilight of Posterity," Silverman takes up Merleau-Ponty's critical response to Valéry's essays on Leonardo da Vinci, and then puts this exchange into dialogue with the contemporary artist Jacob Coleman's "intervention" in an exhibition of Leonardo's work at the Louvre. Emphasizing impersonality over the sovereignty of the artist, Valéry argues that what "'raises' [Leonardo's work] to such a 'high degree' is therefore not 'his precious personal *self*' but rather a universal 'self'— one that includes the pattern of the world" (2009: 135). Valéry rejects any biographical interpretations of Leonardo's work. Merleau-Ponty, however, argues that the biography must be taken into account: "The truth is that the *work to be done called for that life*" (quoted in Silverman 2009: 136). Yet while Merleau-Ponty brought Leonardo's paintings and life closer to each other, he also greatly expanded who could be the author of the art. For the artist "must wait for this image to come to life for other people" (136). As Silverman remarks, "Merleau-Ponty thus encourages us to think of Leonardo's life the way Rilke thinks of his: as 'more than just a private event.'

The same is true of us. Each of us has a biography that is distinctly our own but does not belong to us" (136).

Indeed Leonardo's life and paintings also showed that he saw the artist not as an imitator or transmitter of identity but as a receiver of the world; he chose his apprentices on the basis of beauty, "not on the eagerness to mimic him." Living at the limits of a unique identity, Leonardo allowed for his self—or his "psychic particularity"—to be put "at the disposal of the world" (Silverman 2009: 154). Silverman makes a similar point about the relationship between limits and openings in Leonardo's painting *Virgin and Child with Saint Anne*. Mary sits in the lap of her mother, St. Anne; Mary's arms are outstretched toward the infant Jesus, who seems to be slipping off her lap; Jesus' arms are outstretched to a lamb on the ground while looking up at his mother. Instead of interpreting the figure initiating the fall as "the good-enough mother," Silverman argues that the painting is "concerned less with the limits to which we need to accommodate ourselves than with the opening that these limits create. Because we are finite, this extraordinary painting shows, our capacity for relationality is infinite. Few subjects ever manage to forgive the mother for not satisfying their infantile demands, and far fewer see what a gift that was. For those who understand their limits to be the doorway to relationality, the mother ceases to be 'good enough' and becomes, quite simply, 'human'" (156).

▧ These thoughts are capacious. Resemblance provides that primordial "ontological kinship" among all beings. Limits are valued as openings to new relationships rather than as the capacity for compromise. Rather than think of ourselves in terms of possessing identities and passing them down, we can live as receiving or inhabiting the world, a particularly attractive idea. Yet, turning to my friends in La Pincoya, the crucial question in my relation to the other takes a different tone. Silverman's desire for ontological connection starts with the integrity of identity (its uniqueness) and seeks to move beyond it. But in doing so, it steers around doubt with regard to myself and others. In responding and failing to respond to neighbors and kin, however, what is at stake *is* the reality of others, which can be denied in ordinary ways (see Laugier 2011). It is a world in which Ruby might not be able to receive a neighbor's critical moment because she is exhausted, numb, overwhelmed, or aggravated. Or one in which Susana invites Sara's kids over for lunch, a kindness by *pretense*, after catching what could or could not be a critical moment.

Thus it is a world in which a preoccupation with limits may be emphasizing not the integrity of identity as sovereign self but rather the problems of responsiveness within and across the self's relational modes. In this world, the kindness that I engage cannot be taken as an actual or potential given, neither in terms of the certainty of what is occurring (Is this a critical moment?) nor in terms of the consistency of responsiveness. (I'm too overwhelmed, and I avoid those seeping signs, or I am simply not even struck by them.) The difficulty of kindness is that there is no primordial nature or "ontological kinship" on which it rests. It rests on nothing but this flesh-and-blood self.

But is there not a different desire also expressed in this notion of "inexhaustible depth" or "infinite relationality," of the potential to receive the world and others differently, or to make new connections through resemblance? Engaging this everyday life, I might express a similar desire, but through a turn to the ordinary. Between neighbors there is a double sense to kindness. Just as those critical moments are concealed within a domestic scene, kindness is concealed by pretending. It occurs through achieving a likeness to everyday life, while responding to it. The nature of kindness is therefore thoroughly intertwined with boundaries in this world—between friend and neighbor, "home" and "the street"—that inform the small but significant slip from asking to begging. But it is just as intertwined with *engaging* those boundaries, shoring them up by subtly overcoming them in the face of another's critical moment. In catching and responding to the critical moment, Susana makes her neighbor's present her own, but by first making her present *hers*. In acknowledging her neighbor, Susana makes herself available not only as an actual neighbor but also potentially as a friend, who shares and is remembered in a biography. I return to Silverman's rich phrase, "Each of us has a biography that is distinctively our own but does not belong to us," and I might follow with a question that comes from ethnographic experience: What is at stake in *making* that biography mine?

◼ Let me return to the difficulty of kindness in anthropology. Why do I feel dissatisfied with its conversion to sentimentality or to a compassion that asserts "ahistorical solidarity," an illusory equivalence of lives, or to kindness's quick absorption into the play of social interests? What might be so difficult in kindness is that it may be that disturbing experience of "power and powerlessness" (Phillips and Taylor 2009: 114) that comes with being in another's present. The point is not to assert that everyone is commonly vulnerable. Rather, that *that* vulnerability is mine to respond to: "We are endlessly separate, for no reason. But then we are answerable for everything that comes between us" (Cavell 2002: 379).

Such "being in another's present" might be contrasted to poverty programs in which women must sign a family contract, promising to improve their conditions over time, despite economic precariousness, or the social worker's regard for poor families as a "burden" to the state. In both instances women are integrated into the state's time of individual and family progress, which emphasizes and delineates difference. It is here that we might wonder how such difference displaces any moral and political thought of what *could possibly* be shared—here I too desire that "inexhaustible depth," a depth that might lend itself to a more just world. Yet attending to an ordinary kindness and its concealing brings with it a doubt that must be lived: that the first obstacle to acknowledging the other is not the other but myself. The "truth" of perception lies in acknowledging that separateness, such that our perception might be "true" or "proper" to a world and capable of being repudiated. Such truth, however, carries a requirement of "self-revelation"—as Cavell puts it, "Our position is to be discovered in the painful way that it is always done"—in which blindness and insight are revealed contemporaneously.

NOTES

1. It is quite interesting to me that the "moral sentiments" that the literature on humanitarianism criticizes are located within an assumed "we" of the wealthy, Western societies, organizations, or individuals. The figures of the poor, the illegal, the immigrant, the orphan, however, are almost always drawn on in terms of their furnishing "proof" (the scar, the document, the diseased condition, the testimony of suffering) for inclusion. It is striking how little engagement there is with their "moral sentiments," or more broadly put, the textures of their feelings. I do worry that this critique of humanitarianism, by staying within an opposition between those who perform distinctive labors of feeling compassion and those who perform the labor of providing proof through their bodies, keeps in place those "poor" that philosophy requires for thought. That people in conditions of poverty have elaborated ideas about and aspirations for equality and dignity, among other concerns, rather than being wholly occupied in toiling to create pleas for charity to be heard by the "institution," seems to elude much of the literature.

2. It is important to note that the anxieties over the Church's place within politics and public life in Chile were quite different from Catholic countries in

Europe. While the French Revolution implicated an upheaval against both the monarchy and the Church, the revolution for Chilean independence overthrew Spanish rule but did not threaten the Church's place within political or public life. Rather it generated questions about how that place would articulate with liberal parties. Thus accounts that assert the grounds of modern secularism in Christianity or create a sharp distinction between "the secular" and "the religious" not only assert problematically "Christianity as the fundamental frame for understanding our so-called 'secular' world" (Asad 2011: 673), but they also center the problem of Christianity for democracy within European revolutionary experience.

3. I only realized as I was finishing this essay that my notion of contemporaneity had striking resonances with Merleau-Ponty's notion of "vertical time," or the dimensionality of time. In his writings on Rodin's sculptures, Merleau-Ponty suggests that the sculpture has a simultaneity of times, which offers the sculpture movement (Merleau-Ponty and Johnson 1993; see Slatman 2009).

4. One of the anonymous reviewers asked whether the receiver also "pretends," and how the pretending of the receiver might relate to Mauss's notion of the obligation to receive. The concealing that I attend to in this essay, however, is not simply illustrating the fulfillment of social obligations. Rather such concealing points us to the style or manner in which need is acknowledged and, as I elaborated in later sections, the achieving and failing to acknowledge that need. The point is to attend to the artifice of everyday life. Das's (2012a: 140) perceptive discussion of ordinary ethics is helpful: "Thus while gift-giving can be explained as the 'normal' or 'routine' gesture one performs when visiting a relative or friend as well as on ritual occasions, its mode of performance draws on a register of normativity other than simply fulfilling a social obligation."

5. Please note that Cannell (2004) seems to take "asceticism" as self-renunciation.

6. Adamson (2005: 177) is helpful in clarifying this thought, that the body is "not any particular measure; rather, it is a thing that measures, an element of the natural world that brings measurement to the things it encounters, thus bringing meaning into our experience. . . . The body does not introduce distinctly human norms into our engagement with nature, as if to impose structure on our experience. Instead, the body measures nature by *taking up the things of nature in a normative way*" (emphasis in original).

7. Galen Johnson remarks that Merleau-Ponty's notion of the Flesh was informed by his reading of Heraclitus. The incarnate principle of the Flesh, or Being itself, "is imbued with a kind of energy, longing, desire, or *conatus*" (Johnson 1993: 49).

8. There are serious limitations with reliance on a unified "Christian narrative." The historian Peter Brown (Brown [1996] 2003) has elaborated much more variegated and complex histories of "micro-Christendoms" in late antiquity that

implicated very different understandings of the self, of the relationship between the divine and "saeculum," and between the living and the dead.

9. It is difficult to understand why "unique identity" would be a problem in the Christian tradition without placing it within a genealogy of thinking from late antiquity to the late Middle Ages (before the modern period) on resurrection, the integrity of the body, and divine matter (Bynum 1995, 2011).

CHAPTER 4

Ethnography in the Way of Theory

João Biehl

SUBTRACTION

■ Fragment of a conversation with Clifford Geertz at the Institute for Advanced Study in Princeton, May 2003:

"I am so tired of hearing the question 'What is your contribution to theory?'" I told Geertz. "How would you respond?"

Geertz replied without missing a beat: "Subtraction."

TRANSIENCE

Let me begin by quoting at length from an unexpectedly anthropological text: "Not long ago, I went on a summer walk through a smiling countryside in the company of a taciturn friend and of a young but already famous poet. The poet admired the beauty of the scene around us but felt no joy in it. He was disturbed by the thought that all this beauty was fated to extinction, that it would vanish when winter came, like all human beauty and all the beauty and splendor that men have created or may create. All that he would otherwise have loved and admired seemed to him to be shorn of its worth by the transience which was its doom."

A pause, and the author continues: "I could not see my way to dispute the transience of all things. . . . But I did dispute the pessimistic poet's view that the transience of what is beautiful involves any loss in its worth" (Freud [1915] 2005: 216).

The year is 1915, and Sigmund Freud is recalling an "ordinary affect" (as Kathleen Stewart [2007] would put it) that led him to ponder the different impulses in the mind that the proneness to decay (or precarity) of all that is beautiful and perfect can give rise to. "What spoilt their enjoyment of beauty must have been a revolt in their minds against mourning," Freud argues ([1915] 2005: 217). "Mourning is a great riddle, one of those phenomena which cannot themselves be explained but to which other obscurities can be traced back." An affect that helps to map obscurities, the one in question being the human capacity for love. According to the psychoanalyst, libido "clings to its objects and will not renounce those that are lost even when a substitute lies ready to hand. Such then is mourning" (218).

Yet Freud also realizes that what looms above any attempt to produce a universal theory of the libido vis-à-vis the poet's encounter with transience is the historical moment, the milieu—war on its way.

"A year later," Freud continues, "the war broke out and robbed the world of its beauties." Destroying natural beauty, works of art, pride in civilizational achievements, and faith in philosophy, art, and science, the war "revealed our instincts in all their nakedness and let loose the evil spirits which we thought had been tamed. . . . It robbed us of very much that we had loved, and showed us how ephemeral were many things that we had regarded as changeless." Because the war had made so plain the transience of things, the "libido, thus bereft of so many of its objects, has clung with all the greater intensity to what is left to us" ([1915] 2005: 218).

Freud's insight here is that the precarity of our lives is not merely happy or sad happenstance; it is part and parcel of small- and large-scale constellations and historical shifts and colors our every experience. The Oedipal archaeology is not enough. Libido follows world-historical trajectories. And here is where ethnographic work comes into the picture. As ethnographers we are challenged to attend at once to the political, economic, and material transience of worlds and truths *and* to the journeys people take through milieus in transit while pursuing needs, desires, and curiosities or simply trying to find room to breathe beneath intolerable constraints.

UNFINISHEDNESS

To capture these trajectories and milieus, the philosopher Gilles Deleuze has argued for a cartographic rather than an archaeological analytic of the subject (Biehl and Locke 2010). Archaeologies assume the subject as dependent on past traumas and unconscious complexes, as in Freud (1957), or overdetermined by regimes of power and knowledge, as in Foucault (1980a). In arguing for life's immanence and its horizontal transcendence, Deleuze (1997b : 61) writes, "The trajectory merges not only with the subjectivity of those who travel through a milieu, but also with the subjectivity of the milieu itself, insofar as it is reflected in those who travel through it."

Nearly a century of critical theory, including feminist and postcolonial critiques, has indeed dislodged the sway of crude universals to attend more closely to the specificity and the world-historical significance of people's everyday experience (Berlant 2011; Morris 2010; Scott 2011). The anthropologist Kathleen Stewart (2007, 2011), for instance, has argued for the plurality of ways in which ethnographic rendering can open up new attention to people's arts of existence and the political stakes that make up the ordinary. The slow, granular excavations that ethnography renders visible highlight how affects, raw concepts, and mundane details make up the friction-filled, para-infrastructures of everyday living that are articulated against the background of institutional decays and rifts that deepen (Biehl and McKay 2012; Biehl and Petryna 2013).

The disparate registers of precarity engaged by anthropologists can thus hold off what Stewart (2011) calls "the quick jump from concept to world—that precarious habit of academic thought." She incites us to develop a distinct perceptual capacity out of what is in flux, to become part and parcel not of Life or the Void but of "live forms."

How can we ethnographically apprehend these worldly fabrications and the lives therein, constituted as they are by that which is unresolved, and bring this unfinishedness into our storytelling?

How are long-standing theoretical approaches able to illuminate these political, economic, and affective realities on the ground?

How can the lives of our informants and collaborators, and the counterknowledges that they fashion, become alternative figures of thought that might animate comparative work, political critique, and anthropology to come?

In this essay I explore these questions by returning to my engagements with people in the field (Biehl 2005). I return to the ethnographic not only to address the specific circumstances and trajectories I encountered therein, but to make a case for allowing our engagement with Others to determine the course of our thinking about them and to reflect more broadly upon the agonistic and reflexive relations between anthropology and philosophy (Jackson 1998, 2009). I do so in order to suggest that through ethnographic rendering, people's own theorizing of their conditions may leak into, animate, and challenge present-day regimes of veridiction, including philosophical universals and anthropological subjugation to philosophy. This is not to naïvely assume the ethnographic to be metonymic with a bounded ethnos, but rather to consider what is at stake in the ways that we as anthropologists chronicle and write about the knowledge emerging from our engagement with people.

I am interested in how ethnographic realities find their way into theoretical work. Using the mutual influence between the anthropologist Pierre Clastres and Gilles Deleuze and Félix Guattari as a case study, I argue against reducing ethnography to proto-philosophy. The relationship in fact may be more productively seen as one of creative tension and cross-pollination. This sense of ethnography in the way *of* (instead of *to*) theory—like art—aims at keeping interrelatedness, precariousness, uncertainty, and curiosity in focus. In resisting synthetic ends and making openings rather than final truths, ethnographic practice allows for an emancipatory reflexivity and a more empowering critique of the rationalities, interventions, and moral issues of our times. I conclude with a literal return to the field and reflect on how the story of lives continues.

"I WANT TO KNOW WHAT THEY WROTE OF ME"

"When will you come back?" asked Catarina, seated on a wheelchair in Vita, an asylum in southern Brazil where the mad and the ill, the unproductive and unwanted, are left to die.

Tomorrow, I said—but why do you ask?

"I like to respond to what you ask. . . . You know how to ask questions. Many people write, but they don't know how to get to what matters . . . and you know how to make the account."

I thanked her for her trust and told her that in order to make the account, I would try to find her medical records in the psychiatric hospitals where she said she had been treated.

Catarina agreed and said, "I want to know what they wrote of me."

■ After many frustrating calls to Hospital Espírita, I got hold of a social worker who was kind enough to search the medical files thoroughly. When I anxiously called back, she told me, "Catarina had several admissions here. She has a history of mental illness in the family. A maternal uncle committed suicide." That was supposed to explain Catarina's condition: a madness that ran in her blood. "More I cannot tell you," she added.

The hospital would release the records only if Catarina requested them in person. She was brave enough to come along. On the way back to Vita,

Catarina was quiet. When asked why, she admitted, "I was a little afraid." Of what? "That you would leave me there."

■ I had retrieved some intriguing notes on Catarina's last hospitalization. The doctor wrote that you were hearing voices.

"That's true," said Catarina.

Which voices?

"I heard cries, and I was always sad."

Where did the voices come from?

"I think they came from the cemetery. All those dead bodies. They had nicknamed me Catacomb. . . . Once I read in a book that there was a catacomb and that the dead ones were in there, closed up. And I put that into my head. One mummy wanted to get hold of another one, who was suffering too much at the hands of the bandits."

And how did the story end?

"They imprisoned her there too."

How did you think these voices got into your head?

"I escaped and read the book. I was sad. I was separated from my ex-husband. He went to live with the other woman, and I went to live alone. Then my house was set on fire."

Dead in name, buried alive, looking for a story line in a book found as she escaped from home.

Was it then, when the house burned down, that you began hearing voices?

"No, it was much earlier—immediately after I separated."

The split of the I. "Separated." Catarina was no longer the person she had struggled to become. The ex-husband, the ex-home, the ex-human she now was.

THE RETURN OF THE ETHNOGRAPHIC SUBJECT

"Why does he not let Catarina finally rest?" a leading anthropologist recently asked at a conference, after hearing an abridged first draft of this essay. As anthropologists, I suggested, we are challenged to listen to people—their self-understandings, their storytelling, their own concept-work—with deliberate openness to life in all its refractions.

I was taken off guard and felt my colleague's question as an epistemic violence.

Being referred to in the third person—"Why does he not . . ."—rather than addressed directly and cast as repeating myself did, of course, create some anxiety. But these were not the only reasons for my discomfort. I knew that such provocations were part of academic theater. What bothered me most deeply was the implication that Catarina and her thinking had been exhausted and that this visceral ethnographic encounter and the events it precipitated no longer had any creative relevance.

Catarina most certainly would not want to be put to rest, I told myself. And she loved to hear how her story was reaching broader audiences. This moot moment (or academic nonconversation) did nonetheless push me to think even more rigorously about why I continue to return—why I must and will return—to our dialogues and to the difficult questions Catarina's life and abandonment compelled me to reckon with over a decade ago.

Ethnographic subjects allow us to return to the places where thought is born.

Catarina refused her own erasure, and she anticipated an exit from Vita. It was as difficult as it was important to sustain this anticipation: to find ways to support Catarina's search for ties to people and the world and her demand for continuity, or at least its possibility. Attempting to grasp the intricate infrastructural and intersubjective tensions at the core of Vita and Catarina's life not only revealed the present as embattled and unfinished; it also displaced dominant analytical frameworks, thus marking the ethnographic work as a birthplace of sorts, out of which a mode of inquiry and a method of narration as well as the possibility of a distinct public came into existence. I say *public*, for ours is a practice that also begs for the emergence of a third, a reader, a community of sorts, that is neither the character nor the writer, which will manifest and carry forward anthropology's potential to become a mobilizing force in this world.

Significantly the ethnographic work also made it possible for the anthropologist to return to this other "home" and to know it, through the workings of time, anew. "And the end of all exploring," in the words of T. S. Eliot (1968), "will be to arrive where we started and know the place for the first time."

Put in more scholarly language, I think I return to Catarina, in and out of Vita, much as a field of discourse refers back to its founder or founding moment at each step of its testing and evolution. In his lecture "What Is an Author?" Foucault (1999: 219) reminded his audience that "the return to" is not merely a historical supplement or ornament: "on the contrary, it constitutes an effective and necessary task of transforming the discursive practice itself."

As I am drawn back to Catarina—and as new, variably positioned cohorts of readers and students are affected by her thinking and struggles in different ways—both the force and the meaning of her life and thinking and the anthropologies it has generated remain open and in flux, forbidding any false sense of closure or certainty.

I feel that I owe these returns, and the unfinishedness they sustain, to Catarina. For me this raises the question of what distinguishes the subject of anthropology from that of science. "The fact is that science, if one looks at it closely, has no memory," states Lacan (1989: 18). "Once constituted, it forgets the circuitous path by which it came into being." Is it, in part, this form of forgetting that permits the sense of certainty in scientific claims to truth?

In science (and in philosophy, for that matter) human subjects appear, by and large, as sharply bounded, generic, and overdetermined, if they are present at all. But ethnography allows other pathways and potentials for its subjects—and for itself. In our returns to the encounters that shaped us and the knowledge of human conditions we produced, we can learn from our experiences anew, live them differently, acknowledging an inexhaustible richness and mystery at the core of the people we learn from. In contrast to the subjects of statistical studies and the figures of philosophy, our ethnographic subjects have a future—and we become a part of it, in unexpected ways.

IN THE MIDDLE WAY

One thinks of what allowed Lévi-Strauss ([1955] 1992: 44) to write *Tristes Tropiques*: "Time, in an unexpected way, has extended its isthmus between life and myself," he recalls. "Twenty years of forgetfulness were required before I could establish communion with my earlier experience, which I had sought the world over without understanding its significance or appreciating its essence."

Lévi-Strauss also spoke of the physical objects and sensations that can help us to feel and think through the precarity of the people and worlds that become a part of us. He opens *Saudades do Brasil* (Nostalgia for Brazil), a collection of photographs, with this beautiful moment of Proustian precarity, the curious memory of an odor: "When I barely open my notebooks, I still smell the creosote with which, before setting off on an expedition, I used to saturate my canteens to protect them from termites and mildew. . . . Almost undetectable after more than half a century, this trace instantly brings back to me the savannas and forests of Central Brazil, inseparably bound with other smells . . . as well as with sounds and colors. For as faint as it is now, this odor—which for me is a perfume—is the thing itself, still a real part of what I have experienced" (1995: 9).

Photographs may not incite this same return to lived experience. "Photographs leave me with the impression of a void, a lack of something the lens is inherently unable to capture," Lévi-Strauss laments (1995: 9). They exhibit the deadly force of modern times, the evisceration of the diversity of humans, animals, plants. The anthropologist gives us both forms of memory together, the hollow clarity of the photographic anthology and the tantalizing whiff of distilled tar inviting anew the imagination of what lies between these images.

Ethnography always begins in the midst of social life, and so it is with our writing—we are always "in the middle way," as Eliot (1968) puts it, "trying to learn to use words," painfully aware that "every attempt is a wholly new start, and a different kind of failure. . . . And so each venture is a new beginning, a raid on the inarticulate."

There are of course many different ways, both figurative and literal, of returning to our ethnographic sites and subjects or of reengaging notes, memories, and visual archives. Revisiting earlier work, we might bring into view the broader academic drama in which the ethnographic account and critique were imbricated (as in Paul Rabinow's [2007] pioneering *Reflections on Fieldwork in Morocco*) or highlight the potential of photography to capture the singular against the generalizing mandates of sociological study (as in the case of Paul Hyman, explored by Rabinow [2011] in *The Accompaniment*).

I recall the time I returned to Vita with my collaborator and friend, the photographer Torben Eskerod. It was December 2001, and Torben was finding it quite difficult to make a portrait of Catarina. She was constantly moving her head and trying to pose like a model. Torben asked me to tell her to try to stay still, to look straight into the camera, and "just be natural," which I did. I then added that, as an artist, Torben wanted to capture her singularity, that he did not stop till he found the person's soul, so to speak. To which Catarina replied, "But what if in the end, he only finds his own?" The smile that ensued is what we see in Torben's portrait.

It is the artist's greatest gift, as Stephen Greenblatt (2009: 8) reminds us, to insist on the uniqueness of each one of us, fated to walk the earth at a particular place and time, at times alone and at times carving out a home

Fig 4.1. Catarina. © Torben Eskerod.

or a story with another "irreplaceable being." And to register the human struggle and inexorable loss in the face of Time that Shakespeare so beautifully captured when he said to a youth (in his fifteenth sonnet): "And all in war with Time for love of you, / As he takes from you, I engraft you new."

Literally returning to our ethnographic sites—to say more honestly what we saw or to rectify misrenderings and face the pain one's interpretations and texts have caused (as Nancy Scheper-Hughes [2001] has done for *Saints, Scholars, and Schizophrenics*), or to understand what war and merciless political economies have done to generations (as in Michael D. Jackson's [2004] poignant *In Sierra Leone*)—causes a distinctive longitudinal perspective to emerge, allowing insight not only into how time works on our own senses and sensibilities but also (and perhaps most important) into how the world itself shifts.

Such literal returns enable us to trace the tissues connecting then and now, opening up a critical space for examining what happens in the *meantime*: how destinies have been avoided or passed on, what makes change possible, and what sustains the intractability of intolerable conditions.

DETACHING ONESELF FROM WHAT IS ACCEPTED AS TRUE

Abandoned in Vita, Catarina ceaselessly wrote and demanded another chance at life. The drug Akineton, which is used to control the side effects of antipsychotic medication, is literally part of the new name she gave herself in the notebooks: Catkine. As I engaged the "it" Catarina had become— "What I was in the past does not matter"—I was in my own way becoming something else back home: an anthropologist. Yes, a pedagogy of fieldwork is hierarchical, but it is also mutually formative, as Rabinow (2003: 90) notes: "As it is hierarchical, it requires care; as it is a process, it requires time; and as it is a practice of inquiry, it requires conceptual work."

In my engagement with Catarina, I was particularly concerned with relating her own ideas and writing to the theories that institutions applied to her (as they operationalized concepts of pathology, normality, subjectivity, and rights) and to the commonsensical knowledge people had of her. Rationalities play a part in the reality of which they speak, and this dramaturgy of the real becomes integral to how people value life and relationships and enact the possibilities they envision for themselves and others. The psychiatric process required that the plurality, instability, and flux that composed Catarina's environment and experience be ignored and that her inner life be restrained, annulled, even beaten out of her. Ethnography can capture this active embroilment of reason, life, and ethics, and the anthropologist can learn to think with the theories, however articulate or inarticulate they may be, created by people like Catarina concerning both their condition and their hope.

Comprehension was involved. The work we began was not about the person of my thoughts and the impossibility of representation or of becoming a figure for Catarina's psychic forms. It was about human contact enabled by contingency and a disciplined listening that gave each one of us something to look for. "I lived kind of hidden, an animal," Catarina told me, "but then I began to draw the steps and to disentangle the facts with you." In speaking of herself as an animal, Catarina was engaging the human possibilities foreclosed for her. "I began to disentangle the science and the wisdom. It is good to disentangle oneself, and thought as well."

For all of his exploration of the subject as a function of discourse, Foucault (1997: 327) saw this work of detaching oneself "from what is accepted as true" and seeking "other rules" as "philosophy in activity": "The displacement and transformation of frameworks of thinking, the changing of received values and all the work that has been done to think otherwise, to do something else, to become other than what one is—that, too, is philosophy."

By way of her speech, the unconscious, and the many knowledges and powers whose histories she embodied, there was plasticity at the heart of Catarina's existence. Facing changing social and medical realities, she dealt with a multiplicity of bodily symptoms and desperately tried to articulate a symbolic function that had been lost, searching for words and identifications that might make life newly possible.

Symptoms are born and die with time. They take form at the most personal juncture between the subject, her biology, and interpersonal and technical recordings of "normal" ways of being in local worlds. Hence symptoms implicate those people, institutions, and things standing for common sense and reason in the unfolding of such disorders. Symptoms are also, at times, a necessary condition for the afflicted to articulate a new relationship to the world and to others. Ethnography, I believe, can help us resituate and rethink pathology within these various circuits and concrete struggles over recognition, belonging, and care.

PHILOSOPHY IN THE FIELD

The problem for an anthropology of the contemporary, Rabinow (2007: xxiii) says, "is to inquire into what is taking place without deducing it beforehand. And that requires sustained research, patience, and new concepts, or modified old ones."

While in the field, I read some of Deleuze's work with the psycho- or schizoanalyst Guattari. Their ideas about the powers and potentials of desire (both creative and destructive), the ways social fields leak and transform (power and knowledge notwithstanding), and the in-between, plastic, and ever-unfinished nature of *a* life struck me as refreshingly ethnographic. Deleuze (1995: 170) was particularly concerned with the idea of becoming: those individual and collective struggles to come to terms with events and intolerable conditions and to shake loose, to whatever degree possible, from determinants and definitions—"to grow both young and old [in them] at once." Becoming is not a part of history, he wrote: "History amounts only to the set of preconditions, however recent, that one leaves behind in order to 'become,' that is, to create something new" (171).

Thinking about Catarina's abandonment and subsequent struggles through the lens of becoming rather than bare life, for example, has allowed me to learn from her writing and her desires in a way I might not have been able to otherwise. The philosopher Giorgio Agamben (1998: 4) has significantly informed contemporary biopolitical debates with his evocation of the *Homo sacer* and the assertion that "life exposed to death" is the original element of Western democracies. This "bare life" appears in Agamben as a kind of historical-ontological destiny—something presupposed as nonrelational and desubjectified. A number of anthropologists have critiqued Agamben's apocalyptic take on the contemporary human condition and the dehumanization that accompanies such melancholic, if poignant, ways of thinking (Das and Poole 2004; Rabinow and Rose 2006).

Whether in social abandonment, addiction, or homelessness, life that no longer has any value for society is hardly synonymous with a life that no longer has any value for the person living it (Bourgois and Schonberg 2009; Garcia 2010). Language and desire meaningfully continue even in circumstances of profound abjection. Against all odds, people keep searching for connection and for ways to endure (Biehl and Moran-Thomas 2009).

"Dead alive. Dead outside. Alive inside," Catarina wrote. "I give you what is missing. João Biehl, Reality, CATKINE."

There was something in the way Catarina moved things from one register to the other—the past, life in Vita, and desire for an exit and a tie— that eluded my understanding. This movement was her own evolving language for abandonment, I thought, and it forced my conceptual work to remain tuned to the precariousness and unfinishedness of life even in its most overmedicated and depersonalized state.

When I was beginning to write the book *Vita* (2005) I remember telling my editor Stan Holwitz about reading Deleuze in the field. He replied, "I don't care what Deleuze thinks. I want to know what Catarina thinks!"

I got the point. Perhaps anthropologists have been too enamored with philosophy as the power of "reflecting on." And people and the social worlds they navigate are more complicated and unfinished than philosophical schemes tend to account for. The editor as reader was rightly concerned with the conceptual fecundity of people's practical knowledge. Or as Catarina wrote, "I am like this because of life."

Certainly, to carry out our analyses, we need models, types, theories—abstractions of various kinds. But what if we broadened our sense of what counts as theoretical and methodological innovation and left aside, even if for a moment, the need for central discursive engines—the modus operandi that shaped much of anthropology in the twentieth century? Amid the lure of formalizing the new via "designed spaces of experiment and intervention" (Marcus 2012: 432), what becomes of local, situated, subjugated knowledges?

Epistemological breakthroughs do not belong only to experts and analysts. Simply engaging with the complexity of people's lives and desires—their constraints, subjectivities, projects—in ever-changing social, economic, and technological worlds constantly necessitates rethinking. So what would it mean for our research methodologies and ways of writing to consistently embrace unfinishedness, seeking ways to analyze the general, the structural, and the processual while maintaining an acute awareness of the tentativeness of our reflective efforts?

As anthropologists we can strive to do more than simply mobilize real-world messiness to complicate—or serve—ordered philosophy, reductive medical diagnostics, and statistics-centered policy approaches. Both the evidentiary force and theoretical contribution of our discipline are intimately linked to attunement to the relations and improvised landscapes through which lives unfold and to trying to give form to people's arts of living. At stake is finding creative ways of not letting the ethnographic die in our accounts of actuality. And attending to life as it is lived and adjudicated by people in their realities produces a multiplicity of approaches, theoretical moves and countermoves, an array of interpretive angles as various as the individuals drawn to practice anthropology.

The point is not to move our interlocutors in the field up to our level in the hierarchy of epistemological authority—or to that of the European White Male Philosopher—but to argue for an equality of intelligences and to find novel public and scholarly ways to harness the creative conceptual and relational work activated in the field. Accounting for "tragedies generated in life" (as Catarina would put it), social determinants, and institutional and human heterogeneities may not be new or easy, much less the key to an ultimate critical theory, but it never gets old or less valuable.

"One does not have an idea in general," Deleuze (1998: 14) argues in the lovely essay "Having an Idea in Cinema": "Ideas are potentials that are already engaged in this or that mode of expression and inseparable from them." Thus, according to Deleuze, philosophers *try* (trying is a crucial tentative verb here) to invent concepts, filmmakers invent "blocks of movement/duration," and scientists "invent and create functions" (15).

So what does having an idea in anthropology today entail?

Given that we work with people and are concerned with knowledge of the human condition, it would seem to me that our ideas should come out of that engagement: life bricolage, what people make, often agonizingly, out of whatever is available to them to endure, understand, and desire against all odds. Our characters are those who might otherwise remain forgotten, and they want to be represented, as Catarina did: to be part of a matrix in which there is someone else to see and to think with and through their travails. Our characters are those who might otherwise remain forgotten, and they want to be represented, to be part of a matrix in which there is someone else to see and to think with and through their travails.

In the contemporary politics of knowledge, anthropologists defer too readily to philosophers, seeking authorization in their pronouncements, but as Deleuze (1998: 14) himself stated, "No one needs philosophy for reflecting."

So do we need philosophy to reflect on our fieldwork?

If our business is not to do what philosophy does—"creating or even inventing concepts"—what is it that we make?

Can philosophy—really—transform the characters and realities we engage and the stories we tell (if this is what we do) into figures of thought?

This set of questions frames the problem as one of clarifying the distinctions between separate styles of thought, knowing, and creativity. But overlaps, entanglements, two-way exchanges may be what is at stake here: social fields always leak, intermingle, deterritorialize—and that goes for academic disciplines too. Meanings and concepts flow freely across fuzzy boundaries and change in the process.

In fretting that anthropologists are too subservient to philosophers, we forget how much philosophical concept-work has been stimulated by ethnographers. Who remembers that Deleuze and Guattari ([1980] 1987) owe their notion of "plateau" to Gregory Bateson's (1976: 113) work on Bali?

Bateson, they wrote, "uses the word plateau to designate a continuous, self-vibrating region of intensities whose development avoids any orientation toward a culmination point or external end" ([1980] 1987: 22). The plateau is about people's plasticity. It is a kind of intersubjective medium—a "bizarre intensive stabilization"—for finding footholds in the flux of social life.

"Flux" too is a concept Deleuze and Guattari owe to an ethnographer—in this case, Pierre Clastres, whose thinking found its way into *Anti-Oedipus* ([1972] 1983, the work that preceded *A Thousand Plateaus* ([1980] 1987). Nomadism, the encoding of fluxes, the war machine: all of these key insights come from Clastres's attempt to theorize "primitive society" as a social form constantly at war against the emergence of the state.

"As for ethnography, Pierre Clastres said it all or, in any case, the best for us," Deleuze and Guattari stated in a 1972 debate about *Anti-Oedipus*. "What are the flows of a society, what are the fluxes capable of subverting it, and what is the position of desire in all of this? Something always happens to the libido, and it comes from far off on the horizon, not from inside" (in Guattari 2008: 89).

Clastres, who was there at the debate, said that Deleuze and Guattari were far beyond tedious comparativism: "They show how things work differently. . . . It seems to me that ethnologists should feel at home in *Anti-Oedipus*" (in Guattari 2008: 85).

What precisely ethnologists did was still a matter of debate for each of them. For Clastres (2007: 20), ethnology is an encounter that exceeds the conditions of its existence: "When the mirror does not reflect our own likeness, it does not prove there is nothing to perceive."

For Deleuze and Guattari, the ethnologist can best be seen as an act of art in life. Fascinated by Bateson, they view him as the living pursuit of flows (see Jensen and Rödje 2012). Bateson-*cum*-ethnographer himself becomes the figure of their own philosophy, his career retold in their fantastic terminology: "Gregory Bateson begins by fleeing the civilized world, by becoming an ethnologist and following the primitive codes and savage flows; then he turns in the direction of flows that are more and more decoded. . . . But where does the dolphin flux end, if not with the basic research projects of the American army?" (Deleuze and Guattari [1972] 1983: 236).

According to Deleuze, creation comes out of necessity. What is it that we anthropologists need to do? What necessitates our work?

For Clastres, the answer is not straightforward. He was already engaged in high-stakes theoretical debates before his encounter with the Guayaki, and his desire—his *necessity*—to dismantle the evolutionism and economic determinism of Hegelian Marxist thinking motivated and shaped his fieldwork. The intellectual historian Samuel Moyn (2004: 58) goes so far as to say that "hoping to find an extra-European point of view on European society, Clastres made up at home those whom he claimed to discover someplace else." But I would say that Clastres's experiences in Paraguay actually added a new need: to find a channel for grief and moral outrage at the death of the Guayaki.

MUTUAL BECOMINGS

Clastres fought the erasure of "primitive society" both in theory and in reality. As Clifford Geertz (1998: 2) poignantly noted in his review of Clastres's *Chronicle of the Guayaki Indians*, "The threnodic first-person voice, breaking every now and again into moral rage, suggests that there may be more going on than mere reporting of distant oddities." Indeed the text written is always so much more than the sum of its sentences—other meanings, histories, and contexts proliferate between and beneath the lines.

Later, in the same review, titled "Deep Hanging Out," Geertz wrote that Clastres believed in total field immersion as "the royal road to recovering" what is socially elemental. By not doing a lineage of ideas, Geertz casts Clastres as drawing near a confident empiricism—as opposed to the work of James Clifford, with his hanging back and "lucid uncertainty" (1998: 9). Geertz took a stab at *Writing Culture*: "There is very little in what the partisans of an anthropology in which fieldwork plays a much reduced or transformed role . . . have so far done that would suggest they represent the wave of the future" (10).

So it might be a nemesis that compels us to work: the politics of writing-against (on all generational sides). From Malinowski's (1927) critique of the universalizing claims of Western psychoanalytic and economic theories to Geertz's (1983, 1995, 2000) suspicion of functionalist and structuralist approaches, anthropologists are always fighting reductionist hegemonic analytical frames, even as we struggle to articulate and theorize the conditions of our subjects' becomings. The enemy is in the titles: *Society against the State. Anti-Oedipus. Anti-antirelativism.*

Academic debates can become suffocatingly polarizing. In writing-against, do we not risk being consumed by the nemesis, risk producing more monstrous abstractions—the socially elemental and society without a state for Clastres, or revolutionary society and the outside without an inside for Deleuze and Guattari? But then can the person and the social actually be accessed or created without the framework of a preexisting theoretical disagreement?

Affinities and antagonisms, exchanges and indebtedness abound in the anthropology-philosophy interface (or face-off). Having created crucial evidence for Deleuze and Guattari's concept-work, Clastres praised them for not taking ethnographers lightly: "They ask them real questions, questions that require reflection" (in Guattari 2008: 85). And yet he remained worried about the primacy of debt over exchange in their general theory of society and whether their idea of earth did not "somewhat crush that of territory" (in Guattari 2008: 85).

Clastres (1998: 97) insisted on radical alterity throughout his career, viewing even his own ethnographic work with the Guayaki to have been possible only through *his* world having wounded their own so violently: "The society of the Atchei *Iroiangi* was so healthy that it could not enter into a dialogue with me, with another world. . . . We would begin to talk only when they became sick."

Scribbled a few days before his untimely death, "Marxists and Their Anthropology" is Clastres's most antagonistic essay. He named structuralism "a godless theology: it is a sociology without society" ([1980] 2010a: 224) and denounced the "radical nullity" of Marxist ethnology, "a homogenous whole equal to zero" (221) that reduces the social body to economic infrastructure (234). In the logic of Marxist discourse, primitive society or the Guayaki "quite simply cannot exist, they do not have the right to autonomous existence, their being is only determined according to that which will come much later, their necessary future" (234–35).

But one could also ask whether the "primitive" Guayaki do not work in Clastres as the precursor of the theory of civil society he was advocating at the time, against a feared and condemned state. Ethnography is always engaged in its own politics-of-critique (Biehl and McKay 2012), and there is an instructive irony in the fact that Clastres named his movement *political anthropology* even as he argued that the Guayaki did not practice politics as we know it. At any rate, in his final text Clastres ([1980] 2010a: 227) gets back to Deleuze and Guattari only to leave the cryptic note that, after all, what he identifies under the category desire "has very little to do with how [they] use it."

Clastres's post-fieldwork theoretical moves and entanglements—from his affinities with and swerves from Deleuze and Guattari to his frustration with Marxist anthropology—throw into relief how epistemological hierarchies constantly push ethnographers to harness their evidence to the philosophical and political debates of the day. I sense a profound wisdom in Geertz's seemingly flippant, grouchy answer—"subtraction"—to the question of his "contribution to theory" that opened this essay. If theory is one way that ethnographers establish the connectedness of the things they describe, theory also circumscribes the ethnographic view. At times, this circumscription importantly allows for the analytical pauses that make alternative knowledge viable; at others, it risks reifying ethnographic moments, sacrificing the sense of the unfinishedness of everyday life that makes ethnography so exciting to begin with.

I am reminded of Bateson's (1958: 257) epilogue to *Naven*, in which he makes very clear that the complexity and force of his ethnographic materials would always exceed the conceptual frames he invented to think about them: "My fieldwork was scrappy and disconnected. . . . My own theoretical approaches proved too vague to be of any use in the field." In their shared ambivalence toward theory, Clastres, Geertz, and Bateson all pose the problem of how to maintain integrity to the mutual becomings activated in the field upon return to the academic milieu as well as the question of conceptual innovation via writing. As Bateson put it, "The writing of this book has been an experiment, or rather a series of experiments, in methods of thinking about anthropological material" (257).

People must come first in our work (Biehl and Petryna 2013). Insular academic language and debates and impenetrable prose should not be allowed to strip people's lives, knowledge, and struggles of their vitality—analytical, political, and ethical. Like literature and documentary filmmaking (Rouch 2003), ethnographic writing can push the limits of language and imagination as it seeks to bear witness to life in a manner that does not bound, reduce, or make caricatures of people but liberates, if always only partially, some of the epistemological force and authority of their travails and stories that might break open alternative styles of reasoning. In Clastres's ([1980] 2010b: 92) words, "Each is refused the ruse of knowledge, which in becoming absolute, abolishes itself in silence."

REREADING THE ETHNOGRAPHIC AS PHILOSOPHICAL

In his imaginative introduction ("The Untimely, Again") to Clastres's posthumous collection of essays *Archaeology of Violence*, the anthropologist Eduardo Viveiros de Castro (2010: 17) calls for a rereading of the anthropologist: "*Resisting* Clastres, but not stopping to read him; and resisting *with* Clastres, too: confronting with and in his thought what remains alive and unsettling." A resourceful anachronism is unleashed as Clastres is re-read today: "If it is worth doing, it is because something of the era in which these texts were written, or better, against which they were written . . . re-mains in ours, something of the problems of then continue with us today. . . . What happens when we reintroduce in another context concepts elaborated in very specific circumstances? What effects do they produce when they resurface?" (17, 18).

Clastres was writing against Marxism and ethnocentric European so-cial philosophies that privileged economic rationality over political inten-tionality, and as Viveiros de Castro (2010: 13) explains, "Clastres discerned, in his 'primitive societies,' both the political control of the economy and the social control of the political."

According to Viveiros de Castro (2010: 15), "Alterity and multiplicity de-fine both how anthropology constitutes itself in relation with its object and this object constitutes itself. 'Primitive society' is the name that Clas-tres gave to that object, and to his own encounter with multiplicity. And if the State has always existed, as Deleuze and Guattari (1981/1987: 397) argue in their insightful commentary on Clastres, then primitive society also will always exist: as the immanent exterior of the State . . . as a multi-plicity that is non-interiorizable by the planetary mega-machines."

As "The Untimely, Again" unfolds, Clastres's ethnography acquires its meaning in retrospect, mediated by Viveiros de Castro's interpretation of Deleuze and Guattari. And perhaps because Viveiros de Castro takes such great care to avoid fetishizing the ethnographic encounter, his critical re-reading of Clastres begins to sketch the lines of a theory-ethnography bi-nary. This dichotomy is particularly noticeable when he takes Clastres's work as defining "an indigenous cosmopraxis of immanent alterity, which is tantamount to a counter-anthropology . . . located in the precarious space between silence and dialogue" (2010: 41). In this rendering, one could argue, Clastres's own ethnographic approach is so subservient to the theorists who read him (or the concept-work through which he is read) that he is por-trayed as writing against anthropology itself.

Viveiros de Castro (2010: 34) praises Deleuze and Guattari for having identified the "philosophical richness" in Clastres: "[They] completed Clas-tres's work, fleshing out the philosophical richness that lay in potential form therein." Both Clastres and (later) Deleuze and Guattari argued against the notion that exchange is a "founding principle of sociality." However, "at the same time that they take on board one of Clastres's fun-damental theses, when they affirm that the State, rather than supposing a mode of production, is the very entity that makes production a 'mode,' Deleuze and Guattari blur the overdrawn distinction made by Clastres between the political and economic" (37). Occupying the privileged epistemic position of philosophers, Deleuze and Guattari thus appear as distilling and perfecting Clastres's apparently crude (ethnographic) insights.

The erudition and insight of Viveiros de Castro's analytical work is indisputable. I am only suggesting that in this moment of his rereading, the creative exchange that existed between Clastres and Deleuze and Guattari is markedly unidirectional. Clastres's ideas thus sound "Deleuzian" (where did Guattari go?), and the force of Clastres's ethnography is either muted or evaluated as philosophy in potential. Clearly, if we read anthropologists in the terms of their philosopher-interlocutors, the ethnography seems brittle and unneeded once the philosophy has been written.

Viveiros de Castro, of course, reads Clastres not merely as an affirmation of a philosophy but also in a more generous mode. Herein Clastres's humanism and sense of the political are newly unleashed: "'Primitive society . . .' is one of the conceptual embodiments of the thesis that another world is possible: that there is life beyond capitalism, as there is society outside of the State. There always was—and for this we struggle—there always will be" (Viveiros de Castro 2010: 15).

Yet taken as an anthropology of the contemporary, this project certainly begs for critique or at least deeper specificity: What about life *inside* capitalism? Why this investment in a counterideology to capitalism that rests on the imaginary of a capital's *outside*? How to make sense of contemporary realities of society inside the state and people who mobilize to use the state, forging novel, tenuous links between themselves, the state, and the marketplace?

The concept of "primitive society" was born out of Clastres's ethnographic work, moral outrage, and critical engagement with social philosophy, but it was also a way of articulating a political anthropology for the times. There are two key challenges here: to assess Clastres in light of contemporary ethnography rather than by how his ideas measure up to the often vacuous concepts of critical political theory and to let the unfolding of the ethnographic present—in all its repetitions, singularities, and ambiguities—guide our imagination of what is socially possible and desirable.

Such work is ongoing. Lucas Bessire, for example, has been chronicling the postcontact travails of one of the world's last voluntarily isolated group of hunter-gatherers, who walked out of the forest in northern Paraguay about a decade ago. Using multiple genres of engagement—deep ethnography, film, and concept-work—Bessire (2006, 2011) shows how the Aroyeo new people are not a society against the state but rather "ex-primitives" struggling to survive and make a future in a context shaped by deforestation, humanitarianism, and neoliberal economic policies. They self-objectify their objectification to unexpected ends, both vital and deadly.

In the essay "Savage Ethnography," Clastres's ([1980] 2010b: 90) own words point to the force of the ethnographic encounter that, while rejecting pure positivism—"the academicism of simple description (a perspective close to and complicitous with the most tiresome exoticism)"—is certainly not dependent on the theories of philosophers: "In reality," Clastres writes, "the meager categories of ethnological thought hardly appear capable of measuring the depth and density, or even the difference, of indigenous thought" (88–89).

Are we really to believe that theory can so easily answer the questions that left "ethnological thought" so thoroughly baffled? Clastres ([1980] 2010b: 89) continues, "Anthropology uncovers, in the name of who knows what pallid certainties, a field to which it remains blind (like the ostrich, perhaps?), one that fails to limit concepts such as mind, soul, body, and ecstasy but at the center of which Death mockingly poses its question."

Ethnography is not just proto-philosophy but a way of staying connected to open-ended, even mysterious social processes and uncertainties—a way of counterbalancing the generation of certainties and foreclosures by other disciplines.

This ethnographic vision carries both a hermeneutics and an ethics of intersubjectivity. As Catarina told me, "There is so much that comes with time . . . the words . . . and the signification, you will not find in the book. . . . Nobody will decipher the words for me. I will not exchange my head with you, and neither will you exchange yours with mine. One must have a science, a light conscience. One needs to put one's mind in place. . . . I am writing for myself to understand, but, of course, if you all understand, I will be very content."

Catarina's openness to the existence of a third, so to speak—neither I nor You, an It, an indefinite, neither text-performer nor reader-spectator, but something that, in coming about in the provisional encounter between them, generates new fields of understanding and possibility—is exactly what I long to see more often in interactions among anthropologists as well as between anthropologists and their interlocutors in the field. Along with "the anecdote, the vignette, the ethnographic incident, the organic local theorist," as Michael M. J. Fischer (2010a: 338) beautifully puts it, this third field—fundamentally relational, the exclusive property of no single individual—can also act as "pebbles and labyrinths in the way of theory."

EVERYTHING HAS A STORY

Philosophers tell stories with concepts. Filmmakers tell stories with blocks of movements and duration. Anthropologists, I would say, tell stories with instances of human becomings: people learning to live, living on, not learning to accept death, resisting death in all possible forms.

What does anthropology's storytelling with ethnographic materials invent?

Inventing something is a very solitary act—Deleuze does not believe in giving voice; in creating we are thrown back to ourselves. "But it is in the name of my creation that I have something to say to someone" (1998: 16).

Consider the following statement: "If all the disciplines communicate together, it is on the level of that which never emerges for itself, but which is, as it were, engaged in every creative discipline, and this is the constitution of space-times" (Deleuze 1998: 16).

What we engage with will never emerge for itself. Our creative work, the necessity we address, the mode of expression we are familiar with speaks to this real, reducible neither to time nor to space (nor the Unconscious or History, the Social or the Scientific Function). "Deserted ground is the only thing that can be seen, but this deserted ground is heavy with what lies beneath" (Deleuze 1998: 16–17).

Like a poet, Deleuze speaks of things that are irreducible to any form of communication, bringing a word of caution to our own ideological and humanitarian impulses to communicate the "true" truth of the human condition. Such impulses issue order-words and ultimately partake in systems of control.

So should we be mute? Not engage, not represent?

For Deleuze, we are not just left to an endless self-reflexive and paralyzing mode of inquiry. Our works should rather stand "in contrast" to the "order-words" of the control systems we inhabit: "Only the act of resistance resists death, whether the act is in the form of a work of art or in the form of a human struggle" (1998: 19). Resisting death in all possible forms:

historical oblivion, social abjection or immobility, biological life. And the act of resistance has two sides: it is human, political; and it is also the act of art.

"Medical records, ready to go to heaven," Catarina wrote. "When men throw me into the air, I am already far away." "I am a free woman, to fly, bionic woman, separated." According to Deleuze (1997b: 4), "The ultimate aim of literature is to set free, in the delirium, this creation of a health or this invention of a people, that is, a possibility of life." This vision for literature can also inspire anthropologists: listening more as readers and writers than as diagnosticians or theorists, our own sensibility and openness become instrumental in spurring social recognition of the ways ordinary people think through their conditions amid new rational-technical and politico-economic machineries.

As Catarina put it: "Die death, medication is no more." "I will leave the door of the cage open. You can fly wherever you want to." The fact that such efforts often falter or even fail to change material constraints does not negate the intrinsic force of this struggle to connect and the human resilience it reveals.

In sum, as ethnographers we must attend to the ways that people's own struggles and visions of themselves and others create holes in dominant theories and interventions and unleash a vital plurality: being in motion, ambiguous and contradictory, not reducible to a single narrative, projected into the future, transformed by recognition, and thus the very fabric of alternative world-making.

With our empirical lanterns we can capture elements of this ongoing—agonistic and inventive—conversation between the plasticity of life and the plasticity of death. I say *agonistic* because people struggle to manage time and meaning and find a plateau in the face of impossible choices; I mean *inventive* in the sense of desiring and trying to make things otherwise.

Just as Catarina refused to be stratified out of existence and anticipated an exit from Vita, I would not want her and her story to be confined to a book. Life stories do not simply begin and end. They are stories of transformation: they link the present to the past and to a possible future and create lasting ties between subject, scribe, and reader.

THE AFTERLIFE OF A STORY

It was eerie to return to southern Brazil in August 2005 knowing that Catarina would not be there. (She passed away in September 2003, a few

Fig 4.2. Catarina's headstone. © Torben Eskerod.

weeks after I last saw her.) I wanted to make a headstone for Catarina's grave and decided to visit Tamara and Urbano, the adoptive parents of her youngest daughter, Ana. The couple had helped to organize Catarina's burial in Novo Hamburgo's public cemetery.

Quiet, Ana was helping at the family's restaurant when I arrived. At thirteen years old, she had a face and gaze that were indeed extensions of Catarina's. Tamara did most of the talking. She lambasted every single member of Catarina's family, saying how "fake" they had all behaved during the funeral. Only Nilson, the ex-husband, had shown "respect" by offering to help to defray some of the funeral's costs.

It was striking how Catarina's story continued to shift in the years following her death. In recollections she was no longer referred to as "the mad woman." Both Tamara and the relatives I saw later that week now spoke of

Catarina as having "suffered a lot." As true as this was, such renderings left unaddressed the everyday practices that compounded her intractability—most obviously, the cold detachment that accompanied care conceived as technological intervention rather than relational practice. Indeed the plot of a life story is never securely in the possession of its subject. It is part of the ongoing moral work of those who live on.

One morning that August, Tamara and I drove to the cemetery. I used to visit this place as a child with Vó Minda, my maternal grandmother. We would make the hour-long walk uphill, time and time again, to wash the white pebbles adorning her son's grave and to leave flowers from our back-yard. Nowadays the cemetery covers the whole hill, overlooking a city that has also changed beyond recognition. It now has become a site of pillage. Anything on the graves that might have had some monetary value, from the metallic letters spelling out the deceased's names to religious icons, had been looted. So much for the value of memory, I told Tamara. She shrugged, not knowing how to respond. I was not sure what I intended by my comment either, beyond giving voice to mourning.

The story of a life is always also the story of a death. And it is up to us to project it into the future, helping to shape its afterlife. Catarina had been buried in a crypt together with her mother's remains. I made sure that the crypt was fully paid for, so that in the future their remains would not be thrown into the mass grave at the edge of the cemetery. And Tamara was going to oversee the making of a marble headstone with Catarina's name engraved, along with a photo taken by Torben: the beautiful image of Cata-rina smiling that no one could take away.

NOTE

This essay draws from my collaboration with the photographer Torben Eskerod and from conversations with Michael M. J. Fischer, Stephen Greenblatt, Michael D. Jackson, Paul Rabinow, João Moreira Salles, and Nancy Scheper-Hughes, I am deeply grateful for their generosity of time and creative insight. I also want to thank Peter Locke, Ramah McKay, Amy Moran-Thomas, Joshua Franklin, Raphael Frankfurter, Alexander Wamboldt, and Naomi Zucker for their engagement with this work and for their wonderful support. A first version of this essay appeared in *Cultural Anthropology* 28(4), 2013, as "Ethnography in the Way of Theory" © João Biehl.

CHAPTER 5

The Search for Wisdom:

Why William James Still Matters

Arthur Kleinman

For Joan Andrea Kleinman

September 4, 1939–March 6, 2011

THE SEARCH FOR WISDOM

In 1997 I delivered the William James Lecture at Harvard for the first time and some months later the Tanner Lecture at my alma mater, Stanford. Both occasions provided me with the legitimacy to extend the angle of my perspective beyond medicine and anthropology. The William James Lecture is one of the many ways in which the legacy of William James, the nineteenth-century thinker and Harvard professor, lives on more than a hundred years after his death. When I had the honor of giving both lectures, I sought to articulate a theory of experience that could be read and used by social theorists and philosophers and any educated person interested in ideas and their moral applications (Kleinman 1999, 2006). This theory has grounded my work over the past decades of intellectual endeavor in medical anthropology, global psychiatry, China studies, and the medical humanities.

In the early 1990s I had in fact proposed to the then chair of philosophy at Harvard, himself a noted moral philosopher, who headed a committee in the core curriculum for undergraduates, that I would replace a popular course I taught on medical anthropology with a new course on moral theory and experience from an anthropological perspective. He told me that in his view moral theory could not be taught from such a perspective.

From experiences such as these, I came to realize that philosophers and even many social theorists do not take anthropology (or psychiatry) seriously as a way of framing the moral features of human experience. I also came to see that when such scholarly excursions have to do with a search for wisdom to aid the art of living in a time of danger, uncertainty, and dislocation, the same absence of interest characterizes philosophy and too often anthropology. This quest is seen as not pertinent or even legitimate in the university's current program of scholarship and training. William James encountered similar institutional resistance from the Harvard Philosophy Department when he fought for permission to teach the first psychology course in America in 1875 (Richardson 2006). *Plus ça change, plus c'est la même chose.*

One of the topics in moral theory that has preoccupied me, both personally and professionally, for the past decade has been the quest for wisdom and meaning that, at times of crisis and loss, figures large in the lives of many worldwide. This search for wisdom takes different forms and significance, whether it is structured within an orthodox collective religious framework or a highly subjective search for moral meaning in the more secular intellectual and moral worlds of literature and philosophy. Either way, however, it becomes part of the practical, painstaking art of living that people everywhere fashion as the existential core of human conditions. So where does that quest fit into academic life? Some will respond that academia is for investigators, not for seekers. But I sense that many humanists and interpretive social scientists believe it should be and often is part of academic discourse. I think many clinicians and religionists would agree. James clearly thought that the search for knowledge to assist the art of living is at the very core of what a life of ideas should be all about. In those moments, when we need these answers, indeed nothing could be more important.

In this chapter I discuss two crises in my own life that made a quest for wisdom, not just any meaning, crucial, and the practices of reading, writing, and caregiving that offered guidance. My intention is to ask what we learn more generally from such a quest for wisdom that illumines the place of meaning, practices, and vulnerabilities and aspirations in ordinary lives. Having recently written, based on field research, about quests for meaning in China today, my perspective is more than parochial. I seek to extend my reach beyond Euro-American worlds to human conditions in other environments and histories (Kleinman et al. 2011).[1]

I began my own life of the mind in the confines of a Jewish enclave, an upper-middle-class circle in New York in the 1940s and 1950s. By the 1960s a combination of forces—a university-based liberal education, a medical career, marriage outside my faith community to a life partner from a Protestant European background, introduction to Chinese culture as the core of my research, and wide reading in literature, philosophy, and social theory—had set me on my own road less traveled. During the Vietnam War era I was a U.S. Public Health Service officer and National Institutes of Health fellow stationed in Taiwan (1969–70). I was struggling to find direction, and in the evenings after my duties were finished, I read searchingly. I felt unmoored, struggling with a different culture and language, affected by the civil rights and antiwar movements, increasingly uncomfortable with the expectations and assumptions that seemed to be guiding my professional life, and worried over the new needs and responsibilities of my young family. I kept a journal from that time, filling it with a collection of earnest phrases and instructive quotes collected from my reading. Many of the works I was reading at that time were by twentieth-century Continental philosophers, including Bergson, Cassirer, Dilthey, Merleau-Ponty, Husserl, and Ortega y Gasset. The philosophy I excerpted responded to a dual yearning: on the one hand a desire to compile a guide to the art of living with the uncertainty I faced in my lived world, and on the other the need to orient myself intellectually in the world of ideas. Since I was a young man I had an ardent desire to be intellectually serious, and to be regarded as such. Reading and working with philosophical ideas in this sense fit my temperament. It was also a passion and concern I shared with my wife, and it permeated the domestic and professional conversations between us. I had questions about what the world meant and about my place in it. Who should I petition but the great thinkers of the past century, who had, in their time, reworked philosophical paradigms to fit the worlds they encountered?

In 2011 my wife and collaborator for many years, the sinologist Joan Kleinman, with whom I had shared life and work for almost fifty years, died—after many long years of suffering—from neurological degeneration. After her death I was inconsolable: filled with grief and overwhelmed with memories of the times we'd shared. I missed her presence and her companionship—both the sparkling moments of connection between us and the everyday comforts of the daily rituals of first her health and then even her illness, which had structured the better part of my life. I felt a sense of desolation. Not knowing where else to turn, I dug out the journal I kept during my time in Taiwan, opened its dusty cover and reread the lines that I had carefully copied down decades before, looking once more for solace from philosophy.[2]

I knew, on some level, that my old journal's wisdom could not sublimate the overwhelming emotions of sadness and yearning I was experiencing, but I hoped to find something: some insight, some phrase, some assistance. As I sat and reread the yellowed pages, I became intensely, embarrassingly aware of the emotional parallels between this moment and the moment in which I had carefully recorded these excerpts. This was the second time, though this time with much greater cause, that I had struggled to come to terms with what legitimacy and intellectual authority philosophy could offer in the way of realistic insight on the great challenges and tragedies of everyday life. When I was younger I needed to have my intuitions and my inchoate insights, which had begun to feel ungrounded and overreaching, validated through reference to a lineage of inquiry. I was searching for a moral, as much as for an intellectual, foundation. I found at least the beginnings of an intellectual foundation. By the end of my time in Taiwan, I was preparing to make what I knew could be a decisive shift, one that would take me away from the clinic and the laboratory. I had felt at home in the humanities as an undergraduate, and I decided that I wanted to continue on that path, toward anthropological fieldwork and a different kind of psychiatric practice. This was no more than an uncertain, anxious dream at that moment, the consequences of which I could hardly anticipate, but I felt frustrated and stifled in the world of medicine. I wanted to pursue a path informed by wisdom, not just information as knowledge, one that would animate my career with powerful ideas and a compelling agenda. As I read during those long nights in Taiwan, I searched for a means of calming a restlessness I felt: the unsettled desire for meaning that beset me. That feeling returned suddenly and powerfully following Joan's death, familiar and even more powerfully discomfiting than I had remembered.

If these two moments of unrest in my life seem confused, it is because I experienced them as confused. In both eras I was seeking reassurance, looking for confirmation that the foundations of my intellectual career and the subjectivity of my lived experience were legitimate, stable, and real. I was uneasy with the assumptions that I was expected to live with as a doctor. I wanted to reinterpret illness and understand it in terms of the suffering I saw around me but felt I had limited ways of validating or understanding through clinical practice. I wanted to rethink medicine as a part of culture, even though I knew that many medical academics thought that my quest to develop a novel social theory of medicine and health was at best presumptuous, and at worst, impossible.

After Joan's death the sense of agitation that had so clearly marked those formative years returned, a seething morass of emotion. I again became obsessed by the lack of unambiguous markers by which to live life and was preoccupied also by something large and personal: the absence of the miracle that had been my marriage. My relationship with Joan had so defined my adult life that surviving without it seemed unimaginable. It had been the absorbing love and adoration that I felt for her, and that she felt for me, that had fueled and sustained us through the stressful and uncertain years of building our family and our careers. I remember those years as though through a golden haze, colored by the joyful companionship and fierce love that we shared and by the stable shape of our world, a place that was made ordered and good by our daily collaboration. These memories motivated and strengthened my caregiving and Joan's care-receiving during the awful years that followed, as she suffered slowly through neurodegeneration, which brought on blindness and then dementia, paralysis, and death. Love made it possible for us to endure her illness but gave me no guidance after her death.

And so I read from Bergson: "To endure means to change, to grow, to become." And below it, "The basic reality is my life," from Ortega y Gasset. On the next page of the notebook I quoted Wittgenstein: "A philosophical problem has the form: I do not know my way about." Later on, from Bertrand Russell: "To teach how to live without certainty, and yet without being paralyzed by hesitation, is perhaps the chief thing that philosophy, in our age, can still do for those who study it." (But how was that to be accomplished?) And then, from Michael Oakshott, again, unhelpfully: "Whatever is real has a meaning." (I knew that, but where was I to go with it?) The quotations continue across dozens of handwritten pages.

I have always had an affinity for existential and phenomenological philosophy. There are personal reasons why this work appeals to me, but I also connect with it because these writers formed a bridge to the insights of theorists such as Peter Berger, Georges Canguilhem, Pierre Bourdieu, and Max Weber, thinkers whose ideas were instrumental to me in developing my own theories about stigma, social suffering, illness experience, and the moral enterprise of medicine. Creating documents like this journal, in which I collected and collated philosophical fragments that spoke to me, was part of a process that led to the development of an abiding sense—informing all of my work—that social theory is important. It is important not just because of the insight it provides but because it illuminates the practical implications of empirical studies. It helps to redirect them and make them coherent, transforming them into practical actions that repair and remake the world in new ways, working against the grain of conventional thinking.[3]

But even though these theories offered me professional guidance, philosophy did not offer the wisdom I was seeking during moments of crisis, not in 1969 and not in 2011. It did not offer solace either, in making sense of the crisis points I reached in my career, in managing the peaks and valleys of love and family, nor finally in interpreting the crippling existential blow that the loss of Joan delivered to me. None of these writers, none of the wise words they penned, helped me to manage the defeat and disappointment I felt at these moments. Philosophy had encouraged me in my thinking toward the anthropological career I eventually followed but seemed trite in the face of crisis. But neither did any other source or genre offer me the key—not religious texts, not poetry, not art.

I can see now that this quest was always destined to fail. I could not succeed here because my object of inquiry was wrong. I was trying to understand illness as symbol, life as perception, medicine as culture, but the answers to these questions are not what really matters in a time of crisis. The philosophers and other moral thinkers had helped me to see that all experience, everywhere, is a moral condition, one determined by what is at stake for individuals living in constrained circumstances of uncertainty and threat. Yet those ethically influential thinkers—from Tu Weiming to Mencius, and from Sartre to Montaigne—couldn't help me at these times. What I needed to be able to do was to understand my own subjectivity—my sensibility, self, will, and commitments—not as moral theory but as legitimate values and impulses that would nourish me in my work in the world and bind me to the people who mattered most. I had been treating experience as a philosophical problem, a relevant but inadequate formulation, when what I was really after was understanding experience as practice.

Practice is never just theory; it is always about how we move among others, how we act upon others, and, best of all, what we do for others. This is the art of living. The true subject of my quest for wisdom did not emerge while reading philosophy; rather I discovered it through caregiving and mentoring, as a doctor, a husband, and a teacher. This is what I unsuccessfully sought in my reading of eminent thinkers, what I now see as my romantic reading. I was drawn to what James (1902: 280) called "the strangely moving power of passages . . . irrational doorways as they were through which the mystery of fact, the wildness and the pang of life, stole into our hearts and thrilled them."

CAREGIVING

This exploration, this hunt for wisdom, had been an unfulfilled mission but, as I discovered with caregiving, not necessarily one that was unfulfillable. If crises, especially of health and loss, are one of the central ways we realize failure, mortality, and destabilization in the world, then caregiving is a tangible response to the chaos. It is a practical ritual of love, resilience, and service that helps to reorder the local moral world when it seems to be splitting at the seams. Caregiving comes as close as anything I have encountered to offering an existential definition of what it means to be human. When I was young I learned about caregiving a little in medical school, in clinical practice somewhat more, but mostly I learned about it—suddenly and intensely—from the immersive experience of being Joan's caregiver throughout her catastrophic illness.

Joan suffered from Alzheimer's complicated by occipital lobe atrophy of the brain, which was diagnosed almost a decade before her death. As her deterioration progressed with time, she became functionally blind. Her memory was severely affected, and she lost her independence. She became nearly fully dependent on me, on her home health aide, and her adult children. Although she was physically healthy aside from her brain disease, as it ravaged her mind she became more and more incapacitated. For years of her illness, while she was still well enough to live at home, I would wake her in the morning, take her to the toilet, hand her the toilet paper, flush the toilet, turn the faucet in the sink off and on as she washed her hands. I would hand her the soap and the towel. I would take off her nightgown, help her don her undergarments, lay out her clothes for her: tights, skirt, shirt, and sweater. I put on her shoes and tied the laces. A whole new world of intimacy with her everyday habits opened up to me.

Then I would make breakfast, then later lunch, and then dinner. At the table I would serve her, hold the knife, cut her fish and meat, hand her the water or wine in a glass. I cleared the table, washed the dishes. At every moment of the years over which she slowly slipped away, Joan was determined to do as much as she could. She would stand and dry the dishes and wipe the cutlery. Then I would lead her around the furniture to her seat, opening doors for her and guiding her, lest she become fearfully lost in her own home, every wall and corner suddenly aggressive. And then with time, even this became much more than she could manage. When she became desperately agitated, she might not recognize me, which added greatly to her distress and mine. As disturbing as this picture is to recall, it conveys her condition several years before her death. From this point, the deterioration picked up speed and power; at the end she was completely helpless, without control of bladder, bowels, vision, arms and legs, words or thoughts. At the last she had only one word left, a word that emphasized the burden of moral responsibility I felt: "Arthur," she would say, "Arthur."

Before this, for thirty-five years of marriage, Joan had not only been fully independent, she had been highly effective: responsible for taking care of our home and raising our two children, while along the way she earned her MA in Chinese and collaborated with me in research and writing. With her help, I lived the life of a scholar full time. In retrospect it seems incredible to contemplate the gift she gave me by caring for me all of those years by managing the details of my existence and helping me manage my chronic illnesses (asthma, hypertension, gout), and then the gift she returned by showing me what it was to give that care to her. Suddenly, unexpectedly, I was the principal caregiver.

Caregiving was clearly a burden, but to the end it also strengthened and even ennobled me. I learned to cook and clean, to manage our finances, to shop for food, to send birthday cards, buy gifts, deal with plumbers, electricians, gardeners, auto mechanics, and more. Still, frustration, anger, sadness, disappointment, hopelessness, pain—at every moment they could arise. I lived without hope, and endured that too. Over time, what earlier seemed unbearable was borne. I didn't imagine I could lead my spouse about by the hand for hours. I didn't imagine I could watch her slowly lose the capacity to manage life, and then eventually slip away entirely. I didn't imagine I could survive it. This process of coming to terms with what life brings, making do, getting through, and doing it in a way that is at times emotionally and aesthetically uplifting while at other times just barely endurable, is the art of living: a moral art.

Since Florence Nightingale's nineteenth-century *Notes for Nurses*, health professionals have explicitly defined caregiving around practical acts of protecting and assisting people who are suffering, including the corporeal tasks of bathing, feeding, dressing, ambulating, toileting, and the like. And they have recognized as well that caregiving also includes emotional acts of comforting, supporting, listening, explaining, and the like. It is in the twentieth century that it has become increasing widely recognized that caregiving also involves moral acts of acknowledgment, affirmation, and presence, to name just a few. These moral tasks, as I learned in becoming a primary caregiver myself, are carried out largely within the family and friendship network, and less and less by professionals. Indeed it is well understood today that medicine has relatively little to do with caregiving. Nurses, social workers, occupational and physical therapists, and family members are the artisans of caregiving. And as historians point out, they, like the vast majority of home health aides, are women and often members of immigrant and ethnic minority groups. Although I have had a career-long interest in caregiving, in retrospect I did not learn to be a caregiver in terms of the practices just outlined in medical school, postgraduate training, research, or even professional clinical practice. I learned to be a caregiver by actually performing the activities in caring for my wife. That is, as a primary caregiver, I finally learned what caregiving is all about.

I also learned that primary caregivers experience divided selves, as James (1902: 139) understood when he wrote about the divided self in religious experience. That division in subjectivity is well illustrated in Picasso's only painting of a medical student (*The Head of a Medical Student*) in which one eye is open as if to the caregiver's needs and responsibilities, while the other is closed to protect the self from overinvolvement and to take care of the caregiver's self. These are practices I encountered and learned as a primary caregiver. My role involved a moral as much as a practical aspect. In my experience, this side of caregiving as moral experience receives relatively little attention, as does the moral experience of mentoring and other forms of everyday living that involve taking care. The feminist philosopher Joan Tronto (1993) wrote about this aspect of moral life in her treatise on care, but few other theorists have given it the centrality it so clearly deserves.

WILLIAM JAMES AND THE ART OF LIVING

In my own quest for the art of living, William James, the man whom Alfred North Whitehead called the "only truly original American philosopher," has been perhaps the most helpful thinker.[4] James's prose is extraordinary, filled with resonant cadences, vivid images, and memorable metaphors, all enlivened by his vigorous yet vulnerable humanity. His work invites a dialogical flight of feelings and ideas and a freedom of interpretation that reels in just the right things from the bricolage of ordinary living. It gifts the reader with a broad and suggestive net for meaning making. My reading of James, before and during these crises, gave me a sense of larger significance and happiness. It not only assisted me in smoothing the path to my own ideas, but it contributed in a way no other thinker has to an intellectual dialogue, a conversation that has sustained my work, a long, rhythmic exchange of inspiration and metaphor that has made a kind of music of experience lived and witnessed over time. He approached existential struggle both seriously and practically. He wrote in *The Will to Believe*, "If this life be not a real fight, in which something is eternally gained for the universe by success, it is no better than a game of private theatricals from which one may withdraw at will. But it *feels* like a real fight—as if there were something really wild in the universe which we, with all our idealities and faithfulnesses, are needed to redeem" (1896: 62).

James was for me a different kind of interlocutor, one whose words illuminated my life from within, not guiding exactly, but making me feel less alone. Perhaps that touchstone could have been a poet instead, Shakespeare or Montaigne or Auden or someone else. Instead, for me, it was James; books like the great *Principles of Psychology* and *The Varieties of Religious Experience* spoke and made sense to me. James's words gave me a strange push, as though they were an uncanny echo of something I already knew. There was no specific answer there or exact words, just a feeling that emerged over many readings, that mattered to me and helped me along my way. And although James spoke little of practice and not at all of caregiving, he understood that living life itself is a struggle worth investigating. In his classic pedagogical text *Talks to Teachers* he writes, "The solid meaning of life is always the same eternal thing—the marriage, namely of some unhabitual ideal, however special, with some fidelity, courage and endurance, with some man's or woman's pains" (1899: 154).

Perhaps it sounds trite. And yet words like *fidelity, courage, endurance,* and *pain* are infrequently evoked by social theorists today, though they inspire important imaginings about how moral subjectivity is central to life and thought. These were words that Weber and other early social theorists used often because they understood that social thought was meant to respond to real life. Weber and James would have understood what I (together with Veena Das and Margaret Lock) meant by social suffering—our idea of the way that institutions can affect lives—which moral theorists often seem to overlook. For James, philosophy was lived, it was not an abstraction: it was a labor of love. He did not have the answers, but he sought them clearly and with great seriousness through his intellectual and personal pursuits, while maintaining always that his answers should also be useful for others.

James was on my mind recently, when I was reflecting on the moment of Joan's death for a piece published in *The Lancet*:

> I [saw] my wife's living death mask, the fine skin pulled tight across her high cheekbones, her unseeing eyes, her final breaths, and the feeling that I was floating away, no longer anchored. I had a real fight on my hands, and in my being. The wisdom I needed came out of my readiness to respond to James' pushing at a certain time when I was faced with a problem central to the human condition: a problem that connected me up with the grain of life and with the existential uncertainty of our being. And that fostered a feeling of recognition and recovery. And that is how it perhaps always works. Wisdom needs to be experienced to be effective, and is effective not as an idea, but as a lived feeling and a moral practice that redeems our humanness amidst inevitable disappointment and defeat. Perhaps just so does our readied response at times of deep trouble and anguish to paintings, music, and works in the humanities redeem the felt moral experience of the doctor and the patient in the family—I am here all three—while the impossible fight over life goes on and the quest for wisdom remains ordinarily unfulfilled, yet over time not unfulfillable. (Kleinman 2011: 1622)

James affected me—as an anthropologist, as a psychiatrist, and as an ordinary person.

RELIGION AND MORAL EXPERIENCE

Some years ago I cotaught a course entitled "Religion and Medicine" with a distinguished former faculty member of Harvard Divinity School, Sarah Coakley.[5] Half of the students came from Harvard Divinity School and half from Harvard Medical School. In it we read James's *Varieties of Religious Experience*. The *Varieties*, based on the Gifford Lectures that he delivered at Edinburgh University in 1901–2, is a seminal text on religion. But I also consider it an early phenomenological ethnography of experience. James asserts in the preface his "belief that a large acquaintance with particulars often makes us wiser than the possession of abstract formulas, however deep," and proceeds to structure the text around experiential passages from writers, saints, diarists, and clergymen and accounts of the religious experiences of a range of everyday people. James argues that the foundation upon which religion is built—the core of religion—is not the edifices, hierarchies, institutions, or texts that order it. It is rather the transformative moments of conversion, crisis, and dissolution experienced by individuals, great and humble, that are the building blocks for organized religion. He was interested in religion as an art of life and experience, and he, like me, was interested in it personally. In an era before the advent of many of the real (and sometimes false) cures of modern medicine and psychiatry, James watched many of his close friends and family suffer and in some cases die from the ravages of ills such as tuberculosis, cancer, alcoholism, and depression. He was touched, fascinated, and ultimately inspired by the spiritual and intellectual depths that they plumbed through suffering and, desiring to better understand this, took it as an object of inquiry (Richardson 2006). For him, surviving the ravages of life was a matter of the therapeutics of experience, of which religion was but one balm and medicine but another.

Crucially the *Varieties* focuses on the experiences that help us to make sense of the world. Though most of the experiences he discusses are ecstatic ones, they are also everyday experiences, in the sense that anyone can have them. James focuses in his text on the most dramatic examples of religious fervor, but he uses them illustratively and broadly. He cracks open the unity of religion, using the term as a category with which to describe "man's total reaction upon life," and conversely concludes, "Why not say that any total reaction upon life is religious?" Religion as he broadly interprets it is no more and no less than the serious, considered, individual answer to the question "What is the character of this universe in which we dwell?" (1902: 35). And how can I act upon it?

For the medical students in the class we taught, to a person, James's understanding of religion as based in psychological processes was convincing. That perspective was deemed entirely inadequate by the Divinity School students in the course, for whom its smooth dismissal of theology, religious institutions, and the work of religionists rendered the Jamesian perspective deeply suspect. James's universalist orientation also came in for their criticism, because, as Talal Asad (1993) argues, these students recognized partisan commitments as central to what makes most religions religion. I'm not here to defend James; he needs no defenders. The mere fact that *Varieties* remains widely read and taught one hundred years after his death speaks for itself. I bring this conflict up to build on James's desire to relate religion to quests for wisdom.

From an anthropological point of view, James's understanding of religious subjectivity clearly needs to be updated to go beyond the deep interiority of faith, commitment, and habit to include the interpersonal practices of ritual, presence, and embodiment. James tended to see these largely as individual behaviors rather than the collective moral practices they most decidedly are. And I do not mean to suggest that the experiences he describes (by his own admission the most illustrative he could find) are the only way that a moral crisis can be experienced. I saw in my experience, for example, a kind of conversion that echoed James, but not one that came through a single sudden experience, rather one that emerged slowly through survival, practice, and empathy. But I raise it to illustrate the seriousness of his engagement with the question of how individuals make sense of suffering. His synthetic, interdisciplinary pragmatism did not shy away from the idea that the study of experience can assist us in living our own lives. And of course, for James's (1977) radical empiricism all knowledge had to be seen as coming out of experience broadly understood.

WISDOM AND ETHNOGRAPHY

In our 2011 coauthored book, *Deep China*, my former students and I examined various quests for meaning in China and among the Chinese today. Clearly, one of the most urgent is the quest for what some Chinese call spiritual meaning. Six decades under communism, including most recently powerful market reforms that are central to the global economy—which some Chinese sardonically define as the longest and most painful road to capitalism—has brought China prosperity but also deep social and health disparities as well as cynicism about both traditional Confucian values and contemporary ethics. Not surprisingly, then, there has been a sense of floating dislocation accompanied by a great upwelling of popular interest in Buddhism, Christianity, and, especially among minorities, Islam. By and large this movement has not been characterized by theological passions for theory, nor even by a Chinese version of theodicy, but rather by the most practical involvement with rituals, presence, and embodiment. There is also intensified interest in the consequences of religion for societal values, business ethics, professional standards, and policy regulations. Amazingly, during the era of the most rapid economic expansion experienced by any country on earth, China uncynically hosted several national debates that welled up from ordinary people on the meaning of life in a world dominated by overly materialistic, consumerist, and hyperindividualistic interests. Questioning ultimate political authority of the party-state was not tolerated, of course, but the normally repressive regime allowed, and even enabled, the national debate on the existential human condition without using stories of life's bitterness to critique bourgeois society, as it had done in the radical Maoist past, or using more positive tales to glorify the communist project. Rather these debates acknowledged, as I do, that the existential human condition is grounded in social suffering. This suffering is in response to catastrophes that upend life plans and intimate relations, structural violence that injures especially those with marginal resources who are least protected in societies worldwide, and the serious troubles of everyday life that affect each and every one of us, owing to chronic illness, aging, and the multiple vulnerabilities that make life everywhere uncertain and insecure.

In the face of this universal human condition, people turn to religion (along with other sources of wisdom I have mentioned). Theodicy looms large here, especially for the intellectually oriented, but so does the very practical quest of trying to exert greater control over the exigencies and conditionalities I have described. The quest for wisdom, ethnographies and social histories suggest, is first of all an attempt to normalize, cope, and sustain resilience through the art of living—a truth that James emphasized not just in the *Varieties* but in the *Psychology* and much of the rest of his writing. It is also a moral response to the human tragedy: ultimately all actions fail. Resilience takes people only so far. Moral experience pivots from doing what it takes to survive to living with disappointment and defeat.

James saw religion, like philosophy, as a resource for getting through life. It was a means of strengthening men and women for the unequal and unwinnable struggle against our common fate and destiny. Religion for James also meant fortifying us to not be afraid of life. How religion is made use of in this way is not necessarily how scholars of religion interpret texts and rituals. And yet without this popular dimension of the human uses of religion, religious traditions and commentaries would lose much of their capacity to mobilize individuals and groups and to animate processes of repair, restitution, healing, and redemption. Hence this subject needs to become a more serious source of interdisciplinary academic discussion that bridges the study of religion, anthropology, and the humanities as well as the helping professions. Ethnography's contributions loom large here, even though our era's anthropology has lost confidence in the kind of cross-cultural comparison that James and so many other Victorian-era scholars entertained. Indeed it is precisely the study of this lived reality of religion that can connect anthropology to the broad interest in religious quests for meaning in our society and globally.

But James does more, perhaps because he himself experienced a restlessness and vulnerability that I identified with. He approaches the subject philosophically, yet convinced that if we can map all of these experiences, a kind of comparative wisdom, a guide for life, an art of living might emerge. Hence that wisdom is meant to be personally at stake, not just professionally and theoretically pertinent.

In my own way of thinking, this is where religion, medicine, teaching, and caregiving come together, because the quest for wisdom in the art of living is as central to caregiving as it is to mentoring and to the acts of service in moral, clinical, academic, and religious life. James knew this, as do many moralists and religious practitioners today. It is we, the current academic community of scholars, including anthropologists and philosophers, who need to rediscover this quest at the center of what it means to be human for what it is: perhaps the most universal and defining quality of moral and religious experience, a quality that continues to animate the deep sensibility of the modern person as much as the common sense and ways of life of our social networks and communities. Against the cruel and cold indifference of the universe, with the anthropological gaze we see men and women humanize life by first creating or discovering god(s), then by materializing that creation or discovery into a force in the world, and finally in the quest for wisdom for practically getting through life, and eventually wisdom to meet tragedy and defeat. As James knew it to be, the longing after and the struggle to master ways of living amid real danger and great uncertainty realizes what is most at stake in life: namely, not just enduring but creating and sustaining lives of purpose and significance tested by failure, disappointment, betrayal, and loss, yet still buoyed by endurance, love, and often unfulfilled but not unfulfillable journeys of both practical and transcendent meaning.

ANTHROPOLOGY AND PHILOSOPHY

So, other than the fact that James wrote and taught philosophy, what does all of this have to do with anthropology and its relationship to philosophy?

James conceived of the university as a place where wisdom was at home. This is not so clearly the case in the twenty-first century. Claude Shannon's foundational paper predicting the revolution in information technology that has reshaped our times insisted that the issue for scientists, engineers, and policy experts was the generation, collection, and management of *information* (Gertner 2012). For that purpose, the meaning that information held was irrelevant and a distraction. Only information stripped of meaning could be engineered, he asserted. Over time this central commitment of the IT revolution has flourished as the university has become more about applied science, its application in the professions, its remaking of natural and social sciences, and its replacement of the humanities as the core of the modern research university. Along the way both philosophy and anthropology have been dislodged from the university's symbolic center of knowledge generation and transmission to its vulnerable periphery. Both fields, in my view, have played into this sad scenario by understandable yet still destructive compensatory practices, including employing overly technical, jargon-driven, and obscure writing styles that are unfriendly to the ordinary educated reader, and disdain for the very practical mundane concerns of everyday life. This cultivation of the recondite, the otiose, the irresponsibly transgressive, and the merely clever has bemused critics, forging a public consensus that these fields are less relevant today, other than to represent a museum of past greatness whose classic status deserves to be conserved along with the ivied cloisters, antique façades, and quaint memorabilia of earlier times.

Turning away from lived experience has abetted this long, slow decline. And this may be what philosophy and anthropology today share most. Both disciplines are of reduced significance in the academy and outside the academy among the educated public. While reasserting the importance of the search for wisdom for living and moral conditions may not resurrect their place in the university, it would offer a challenge to where these disciplines and the universities of today are headed. At the very least it could be a reminder of why theory and theorizing continue to matter.[6]

Theory can reframe how we look at the world and ourselves. Theory can ask large, original, and discomfiting questions. It can redirect empirical studies; it can rethink what sense to make of empirical findings. It can insist on ends that are serious and significant. And it can coordinate across distinctive domains of life and ideas with the object of creating original formulations and practices that are useful to and good for life. In the arena of caregiving, for example, theory can rethink what caregiving is for, how best to configure and implement care, and how to situate caregiving in the broad array of societal and personal values. Indeed something on this order can already be seen to be happening in anthropology and philosophy.

I believe the best of ethnography still does this, and there is a clear turn to sensibility and the moral, yet the theoretical perspectives that have come to dominate the field have moved farther and farther away from the serious question of human experience. I am not naïve enough to believe that a call for a Jamesian revival will reverse the historical transformation of the academy, with its deep roots in our current political economy and particular global cultural commitments. What it can do is to illustrate why both anthropology and philosophy really do matter for educated people and for society broadly today, because they can ask the truly central questions and because they can contribute to wisdom about the human experience that every one of us could use to enhance the art of living. And that in itself is not only a noble thing to do but the best defense of the humanities and interpretive social sciences. These fields will be revitalized not only by the study of the subjective, social, and moral consequences of science and technology, as some claim, but even to a greater degree by moving the agenda of lived experience to the center of their colloquies. And that in turn will sustain the liberal arts tradition that has long been core in the universities.

Anthropology and philosophy, as I see them, don't just need each other in order to foster this prioritizing of human experience. They both need to change in relation to each other. Anthropology needs to make philosophizing and theorizing about the ethnography of the art of living and moral experience in the context of insecurity, danger, and uncertainty the source of engagement with philosophy. In turn, philosophy needs to make this core empirical reality of living not only more central to its concerns with epistemology, ontology, and ethical principles but an active source of dialogue with ethnography. The upshot would be to revivify quests for wisdom in the university and more broadly in public life on behalf of moral, aesthetic, religious, therapeutic, and subjective experiences at the core of human conditions.

NOTES

I wish to thank Harvard Divinity School's faculty and students for inviting me to deliver the William James Lecture in 2011 and for responding so thoughtfully to the lecture. This essay benefited from the editing of Bridget Hanna and Jan Reid and from the formal responses of David Carrasco and Kimberley C. Patton. I thank Marilyn Goodrich for once again transforming my longhand scratches into computer files.

1. I prefer the term *human condition* or *conditions* to *human nature* because determining what precisely constitutes human nature is so ideologically divisive and unclear, whereas among the myriad possible ways of living there appears to be only a relatively limited number of empirically documented states that define our shared human condition. Among them are love, loss, intellectual and moral aspiration, and failure—the ones pertinent to this chapter. And if this is what human experience is about, surely it must have a place in knowledge generation and transmission in the academy. Perhaps its broader significance, in fact, is to reclaim, following James, the idea that a practical contribution to how we live is inseparable from what a university at its finest should be about.

2. This section of this chapter is a revised and rewritten version of my article "A Search for Wisdom" (Kleinman 2011).

3. This perspective on the reason theory matters grew out of my own intellectual trajectory. In 1973, at the very outset of my career, I published four articles that defined my theoretical interests (Kleinman 1973a, 1973b, 1973c, 1973d). These articles were the basis for my major empirical studies: *Patients and Healers in the Context of Culture* (1980); *Social Origins of Distress and Disease: Depression, Neurasthenia and Pain in Modern China* (1986), and others. In turn, these frameworks were reworked based on research in later works, such as *Rethinking Psychiatry* (1988b); *The Illness Narratives* (1988a); *Writing at the Margin* (1995); and *What Really Matters* (2006). In a much more compact period of time, Veena Das, Margaret Lock, and I led an SSRC program that set out theories of social suffering, which were the basis for empirical studies by younger colleagues and which in turn led to recasting and reformulating our theories (as can be seen in the three-volume series: Kleinman et al., *Social Suffering* [1997], Das et al., *Violence and Subjectivity* [2000], and Das et al., *Remaking a World* [2001]).

4. My connection to James is overdetermined. Both he and I studied medicine before we turned to moral questions. Besides the fact that I have delivered Harvard's James Lecture on two occasions, I have occupied an office in William James Hall for over thirty years and have frequently participated in seminars on the fifteenth floor, where a portrait of James presides over every occasion. I have cotaught a seminar on James with my colleague Steve Caton, and I have taught James's *Varieties of Religious Experience* on numerous occasions and used quotations from James in several of my books. In my daily routines I often drive by the house James built and lived in on Irving Street in Cambridge.

5. In spring semester 2012, my colleague David Carrasco and I were funded by a Harvard Hauser grant to teach a new course titled "Wisdom and the Art of Living"

that is based on the ideas sketched in this essay. Interested readers can obtain a copy of the syllabus for this course by emailing kleinman@wjh.harvard.edu.

6. James, as well, worried about a version of this in his time, complaining in the 1903 *Harvard Monthly* article, evocatively titled "The Ph.D. Octopus," about the ways the professionalization and bureaucratization of the university system through the insistence on PhDs for teaching positions mistook thesis for wisdom and degree holders for teachers, ultimately impeding the true work of scholarly inquiry.

CHAPTER 6

Eavesdropping on Bourdieu's Philosophers

Ghassan Hage

▦ "It is nerve deafness. I am sorry but there isn't much I can do for you. A hearing aid will not be of help." I still remember those words, very solemnly pronounced by the Macquarie Street, Sydney, ear specialist I went to see sometimes in 1978. Until that point I was very much hoping that there was something he could do for me. But it brought to an end a long period of speculation that began with my noting a year or so earlier that, no, I wasn't failing to understand what people were saying because of their Australian accent. There was no doubt about it. I wasn't hearing very well. Three years or so before that visit, in Beirut, in the middle of the civil war, before I left to continue my university studies in Australia, a bomb exploded very close to me. I could not hear well for a couple of days following the explosion. So I immediately thought it was the obvious culprit. Later tests did not show conclusively that it was. The nature of my nerve deafness and its "curve" were not consistent with an injury, the doctor informed me. There was a possibility that the bomb accelerated already existing damage. After probing into my past, the doctor decided that it could be either a preexisting congenital condition or damage to the nerves incurred from years of being a drummer with a distinct bias toward hard rock music. Suddenly I was confronting the possibility that my deafness was the product of both the highs of Beirut's hedonistic culture and the lows of its barbarism. As the coexistence of this hedonism and barbarism marks every facet of the city, it made my deafness a quintessentially Beiruti phenomenon. But it was in Australia that this Beirutness revealed itself.

After arriving in Australia in mid-1976, and particularly when I started university, I began noticing that I was definitely having difficulties following lectures in big lecture theaters. I assumed that this must be due to the

Australian accent of the lecturers. And for a while I convinced myself that this indeed was my main problem. I did not let the fact that I was not having problems understanding Australian accents in face-to-face or small group situations perturb my reasoning. In any case, it was a short-lived conviction. In the back of my mind, there was another experience that was slowly imposing itself on me and that forced me to confront the fact that I was definitely losing my hearing: I was losing my capacity to eavesdrop.

This was no ordinary loss. Eavesdropping was not something I occasionally indulged in; it was a permanent disposition that was part of my very being. When I was a young boy, my parents often used to take me to what was, for me, excruciatingly boring lunches with their friends and business partners. There were no iPods at the time; even the Walkman had not come into existence. So I directed my attention to the tables around me and started eavesdropping to ease the boredom. Even though the conversations at the tables around me were not necessarily more interesting than what was happening at my table, there was nonetheless a pleasure derived from listening to what seemed like "stolen" conversations. It was an addictive pleasure, and soon I was eavesdropping everywhere, regardless of whether I was stuck at a boring business lunch with my parents or having lunch at my boarding school. I became an eavesdropper, that is, to use language that is important for this essay, eavesdropping became a permanent disposition and an integral part of my being, a *habitus*. Losing my capacity to eavesdrop was a seriously painful loss.

Since I received a cochlear implant in October 2004, I have been writing what I have titled, somewhat inexactly, "an auto-ethnography of my deafness"—inexactly because what I am recording includes reminiscences of when I actually started losing my hearing as well as experiential accounts of hearing with an implant. In 2010 I was working on some of these notes while concurrently offering a seminar on the philosophical dimensions of Pierre Bourdieu's work. That's when it struck me how permeated my ethnographic language was with the very Bourdieuian concepts whose philosophical foundations I was examining. This was particularly true of the concepts relating to *illusio*, such as investment, directionality, and intensity of reality, and to *habitus*, such as capacity, disposition, and habit.

It is of course hardly surprising for someone who has been as deeply influenced by Bourdieu's work as I have to be deploying Bourdieuian categories. I have, after all, sat on some of his courses in Paris in a disciple-like fashion, have closely read all his works, and was intermittently a postdoctoral researcher and a visiting professor in his research center for many years. Nonetheless not everything lends itself to the deployment of Bour-dieuian categories with the same ease. The fact that this account of my deafness did fit those categories drove me to investigate the extent to which I could integrate it into my reflections on Bourdieu's relation to phi-losophy. Initially, and as I show below, some of the moments captured in the ethnography played docilely a function of exemplification of Bourdieu's theories and the philosophies behind them. At times, however, I found that my description of certain states of being and hearing that I had reacquired through the implant pointed to some of the limits in the way Bourdieu con-ceived of being. Indeed some of the descriptions disturbed the stability of the way Bourdieu himself had portrayed the relationship between his work and philosophical writing. It invited a more complex three-way conversa-tion between the ethnography of my deafness and Bourdieu's writing and the philosophies that influenced it. It also highlighted a tension between what belongs to a critical sociological tradition and what belongs to a criti-cal anthropological one in Bourdieu's writing, and how each of these criti-cal traditions relates to philosophy in a different way. I deal with this ques-tion in the concluding part of the essay.

AN INTRODUCTION TO BOURDIEU'S POLITICAL ECONOMY OF BEING

The relationship between Bourdieu's work and philosophy has been the subject of a number of conferences and books, particularly in French (see Meyer 2002; Lescourret 2009). Bourdieu, like many other French sociolo-gists and anthropologists before him (Durkheim, Lévy-Bruhl, Lévi-Strauss), was initially trained as a philosopher and was writing his thesis on Husserl under the supervision of Georges Canguilhem when he left for Algeria and was transformed into an anthropologist and later a sociologist. It is not sur-prising therefore that there are many explicit and implicit critical dialogues with philosophy in his work or that this dimension should attract research-ers examining his work. Some have questioned whether Bourdieu uses phi-losophy to do a better sociology or whether he considers his sociological ap-proach as the best way to do philosophy (Lescourret 2009). Whatever the case might be, the elements of Bourdieu's relation to philosophy that are most consistently present in his work are already well known.

To begin with, there is Bourdieu's own ongoing and well-articulated cri-tique of philosophy as a variant of scholastic reason. He sees it as an aca-demic and intellectual reason that fails to examine the conditions of its own production, particularly its structurally privileged position that protects it from the realm of practical necessity. Thus, Bourdieu argues, not only does the thought philosophy produces carry the mark of its remoteness from practical necessity, but in its remoteness it ends up failing to note that there are practical reasons in the world that differ from its own scholastic reason. Consequently his critique goes on to maintain that philosophy ends up positing the kind of reasoning that is peculiar to it into an invariable universal reasoning. In what is perhaps one of the most formulaic of Bourdieu's critiques, philosophy ends up constantly "projecting its own particular relation to the object into the object."

Nonetheless, for Bourdieu, this does not mean that philosophy has no relevance to the social sciences. As he has explicitly claimed, philosophy asks the most complex and intellectually demanding questions about the world. Bourdieu, however, sees it as ill-equipped to produce answers to the questions it asks. This is because the richest answers to its questions come out of empirical research that socially contextualizes the production of knowledge, not from pure reflections on the state of the world that only reinforce the scholastic tendencies of the discipline. As such, Bourdieu calls for, and sees himself as always engaging in, "fieldwork in philosophy" (Bourdieu 1990).

The above constitutes the parameters of what Bourdieu constructs as a competitive relation between sociology and philosophy. He tries to dethrone philosophy from its position as the aristocrat of the human sciences. But it could be argued that in portraying sociology as a kind of submission to a reality principle (empirical reality) that needs to be investigated, and differentiating it from a philosophy perceived as unlimited *jouissance* unhampered by necessity and such a reality principle, the conception of philosophy as having a kind of aristocratic ethos is in fact reinforced.

This idea of philosophy as the unlimited jouissance of a thought that knows no empirical restraints is perhaps behind Derrida's reported quip that Bourdieu relates to philosophy as a man relates to his mistress. This is a very pertinent characterization insofar as the traditional image of the mistress denotes a clandestine relation to someone who provides one with pure enjoyment. Nonetheless one can say that after Bourdieu's critical severity toward Heidegger in *The Political Ontology of Martin Heidegger*, toward Sartre in *Outline of a Theory of Practice*, and toward Kant in *Distinction*, *Pascalian Meditation* represents a succumbing to the philosophical pleasure principle where the relation to the mistress is brought out in the open.

Whatever one thinks of the above, there is no doubt that the philosophical and the sociological are in constant relation to each other in Bourdieu's overall approach such that a lack of awareness of the philosophical dimension of his work leads to a truncated understanding of his sociological categories. It is to avoid such a truncation that I have, in my teaching, always designated his work a "political economy of being" (see Hage 2009).

Bourdieu has often defended himself against a utilitarian understanding of his work that misinterprets his conception of social agents "accumulating capital" as an economistic neomarginalist anthropology that sees individuals as always driven by the need to maximize profit. He once retorted, "It is not true to say that everything that people do or say is aimed at maximizing their social profit; but one may say that they do it to perpetuate or to augment their social being" (1993: 274). Dreyfus and Rabinow (1993: 35) have usefully defined this dimension of Bourdieu's approach as an "empirical existential analytics." It is in this sense that, to me, Bourdieu's work constitutes a "political economy of being." It is a critical mode of understanding the production and circulation of culturally specific ways of perceiving "being" (that is, whatever is contextually sensed as a "good," fulfilling, satisfying, viable, etc. life). That such a perspective is the philosophically richest way to capture the complexities of his analytical apparatus becomes clearer in Bourdieu's later work, where he himself makes it more explicit. In *Pascalian Meditations* he tells us that the social world is defined as a producer and distributor of "reasons for being" and that "one of the most unequal of all distributions, and probably, in any case, the most cruel, is the distribution of symbolic capital, that is, of social importance and of reasons for living" (2000: 241).

What's more, people do not just passively receive a certain amount of being from society. Some might inherit a social or class location along with various material and symbolic resources that make the accumulation of social being relatively easy for them. Others might begin with very little being and have to feverishly struggle for their life to even begin being meaningful in their own eyes and in the eyes of others.

This vision of society as an assemblage concerned with the production and distribution of social being pervades Bourdieu's work. So does his conception of social agency as a struggle to accumulate it: the key concepts of capital, illusio, and habitus each delineates a dimension of this struggle. Illusio denotes the mode in which the social subject is gripped by the social and becomes driven by something that gives his or her life a meaning. This is what Bourdieu's co-researcher Louis Pinto (1998) has called "l'accumulation des raisons d'être." Capital in its variety of forms refers to the accumulation of being in the form of recognition. Finally, habitus, which is what I will mostly be concentrating on here, is the principle behind the accumulation of being in the form of social or practical efficacy.

To begin with, I want to go through a short exploration of habitus's philosophical genealogy, particularly in its relation to notions of capacity and disposition. In the process I will show how some of my reflections on hearing and deafness can be used to exemplify the key issues that Bourdieu's dialogues with philosophy are trying to highlight in relation to this concept.

HABITUS, CAPACITY, DISPOSITION

The term *habitus* has a long presence in Western thought, and much has been written about its genealogy, especially in French. Some ancient and modern philosophers and sociologists have used the more mundane term *habit* in English, or *habitude* in French, to convey the same key idea of a generative mechanism that habitus has aimed to capture. Merleau-Ponty used *habitude*. Husserl used *habitus*. Which word a particular thinker chooses, *habit* or *habitus*, was and is a somewhat arbitrary choice. It is so in the sense that regardless of whether *habit* or *habitus* is used, those using it for analytical intentions tried to grapple with the same question: How is it that human beings, by repetitively engaging in or mimicking the behavior of people, animals, and even certain objects around them, end up being more than just automatons and develop a creative "generative" capacity out of what Aristotle called the "sedimentation" of previous experiences?

In a well-known piece, François Heran (1987) has shown the evolution of the concept not only in philosophy but also in early medical language, where *habitus* referred to the symptomatic, manifested, state of the body in relation to a specific illness affecting it. *Manifested* here means an outward appearance generated by an inner state. As Heran informs us, the word *malade* in French, meaning "sick," which still exists in English in the form of *malady*, has its roots in this usage and is a contraction of *mal habitus*—a not so good outward state of the body generated by something wrong happening in the body. This idea of the body's visible, outward deployment in space and time as a product of the inner body perceived as a generative mechanism has been one of the core meanings conveyed by the philosophical deployment of habitus: the internalization and sedimentation of experience, on one hand, and the production of a generative capacity and the externalization of this capacity, on the other, are perhaps the most well-known tropes associated with habitus generally and with Bourdieu's own conception. Earlier I spoke of my capacity to hear and my disposition to eavesdrop. To understand the significance of such a terminology we need to further analyze the significance of these tropes.

It is agreed in Bourdieu scholarship that the earliest and perhaps still the most important philosophical usage of the concept of habitus comes from Thomas Aquinas (2000), who used it to translate Aristotle's (1999) notion of *hexis*, a concept that Bourdieu also uses along with habitus. Aristotle's hexis already contained some of the core dimensions of what has come to characterize habitus, for Aquinas to begin with and later for those after him, including Bourdieu. Most important is the way the notion of hexis denotes a fusion between the notions of "having" and "being." In its common everyday usage the verb *to have* indicates "possession" of something and presumably the possession of its capacities. As important, *to have* indicates something that is outside of me but that I can access, and as such, by accessing it, I access its properties. As such, it enables me, in the straightforward way that having a car or a bicycle enables me to be mobile on certain surfaces. Aristotle illustrates the problem with the category "to have" by reflecting on, among other things, the idea of "having a coat." For him, a statement such as "I have a coat" tells us that the person making the utterance has access to a coat that is outside of her. This gives her access to its capacities to shield her from the cold and the rain when necessary. But this does not tell us where the coat is: the person can have it at home, for instance. Consequently it might well rain and be cold and the person is left without her coat to shield her even though "she has a coat." This is the kind of having that Aristotle is keen to disassociate from hexis. The kind of having he wants to emphasize with the latter notion is a habitual and ongoing having whereby what is outside of me becomes an inseparable and durable part of me; it becomes me. There is a movement and a fusion between what I have and what I am. Hexis is a kind of coat that becomes part of me and is always accessible. It allows me to always have not just the occasional capacity, such as when I have a coat at home, but the continuous practical capacity to shield myself from the rain and the cold as soon as I need to do so. Never would I have to say "I left it at home" because the coat in a sense has become part of me. In fact it *is* me or, perhaps better still, it is within me to become a coat. That is, it becomes part of the way my body efficiently deploys itself in the world, what Spinoza calls "perfection." In an important sense, habitus for Bourdieu is both a manifestation and a measurement of this "perfection": How well is a body capable of deploying itself in a particular environment? For Bourdieu, the answer is always: as well as the body has internalized this environment.

If what I have becomes what I am, it means that what was outside of me has also become an internal part of me. It is here that emerges the dominant trope of an "internalization" that creates in me a "durable" disposition, a durable mode of being. The easiest way to think of this internalization is by thinking about how a body acquires physical fitness after years of regular exercise. Fitness becomes a durable quality of one's body, something one always has rather than something one can have or not, which means it becomes something one is. Habitus, however, is not just general fitness; it is fitness to meet the challenges that a specific social milieu throws at you by the mere fact of your living and evolving in it. Because both the body and the space in which the body is immersed are continuously evolving, internalization is also a process of "coevolution." Dispositions are the transformation of the body's capacities such that it becomes more inclined to, geared toward establishing a particular mode of encounter with the social rather than another.

What I described as my disposition to eavesdrop can help us explore this matter further. As I briefly described earlier, when I began eavesdropping I was repeatedly in a social situation that was of no interest to me (the table where my parents were discussing work matters with others). I had no desire to invest myself in a conversational space that had no meaning to me. So I began investing myself in the discussions happening at the tables around me, which proved to be far more interesting (if only because of the naughtiness of it all). This investment of the self in situations where one can augment the meaningfulness of one's life is what Bourdieu calls illusio. The illusio is therefore always at the root of the coevolution of bodily capacities and the imperatives of a specific social space, or what Bourdieu refers to as the complicity between habitus and field. From a situation where I was eavesdropping because I was not interested in the table I was sitting at I gradually developed, through repetition, a desire to eavesdrop regardless of where I was. The space of the other tables and my body developed an intimate relation so that I became always geared to direct myself at this other space, rather than or alongside the space of the table where I was sitting. It is in this sense that eavesdropping became a constant natural mode of deploying myself in the world, a disposition that I found rewarding. It augmented my being. Maybe it did so perversely, but it did.

We can move now to analyze a crucial distinction between understanding my disposition and understanding Bourdieu's habitus. I spoke of my *capacity* to hear what was going on at the other tables and my social *disposition* to eavesdrop. One can say that this differentiation between capacity and disposition is at the core of Bourdieu's notion of habitus. Yet it is by no means an easy differentiation to establish. The first thing one can say about this is that a disposition is a social transformation of a capacity in the process of becoming part of a specific social field. Becoming part of any social space involves the transformation of biological capacities into social dispositions. The disposition to speak Arabic is the result of a biological capacity to speak that has internalized, and coevolved with, an Arabic-speaking social space. One cannot internalize a space and develop a bodily disposition toward something without first having the capacity to develop such a disposition. I cannot develop a disposition to eavesdrop without a biological capacity to hear. Likewise I can continuously expose myself to the flight of a bird, but doing so is not going to make me fly. One should note, however, that this might create in me a disposition to fantasize about flying.

The complexity of the situation lies in that the transformation of biological capacities into social dispositions does not mean that the biological is always a capacity and the social always a disposition. A body's power is not always either a capacity or a disposition across social space and time. Capacity is a "raw" or "pre-social-field" power that the body brings into a field before being transformed within that field into a disposition. My biological capacity to hear was the raw material that was transformed by virtue of my being born in Lebanon into a disposition to hear Arabic. But this disposition to hear Arabic stands in relation to my disposition to eavesdrop as a capacity. I brought with me one day to the dinner table my capacity to hear Arabic, and, with time, because of the social and historical circumstances I have already related, my capacity to hear in Arabic was transformed into a disposition to eavesdrop on people speaking Arabic. A disposition is therefore a capacity, social or biological, that has been transformed through the process of coevolution with a particular social space or field.

Note that when I started losing my hearing I didn't immediately lose my disposition to eavesdrop, even though I was losing my capacity to do so, which was really losing my biological capacity to hear. The relation between capacity and disposition is not unidirectional in a simple way. Indeed for a while I was in this frustrating state where I had the disposition to eavesdrop without the capacity to do so. This raises another important question that has occupied Bourdieu and his philosophers: In what way is a disposition a different kind of bodily power, a different phenomenon, from a capacity?

This was an important dimension of the notion of hexis that Aristotle had to grapple with and that other philosophers and theorists after him have continued to grapple with: What is the significance of this idea of a durable state of being that ends up being a *dispositional* state? What does it mean to say that I have a bodily disposition, and in what way is that different from saying that I have a bodily capacity? What kind of ontology is assumed by the notion of dispositionality? As far as I was concerned, to say that I have, like all hearing people, a capacity to eavesdrop simply means that I have what it takes to do it. It does not mean that I feel or that I really want to do it. This is not the same as saying that I am disposed to eavesdrop, which clearly means more than having what it takes to do it. It means that I get the urge to do it, that I desire to do it, that I am driven from within to do it. I think the difference is obvious, but its significance is not.

One thing should be clear: take two situations, where (a) I have the capacity to eavesdrop and (b) I have the disposition to eavesdrop. The difference does not entail that in the case of (b) I will definitely eavesdrop, while in the case of (a) I will not eavesdrop. This is where the difficulty lies. For neither having a capacity nor having a disposition determines what I will actually do. I might well be disposed to eavesdrop, but that doesn't mean that I will do so. Indeed if I am in a transitional state following visits to Eavesdroppers Anonymous, I can even say that I am disposed to eavesdrop but have worked out a way to stop myself from doing so. Conversely, at the same table that night, somebody who doesn't have the disposition to eavesdrop might be eavesdropping on the table next to us because he really wants to know what is happening at that particular table. This is what bothered many ancient and modern philosophers about the notion of "disposition": What is a "dispositional power," and does it really exist? How can I say that I have a disposition to do something and then not do it? Is it not a bit meaningless? For instance, in the case where I say I am disposed to eavesdrop but have not done so for a while, why not say that I also clearly have a disposition not to eavesdrop since at least I can provide empirical examples of its being the case?

This has led some philosophers to dismiss the concept of dispositionality as a mystification rather than a clarification of reality. Bourdieu himself follows in the Aristotelian tradition by seeing dispositionality as referring to an actual, not virtual, constant empirical presence. His conception is similar to the notion of "tendency" as analyzed by the transcendental realism of Roy Bhaskar (2008): a dispositional force is a causal force. It is always present, and it causes something to happen even when it does not cause the subject to do what it is disposing her to do. So if I am sitting having dinner at a restaurant and I have a disposition to eavesdrop, even if I don't eavesdrop, this disposition will explain why I have to concentrate harder than others to stay tuned to the conversation happening around my table. I will be more tired than others by the end of the dinner, and my tiredness can be explained only by the fact that I had to fight my disposition to eavesdrop in order not to do it. Unlike "having a capacity," "having a disposition" is an active variable in a given social situation. It has a specific type of causal power even when it does not cause the body to do what it is predisposed to do.

This notion of dispositionality as a force emanating from the body is crucial for understanding Bourdieu's habitus; without it we cannot understand syncretic cultural forms. For example, I am a native French speaker and therefore I have a disposition to speak French. I am learning English, and the teacher asks me to say the word *table*. I look at it and I say *tébeuhl*. One can see that it is not the pronunciation of *table* in French, *tahbl*, that is haunting me; rather it is the task of producing the phonemes *tay* and *ble*. An accent is not a cognitive lack but a state of the body subjected to multiple directionality: words uttered, meaning a movement of one's facial muscles and vocal chords in a direction against the direction that those muscles are usually predisposed to go under the effect of the dispositionality of one's facial, mouth, and tongue muscles and vocal chords. The fact that I eventually might succeed in saying effortlessly and unreflexively *table* in the proper English way, without an accent, means that I have the capacity, but it takes time to have the dispositionality.

Before moving away from the question of dispositionality, there is something quite important that needs to be emphasized. There is sometimes among phenomenologically inclined Bourdieuians an equation of habitus with dispositionality. This is really reducing his anthropology to philosophy. For it is true that habitus as understood by phenomenologists like Husserl or Merleau-Ponty can be understood as a form of dispositionality, but it is not true in the case of Bourdieu. Indeed if that was the case, Bourdieu would not have really added much to the philosophical understanding of habitus and would be seen as simply aiming to apply it in empirically grounded research. However, that is not the case. For Bourdieu, a habitus is not just a dispositionality but the structure of this dispositionality. One needs to recall here the famous definition of *habitus* in *Outline of a Theory of Practice* (Bourdieu 1977) as "a structured structure" and a "structuring structure" and so on. What is the relation between a dispositionality and a structure?

Let me again go back to my eavesdropping. It is a disposition, but it also has a general structure: in eavesdropping, you are physically positioned within one specific space, the table you are sitting at, and yet your attention is also or mostly directed at an "other space" nearby, the space of the other table. Now, if you visit a museum and you are looking at a painting and your attention cannot stay only on the painting but keeps shifting to the surrounding paintings, we can say that you have a similarly structured disposition when it comes to visual experiences. And if you are eating from your plate at a restaurant but you cannot help yourself from being totally interested in what's on the plate of the person next to you, yet again we can say that you have a similar structure of experience involving all your senses. It is the shared structure of these dispositions that represents habitus for Bourdieu, not the disposition itself. This is why he calls it a "transposable structure." Theoretically speaking, the lineage of this conception of structure is in Merleau-Ponty's notion of *généralité du corps*; Merleau-Ponty uses the examples of how writing on paper and on a blackboard involves distinctively different muscles, and yet the general movement of those muscles ends up producing in each case similar handwriting. An actual disposition that is located in a modality of a particular part of the body cannot be transferred to another part of the body, but the general nature of it can. In much the same way, a hearing disposition cannot be transposed into the domain of smell, but its structure can. This is habitus for Bourdieu, not the disposition on its own.

For Bourdieu, therefore, my disposition to eavesdrop is only a social habitus insofar as this structure is reproduced in other spaces. In my case, it is. Indeed I wonder if this disposition to be in one place while directing my attention to what is around me also structures the way I do my research. Even this very piece on Bourdieu involves attention to the "philosophical table" next to me while sitting at Bourdieu's table, as it were. This is why it can be suitably called "eavesdropping on Bourdieu's philosophers."

I want to now move to Bourdieu's conception of the habitus–social reality nexus that he has developed in dialogue with Husserl's notion of *Umwelt*. This underlies Bourdieu's notion of politics as a struggle, not between views of reality but between realities. Again some reflections on my eavesdropping and later deafness can help illuminate Bourdieu's conceptualization.

CONCERNING REAL SOCIALLY CONSTRUCTED REALITIES

The habit of eavesdropping involves not merely listening to people you are not supposed to listen to; it also situates the listener in a different "hearing reality." I am saying a different hearing reality because just as it is clear that eavesdropping involves a different way of deploying oneself (one's hearing) in the world, it also involves a different way in which the world makes itself present to us. Generally speaking, for example, there is a positive correlation between the intensity with which one hears a sound and the shortness of the distance between the listener and the source emitting the sound. The closer the sound, the clearer, sharper, and louder it is heard by a hearing person. For an eavesdropper, this order of things is reversed: one occupies a world in which the sounds closest to us are experienced as faint, while those farther away are sharper. It is important to stress here that this is not a mere take on reality but a reality, or rather both. Indeed when I lost my capacity to eavesdrop it wasn't "a point of view" on or a representation of reality that I lost but a whole reality that I had been inhabiting and that was no longer available to me to inhabit. It is this social space, subjectively produced as a result of one's specific interests, social location, and power, but nonetheless practically existing that marks Bourdieu's perspectivism. It is a perspectivism that he has produced by blending Nietzsche's perspectivism with Husserl's Umwelt. Perspectives for Bourdieu are part and parcel of the social realities they bring about, but neither these perspectives nor those social realities are mere subjective takes on reality. They are realities as such, produced by the historical unfolding of a particular habitus and the environment it is part of and that it has brought into being.

This conception already had, yet again, an embryonic existence in the Aristotelian notion of *hexis*. But it was taken up by Husserl and further developed in his conception of the Umwelt. It should be remembered here that Husserl was the subject of Bourdieu's doctoral thesis. Bourdieu fully activates this Husserlian notion while politicizing it with Nietzsche's perspectivism, arguing that habitus is always metonymic of a larger social reality that is integral to it. Consequently insofar as life is a struggle between differently dispositioned people, each with a different habitus, life is also a struggle between different realities. This constructivism is radical in that it is not a relativism. Perhaps we can say that Bourdieu's realities are social constructions in the sense of a chair being more a social construction than a tree. While this analogy does not entirely capture Bourdieu's position, it nonetheless conveys the key idea in Bourdieu's perspectivist social constructivism: to say that something is socially constructed is not an ontological statement regarding how real it is.

I have often struggled to find a good way of communicating this notion of a "real constructed reality" to people who, for a variety of reasons, find it hard to imagine. I'll allow myself to deploy here the same wild example that I have allowed myself to deploy many times while teaching, only because, despite its unrealness, it has been so far relatively effective in conveying what Bourdieu has in mind. So here we go.

Skis allow you to move better on snow if you master them. Fins allow you to move much more easily in water if you master them. In Bourdieu's world, there is a Darwinian-like process where the body trying to move on snow eventually develops ski-like features and the body trying to move in water develops fin-like features—bodily dispositions that allow one to operate maximally in one's environment. This is what Spinoza refers to as "perfection," the maximal ability to deploy oneself efficiently in the world. The "augmentation" of this perfection is what Spinoza says causes us to experience joy. The influence of this Spinozist paradigm on Bourdieu's conception of practical efficacy is clear. Bourdieu explicitly uses a Spinozist concept, *conatus*, to describe the core part of the habitus that always aims to reproduce itself in its being.

To go back to our example, in Bourdieu's world of skiing people (the world of people with a skiing illusio), they acquire a skiing habitus and accumulate being by pushing themselves to master skiing in the best possible way by accumulating varieties of "skiing capital": strength, technique, grace, better equipment, and so on. Likewise in the world of swimming people (the world of people with a swimming illusion), they strive to accumulate "swimming capital." So far so good, one might say, in that there is a very Spinozist struggle to seek joy happening through the accumulation of practical efficacy within the world of skiing where the world is mainly snow, and within the world of swimming where the world is mainly water. The difficulty in understanding Bourdieu's concept of habitus is that it highlights another important dimension to this struggle, one that takes us away from the Spinoza-inspired accumulation of practical efficiency.

To understand Bourdieu here you have to imagine—and this is where I am asking you to stretch your imagination a bit—you have to imagine that the snow-full reality of the skiers and the water-full reality of the swimmers are not something given, like an unchanging environmental reality: the bodies equipped with skis are also equipped with mini-personal snow-making machines. They are personally and collectively busy creating the very world in which they can operate best. Indeed their snow-covered world will exist only insofar as they succeed in creating the snow on which they can maximize their movement. Likewise with the bodies endowed with fins; not only do they have fins, but they are also equipped with flooding devices trying to turn everything into a swimmable reality. It is here that we come to the struggle that is of interest to Bourdieu: while the struggle for practical efficacy among skiers and swimmers is important, the most far-reaching struggle is the one between snow-producing skiers and water-producing swimmers. Here the competition is not merely about who skis or swims better but about whether the world itself is going to be a skiing world or a swimming world. The winners impose both their reality and their practical mastery over reality. If the skiers win, you end up with a lot of people looking ridiculous wearing swimsuits and fins and trying to walk in the snow. And if the swimmers win, you get the equally ridiculous situation of a bunch of people in full ski gear trying to cross the lake of life, as it were. This is what Bourdieu calls "the struggle to 'make and unmake' social worlds."

I will stop here with this wild heuristic analogy as it is already beyond the pale to stretch it further. But for what it's worth, you need to also remember that for Bourdieu, even if snow reality dominates, water reality will still have a minor existence to the extent that there remain people with fin-like habitus. There are dominant and dominated people within a reality, but just as, if not more, important, there are dominant and dominated realities.

It is this conception of a struggle between opposing "habitus-realities" that constituted the basic framework Bourdieu used in his early work, even before he developed the notion of habitus, to understand and analyze the practical decision-making processes of the Algerian peasantry in the face of social change. He aimed to show that capitalism did not merely introduce new practices that the peasants were not capable of mastering; rather these practices forced on the peasants a new reality: they actually robbed the peasants of the very reality in which they could operate, or at least made that reality a minor dominated reality.

In this sense, the accumulation of being that is generated by the habitus not only pertains to a technical domain of accumulation of practical efficiency. It also embodies a more existential domain that we can call the accumulation of homeliness. One can say, continuing along the same phenomenological Husserlian-Heideggerian bent, that habitus is a principle of homing and building, of striving to build the space where one can be at home in the world, a struggle that is never-ending.

When we say that a habitus "fits" in its environment, this does not mean that there is some kind of imaginary "total fit." Rather it means that the habitus is part and parcel of an environment where it is capable of generating actions that strive to make us at home. As Heidegger famously put it, we are at home insofar as we feel we can strive to be at home. Likewise for Bourdieu, the habitus is at home insofar as it can generate what he calls strategies. Strategies are both an indication that the human agent is not totally at home and the fact that she is. I was at home in my eavesdropping hearing world. And its loss was, as I have argued, the loss of a home, not the loss of a subjective perspective on the world. Even more clearly, when I lost my capacity to hear I lost the world that my hearing both created and allowed me to inhabit; I didn't lose a subjectively conceived hearing "perspective" on the world. From such a perspective, our sensorial reality is always the fusion of a multiplicity of realities produced by the encounter of the world with each of the senses.

This conception of social realities as "real constructions," emanating from an encounter with multiple potentialities of the body and the multiple potentialities of the surrounding environment, as it were, is perhaps one of the more critical and far-reaching aspects of Bourdieu's work. I see it as prefiguring the "multinaturalist" turn developed in the work of Latour (2012) and Viveiros de Castro (2009). But it also takes us to where one encounters the limits of Bourdieu's conception of those realities. I will now move to those aspects of my experience of deafness and hearing that point to some of those limits.

HEARING, LISTENING, BEING, AND SOCIAL BEING

The first experience associated with deafness that I want to highlight has to do with the loss of the symbolic capacity of speech. Being partially deaf meant that I still heard speech, but the deafer I got the more speech became slowly unrecognizable and meaningless. Those differences in phonemes and morphemes set against each other and that Saussure tells us are the basis of the production of meaning start to disappear, and every word or sentence becomes a certain duration of sound that lacks clear differentiation or meaning. Later, when I received a cochlear implant, I recovered some of this capacity to capture those differences that made sound meaningful, and in the process some of the symbolic sharpness of the world returned.

But here something interesting happened. After an exhilarating period when I gradually felt I was hearing better again, I started to yearn every now and then for the world of deafness, which was not as dominated by symbolic and symbolizable dimensions. The way I associated the symbolic domain, or symbolized life, with the "sharpness" of sound was itself interesting to me. I felt that as a deaf person I had greater access to what I might call the libidinality of the world, and a certain subliminal jouissance came with this slightly less sharp and symbolic relation to what was around me.

Let me be clear that what I experienced and what I am describing is not an either/or situation (that is, either symbolic or not) but a case of more or less. Perhaps from a Lacanian perspective, I can say that the imaginary dimensions of life became a little bit more important as I lost the capacity to hear because the symbolic or representational dimension becomes a little bit less pronounced. It is not a world without words, but rather even words themselves, as they lose this sharp differentiation, start conveying less a symbolic meaning and more an emotional charge, and instead of differentiated meanings they produce differentiated intensities, something perhaps more akin to Kristeva's (1977) *chora*. How can one think that perspective on reality as a sui generis reality as conceived in the Bourdieuian-Husserlian approach described earlier? Before attempting to think through the answer to this question, I want to relate a second experience. It has to do with something I became aware of only after I received my implant.

Going deaf means that listening requires an exceptional amount of concentration. As you are scraping the bottom of the barrel for a bit of meaning here and there in order to reconstitute the totality of what is being said to you, you simply cannot afford to lose or not capture anything that is possible to capture. Hearing always takes the form of intense listening and is an exceptionally tiring practice.

When I received my implant and gradually recovered some of the capacity to hear sounds in my surroundings, such as birds, planes, the wind, cars in the background, and waves, slowly I regained something I had forgotten about completely: that hearing is not always a purposeful act. One simply hears. It is a way of being constantly deployed in the world, not in the sense of deployment associated with Bourdieu's habitus, where the body is always deployed directionally to do this or to do that. Here is a passage from the auto-ethnographic notes I was taking during the early period when my cochlear was being fitted and fine-tuned for me:

> This morning, following the cochlear adjustment session, I sat in the park facing St. Vincent's hospital. The session involved only mild adjustments, but for some reason, as I was going down the elevator, I felt a sense of qualitative difference in the sounds I was hearing. . . . I thought the same as I did a few weeks ago: "more human and less

computer-like." As I settled on the park bench I became emotional again hearing the birds just as I did two weeks ago. I was hearing them even better . . . like I remembered them to be. . . . I felt lucky and grateful that I've had the opportunity to hear them again . . . and I sat down enjoying the sun in the park. Then my thoughts drifted to the paper I was writing and I got immersed thinking about it. Suddenly, as I slowly moved back to thinking about more everyday practical things, something struck me: I never stopped hearing the birds, the traffic, car doors slamming, while I was thinking about my writing. I was hearing them in their distinctness even though I was not aiming to hear them. This was definitely a "regained" experience: hearing my surroundings as a distinct and recognizable sound rather than a general hum, and, as important, hearing it without concentrating all my energy in order to do so.

As I reflected on these two realities and experiences in conjunction with thinking about Bourdieu's theory and its relation to philosophy, there was a disruption of the relatively smooth and complementary way in which the relation between the three operated. In concluding this chapter, I want to suggest that this disruption comes because these experiences denote an experience and a reality that lie outside the dominant modern conception of being that Bourdieu works with. As such they require an anthropology of radical alterity that demands more than the kind of relation Bourdieu's work has with philosophy.

PHILOSOPHY AND CRITICAL ANTHROPOLOGY

Despite the pertinent and powerful critique of rational choice theory that underlies his conception of habitus, Bourdieu's subject is still an "oriented" subject who derives meaningfulness from having a purpose in life, or to put it differently, a subject that encounters the world purposefully. "Sense" as meaning and as direction plays an important role in Bourdieu's conception of the subject. This is so even if that purpose, unlike for rational choice theory, is inherent in the orientation of a social body to the world rather than in a presumed universal calculative rationality. This is the significance of the close relation between habitus and illusio in Bourdieu's work: to be deprived of purpose and orientation is to simply be deprived of raisons d'être, to be deprived of being.

Let us listen to him speak about the chronically unemployed in his preface to Lazarsfeld's work on the unemployed of Marienthal, whom he sees as "dispossessed of the vital illusion of having a function or a mission, of having to be or do something":

> What transpires is a sentiment of abandonment, despair, even of absurdity, that imposes itself on these men suddenly deprived not just of an activity and a salary, but of a social justification and motivation for being. They are thus thrown back to face the naked truth of their condition. Withdrawal, retirement, resignation, political indifferentism (the Romans called it quies) or the escape into a millenarian imaginary are so many manifestations . . . of this terrible state of rest that social death is.
>
> In losing their work, the unemployed have also lost the countless tokens (the thousand nothings) through which is realised and can manifest itself a socially known and recognized function, in other words the whole set of goals posited in advance, independently of any conscious project, in the form of demands and commitments—"important" meetings, cheques to post, invoices to draw up—and the whole forthcoming already given in the immediate present, in the form of deadlines, dates and timetables to be observed—buses to take, rates to maintain, targets to meet. Deprived of this objective universe of incitements and indications which orientate and stimulate action and, through it, social life, they can only experience the free time that is left to them as dead time, purposeless and meaningless (emptied of all significance). If time seems to be annihilated, this is because employment is the support, if not the source, of most interest, expectations, demands, hopes and investments in the present, and also in the future or the past that it implies, in short one of the major foundations of illusio in the sense of involvement in the game of life, in the present, the primordial investment which—as traditional wisdom has always taught, in identifying detachment from time with detachment from the world—creates time and indeed is time itself. (Bourdieu 1981: 7–8)

This is, at least to me, Bourdieu at his best, explaining very powerfully, and quite poetically to boot, what it is like to be deprived of social being, and the loss of reality this entails. However, and this is my point, what is striking is that he is unable to find anything positive, anything redeeming or worthwhile, existentially or politically, in this state of nonsocial being. It seems clear from this that being, for him, is entirely reduced to modern purposeful social being. Despite his capacity to think of realities as constructions and as multiple, he is not able to think of this state of nothingness as itself a reality, let alone consider it a viable reality. For him it is a nonreality.

It is in this sense that this limitation of Bourdieu's work is also at the point of tension between a sociological tendency that takes a unified and given modern ontology for granted, and an anthropology of radical alterity where forms of being are not only seen as multiple but are also radically other to our own, demanding from us an effort to think about the possibility of viable modes of life that are not close to ours and that are not reducible to states of purposefulness.

The realities of hearing "nonsymbolically" and of being diffused rather than oriented in the world that I have described require one to move outside of a modern conception of purposeful being. What we have is a reality where one is differentially enmeshed in the symbolic and where the affective and libidinal dimensions of life come to the fore, and another reality where one's being is not directional and purposeful, where being is not a "being for" but simply "being." These realities are more akin to Lévy-Bruhl's ([1923] 1985) concept of participation: modes of life that are other, and sometimes radically other, to the dominant modern modes of thinking reality. Bourdieu, however, offers no conception of such radical otherness. His realities, despite their multiplicity, are inescapably modern. Even his Algerian peasants, struggling to accumulate being in the face of an imposed capitalist reality, are precapitalist but not premodern (Bourdieu and Sayad 1964). Certainly Bourdieu pertinently critiques the modern "rational choice" conception of the purposeful life but only to replace it with the purposeful body. For him, the body that is "simply there" is a socially pathological body.

The critical anthropology that deals with such radical alterity has a different relationship to philosophy than Bourdieu's sociological anthropology— and in that sense is an anthropology pertaining to the modern. The latter, already sharing a common ontological ground with philosophy, is happy letting this philosophy do the ontological questioning while it devotes its energy to a complex empirical exemplification of philosophical problematics. It is in this sense that Bourdieu saw his sociology as competing with philosophy at giving better answers to philosophical questions.

A critical anthropology that captures a mode of being and thinking that philosophers have no access to, on the other hand, has to struggle, not with the explanation of an already philosophically questioned reality but to find the concepts needed to apprehend such a reality as reality. As such it competes with philosophy about the fundamental ways of asking questions rather than about providing answers to already philosophically formulated questions concerning particular realities. Martin Holbraad has perceptively pointed to this regarding a critical anthropology that sees as its object radically other ontologies. One does not have to agree with Holbraad's polarization between the cultural and the ontological to appreciate that, as he put it:

> the key tenet of an ontological approach in anthropology . . . is that in it anthropological analysis becomes a question not of applying analytical concepts to ethnographic data, but rather of allowing ethnographic data to act as levers—big Archimedean ones!—for the transformation of analytical concepts. Instead of worrying about how best to use the concepts we have at our disposal in order either to "explain" what we find in our ethnographies or to "interpret" it (the contrast between explanation and interpretation being the *ur*-dilemma of culturalism), we should be worrying about the fact that when push comes to shove in ethnography the concepts we have at our disposal may be inadequate even to describe our data properly, let alone to "explain" or "interpret" it. Our task then must be to locate the inadequacies of our concepts in order to come up with better ones—a task one associates more with philosophy than with any form of science or the softer "arts." So if there were to be a one word slogan for an ontological approach in anthropology it would be one that some philosophers like to think of as their own: "Conceptualization!" (quoted in Carrithers et al. 2010: 180)

It is because of this that the experiences I have related not only escape Bourdieu's paradigm but also disrupt the relation he has established between his work and philosophy.

NOTE

A version of this essay appeared in *Thesis Eleven* 114.1 (2013): 76–93.

CHAPTER 7

How Concepts Make the World Look Different:
Affirmative and Negative Genealogies of Thought

Bhrigupati Singh

FINDING A QUESTION

■ I begin with a simple and yet immeasurably difficult question: What is philosophy? The answer I consider comes from postwar Continental philosophy. Why here? Where else? Anthropology may signal an elsewhere. For now let us stay with the question. In their book *What Is Philosophy?* Gilles Deleuze and Félix Guattari (1994: 2) suggest that "philosophy is the art of forming, inventing and fabricating concepts." An answer may begin rather than end a conversation. Unlike a sage's utterance, Deleuze and Guattari (1994: 3) contend, a philosopher's answer is usually followed by a counterquestion or a challenge, for instance, What are "concepts"? Do only philosophers produce concepts? I enter this conversation as an anthropologist. Dare I pose as open-ended a question to myself: What is anthropology? There are many answers, among which I propose the following: anthropology is a mode of heightened attentiveness to life. This answer too prompts counterquestions: Attention toward what, and in what way? Some say there was a time when anthropology had a definable set of research questions. Do we now seek wholly at random?

We might notice that in recent years a significant measure of anthropological order, we might even call it standardization in some cases, has emerged through the influence of particular philosophers as interlocutors or guides: Foucault, Benjamin, Derrida, more recently Agamben, and in my case, the philosopher I am most drawn to, Deleuze. These names may be a symptom of decline, a loss of anthropologically generated theory. Or they may signal an infusion of vitality from a neighboring field. Does quoting philosophers mark a loss of self-reliance for anthropology? Consider a counterquestion: Would the avoidance of philosophy liberate us from philosophical pressures? Or a different question about these pressures: Are the anthropological turns to philosophy dictated by little else than passing fashions? We might pause to wonder at how thought moves, in more or less transient ways, and the impact these changes have on how we view the world through ethnography.

Rather than stand-alone concepts or theorists, in this essay I describe a long-standing philosophical antagonism between what we might call dialectical and nondialectical genealogies of thought, and how this difference may implicitly or explicitly impact our ethnographic ways of perceiving the world. According to *What Is Philosophy?* philosophers are "conceptual personae" (Deleuze and Guattari 1994: 61), signaling routes of thought. For me, Deleuze, or Deleuze and Guattari, named an opening, a way into nondialectical thought. Through conceptual and empirical instances, I will describe how this philosophical antagonism surfaced for me, in thinking about power, ethics, and life itself in the ethnographic setting of rural central India that may otherwise seem so distant from the concerns of Continental philosophy. Concepts may be reterritorialized and illuminate the world differently. The *non*dialectical that I invoke, as the kind of illumination to which I was drawn, is not just a negation but also a way of thinking about the "meta"-physical, not in the sense of a transcendent other world but rather the play of forces that compose this world. Prior to Deleuze, Nietzsche is a predecessor, a preceptor into this mode of nondialectical thought. Three concepts in particular describe my sense of what this philosophical genealogy might offer anthropology: polarities, thresholds, and intensities, each of which I will explore.

When do anthropologists need such concepts? Perhaps not, or not explicitly, while attempting an ethnographic immersion into a milieu. What does it mean to think ethnographically? This too is a standing concern of this essay. At first we gather impressions. Then we try to express those impressions as thoughts. Concepts come more explicitly to the surface as impressions grow into thoughts. Then again, concepts are present, perhaps implicitly, even at the point of impressions, in what we sought. Philosophy is one mode in which we may reconsider the concepts that inform seemingly straightforward impressions of the world. We may express a genealogy of thought, explicitly or implicitly. Dialectical modes of thinking such as the domination/resistance paradigm (Scott 1990) or a significant fraction of postcolonial theory and subaltern studies often do not explicitly claim to express a particular philosophical genealogy. A philosophical-genealogical antagonism that is only implicitly and vaguely (although insistently) present in some instances may become sharper in other juxtapositions, as in a contrast I draw between Deleuze's nondialectics contra Agamben and the many anthropologists drawn to this recent avatar of a (quite illustrious) negative dialectical lineage of thought. The conceptual company we keep impacts our modes of perception quite directly.

We may also arrive at these ways of perceiving the world without academic philosophy, since what is at stake are ways of thinking and perception. One of the central themes of *What Is Philosophy?* is how philosophy relates to and draws on nonphilosophy. Thought is composed of "percepts, affects and concepts" (Deleuze and Guattari 1994: 163). A concept may reorient our affects or percepts and vice versa. In mapping these antagonisms of thought and feeling, I began to find a different set of coordinates than the received wisdom of anthropological and critical theory in the late twentieth century, which grouped a number of quite divergent philosophers within easily assimilated shorthand, such as postmodernism and poststructuralism. Let me set out the antagonism somewhat more systematically, after which I will turn to my own ethnographic work to ask what anthropology might gain from these conversations or add to them, with its own modes of examining life.

A PHILOSOPHICAL ANTAGONISM

In speaking of philosophy, I am not invoking a unified field. Differences are usually cast in geographical ("Western" vs. "non-Western") or national ("Indian" or "French") or subdisciplinary (analytic vs. continental) terms. In emphasizing the difference between dialectics and nondialectics, I am referring to a tension that may exist *within* a philosophical tradition, Western or non-Western. Such conceptual differences may also be expressed in a thoughtful moment of an ordinary conversation, even by those untrained in scholastic traditions.

For now let us stay with the antagonism in its academic, Continental avatar. Recent work in critical theory has begun to show the sharp differences glossed over by a label such as *poststructuralism*. Daniel Smith (2003: 49), for instance, describes the sharply divergent trajectories of Derrida, expressing a tradition of negative transcendence (différance, an absence that transcends "a" and "not a"), as distinct from Deleuze, expressing a tradition of affirmative immanence (the immanent flux and copresence of "a" and "not a," the self-differentiating intensities of "a"). What might anthropology make of these seeming abstractions? In "Theatrum Philosophicum," Foucault (1977: 165) makes the enigmatic assertion, now often quoted (particularly by publishers on the cover of books by Deleuze), "Perhaps one day this century will be known as Deleuzian." Have we arrived at such a century? Anthropologists close to this field of thought, such as Paul Rabinow (2011: 121), declare that Deleuze is "notoriously esoteric." Anthropology has profitably received a clutch of Deleuzian terms: *assemblages* (Ong and Collier 2005), *deterritorialization* (Ferme 2004), *becoming* (Biehl and Locke 2010), to name a few. Given Deleuze's stress on multiplicities and excess, we are warned not to reduce his thinking to a "system" (Rabinow 2011: 121). Rather than a closed system, I will refer to a genre, a way of thought exercised and extended through different instances. Through a series of books on Spinoza, Bergson, and Nietzsche, as well as two texts central to his oeuvre, *Difference and Repetition* (1994) and *The Logic of Sense* (1990) Deleuze builds a countertradition of European philosophy distinct from the dialectical lineage that moves from Aristotle to Hegel and into the twentieth century, the consequences of which are only beginning to be tracked for critical theory.[1] As anthropologists we remain interested in genealogies and kinship charts. To belong to a lineage is not necessarily to say that it remains the "same" or that nothing new happens from one generation to the next. And yet, as we know from anthropology, feuds between clans can remain long standing.

Deleuze's hostility to dialectics is polemically articulated in his early text *Nietzsche and Philosophy* (1983), which reinterprets Nietzsche's thought within a countertradition. In the chapter titled "The Overman: Against the Dialectic," Deleuze tells us, "We will misunderstand the whole of Nietzsche's work if we do not see 'against whom' its principal concepts are directed. Hegelian themes are present in this work as the enemy against which it fights" (162). Evidence for such a reading is amply present in Nietzsche's (1969: 223) own writings: "My readers know perhaps in what way I consider dialectics as a symptom of decadence." Deleuze (1983: 195) contends, "There is no possible compromise between Hegel and Nietzsche." What is at stake here? Deleuze: "Three ideas define the dialectic: the idea of a power of the negative as a theoretical principle manifested in opposition and contradiction . . . the valorization of the "sad passions" as a practical principle . . . and the idea of positivity as a theoretical and practical product of negation itself" (195). The Hegelian dialectic, Deleuze and Nietzsche contend, expresses primarily reactive forces: "For the affirmation of self it substitutes the negation of the other, and for the affirmation of affirmation it substitutes the famous negation of the negation" (Deleuze 1983: 196). The result: *ressentiment* and bad conscience: "The unhappy consciousness is the subject of the whole dialectic" (196). Many of the fields in which I was formed—postcolonial theory, critical theory, cultural studies—are descendants of negative dialectics. I could not help but feel implicated in the disputes of these warring philosophical clans.

Affirmative nondialectics does not try to "end" dialectics. Instead it aims for what Nietzsche (1990: 53) calls the "spiritualization of enmity," which "consists in profoundly grasping the value of having enemies . . . the opposing party should not decay in strength." The task is to preserve and sharpen oppositions rather than to resolve them into a "higher" synthesis. Deleuze continued to extend his nondialectical lineage in different ways throughout his oeuvre, including the books coauthored with Guattari. For instance, Deleuze and Guattari's two-volume magnum opus, *Anti-Oedipus* (1983) and *A Thousand Plateaus* (1987), together subtitled *Capitalism and Schizophrenia*, could less dramatically be subtitled "Capitalism and Nondialectical Thought" (if we take "schizophrenia" to be a nondialectical expression of different polarities held together). In recent years we can see a counterwave of contemporary dialecticians writing against Deleuze to restore the primacy of dialectics (Badiou 2000; Jameson 2009; Žižek 2004; Nesbitt 2005).

A different contribution to this dispute from within anthropological thought might be Lévi-Strauss's (1985: 185) essay "Cosmopolitanism and Schizophrenia," which shows how Chinook myth (nondialectically) "uses the notion of a split to create a philosophy." Deleuze (2004: 170) deeply admired Lévi-Strauss, even making an argument for the dynamism and temporality of the structure, as distinct from dialectical historicism and the Freudian unconscious. In this sense a term like *"post"-structuralism* signals a danger for the anthropological spirit. "It smells offensively Hegelian," as Nietzsche (1969: 270) would say, as a determinate negation, followed by a "higher" synthesis. This is not to suggest a "return" to structuralism. Deleuze gives us a range of concepts with which to inhabit a plenitude of life that exceeds structural or binary tensions, while not necessarily negating the analytical potency of particular oppositions.

In the remainder of this essay I take up not so much the history of anthropology or philosophy as themes in my own ethnographic work in rural central India to describe a few nondialectical terms that I found helpful for thinking about power, ethics, and life. I want to begin this part of the essay not from a conceptual point but rather from ethnographic experience, seeking to understand how one thinks ethnographically and what role philosophical allegiances might play in these modes of perception. To put it simply, I didn't go to Shahabad looking to instantiate Deleuzian concepts. And yet I didn't go there a tabula rasa. After fieldwork I returned, differently, to texts I had been reading prior to my departure. Between these moments of departure and return lay a whole world, full of life.

ETHNOGRAPHIC BEGINNINGS

Shahabad is a subdistrict of 236 villages in Rajasthan, where I lived for a year and a half. The main focus of my research interests were the Sahariyas, among the lowest status group in Shahabad, governmentally classified as a "primitive tribe," known locally as Adivasi ("original inhabitants," indigenous), but also as one among many local *jatis* (a common word for caste and tribe), an overlap that signals a classic debate in South Asian anthropology.[2] The Sahariyas constitute 34 percent of the population of Shahabad (TRI 2004: 2), alongside the Kiraads (a cultivator caste, 30 percent) and the Ahirs (a pastoralist caste, 10 percent), both governmentally classified as Other Backward Castes, to whom previous generations of Sahariyas and Chamars (a Scheduled caste, 15 percent of the population)[3] served as bonded laborers, a relation involving intergenerational servitude and nonnegotiable indebtedness. Starting in the 1960s, nationwide laws were passed against bonded labor, leading neighboring groups such as the Sahariyas and the cultivator Kiraads to renegotiate their transactional relations, usually to more temporary, seasonal arrangements. At present most Sahariya families earn their livelihood by cultivating small landholdings assigned to them by the state in the course of postcolonial land reforms while also working as agricultural wage labor on the lands of neighboring high and low castes.

I returned from fieldwork in Shahabad full of fervor and fondness for those I got to know there. I wanted nothing more (and nothing less) than to express life as I had experienced it there, in its vitality and struggles. The struggles often expressed relations of power. That said, over time I also began to notice other modes of spiritual and material relatedness that would be lost if I were to tell a story that was only a variant of a master-slave dialectic. Roughly midway through fieldwork I chose a few themes to follow more closely with no overarching plan in mind: particular modes of social conflict and cohabitation, two deities among the many that inhabit Shahabad, different ways in which state power manifests itself in Shahabad, the emerging water shortage in the region, and the life stories of two people whom I found particularly admirable, a Sahariya man, Bansi, a former bonded laborer, who gradually became a famous ascetic in the region, and a woman, Kalli, also a former bonded laborer turned social activist.

Any anthropologist might write on such themes, so I'll have to clarify how "nondialectics" came to be involved in this conversation. How do we piece together a world? At the outset what united my catalogue of ethnographic curiosities was nothing more than what I had instinctively found most significant and interesting in Shahabad. I began with a series of specific problems. It was only later that I came to review the answers I came up with in each instance and how these thoughts were linked to my philosophical allegiances. I turn to the first of these questions, of how we might think about state power.

POLARITIES: SOVEREIGN POWER AS MITRA AND VARUNA

I wanted to understand the ways in which state power is implicated in the lives of the Sahariyas and their neighbors. The most palpable presence of the state was through the punitive power of local Forest Department officials. Environmental historians of India have described the colonial origins of the Forest Department and the ways these powers have been recurrently contested, well into the postcolonial period, by castes and tribes living in the vicinity of forests (Guha 1983: 1991). The kingdom of Kota that included Shahabad (until Indian independence in 1947) came under colonial "indirect" rule (Peabody 2003: 148). According to most people in Shahabad, colonial and governmental powers more generally were a relatively distant presence until as recently as the 1960s. Older residents of Shahabad name the 1970s and the 1980s as the years in which the Forest Department became a more palpable, everyday presence. This period marks the provision of heightened coercive powers for Forest Department officials, in particular the assistant conservator of forests, to evict forest dwellers accused of "encroachment," impose arrests, seize crops, and confiscate property. I witnessed such punitive instances during the course of fieldwork.

There were other ways, however, in which the state was present at an everyday level in contemporary Shahabad, for instance as a guarantor of employment for the rural poor, as part of a nationwide "100 day employment guarantee scheme" that emerged from public pressure and a history of relief measures during crisis periods (Khera 2006: 17). During one such crisis, a drought in 2002–3 in Shahabad and the surrounding region, this element of state intervention had intensified. In 2002 only 25 percent of Sahariya families were officially below the poverty line, described as BPL in government-speak. During the drought period all Sahariyas were declared BPL, which entitled each family to 35 kg of government-subsidized wheat every month, among other welfare provisions. Other neighboring castes and tribes often resentfully described the five-decade long history of government programs favoring the Sahariyas that ranged from land grants to educational initiatives to beekeeping and Joint Forest Management programs. "The government has done so much for them and they are exactly where they were [vahin ke vahin]" was the common refrain. A chorus of journalist and activist accounts of the region described state "failure" and incapacity. I wanted to reconsider my own understanding of the state. Talal Asad (2004: 280) tells us that the word *state* issues from the Latin *status*, invoking the "standing of rulers." How do we come to measure this standing? The answer I sought was not numerical but, prior to that, a question of how we conceive of the state and the hopes and disappointments that issue from those conceptions.

I turned back to current anthropology, which was abuzz with discussions of sovereign power,[4] drawing mainly on the work of Giorgio Agamben (1998), in ways that invariably led to global and local declarations of catastrophe, with sovereign power exerting a near totalizing force over an abyss of "bare life." While this may be a compelling perspective in some cases, are there other ways to conceive of sovereignty? Crucial to Agamben's conceptual architecture is Carl Schmitt's (1985: 36) famous assertion that modern concepts of authority such as the state are "secularized theological concepts." Schmitt's theological assumption of an omnipotent god (via Hobbes) led him to posit a "decisionist" totalizing authority (36). A different sense of *theos* might open up other ways of thinking about sovereign power.

For instance, how might we imagine a political theology that enfolds more ambivalent potentialities, such as violence and welfare? I turned to Deleuze and Guattari's habitation (1987: 351) of a "bipolar" theos outlined by the comparative mythologist Georges Dumézil in *Mitra-Varuna: An Essay on Two Indo-European Representations of Sovereignty* (1988).[5] Dumézil's analysis draws striking parallels between the Vedic sovereign deities Mitra and Varuna and the legendary founding figures of Ancient Rome: Romulus, with his warrior ambitions, and Numa, the "peaceful elder" who establishes the rule of law. According to Dumézil, Romulus and Varuna express force, the "terrible" and violent aspect of sovereign power, while Numa and Mitra embody contract, the "friendlier," "pact-making" aspect of sovereignty (46). Understood as complementary, Dumézil argues, force and contract together constitute sovereignty (80). I take force to mark a potentiality for coercion, and contract to signal a variably negotiable bond, involving different modes of give and take. I call this concept of sovereignty bipolar, resonant with Deleuze and Guattari's term *schizophrenia*, inasmuch as it marks an unresolved, nondialectical tension. In comparison I contend that Agamben's transcendentally negative dialectical concept of sovereignty entails a totalizing elevation of Varuna (the terrible) in such a way as to wholly eliminate the potentialities, threats, and possibilities of Mitra.

I found these bipolar tensions recurrently expressed in different political and everyday forms. For instance, in Shahabad the most fearsome representative of the punitive Varuna aspect of the state is the assistant conservator of forests. During my fieldwork this post was held by a young man, let us call him Vignesh. I spoke to him numerous times, even challenging him with maps and statistical evidence that I gathered about the confusion over land allotments, that showed how in some instances Sahariya and others in Shahabad were being fined by the Forest Department for land they had been legally assigned by the Revenue Department, since demarcations were sometimes confused even between different offices of the state. He would offer counterarguments, saying how he stayed away from cases where he felt sympathetic. Over time our conversations became less formal. "Do you think you do your job well?" I asked him one afternoon. "I would do it better if I was a robot," he replied, "but I am a human being. So some bias enters. My major problem is the repeated contradictions in the chain of command. One week I'll get a circular saying 'Give rights and concessions to the poor.' Then next week I'll get another circular saying 'Tagdi karyavahi karo [Take forceful action].'" Sitting next to Vignesh was Deepa, the district forest officer, the highest rank in the local Forest Department hierarchy. Deepa had recently begun her tenure in the Forest Department. "It's very hard," she added. "You feel terrible when people fall at your feet crying. Even those with tractors are poor farmers, repaying loans. It's even worse when you have to seize their crops. I wanted to be a giver, like those in the development field, not a taker." Rather than contradictions between "givers" and "takers," I understand this as ongoing fluctuations between two polarities of sovereign power: violence and welfare, Mitra and Varuna.

Other anthropologists have reached a resonant thought from different routes. Didier Fassin (2005a), for instance, in studying French immigration policies has described the state as embodying a simultaneous "compassion and repression." Through Mitra and Varuna I seek to signal a wider range of forces (of which "repression" would be one) and forms of contract (modes of give and take that are not exactly captured by the idea of "compassion").

Do Mitra and Varuna actually exist? It depends on what we mean by *exist*. In Deleuzian terms, they exist as potential tendencies of power, two forms among others that power over life may take. Tendencies are not static or "ahistorical." We might track the modern transformations of Mitra and Varuna through the work of Foucault, whose career may be reread in light of his mentor (some say his lover), Dumézil, as a series of studies on the transformation of Varuna (as punitive power and force morph into a range of disciplinary mechanisms) and Mitra (as a producer of welfare and health and productive economy). Tendencies too may morph and take new shapes.

To inhabit Mitra and Varuna is to not give up all political hopes and criticisms. Dialectical political logic often offers a "higher" synthesis of re-demptive hopes, a final purifying battle, as with the political theology of the Internationale. Such hopes may be life-giving, but they can also turn toxic when they are disappointed. We then oscillate from redemption to catastrophe, as with Agamben and other "secular" critical theorists. With Mitra and Varuna we are not giving up hope, but the project becomes more specific: to track the particular degrees of force (many of which may be morally objectionable) and the modes of contract that are available in a polity. A small shift in the modality of force or a widening in the range of available contracts may hold the difference between a feeling of freedom or exploitation.

What, then, does a concept offer to ethnographic inquiry? It can shift or revise the locus of our hopes and disappointments. As crucially, a con-cept gives us coordinates along which to pay closer attention. To inhabit polarities (as the coordinates are in this instance) is not necessarily a re-turn to structuralist "dualisms," although with Mitra and Varuna we are undeniably in the region of structural-potential tendencies. Deleuze spurs us further, to explore a range of actualizations of these potentialities and the shifts and fluctuations within the tendencies themselves. Conceptually, nondialectical thought breaks with one of the first principles of dialectical logic, namely the law of noncontradiction (associated most famously with Aristotle), which states that an entity is either "a" or "not a." In *The Logic of Sense* Deleuze (1990: 9) explores his affinity to Lewis Carroll: as Alice grows bigger, she simultaneously becomes smaller. Let us keep this form of logic in the background, as an orientation, as we move to a specific life I was drawn to, that of Kalli Sahariya.

THE WAXING AND WANING LIFE OF KALLI

I first heard about Kalli from her colleagues at Sankalp, an NGO, who were my hosts in Shahabad. "She is fearless and has an amazing ability to bring people together" was the general refrain. I was drawn to the vitality that Kalli seemed to embody, a kind of life-force that an older generation of social science would have called "agency." As a bonded laborer, she had burst an earthen pot on the head of a leading agriculturalist in the area, when he made a lewd remark directed at her. In 2002 she led a rally to a local police station, successfully demanding the arrest of a middle-caste cultivator who beat up a male relative of hers. People in her vicinity had persuaded Kalli to stand for village-level elections in 2005 and organized rallies in her support. Her reputation remained unscathed even though she lost the election, since the rival candidate, from the Meena tribe, was said to have won through bribery and a miscounting of votes.

Kalli's village is composed of two main neighborhoods, with fifty Sahariya families in one and thirty Nagar (cultivator caste) families in the other. Perhaps the most "logical" way to speak about Kalli, in describing her journey from a bonded laborer to a local activist, would be through forms of dialectical negation and contradiction, domination and resistance. Life sometimes exceeds negations. One afternoon I was attending a Sankalp meeting. A senior male colleague from the cultivator caste had just returned from Kalli's village. He had gone there to argue against a few Nagar cultivators over a portion of disputed land claimed by them, which had been assigned to Sahariyas as part of a Joint Forest Management program. He called on Kalli for help in a public meeting. The Nagars stood up, declaring, "Voh tau hamari behen hai [She is our sister]." "Kalli took their side!" our colleague exclaimed, much to the consternation of everyone in our meeting. "I left," our narrator concluded, "saying, 'You and your sister know best.'" Had Kalli sold out?

Through Kalli I came to understand a more intricate weave of relations with the dominant cultivators, specifically her shifting relationship with three brothers from the cultivator caste, local strongmen, let us call them Ajay, Vijay, and Sanjay. Kalli's son worked for Ajay, positioned somewhere between indebted and free agricultural laborer, since he occasionally borrowed sums of money from Ajay and worked for a few months to return it, while also taking up other occasional jobs. Ajay's elder brother Vijay was the one who beat up Kalli's relative and whom she subsequently got arrested. "Didn't that fight permanently affect your relations with their family?" I asked. "How come he calls you his sister?" "Sometimes we fight, sometimes we make up. Or the fight is with one brother but not the other," Kalli replied. "I didn't talk to them for a long time after the arrest. They used to be very *ladaka* [belligerent] during the drought [2002–3]. They even drove past our office on a jeep once, shouting 'We'll kill her, we'll bury her.' But I am a daughter of that village. Their [the Nagars] children call me Buaji [aunt, father's sister]." Over the next two years tempers cooled, and in 2005 many families in her village, including the three Nagar strongmen, supported Kalli's election campaign. The eldest brother, Sanjay, was supposed to be Kalli's representative during the counting of votes. "On the day of the election, the Meena [the rival caste/tribe] men provoked Sanjay, saying, 'Have you forgotten? She is the one who got your brother arrested.' So then Sanjay went over to their side. Everyone in charge of the polling booth was a Meena. Sanjay could have stopped them, but he betrayed us and let them forge votes. That's why the Nagars are called a *dhokli jaat* [a caste of betrayers]."

"So then why did you help them with their land?" I wondered aloud. "When the [Joint Forest Management] plot was demarcated, Ajay, Vijay, and some eight or ten Nagars' lands came into it. They went to the forest surveyor, but he wouldn't listen to them. They went to Vasundhra [the chief minister of Rajasthan], and she wouldn't do anything for them. Then they came to me! [Laughs] They said, 'Tell the forester to free our land.'" Although Kalli was illiterate, she was known for her argumentative skills with local government officers. She was also one of the leaders of the village-level forest committee in question. "I made the forest surveyor come back with me. He said, 'If you agree, then we'll move the boundary wall of the forest enclosure.' So the Nagars got their land back. During the elections Sanjay took his revenge against me. But when his land got stuck with the Forest Department, I didn't take revenge, thinking that they are from our village and they have an old *kabza* [occupation/cultivation]. So I helped them." Fortunately Kalli's colleagues at Sankalp understood these complexities, and this episode did not harm her reputation. She continues to work for the rehabilitation of indebted laborers in the area and currently heads a human rights center started by Sankalp.

Engaging the varying relations of Kalli and, more generally, between neighboring castes and tribes in the region, led me back to an old anthropological question: How do we conceptualize relations between potentially hostile neighboring groups? (Singh 2011). I sought a term to describe everyday relations between the Sahariyas and their neighbors at a historical juncture when hierarchies of caste and tribe are present but also deeply contested, in ways not overwritten with a wholly negative valence of contradictions, such as the domination/resistance paradigm (Miller et al. 1995; Scott 1990). Nor was I drawn to primarily affirmative ideas of trust, community, and "social capital" (Halpern 2005; Putnam 1993). As a picture of relatedness predisposed neither to oppositional negation nor to communitarian affirmation, I come to the term *agon* (contest), central to Deleuze and to Nietzsche, building on which I offer the term *agonistic intimacy*,[6] as a way to understand the copresence of modes of conflict and cohabitation (Singh 2011). Nearness or intimacy does not necessarily betoken peace. Locally and globally we see that conflicts may at times be most intense between those who are precisely proximate neighbors. And yet life may continue. With the concept of agonistic intimacy, I want to leave open the possibility of a shared and contested future. Ahead, as a further contribution to this question, I will analyze how agonistics and intimacies may traverse different *intensities*. For now let us turn back to differences "internal" to a life.

As I got to know Kalli better, I understood her life not simply as a unidirectional story of "empowerment" or "agency" but as a fluctuation between forms of strength and vulnerability. A few years before my fieldwork, she had had a hysterectomy, for which she and her husband had to mortgage the only plot of land they owned to a well-to-do cultivator. Over the years they gradually saved enough to retrieve a portion of that land. Kalli's recurring health problems constantly threatened to push them back into debt. In her work too, after the initial narratives of admiration, I began to overhear occasional complaints from her colleagues. "Her mind has gone off work totally," some would grumble, after she retreated for a few weeks into the rigors of household life. We might say that this is a condition of life itself, as our particular strengths and vulnerabilities variably express themselves. That said, we are not all equally vulnerable. Perhaps it is a condition specific to economic poverty that a fluctuation may prove to be a fatality. Kalli's mother's brother had been among the best-off in their village, owning two plots of land. He was now among the poorest, a spiral caused by a few family illnesses. Among Sahariyas such spirals were common and sometimes sudden, pushing a family from a position of relative strength into near destitution.

Amid these vulnerabilities there was a certain psychic strength, a fearlessness Kalli exuded that many around her sensed. I once asked her,

"Don't you ever feel scared, taking on strongmen who could kill you?" In this instance we were discussing a labor dispute in a more distant village with a cultivator who was known to be violent. Kalli laughed. "I have always been *poorna pagal* [totally mad], since childhood." Over time I learned that this was not a joke. Kalli's life had indeed been punctuated by periods of mental instability, attributed by her, and others around her, to possession by a Jind (the local word for Jinn), a category of spirit shared by popular Hinduism and Islam.[7] This facet of her life was known to most of her colleagues but not openly discussed in her NGO life. As Kalli realized that, despite being a literate outsider, I would not demean this spiritual potentiality as "superstition," she became more open to talking about the Jinn, who had, it turned out, been a lifelong companion. "When I was a child, so was he. He would play with me. I paid so much attention to him that I forgot about my family. He grew older with me. He would keep coming in my dreams [*barlat*]. We would be walking together in a fort or in a garden." Based on this friendship Kalli is also known as a spiritual healer. People from nearby and far-away villages would occasionally stop by for spiritual cures. However, a relation that can be life-giving may also become life-denying.

As many in Shahabad describe it, Jinn and other minor spirits may also harbor the possibility of madness (*pagalpan*) for their mediums. "After my marriage, he [the Jinn] used to get jealous of my husband. Even now he sometimes gets angry." At present, though, the Jinn was said to be "pacified," "controlled" by a stronger spirit, Thakur Baba, a deity linked to her husband Shrikishan's clan. Her husband oversees the daily worship in their household shrine. Within this relative calm, Kalli told me, over time, about her continuing, albeit less frequent episodes of mental instability, the most recent of which occurred during a visit she made to Bombay in 2003 for the World Social Forum (a global activist convention), where she climbed the roof of a building and shouted, "Where is my home?," until a coworker, also a spiritual adept, gradually pacified her and brought her back to ordinary consciousness.

In Kalli's account, this madness and volatility are an intrinsic part, an enabling and potentially disabling threshold of her ordinary self. "Some people say that I am brave, but I am brave because I am mad," Kalli reiterated. I accepted this formulation. Volatility may be distinguished quite sharply from mental illness. Or these states may stand apart by only a few degrees of intensity. Each increasing degree courts death, but they may also court life. Let us mark this as the differential intensities that compose a relationship and a self. The entry of the Jinn and other spirits takes us to a different kind of intensity, for which I also sought a conceptual language.

VARYING THRESHOLDS OF LIFE

A few paces from Kalli's house stands one of the most ubiquitous sights in Shahabad, a small roadside shrine depicting a headless horseman called Thakur Baba, the deified ghost of Rajputs (members of the warrior caste) said to have died in battle. "Which battles were these?" I asked. Answers to such historical questions were always vague: "Who knows? There must have been battles in the time of kings." The deity's power was not to be found in any historically locatable royal lineage. Further, unlike most other Hindu deities, there is no elaborate mythology connected to Thakur Baba. Instead I encountered descriptions of ritual, mainly of three types. The first regarded troublesome ancestral spirits known as Preet, those in one's lineage, particularly unmarried males who died an *akaal mrityu* (untimely death), as well as companion spirits such as Jinn. Thakur Baba is said to keep such wandering spirits under control. A second ritual task involves requests for childbirth (*santaan prapti*) addressed to Thakur Baba, and the third involves healing a disorder, usually by expelling a weaker spirit causing the ailment. Almost every household in Shahabad, high and low castes and tribes, maintains ritual links to particular shrines through spirit mediums.

These forms of life led me back to one of the oldest of anthropological curiosities: How might we think of the dead and the unborn and spirits and deities as participants among the living? (see Singh 2012). Let me ask the question differently: What conception of life would this require (as distinct from, say, the negativity of "bare life")? Following Deleuze, I offer the term *varying thresholds of life* as a way of engaging ancestors, spirits, the undead, and the unborn who subsist alongside the living. I use *thresholds* in two senses: first to denote points of passage across phases of life—initiations, births, marriages, and deaths—that often occasion ritual commemoration. Second, *thresholds* also refers to varying degrees of intensity that may continue after death, as a spirit is preserved or recedes, through possession or in visions or memories, enduring in potentially multiple dimensions. As such, I neither doubt nor prove the "existence" of spirits. A memory, a dream, even a hallucination is also a threshold of life.

We are at a delicate point here, central to the theme of this volume, a point at which anthropology and philosophy have separated in the past, over an ontological difference, in their mode of immersion in the metaphysical. In one of his earliest published writings, a review of his teacher Jean Hyppolite's book on Hegel, Deleuze (1997a: 191) writes, "That philosophy must be ontology means first of all that it is not anthropology. Anthropology wants to be a discourse on man." A knee-jerk anthropological reaction would be to argue back that ontology is a philosopher's fiction; ontologies are "socially constructed." And what, by the way, is "the social"? (Is it "our" version of the transcendent/immanent metaphysical?) How many dimensions is "our" metaphysical composed of? Here I want to mine a different possibility within a "founding" conceptual moment in anthropology, in Durkheim's *Elementary Forms of Religious Life.*

According to Durkheim (2001: 140), religion is an engagement with a vital animating principle, "a kind of anonymous and impersonal force. . . . None possesses it entirely and all share in it." Spirit mediums in Shahabad, such as Kalli and others, often say that genuine states of possession are akin to receiving an electric current. Durkheim concurs: "When we say that these principles are forces, we are not using the word in a metaphorical way: they behave like real forces. . . . If an individual comes into contact with them without taking the necessary precautions, he receives a shock that can be compared to an electric charge" (142). A few pages later: "Spirits, demons, genies, gods of every rank are the concrete forms that capture this energy, this 'potentiality'" (148). A remarkable formulation, except that at this promising juncture Durkheim reduces this vast potentiality to his signature form of the metaphysical: "the moral authority of society" (155). "The basic purpose of the religious engagement with life is to reawaken solidarity. . . . The cult really does periodically recreate a moral entity on which we depend, as it depends on us. And this entity does exist: it is society" (258).

We may call this an exhausted formulation, or we may call it a spot ripe for recultivation. Innumerable anthropologists have shown how religion does not necessarily "reawaken solidarity." My question, though, is prior to that: Does anthropology necessarily "reduce" all energies to "the social"? Or is the social one among other dimensions of life? I am thinking here of a "vast continuum of human and non-human life" (Deleuze 2001: 6) that includes but also exceeds the social. This continuum is not timeless or static. Rather it is composed of varying thresholds that move along different rhythms of conscious and nonconscious levels of time. This is not to refuse the very concept of the social. From a nondialectical perspective we have an extension rather than a negation.

To take these thoughts back to Shahabad, how might we understand the "agency" of spirits? We might call it a threshold of life, with its own immanent forms of movement and flux. All spirits are not necessarily beholden to a Hegelian teleological *Geist*. For instance, an abstract spirit of modernity or a secular education does not necessarily result in the "disenchantment" of lower thresholds of deified life such as Jinn or the warrior spirit of Thakur Baba. I met innumerable schoolteachers, NGO and government employees, and other self-professed moderns who could be possessed by Thakur Baba or at least participate in the whispers that convey a manifestation of deified force. Such whispers are not self-evidently "beliefs." In hushed tones my research associate Gajanand, in his mid-sixties, from the low-status Namdev (tailor) caste, would say, "I tell you from my heart, all this is *andha-vishwaas* [superstition]." Then we would reach a spirit medium, and Gajanand, a veteran performer in uncountable "rural education and development" campaigns, would prostrate himself, saying "Baba, I have been troubled for years. What can I do to please my ancestral spirits?"

This was not simply the cunning of self-interestedness. On occasions Gajanand and even I as an "unbeliever" would get goose bumps from the intensities, the "incredible feeling of an unknown Nature-affect" (Deleuze and Guattari 1987: 240), in listening to the slow, deliberate rhythms and the exalted tones of a song to call up a particular spirit. These intensities were not uniform. Spirit mediums would complain, "It's nothing now. . . . You should have seen it in my grandfather's time. When Thakur Baba came to him, he would roar. Even the peacocks in the surrounding forest would call back. At that time people knew how to sing. Everyone would be in tears." Such statements were not mere nostalgia. I too could sense these shifts in intensity, for example in the generation following Gajanand's, who would mock the melodramatic tones in which the spirit was summoned, even as they quickly bowed their heads by a few degrees or honked their motorcycle horn when passing a shrine. From the deity's perspective, we might call this not "disenchantment" but a shift in the quality of life, which, I contend, is not necessarily teleological. When the spirits were better aligned, the intensity would return and young men and women around me would pass out with excitement. Rather than a linear direction to a spiritually impoverished "modernity," ethnographic investigation can be a form of heightened attentiveness to varying thresholds of life, to sense what we might call waxing and waning intensities immanent to a milieu. In what ways might these varying intensities affect our ideas of ethics and politics?

Consider a dialectical picture of negation in ethnographic/historical terms. In *The Coming of the Devi* (1987), the subaltern historian David Hardiman analyzes the rise of a "vegetarian" Mother Goddess among tribes in Western India. Negating any potential for spiritual movements between rival groups, even in what is clearly a form of religious life moving across neighboring castes and tribes, Hardiman characterizes the rise of this Mother Goddess as a form of "Adivasi (tribal) self-assertion" and "resistance" (24). Elsewhere (Singh 2011) I have argued how we might understand these movements, including the "adoption" of vegetarianism and new deities by lower castes and tribes, as a mode of "becoming" (Deleuze and Guattari 1987: 232), distinct both from the "bottom-up" thesis of oppositional negation and from its "top-down" opposite, the idea of spiritual "conversion," to vegetarianism for instance, simply as the "imitation of upper caste values," as M. N. Srinivas, a founding figure of Indian sociology, famously theorized it in his concept of "Sanskritization" (the mimicry of "high" Hinduism by lower status groups). The fatality of these ideas of negation and of imitation is that they obscure the possibility of a spiritual inheritance that may be shared and contested in ways that create the possibility of a cohabited future between neighbors and rivals.

Let me take this insight further, using a question Deleuze (1994: 52) asks in *Difference and Repetition*: "At this point, does the philosophy of difference not risk appearing as a new version of the beautiful soul? The beautiful soul is in effect the one who sees differences everywhere and appeals to them only as respectable, reconcilable or federative differences, while history continues to be made through bloody contradictions." Indeed history might be made through bloody contradictions. And yet, as ethnographers we cannot be as Magi, waiting for the big drama to unfold. Perhaps a signature capacity of ethnographic attentiveness in an "affirmative" lineage of thought, as I am suggesting, is not to deny contradictions but to be able to sense varying intensities of conflict and cohabitation, including the "lower," undramatic thresholds. These intensities may escalate into conflict or remain latent or fluctuate with different valences, informing the politics of everyday life. Let us give this conceptual insight anthropological flesh by asking: What is the difference between a riot and a festival? It is a difference, I contend, of the form of collective energy, or what Deleuze calls "differential intensities" (118).

Play and war may both be latent in the give and take of everyday life, and the difference may not always be clear-cut. Consider the case of an intercaste feud in my research associate Gajanand's village in Shahabad. The feud began some years back on Holi, the most erotically charged of Hindu festivals.[8] A merry musical party of Ahir men entered the Kiraad neighborhood in the neighboring village. A Kiraad woman was bent over outside her house, flush with festive colors. "What are you looking for?" one of the Ahirs asked, drunk and exalted. The story was being narrated to me by his nephew. "I lost my nose-ring," the woman replied, still searching. "Did you look inside your *choot* [cunt]?" the Ahir man yelled, and his companions responded with an appropriately bawdy Holi song. Part of the carnivalesque excitement of Holi is that it can take such forms including in the "obscene" songs sung by women. The Kiraad woman must have complained, however (or maybe this was her agonistic festive ploy), because an hour later the Ahir neighborhood was attacked by a band of Kiraad men, beginning a feud that will last many years, other listeners added regretfully.

Veena Das (2007: 152) has shown how "intimate" insults and neighborhood rivalries can accumulate deadly force, involving state and nonstate actors in situations of collective violence. Such instances of violence (since I am referring here to the shifting intensities between a festival and a riot) are not necessarily a "modern" degeneration of traditional festivity. The epic *Mahabharata*, for instance, describes a war between cousins that begins with a dice game, an intimately playful form of the agon. Heightened intensities are not necessarily "bad," since they may animate new political and social movements or sustain the vitality of collective life. As we saw earlier with the songs for Thakur Baba, intensities may also wane and become deadened. How might ethnographic attentiveness receive the signs of *ascendant* energies within a specific milieu? This too is a challenge implicitly posed by the nondialectical philosophical lineage that Deleuze introduced me to, each member of which foregrounds a concept of vitality: Nietzsche (will to power), Bergson (*élan vital*), and Spinoza (*conatus*). As an anthropologist I respond to this challenge with an ethnographic persona, Bansi Sahariya, a former bonded laborer, now an ascetic well known in this region as Bansi "Maharaj" (an honorific term usually associated with kings but also used for ascetics).

Bansi first became known as an organizer of small-scale village-level sacrifices (Yagya), which gradually grew in scale, now involving thousands. I witnessed two such events over the course of my fieldwork, each of which took three months of preparation, with Bansi staying in the host village and making daily forays with a small team of co-organizers to raise funds for the event. The sacrificial rituals were conducted by Brahmins, specialists brought in from Banaras. Bansi is known as the "officiator" of the sacrifice (Yagya-karta). One of the sacrifices I witnessed was in the Karaal district of Madhya Pradesh. Bansi's host and co-organizer was a schoolteacher from the Chamar (formerly "untouchable" leather-workers) caste. When I first visited Karaal in the initial period of Bansi Maharaj's stay there, his co-organizers were quite nervous. A powerful faction of Brahmin landowners was being particularly uncooperative. While they were not stating their objection explicitly, it was clear to everyone what the problem was, since this was a suspicion Bansi had often encountered in his career: the highest ritual of Hinduism was being overseen by the lowest of the low.

When I left it was unclear whether the event would happen. Two months later I returned, and everyone in the village, including the Brahmins, seemed to be falling over each other to invite Bansi Maharaj home and to help out with the event however they could. The most respected Brahmin of the village, a former schoolteacher who had participated in the Indian freedom struggle, had developed a particularly deferential attitude toward Bansi. After we were introduced, the admiring Brahmin shared his thoughts with me: "He's been staying in our village for the past few weeks. I've been listening to him. He speaks in the local language [i.e., uneducated speech, not 'pure' national Hindi, since Bansi is illiterate and never went to school], but if you listen to him carefully, his interpretations [*arth*] are like Vedanta [the Upanishad philosophical literature]. You must write his *jeevni* [biography]." A few threads of the social fabric had been retied differently.

This is not to say that Bansi is straightforwardly a peacemaker or a sage. I began to pay closer attention to his facility with Sant Vani (a genre of "saintly speech," commonly used to refer to the discourses of holy men and women). Such discourses are not self-evidently charged with sacred force. A host of TV channels in India are now dedicated to Sant Vani, which can also be the butt of jokes and mimicry. Bansi's words, quite differently, expressed a combination of play and a challenge to those in his vicinity. It would surprise me initially to hear Bansi Maharaj playfully insulting the dominant middle-caste Kiraads and Ahirs: "These *dhondan* [cows, a pejorative reference to the central symbol of middle- and upper-caste religious and economic life]—they worship *pathra* [stones, idols]. These stones won't do anything! Don't worship these stones, piss on them [*mooto*]. A dog pisses on them, he doesn't die, why will you die? [Everyone laughs]."

I would often have to ask Gajanand to translate the many resonances at play in Bansi's words. In this case, as the audience received it, what sounds like an insult ("Don't worship the deities, piss on them"), taps into recognizable resonances with the medieval Sant (poet-saint) tradition, a crucial element of which was a challenging mode of address and mockery of the potential emptiness of religious practice, such as Kabir's widely remembered poetic references to idols as "lifeless stones" (Vaudeville 1987: 25) and his aesthetic use of profanities, such as sperm, piss, and shit (Hess 1987: 158).

In other contexts Bansi's words were more explicitly hostile. He had openly declared his antagonism to local Hindu right-wing groups and often held forth against them and their political projects, such as the infamous Ram Janambhoomi movement (demanding the destruction of a mosque in what was claimed as the "birthplace of Ram," an action that led to Hindu-Muslim riots in many parts of India in 1992). "Ek kitaun na Ram! [There was not a 'particle' of Ram there!]," Bansi Maharaj declaimed. "Daughter fuckers, if there was a Ram there and someone harmed him, wouldn't he kill them himself? A home and a birth is for humans, not gods. The birthplace of Ram can only be in your heart. What they made was a Bizooka [a local word for *scarecrow*], to scare people."

I am not presenting Bansi as a "redeemer." And yet I do see him and Kalli as ethical actors. What, then, do I mean by ethics? Recent work in the anthropology of ethics suggests that ethics cannot be understood as simply instantiating "categorical imperatives" and obligations (Laidlaw 2002: 312). Life often produces intensities and conflicts that cannot be accounted for by a priori rules and obligations. For Deleuze, following Nietzsche, ethics is not the instantiation of moral laws or a journey from war (or politics, as the "continuation of war by other means") to a nonagonistic equilibrium of "perpetual peace." Rather ethics has to do with what they call noble or active, as distinct from reactive energies (Deleuze 1983: 55; Nietzsche 2003: 192). Critics of Deleuze call such terms "profoundly aristocratic . . . contrary to all egalitarian or 'communitarian' norms" (Badiou 2000: 12). Contrary to such blockheaded dialectical proclamations of egalitarian ideals, we see how there may be a self-made "aristocracy," higher regions of the self, even among the "poorest of the poor."

What specifically is noble here? In Kalli's case, in relation to the neighboring Nagar cultivator caste, I see nobility in her refusal of revenge, for instance in arguing to free their land from the Forest Department, even if this was done from an agonistic motive, to keep them in her debt. The most characteristic debasement of agonistic ethics, according to Nietzsche (2007: 48), its reactive form, is "to sanctify revenge with the term justice—as though justice were simply a further development of the feeling of having been wronged." With Bansi, through his words and actions the agon morphs into a nobler, more animated form. It comes closer to life than to death.

These singular, energetic expressions of vital life are not just "individual." They have consequences for the ways social groups live together and conceive, even implicitly, of a shared future. For instance, it is well known that caste hierarchies involve rules of commensality, of who can eat together with whom (Dumont 1980: 141). A high point of Bansi's sacrificial events is the *bhandara* (collective feast). Caste and gender divisions are still observed even in the ways queues are formed. And yet allies and rivals, many of whom I came to know, ate together. "And then, they ate," as Vedic sacrificial manuals say, describing a brief respite between the agonistics. Ethics, in this sense, is not a disavowal of agonistics but rather its modulation into nobler forms. Evaluative terms such as *noble* and *base* do not name a dichotomy (like good and evil) but coordinates within which, and in excess of which, life forces flow and way and wane. Ethics examines the conduct of life.

The ethical imperative in Deleuze and Nietzsche is to examine the kinds of life forces we affirm. Negation is not expelled. It is an after thought. What I call the ethnographic element of this imperative is their intuition that what *is* may be richer than any ideal *ought*. We may be embarrassed to expose the modesty of what we affirm in the actual world, after how loudly we negated the imperfections of the world. But we wouldn't know till we looked carefully enough at what *is*. Anthropology and philosophy, then, are two distinct but related ways in which life may be examined.

PHILOSOPHICAL CONCEPTS IN NONACADEMIC FORMS

In conducting such examinations of life, is it only philosophers who philosophize and produce concepts? This question brings me to a point at which I disagree with, and perhaps negate Deleuze and Guattari. To think affirmatively might also mean that our negations become sharper. In this instance, the disagreement may be major or minor, depending on how far we take it or who is willing to back down. The difference hinges on their claim in *What Is Philosophy?* that philosophy is specifically and originally Greek:

> We will see that concepts need conceptual personae. . . . Friend is one
> such persona that is even said to reveal the Greek origin of philo-sophy:
> other civilizations had sages, but the Greeks introduce these "friends"

who are not just more modest sages. The Greeks might seem to have confirmed the death of the sage and to have replaced him with philosophers—the friends of wisdom, those who seek wisdom but do not formally possess it. But the difference between the sage and the philosopher would not be merely one of degree, as on a scale: the old oriental sage thinks, perhaps, in Figures, whereas the philosopher invents and thinks the Concept. (Deleuze and Guattari 1994: 3)

Again, a knee-jerk reaction would be to invoke Eurocentrism. Perhaps we can do more than react. Let us receive the criteria for the definition of philosophy. What is invoked here by Deleuze and Guattari are not just thoughtful moments among friends but scholastic and conversational traditions. And further, philosophy is not sage-like pronouncements, but concepts, open to further questioning. Here I want to return briefly to Bansi, to describe a conversational tradition I was delighted to discover that is often folded into but is distinct from the genre of Sant Vani (saintly discourse), namely *gyan-charcha* (knowledge-talk). Through Bansi (contra Deleuze and Guattari) I rediscovered a point locatable in non-European classical disputation, namely that the position of the "sage" can be unstable, and part of a larger conversational contest culture that may not be between "friends" but is certainly an agon. Within such a culture we find not just "figures" but concepts. For instance, although Bansi had never been to school, there were concepts he regularly returned to in his discourses. Among several different concepts that I could describe within his lexicon, I will mention one for now, *mann* (will, desire). To inhabit this concept we need to enter an actual conversation and a form of life.

In Shahabad, as I learned the rules of participation in "knowledge-talk," I too began to ask Bansi questions in public conversational contexts. For instance, we were sitting outside a tea shop. An impromptu crowd of listeners had gathered, as it often did to hear Bansi speak.

Bhrigu: There are so many deities [*devta*] in Shahabad, Jind, Siddh (deified ascetics), Thakur Baba. What are these deities?
Bansi: There are many. But they are *ekaai* [all-one].
Bhrigu: What is that One that these are all forms [*roop*] of?
Bansi: *Mann* [will, desire].

Not a bad reply, I thought. Writing out this interview, or whatever I understood of it on my own, it came to eight pages. Transcribing the interview with Gajanand, as he explained the embedded wordplay, lyrics, and mythological and local references to me, the same interview filled forty pages. Bansi's reply to my question about deities, for instance, hadn't ended simply at mann. His broader theme had been on how different valences or meanings of a word impose moral judgments of good and bad. His answer to me, in a sentence, was built on a play between the words *mann* and *dhon*: "Sau mann ghate tau ek mann ko dhon hogo, aur dhon tau sabse nikam hogo." Gajanand explained this sentence to me:

> You may have a hundred desires [*sau mann*] to begin with, but you'll have to reduce [*ghata*] some of them in life. This reduction leaves you heavy-hearted because you still remember the other desires you left behind to arrive at the ones you willed [*ek mann*]. The first time Bansi said *mann* he meant "desire." The second time he used the word [*ek mann*] he meant both "desire" and the old (premetric) word for 40 kilos used to measure grains, also called mann. He said that a mann will reduce to a dhon, the premetric term for 20 kilos. But then he used the same word *dhon* differently the second time, for its other meaning of "dirty water" left over after washing clothes or dishes, which is *nikam* [worthless] but also *ni-kam* [prevents you from getting on with your work and life].

So Bansi's response then becomes: Desire is heavy, and in becoming lighter, as it must, it leaves a bitter residue. The deities you ask about are involved in these processes of the limitation and expression of desire. A conceptual answer to rival Freud and Kant!

Gajanand explained the genre further:

> When you asked him the question about deities, you began a type of conversation called *gyan-charcha* [knowledge-talk]. The answer he gave you, like the play with mann, is a knowledge-talk technique called *chod-hara arth* [a "four-sided" meaning], where a word will have two into two meanings. Bansi always had a lot of interest in such conversations. He learned it from Gokal Sehr, Mathura's father [a Sahariya spirit medium we both knew]. Gokal used to play the dholak [percussion instrument]. Bansi couldn't enter the temple [because of hierarchical caste-based temple entry restrictions—a major political flashpoint for lower-caste movements], but he would amaze the visiting Pandits [Brahmins] and ascetics with his questions and answers.

A concept overlaps with and could also be (mis)taken as merely "ordinary" language. For instance, a phrase Bansi often used in his discourses was *lebo-debo* (give and take). This could be taken simply as a "figure" of speech. However, as I began to transcribe the ways Bansi used these words in particular discourses, I realized that he was deploying it as a concept to think through bonded and legitimate labor, power relations, marriage, sacrifice, kinship, intimacy, buying, selling, indeed the very fabric of human relatedness that in many ways depends on different understandings of "give and take." We may also encounter an analogous idea, for instance, in Nietzsche's *On the Genealogy of Morals* in its conceptualization of the centrality of the creditor-debtor relationship, as a way to understand relations between humans, and between humans and gods.

As our conversation ended, a few audience members expressed their delight. "Jai ho Maharaja [Victory to you, rule-giver]!" they shouted appreciatively for Bansi (echoing a common devotional call, often addressed to ascetics and to deities), and I concurred. For us ethnographers, devotees of life in this world, enlightenment is not much more than finding an occasional vital spark. That is sun enough for us.

CONCLUSION: LUNAR ENLIGHTENMENT

What did I find? Certainly not subalterns who could not speak. With respect to Gayatri Spivak, we can see how the assumption of a necessary lack is a Derridean moment of negative transcendence, a void above and within the flux. Instead I have tried to inhabit the waxing and waning plenitude of that flux. To pose this difference in more agonistic terms, I have gestured to a style and a habit of thought—dialectics—variably expressed in anthropology and philosophy and critical theory. I have tried to outline some of the reasons for my attraction to an alternative nondialectical path, via Deleuze and Nietzsche. On the way we encountered a number of long-standing anthropological curiosities: on state power and sovereignty, on relations between neighboring groups, on individual subjectivity and creative action, and on relations with spirits and deities. I proposed a network of concepts that give us coordinates for further exploration in each of these domains: the polarities of Mitra and Varuna, varying thresholds and intensities, logics of a/not-a, ethics and energetics; I hope the list will extend. Rather than dualisms, I have stressed gradients and degrees and varying modes and intensities. A shift of even a degree (say, a different mode of contract or force) could be the difference between social life and death, happiness and despair, or exploitation and freedom. The concepts I outlined are located within the conflicted history of European philosophy, but not necessarily so, since these questions and answers can also be produced by processes of thought and life independent of academic philosophy, in other conceptual-conversational traditions such as gyancharcha, and in everyday life.

Deleuze (1995: 6) uses a provocatively Dionysian image to describe his own engagement with the history of thought: "I myself 'did' history of philosophy for a long time; writing books on this or that author. . . . I saw myself as taking an author from behind and giving him a child that would be his own offspring, yet monstrous. It was really important for it to be his own child, because the author had to actually say all I had him saying." Perhaps I have performed some such maneuver in producing an anthropologically oriented Deleuze. Such orientations or reorientations can also be critical for us as ethnographers. I would have written a very different account of the same ethnographic milieu if, say, Agamben had been my theoretical guide and Deleuze my antagonist. That other account would have been about the rural poor in central India as "bare life," abandoned to "let die" by the state. Such an account would not have been wrong or lacking in evidence. So it is not a question of negating dialectics but of setting out a different style of thought and examining the ethnographic and political consequences that follow.

How might we name these consequences in affective terms? Did I become more "optimistic" following Deleuze than I might have been following Agamben or other negative dialecticians? I contend that simply because Deleuze does not swing between the heightened extremes of redemption and catastrophe, as Agamben does, following a particular reading of Benjamin, this does not necessarily make Deleuze a more "optimistic" philosopher. That said, I may not have been open to receiving Shahabad in the range of moods and intensities, as I try to, or have asked myself what I *affirm* as strongly, had it not been for Deleuze. What is it to "affirm"? As Deleuze argues in *Nietzsche and Philosophy*, affirmation is not simply an acceptance of what is. That would be what Nietzsche calls the "yea of the ass": "The ass does not know how to say no because he says yes to everything which is no" (Deleuze 1983: 184). Rather "to live is to evaluate" (184). Or to put it differently, to affirm is "to release, to set free what lives" (185). As against the dialectic of redemption and catastrophe, I will say that Deleuze and Nietzsche open out to life differently, perhaps allowing for a wider range of the tragic and the comic, the contestable and the forceful.

In drawing out these antagonisms of thought, have I ended up by positing a bit too much of stability? Have I impoverished Deleuze by emphasizing and perhaps fixing his identity as "nondialectical"? Would it have been better to leave things more "fluid" and "complex and contradictory," as many scholars say these days? Can't a dialectical thinker have a nondialectical moment and vice versa? My (nondialectical) answer would be yes and no. I have gestured to tendencies of thought that may be more or less sharply defined. In certain instances the antagonism may be sharp, as it is between Deleuze and Agamben. In other instances it may be less so, say if we were to bring Adorno into the mix. In the absence of ordering distinctions, however, what we have is not necessarily freedom or fluidity. We often end up with more impoverished distinctions, such as "West" and "non-West," built on entirely negative images of Europe, from which perspective postcolonial settings appear with a double negativity from which they can never recover, as we see in many dialectically inspired forms of thought including postcolonial theory and cultural studies.

What might it mean to travel differently along these routes of thought? In reconsidering the antagonism and affinities between anthropology and philosophy, what is it to "follow" a philosopher or a lineage of thought, in ethnographic terms? I suggest that there are at least two distinct phases of ethnographic labor: the first, a form of hunting and gathering impressions; the second, sifting and cultivating expressions. At the initial stage of fieldwork, our conceptual allegiances are vaguely formed orientations, making us attentive in particular ways. In the next phase of our labors, our relation to concepts becomes more explicit, as we turn impressions into considered thoughts. At both these stages, our conceptual allegiances have consequences for and may also be revised by our percepts and affects. What form does this revision take? In the preparatory workshop for this volume I was asked if fieldwork did not "challenge my presuppositions," if I was claiming that my presuppositions came, to whatever extent I was aware, from a specific nondialectical lineage of thought to which I was drawn before and after fieldwork. My questioners seemed to suggest that this was the truly ethnographic form of an insight: Did you "challenge your presuppositions"? I will answer this question by asking another one: How did this particular mode of reflexivity come to stand in for "true" anthropological thought? This too, I contend, is a dialectical habit of thought, the idea that the signature moment of thinking is a determinate negation. Instead I suggest a different possibility, that of extension. I have been describing a style or mode of thought, akin to *gharanas* (lineages) in Indian classical music, or philosophical lineages such as the Stoics or Epicureans in the Greco-Roman world. We might consider thinking, then, as an extension, that is to say, extending but also standing in tension with, a lineage.

In describing my lineage as such, am I "still" beholden to the European Enlightenment? My answer: yes and no. Anthropology is one way among others to receive and extend the light we can yet receive. Regarding "enlightenment" we might ask a more open-ended question: What kind of light do we assume as our image of plenitude? Perhaps the sun is not the best or the only assumption, since it rises and sets with brief twilight, leaving us inattentive to degrees and phases. Plato describes the climax of philosophy as the "form of the good," through the image of the sun. Deleuze (1990: 291), following Nietzsche, describes his project as a "reversal of Platonism." Anthropology too often must head in the opposite direction from Plato, not upward to the sun but farther into the cave, to inhabit the shadows and bewitchments of everyday consciousness. Must we flee the shadows? I will describe my attraction to Deleuze, to Nietzsche, through a distinction critical to Hindu mythology, namely lunar and solar lineages. Reviewing many of my concepts, waxing and waning intensities, fluctuating thresholds, and others I have not spoken of in this essay, the ebbing tide of water, the rise and fall of gods, I recognize the tutelage of the moon, a lunar rather than a solar sense of enlightenment. Blemished and inconstant, waxing and waning, the moon is nondialectical. Thought, we might say, neighbors lunacy.

NOTES

1. On Deleuze contra Hegel, see Baugh (1992).

2. For an informative account of the opposition to the term "Adivasi" by Indian sociologists in the 1940s, see Hardiman (1987: 13).

3. Other groups in Shahabad include Sen (barbers), Dimar (fishermen), Namdev (tailors), Baniya (traders), and Brahmin (priests), among other jatis.

4. On the "return" to the concept of sovereignty in anthropology, see Hansen and Stepputat (2006).

5. Dumézil appears in *A Thousand Plateaus* in Deleuze and Guattari's theorization of the "war machine" (1987: 424), and the Roman "nexum" as a mode of contract (565).

6. The agon is central to the nondialectical thrust of Nietzsche's (1990: 41) thought, including his distrust of Socrates for dissolving the agon in favor of "higher" truths. For Deleuze on Nietzsche's "reversal of Platonism" see *The Logic of Sense* (1990: 253). Within anthropology, there is a rich archive of thought on agonistics, including perhaps most famously Mauss's *The Gift* (1990), Geertz's

(1973) notion of "deep play," and Herzfeld's (1988) descriptions of idioms of contest in rural Greece, among others. In political theory see, in particular, William Connolly's work on "agonistic respect" (Chambers and Carver 2008).

7. On Jinn in Muslim contexts, see Khan (2006) and Pandolfo (2005).

8. On the play and violence of Holi, see Marriott (1966: 211) and Cohen (1995).

CHAPTER 8

Philosophia and Anthropologia:
Reading alongside Benjamin in Yazd,
Derrida in Qum, Arendt in Tehran

Michael M. J. Fischer

■ What would it mean for anthropology to be the empirical means of doing philosophy? Philosophy is the love of wisdom, the wisdom that comes from friendship, worked out in dialogue, disputation, and questioning, address and response, the ear, face, and eye of the other, learning across the tympanum of exchanges between self and other.[1] Anthropology is the speech, account, reason, or logics of the animal operating semiotically, psychically, emotionally, intro- and projectionally between the bestial and the divine.[2] The anthropo-logics include affects and actions that—after giving reasons for actions run out and yet decisions and actions must be taken—leave enduring legibilities, traces, hints, or cues in the rhythms and sounds, the catacoustics of the social text.[3]

In what follows I reread some of my ethnographic work in Iran, attempting to use some of the theorists and philosophers I drew upon for social theory parallels and possible clues in European historical experience with which to create social theory attentive to experiences elsewhere. The hope is that illumination may be cast back and forth, but more important, to provide points of attachment for creative and productive dialogue beyond mere comparison, beyond the dialectic of seeing (theoria) and conceptualizing (theory), attentive as well to the affective body of interpersonal emotions, the tropes of vulnerability and calls for social justice, and the ear, face, and critical apparatuses of the other as places for ethical ethnographic exchange.

At issue are both catacoustics and ringing the changes in Yazd and Washington, D.C.; in Qum and Paris; and in Tehran. My philosophers, lovers of wisdom, are social hieroglyphic characters, here and there, and everywhere.

I plot each of the three sections to evoke a constellation of (a) urban place, (b) historical horizons, (c) communication circuits or infrastructure, (d) new (especially dissertation) ethnographies in which the writers have serious stakes ("skin in the game"); and (e) theorists there and here, then and now.

Section 1 (Washington, D.C., and Yazd) focuses on infrastructure and communication circuits. Section 2 (Qum and Paris) focuses on the critical apparatuses of debate and interpretation. Section 3 (Tehran) focuses on pluralism and the struggle for civil politics.

1. WASHINGTON, D.C., AND YAZD

TAGHI MODARRESSI, NAHAL NAFICY, AND WALTER BENJAMIN

Losing Language, Finding Passion

"Nobody chopped chives for him." "If news reaches the mosque, you'll need an ass to carry all the rumors." These idioms do not quite translate from Persian into English, but they pepper the novels of the author and child psychiatrist Taghi Modarressi. Modarressi was interested in the fivefold resonances among (1) the effective communication of infants using approximation and mirroring; (2) dementia, Alzheimer's, or end-of-life loss of language, again approximating with wrong words but still expecting intimates to know what is meant; (3) the feeling of émigrés of not being at home in either mother or acquired languages; (4) the recognition in "the task of the translator" that by reading passages aloud, one often can catch meanings beyond specific word choices and phrases; and (5) the work of grieving and of comedy in catching the rhythms of language in these five arenas. What's important in these encounters, he would say, is the movement across languages, gestures, and approximations, not so much the content. After some years of not writing, he found a new internal writerly voice "unexpectedly, while listening to the sound of Persian in the streets of Los Angeles and Washington." "It was the sound of Iranian refugees, bargaining in American shopping malls. My new voice did not have any content. It was more like rhythmic humming, perhaps a ghost of a Persian accent. It was like the humming we do when we are intrigued by an idea. . . . That melodious Persian sound could sometimes throw light on forgotten scenes, bringing them out of total darkness and allowing me to invent memories of a time when I wasn't even born" (quoted in Rahimi 2011: 9–10).

Nasrin Rahimi, the translator of Modarressi's last novel, writes, "What facilitated Modarressi's return to writing fiction was the arrival of the wave of Iranian immigrants and refugees in the wake of the 1979 revolution. It was the reinsertion of . . . the tonalities and affects surrounding the use of Persian that revived his passion for writing" (Rahimi 2011: 9–10). Like a good ethnographer, Modarressi writes, "I found myself sitting once again with my friends, but this time we were not in Tehran. We were in Washington or Los Angeles. Once again I was the happy captive audience to the fantasies of Iranian social theorists, with their spicy interpretations of daily events in Tehran, Paris, Washington, the Pentagon, even the Oval Office. I was delightfully engulfed in rumors. . . . The excitement was almost unbearable. My feelings were so intense that I began to wake up every morning between four and five a.m., at which time I would drive to my office and work on a story that was actually an invented memoir" (8).

My own memories of Modarressi are of a wonderful lunch of *chelo kebab* and stories we shared at the Kolbeh restaurant on Wisconsin Avenue in Georgetown, shortly after he had published *The Book of Absent People*, published around the same time in Tehran in Persian (*Ketab-e adamha-ye ghayeb*). It is part of my geography of Iranian Washington, D.C., now indelibly enriched by a remarkable dissertation by Nahal Naficy.

In genre terms, Naficy's dissertation sits somewhere between anthropology (the department granting the degree), belles lettres, comparative literature, and investigative journalism, and provides, as only such a mixed genre could, one of the most remarkable accounts of the culture of paranoia, intrigue, political commitments, and the ability to negotiate the worlds of NGOs, diplomacy, media, and politics in Washington among an émigré community. It is this "structure of feeling," and the cultural references and allusions out of which it is composed, that is the target of the dissertation, rather than, say, a political scientist's evaluation of the strength and effectiveness of particular organizations, although along the way it accomplishes some of that as well. One gets, for instance, the contrast between one NGO dedicated to using the tools of American civic and political engagement and other NGOs that are nursing their resentments and commitments from the 1979 revolution, who see the world in terms of fighting for its reversal, and thus are not part of "this world" (Washington, the present) but primarily of that one (Iran, the past).

That's the mundane surface. The cultural texture is much finer. The ethnography functions like the object of love in Persian poesis: elusive, tempting, motivating, moving, unpinnable, hence alive. In presenting what Naficy calls "actual life," she draws upon the Persian miniature as a social form in which people are always peeping at one another from behind rocks or trees, holding their finger over their mouth in surprise, peering out from curtained windows and doorways ("shades" of Hamid Naficy's diagnostics of "accented cinema": claustrophobic looking through windows, doors, liminal and interior spaces). The mystery of the political is key here: the indirection of language and action, the dispersal of power, the functioning of gossip, organizational charts that, like the geometric divisions of space in Persian miniatures, hint at what they are supposed to describe (active figures on the margins, actions dispersed in spatially separated but juxtaposed frames).[4]

Naficy describes "a landscape of affects" composed by the heady proximity to imperial power, the intensity of Washington's Potomac fever, and by the "character rot," the "primitive within" or "the Count Dracula within" (carrier of a glorious past that lives on unnaturally in the present, out of phase, dysfunctionally). Naficy's painting of efforts at "fixing" alleged pathologies suggests wonderfully human, wacky efforts at self-reform: out-of-phase uses of Sufism/escapism, mourning/memorializing, positive psychology, and the now century-old cultural warfare between cultures of life and cultures of death. Indeed the Ministry of Health announced in January 2009 a program of engineering happiness to offset the rising rates of addiction and suicide after thirty years of philosophical melancholia, stoicism, and gravitas. The cultural warfare has so intensified that one recent ethnography speaks of the criminalization of the youth culture and the turning of social statistics into state secrets (Khosrovi 2007).

As I began to attend to the dynamics of these sorts (of migration, of miniatures, of "actual life" hemmed in by heroic and martyred pasts) in Yazd in the early 1970s, Walter Benjamin kept returning, both as a direct interlocutor for me and through an extraordinary afterlife career with ever more investments of interpretive energy in the global academy. There were extraordinary parallels with the baroque *Trauerspielen* of Spain and Germany he analyzed, and also the transformation in Europe away from valorizing the melancholia that Iran preserves in its Khomeinist strands. Indeed Benjamin (1928b) called the Trauerspielen secularized passion plays, and their point, as with the *taziyeh* or *shabi* in Iran, was to elicit lamentation, plays through which mournfulness finds satisfaction. Both portray the hopelessness of a corrupt worldly condition in which the only moral dignity possible is through stoicism. As one says in Iran, one tries to achieve a *hal-e khosh*, a "good feeling" of quiet determination, a willingness to struggle against even overwhelming odds for moral ends. Even the political structure of the baroque plays aligns with Iranian politics, the conflict between absolute power attempting to bring order to social chaos and actual human limitations, sometimes leading to madness. The stock characters are a tyrant (often a Persian shah or Turkish sultan), a martyr, and an intriguer.

Benjamin as montagist of the dialectical images of ruins-redemption, catastrophe–transformative technologies of urban place, cinema, and theater space, and iconoclastic art that explodes the boundaries between high and low has come to be equally important in thinking about the cultural *Zerstreuung* of Iran. *Zerstreuung* is usually translated in English as "distraction," the distracted mode of attention for which the cinema is a gymnasium of the senses for practicing how to deal with the multiple channels of sensory and information input, the intensities of psychological shock of which Baudelaire and Simmel also wrote. André Breton called it perceptual bewilderment. For Iran I borrowed the term *mute dreams* (*gonge khabide*) from the filmmaker Mohsen Makhmalbaf for the title of my book on Iranian cinema, films that deal with the aftermath of war, society ripped apart, attempting repair, reverberating with traumas, but humanistic and redemptive in a fashion Benjamin might have appreciated (Fischer 2004a). *Gonge khabide* is that moment when one is waking from a dream and, bewildered, tries to make some sense of the images, or in an older messianic fashion it is that feature of prophetic vision impossible to convey, and if it could be described, the people who heard it would be deaf to its message.

The theater spaces that Benjamin attended to were not only that of the baroque Trauerspielen but the transformation of Moscow by modernism, the contrasting porous Neapolitan street with its stage-like staircases half-hidden, half-open to the street, and the contrast between nineteenth-century arcades and the one-way street (1928a), with its signage designed for car traffic and advertising on the walls of consumer society, an accelerating society of speed and intensities. The German word *Zerstreuung* is more violent, dispersive, intensive, not merely distracted or paying attention to many different things at the same time. Sonically, almost homonymically, it is close to *Zerstörung*, destruction, ruination, disturbance.

In the 1970s I described Yazd's urban modernization of the 1930s under Reza Shah as having cut boulevards, Baron Haussmann–style, through the bazaar and old residential quarters, still decades later leaving the insides of houses open to the street, a fitting image of turning the old inside-out, the *anderun* (inside) becoming the *birun* (outside), and the cultural emptying out of the old bourgeois dwelling of which Benjamin wrote, the old Yazdi merchant houses with their many courtyards, contrasting with the sleek Bauhaus, machine houses of glass and steel, and the prefab townhouses of steel frames familiar in new suburb developments from Houston to Ahwaz to Yazd (Fischer 1973). Benjamin contrasts the bourgeois dwelling in which habits are cultivated with the glass and metal houses in which no traces are left but things may be adjustable at will. At issue for Benjamin was the destruction of an older intelligentsia and the rise of mass society both for collective and participatory good and for fascist evil. The war (World War I, the Iran-Iraq War) proved that (as surrealism in France would explore, or iconoclastic contemporary Iranian art) the old boundaries of high and low could not be maintained. Yazd too, like the metropolises of Europe, has exploded, from a population of 100,000 in the 1970s to over a million today, still conservative at its core but with migrants and refugees from the wars bringing diversity. The old mud-brick houses with their elegant wind towers still stand, but some now are transformed into boutique tourist hotels and a water technology museum and other tourist attractions. The old six-wind-tower ice house (*sish bad-gir*) in the center of town is now a fancy *zurkhaneh* that even allows women tourists in to watch the traditional gymnasium exercises done under the beat of the *tambak* drum and the martial songs celebrating Imam 'Ali and the *pahlavans*, hero-athletes of the *Shahnameh*. The zurkhaneh remains a somewhat times-out-of-joint, wonderful, rich icon of moral, spiritual, and athletic calling.

The conservative, bazaari moral core is no more intact, protective, and intimate than when I went looking with Mazyar and Melissa in 2004 for an old friend, one of my high school part-time assistants from the early 1970s. I inquired at a hat shop along the inside-out part of the bazaar, along the 1930s-new boulevard once called Pahlavi. A phone call or two and a request to leave my phone number. Connection clearly had almost been made, but I was not to be given a phone number, lest, it was said, the connection was not the one I meant, the party did not want to connect, the party was not in town, the timing inconvenient, or of course the inquiry of a American foreigner unwanted. (Time was short, and the connection was made only upon my return to Tehran, and meeting only the next visit to Iran, where my wife and I were feted in grand style. My friend had become a successful import-export agent in Tehran, only to have his most lucrative businesses attached by the politically more powerful, and so he had returned in semiretirement to Yazd.)

The cinema, mosque, and bazaar remain theatrical poles of Yazd's urban space, as they do more generally in Iran's culture wars. In the 1970s "defiant" was how I described the middle-class women who appeared unveiled at parties but dared to go to the movies unveiled, among the ordinary folk, only in groups protected by their men folk (Fischer 1980). The first Yazd cinema, opened by a Zoroastrian in the 1930s, closed under pressure; another failed. In the 1970s there were but two, the mood captured in the ditty:

yeki sakht masjid, yeki cinema
yeki gasht gom-ra, yeki rahnema
to khod dideye aql-ta baz kon
Tafavot bebin az koja ta koja

One built a mosque, one a cinema
One leads astray, one guides
You yourself, open the eye of your reason
Observe the difference from where to where.

Haj Mohammad Husain Barkhorda had been persuaded to build yet another mosque, rather than the hospital he intended, as a counter to the two cinemas up and down the street. Thirty years later a brand-new state-of-the-art private hospital was opened by a local doctor, proudly without patronage or portraits of ayatullahs and without loans, making a statement even with the crisply starched white head covering and attire worn by the nurses and female staff.

Times are out of joint from the perspective of both sides, the modernizing classes seeing the revolution as a reversal, the religious classes feeling the global economy using cinema, cell phones, the Internet, and social media as ways of inserting alien aspirations into the youth. The cinema in the late 1970s was a battle ground, target of arson in the early days of the revolution and of seats torn up by unnerved viewers of modernist new wave films such as *Moghul-ha*, itself diegetically about television as destroying film and oral narrative culture (epics recited with a *pardeh* or painted cloth; *rowzeh*s and *khotbeh*s, sermon forms framed by the emotions and story of Karbala).

Benjamin's Berlin, Naples, and Paris were in transformative moments that differ but are analogous to those in Iran. The Yazd of the 1970s was a wonderful stage, literally with Amir Chak Mak (double minaret reviewing stand) and many *husseiniyas* where passion plays and processions intense with sexualized energy were staged during Moharram. Dramatic *rowzehs* also in mosques and homes worked the emotions and calls for social justice into fervent laments, ending with a sudden sigh and return to the world. These ritual forms exercised and prepared people in the tropes and emotions that would be used to mobilize the 1977–79 revolution. The walls of Tehran during the revolution and ever after became animated with revolutionary posters, along with advertising posters of which Benjamin wrote. In 2009 during the month of Muharram (December), the Karbala Paradigm and mass marches were reactivated, with cell phones and social media, this time against the Islamic Republic (Fischer 2010b).

The emotional registers of Iran have dramatically transformed in the past thirty years, but in June 2009 there was a rapprochement across generations, registered in old revolutionary songs that were no longer dismissed by the youth as parental nostalgia. Reciprocally parents acknowledged that the hours their children spent on the Internet were not idle foolishness but means of acquiring vital new infrastructure skills. Anger, silence, and *qahr* (refusal to speak) between generations was replaced by *ashti* (reconciliation), if not between the polarized sections of the society opposing and supporting the government (see Rohani 2009; Behrouzan 2011).

Two points in sum: (1) attention to the technical, social, and emotional infrastructure, and (2) work from ethnography to theory, not the other way around. Theory should be registered in a text like a sudden ray of light that prismatically deconstructs so that one sees its sources and structure; and the immanent resources in social history are illuminated in a flash (*blitzhaft, Augenblick*). There is something more to storytelling than a good story, more to the ethnographic vignette than intrigue and curiosity. Benjamin writes, "Kafka's writings . . . had to become more than parables. They do not modestly lie at the feet of doctrine, as the hagaddah lies at the feet of halakhah. Though apparently reduced to submission, they unexpectedly raise a mighty paw against it" (Benjamin 1968a: 143–44).

I think of Modarressi sitting in Washington listening to the rhythms, tonalities, and affects surrounding the use of Persian in Washington, writing his *Book of Absent People*, like Benjamin redeeming the future from the ruins and catastrophes of the past, pondering the effects of emigration and social transformations. I think of Naficy peering from the margins of her dissertation, refusing to live in the alienated and displaced time of *Reading Lolita in Tehran*, the account of a reading group formed around the

time of President Muhammad Khatami's election, so alienated in oppositional interiorities that they felt the elections not worth participating in;
similarly refusing to be enrolled in Washington NGO paranoias and faction-
alisms; and also refusing to be enrolled in the standard moves of ethnography. She just wants to live her "actual life" of being a happy young woman in
the world.

Baudelaire defined modernity as the ephemeral, the fugitive, the contingent, the half of art whose other half is the eternal and the immutable.

Nahal Naficy wants to live in modernity, not in the eternal.

2. QUM AND PARIS

HASSAN ALI MOINZADEH, HENRI CORBIN, ALLAMEH
TABATABA'I, AFSANEH NAJMABADI, AND JACQUES DERRIDA

Fighting Arguments, Generating Cultural Power

> Suppose I write a book, let us say "Plato and telecom.," . . . on the postal
> agency of the Iranian uprising (the revolutionary role of dis-tancing, the
> distancing of God or of the ayatollah telekommeiny giving interviews from
> the Parisian suburbs . . .
> —Derrida, *The Post Card: From Socrates to Freud and Beyond*

> Now about this science of anthropology, tell me: is it cooked or raw [*pakhta
> ya napokhta*]?
> —Ayatullah Muhammad-Kazem Shariatmadari Qum, quoted in Fischer, *Iran:
> From Religious Dispute to Revolution*

Qum 1975, 2004

Forms of debate—stylized UN debates; formal scholastic debates based on
Qur'an and hadith proof texts; academic debates based on evidence and analysis; media debates deploying visual, sonic, and verbal means of shaping
perception; everyday face-to-face debates among friends and neighbors—
construct and weave, tear apart and reweave, the urban fabrics of Qum and
Paris.[5] Occasionally, as in 1968 in Paris and 1975 in Qum, they ignite into
demonstrations, and sparks can fly, as in 1978 from cassette tapes of Khomeini recorded in Paris to the 1977–79 revolution in Iran.

The shuttles of the Iranian weft fly back and forth through warp ends
anchored in Iran and America.[6] In the 1970s Sheikh Muhammad-Taghi

Falsafi (*falsafi*, "philosopher") famously asked mischievously, with double-entendre intended, midsermon, What rises at night in Qum and retracts in the daytime? Answer: television aerials. In 1975 the coming revolution was rehearsed in the Faizieh Seminary, the same place to which Ayatullah Khomeini would claim to retire after his return to Iran in February 1979. The Faizieh sits along the desiccated river keeping the impurity of the cinema on the other side from the side of sanctity of the golden dome of the Shrine of Fatimeh Hazrat-e Masumeh (sister of the Eighth Imam, whose shrine is in Mashhad), the blue-tiled dome of Masjid-i Borujerdi, and the madrassehs. The cinema would be torched. The lines of sanctity and purity fracture in more complicated ways than a simple desiccated river could draw.[7]

The wall between the seminary and the Shrine-Masjid complex was where, in 1975, the Faizieh students hoisted the red flag of the unavenged martyrdom of Imam Husain on the anniversary of the 1963–64 revolts against the White Revolution, led by Khomeini, and in rehearsal, as it were, of the revolution to come. As I watched from the periphery, the 1975 revolt was quelled by special forces and water cannon. Inside the shrine are the graves of Safavid and Qajar kings as well as leading clerics and founders of the *hoseh elimiyeh* (the center of learning of the seminary system). I lived just outside the Shrine quarters in the lanes between the establishments of two *maraje taqlid* (the highest rank of ayatullah, crowns of imitation, to whom ordinary Muslims should turn for advice on religious duties and law), S. Shahabuddin Marashi-Nejafi and S. Muhammad-Kazem Shariat-madari. My next-door neighbor was a custodian of the Shrine who had helped with the closing of the doors at night and opening in the morning, once done with trumpets and drums. Fired for being an opium addict, he would invite us over to smoke with him. One day we accepted. The next day people from the bazaar and all over town would come up and say, "Dudi hastid? Biya-id khuneh-ye ma" (You're a smoker? Wonderful, come over to our house and smoke with us). It was but one token of the tensions between townies and seminarians. A cross-cutting tension was signaled by the giggles I was met with initially when I was asked where I lived: it turned out the house had been owned by an old woman who rented it for *sigheh*, the temporary marriages in which pilgrims often indulged, sanctioned by religious law.[8]

Like Yazd, Qum has exploded in population since 1975. The new highway enters the city from the other side of town, away from the river, through a large pilgrim plaza of sweets and trinkets and food for sale. A uranium enrichment facility and a space center for rocket launching signal a changing modernity outside the city. New-style rival madrassehs and religious universities have sprung up around the old city center, such as Mofid University, founded by Ayatullah Abdul-Karim Mousavi-Ardebili,[9] an institution granting B.A., M.A., and Ph.D. degrees, with economists, political scientists, and law professors pursuing a general mission of testing whether Western humanism and Islam can get along; in contrast was the more fundamentalist Imam Khomeini Institute associated with Ayatullah Muhammad-Taghi Mesba-Yazdi, an ultraconservative and antidemocracy member of the Assembly of Experts. Digital media have been adopted both for searching proof texts and for sending opinions and responsa (*fatwas*) to followers around the world. Arabs in their distinctive garb wander to and fro, as they never did in the 1970s, talking, if not of Michelangelo, then perhaps of Najaf and Karbala, of Iraqi religious figures S. Motadaq Sadr and Ayatullah S. Ali al-Hussaini al-Sistani Iraq, or Lebanon's S. Hassan Nasrallah, or perhaps just of trade deals in Bahrain and the UAE. Politicians shuttle back and forth from Tehran to Qum in search of support.

Narges Erami's 2009 dissertation on the carpet bazaaris of Qum provides a counterworld to that of the seminaries and contributes to a long line of studies on the moral spheres of the bazaar. Focused on the union (*ettihadiyeh*) or guild (*senf*, pl. *asnaf*) structure used to settle both economic and extracommercial disputes, she develops case studies of how bazaaris deal with a heroin addict and his family's shame, using a local Narcotics Anonymous program to help; of how a "wrong marriage" illuminates status, interpersonal, and disciplining mechanisms; and of why a leading carpet designer's attempts to set up training in both traditional and innovative design is frustrated, and why he returns to producing on commission for wealthy Iranians abroad rather than being able to train a new generation of innovative designers in Iran, even though their markets are being eroded by South, Central, and East Asian competitors.

Like Arzoo Osanloo's (2009) account of family courts in Tehran, or Saeed Zeydabadi-Nejad's (2009) account of negotiations over cinema scripts in the Ministry of Culture and Islamic Guidance, or Rakhshan Bani-Etemad's films on women running for office, Erami provides access to the "actual life" of local moral worlds of everyday life—and of philosophical wisdom achieved through face-to-face interactions, mobilizing friendship networks, soliciting favors or collecting moral credits from previous interactions, in part *parti-bazi* (using connections), in part the male and female interventions of repair of social worlds when things go awry.

Looking Awry

Among the various dissertations on contemporary identity issues, Hassan Ali Moinzadeh's (2004) "Secret of Gay Being: Embodying Homosexual Libido in the Iranian Imagination" is one of the more challenging to the *sensus communis* tightrope separating the sacred and the profane, the mystical and the carnal, the metaphorical and the literal. Written for a clinical psychology degree with a Jungian bent, not an ethnographic one, it ventures into a highly fraught space, only partly acknowledged. It is an American coming-out and ego-affirming story, and it is careful not to make either wider therapeutic or descriptive claims. What it does well is to excavate an ambiguously central and ex-centric tradition in Persian culture and refunction it for contemporary psychology. As Moinzadeh puts it, he wants to "bridge the gap between the metaphysical language I encounter in ancient texts and the meanings I understand as a modern person" (2004: 3). The key task is working out a psychological template (the clinical psychology side), and in the process doing serious new translations of old texts (the cultural critique side).

At issue is the Platonic-Iranian tradition of modeling the training of the self on love for boys, expressed in the poetry of Jami, Attar, Rumi, and Hafez, in the philosophy of Suhravardi, and even, he says, in the hadith and the Qur'an itself. He remains respectful of the ambiguity and undecidability of what is a metaphor about love of the divine and what is physical, while at the same time using those resources to create a charter myth for strengthening self-respect and independence. In American fashion, he begins by saying, "I use the term gay to describe someone who consciously and purposefully recognizes a gay identity in public as well as private life and actively seeks to further the rights and visibility of gay people in society . . . using the conscious awareness that one's same sex desires separate one from the rest of society" and that this conscious alienation includes "premodern folk who have used homosexual love as an engine for their own spiritual transformation" (2004: 5). He explicitly excludes those who engage in homosexual activities only in private and those who use homosexual sex as a tool of domination, topics of concern in today's worlds of sexualized torture in Iran's prisons, of harsh choices in Iran for those accused of homosexuality, and of UN campaigns to stop the recruitment of young dancing boys in Afghanistan who would not organize their identity around same-sex desire of their own free will.[10] The stakes are high in negotiating the discourse on the level of psychological maturation and on the metaphorics of what Lévi-Strauss called the "effectiveness of symbols."

Historical materials include the youth brotherhoods (Malamatiyya, Qandari, Javanmardi), the *rend* (rogue) in poetry, the poetry of Attar, Rumi, and Hafez, the philosophical meditations of Suhravardi (and others), even the love modeled in the Qur'anic version of Yusef and Zulaikha (where, in a simple structural permutation of gender roles, it is the woman Zulaikha who is the lover and Yusef the beloved). But it is a modern hermeneutical tradition—of Henri Corbin, Jung, and Heidegger—that is key for helping Moinzadeh with his critical tools for clinical psychology. This is a fascinating and still half-submerged tradition in the cultural politics of contemporary Iran (and one that Moinzadeh does not explore but that Behrouzan and I have begun to [Behrouzan and Fischer forthcoming]).

Jung provides Moinzadeh tools of depth psychology, using universalized archetypes to teach the self to separate from maternal engulfment and to discriminate one's interior aspirational double and one's interior negative shadow from one's maturing independent self. (The shadow in this case is especially the internalized self-accusations of shame and humiliation for one's gay desires.) Jung, although supplying the hermaphrodite as an image of the original whole self, both male and female, was homophobic in the style of his time, but his methods offer some critical tools. Corbin, much honored in Iran, applied Jungian and Heideggerian ideas to the task of recovering the "theosophical wisdom" of Zoroastrian rhetorical imagery and of the illuminationist (*ishraqi*) philosophy of Iran's mystical traditions represented by Suhravardi. Suhravardi provides a language, imaginal and metaphoric, of steps, stages, and techniques for the self to train toward mature understandings of reality, separate from the mere carnal temptations of the world. Corbin connects Plato's Ideas, Suhravardi's *alam-e mesal*, and his own Catholic Latinate *mundus imaginalis*. Moinzadeh uses Corbin in a Jungian mode of therapeutic working through the shame and humiliations of growing up gay, creating an "effectiveness of symbols" abreaction technique to create horizons of subjectivity that can distance themselves from the shadow self-accusatory self and identify instead with a heterodox but powerful Iranian cultural tradition.

The significance of Jung for Moinzadeh may come more from where he pursued his Ph.D., an American clinical psychology program, apparently with a strong Jungian bent, than from Iranian contexts. But the Jung-Corbin-Heidegger connection is also a nexus of cultural politics in Iran. Corbin worked in Iran with the famed cleric-scholar Allameh Tabataba'i in Qum, and Tabataba'i's circle became quite influential, including such notables as Darius Shayegan (a comparative literature and religion scholar), S.

Hussein Nasr (a guru in the 1970s for Americans seeking Eastern wisdom as well as a university chancellor and founder of the Institute of Philosophy in Tehran), and Mehdi Bazargan (an engineer and head of the provisional government after the revolution, who long mediated between the secular and religious elites). Tabataba'i was also a teacher of Khomeini, Montazeri, Motahhari, and even Mesba-Yazdi, all of whom walked the tightrope between mysticism and puritan orthodoxy. Heidegger, whom Corbin translated into French, has become something of a fad in recent years among conservative philosophers in Iran.

There are more layers to this cultural arena, again, than at first appear, and a valid ethnographic question might be: What qualities of ethnographic tapestries can one weave with thicker versus thinner ethnographic explorations, deeper play versus quicker instrumental assessments, and in what sorts of social spaces can they be appreciated, considered, or rejected?

While Moinzadeh probably cannot go to Iran, Afsaneh Najmabadi's (2013) remarkable ethnography of transsexuals in present-day Iran traverses adjacent sites of the law, clerical interpretations, bureaucratic negotiations, psychiatric oversight, and desires to avoid the kind of politicization that the international human rights and feminist movements would like. It is an example of what Derrida calls *la danse* (a feminine noun in French, *elle*), a mode of life that resists the dogmas of progressive revolution in favor of an ability to live "actual life" (à la Naficy avoiding ideological definition or recruitment into political or identity agendas). This is likely to be, Derrida writes, "a much more important phenomenon . . . outside of Europe" that brings with it "new types of historical research, other forms of reading, the discovery of new bodies of material" such that feminist movements will perhaps have to renounce an all too easy kind of progressivism (Derrida and McDonald 1982: 67).

And indeed Najmabadi's research is among such "new types of historical research," drawing a historian of the modernization of Qajar sexual anxieties and vocabulary (see note 2) into ethnographic modes of research, and thus into "new bodies of material" that include not only the relatively new surgical possibilities of "sex reassignment" but also, as "always already" there, a recognition of stepping into contested streams of previous representations so that there can be no naïve "I" or eye. Transsexuals, Najmabadi writes, "are used to being objects of curiosity" and "have become actively engaged in taking charge of the process of their own production, engaged with numerous organs of government and medical professions on almost a daily basis."

Paris, 1968–2004

It was, of course, Jacques Derrida whom I read as I was composing *Debating Muslims* (Fischer and Abedi 1990). I sent him a copy in appreciation, as I had hosted him at the Center for Cultural Studies at Rice University. He had been a gracious interlocutor to students and faculty alike, even screening a documentary film about him, after years of refusing to allow even his photograph to be published. He sent back a lovely, short, hand-written note of thanks for the book, replying, however, that while it looked interesting, he did not know anything about the subject. There is much to be said about this for a man who played upon his Judeo-Islamic backgrounds, his circumfessions, his claims to deal with the media circuits of globalatinization. I tried to tempt him again with my contribution to Hent de Vries and Sam Weber's 2001 edited volume, *Religion and Media*, to which he contributed the central paper. Alas, he can no longer be coaxed into responsiveness.

But a central claim of *Debating Muslims* is that deconstruction is a continuation of the scholarly apparatuses of Islamic debate, and if we want to make good on our claims to engage the Islamic world, it might behoove us to read such scholars along with Derrida. There is both sophistication in those critical apparatuses and autoimmune dangers. Engaging these critical apparatuses is part of what is often called immanent critique, or critique from within a discursive tradition. It is probing for the terms of debate, the opportunities for enlarging both the field of engagement and the range of participants. There was a transformative generational call in the 1970s sounded by Dr. Ali Shariati that with literacy, Iranians no longer needed to follow mullahs blindly, they could read the texts for themselves. Indeed one of the most important of these enlargements of participation, I argued, were the feminist Muslims who learned to read the tradition as rigorously as the clerics, showing how it could be read otherwise.

This is no mischievous play by an outside, but a call to recognize our own stakes in a cosmopolitan world. Even if Derrida did not trust himself to engage with *Debating Muslims*, with the vigorous internal debates within the ideological worlds of contemporary Islam, this immanent critique is a key affordance of deconstruction. So too is Derrida's embrace both of Levinas's rejection of ontology as a ground of philosophy in favor of ethical struggle in encounters with others as first philosophy and of Hélène Cixous's writing feminine, feminist, and womanly alterities into the blood flow, neurons, and sinews of textuality.

These projects of immanent critique, and of recording the traces of women's and transsexuals' struggles, are ones that Afsaneh Najmabadi and Arzoo Osanloo pick up in charting both the workings of family courts and the negotiations of transsexuals in Iran. The critical apparatuses of *fiqh* interpretation of Qum trained scholars are central in both projects. So too the practicalities of interpretive argument and justification, negotiation and social accommodation are central to both jurisprudence and the struggle for justice. Law and justice are not the same, and courts must shuttle between them, between decisions and conflicting rights. In preparations for family courts, women lawyers coach distressed women how to plead their cases, how to invoke the law's requirements, how to fend off false interpretations, how to strategize among the judges.

Transsexual Activism, 2003–2008

The case of transsexuals is particularly indexical, since, as Najmabadi argues, it is not true that homosexuality is itself criminalized (only sodomy, which would require witnesses, an almost impossible standard of evidence), and in any case transsexuals and homosexuals must not be lumped together, as they frequently are in international gay, lesbian, and transsexual campaigns. Activist transsexuals are often critical and resentful of such lumping and of the documentaries and news articles that portray their lives as objects of pity. Such framings can make them more vulnerable, not only overriding their own agency but, by politicizing their circumstances, limiting their agency to create spaces for the lives they wish to lead (often to meld back into society in their new genders). *Vulnerable* is a key cultural term, a legal, moral, theological, psychiatric, psychological, hormonal, medical, and surgical "switching point." It shifts the grounds from "human rights" language to the less contested, more local and contextual language of welfare, justice, and vulnerability and opens up bureaucratic space, using psychiatry as a procedural means of regulation and defense.

Sex-change operations were first allowable in Iran under the justification of correction for a kind of hermaphroditism, and it was on such grounds that Khomeini first issued a *fatwa* in 1984 in response to the plea of a transwoman, but he was then persuaded to also allow it for conditions that were not physically visible.[11] Legal, biomedical, and psychiatric authorities work with specialized clerics to create procedures for diagnosis, treatment, and financial and social support for both legal recognition and surgeries. The role of activist transsexuals has been critical, as has the Tehran

Psychiatric Institute of the Iran University of Medical Sciences, and such specialized clerics as Hojjat ul-Islam Muhammad Mahdi Karimi-nia. Karimi-nia wrote his Ph.D. dissertation at Imam Khomeini Institute in Qum on the subject, and has become known as a transsexual-friendly cleric to the community as well as a consultant to the courts. Activist transsexuals involve themselves in the halls of the bureaucracy, pushing, monitoring, winning victories, suffering setbacks, but keeping possibilities open. "One day we have a break-through in one ministry and get something in place, then the next day in walks someone hostile and turns all our 'woven cloth back into raw cotton'" (Najmabadi 2013: 4). It is important, for instance, that transsexuals be coded in exemptions in the military service code not under section 33, "mental disorders," but under section 30, benign "diseases of the internal glands," because otherwise they will be virtually unemployable.

The daily fabric of hours of lobbying in which transsexuals engage is ethnographically important in showing how modern moral worlds are constituted, shaped, and created. The proceduralization, the finding of psychiatrists to staff the Tehran Institute of Psychiatry and the several review boards who would be pragmatically responsive rather than punitively disciplining—these help shape the networks of religious, political, and bureaucratic authority. The case of a male-to-female transwoman in 1983–84 was brought to the attention of Ayatullah Khomeini, according to the activist Maryam Khatun Mulk-ara, at the suggestion of then Speaker of Parliament Hashemi-Rafsanjani, who referred her to S. Abdul-Karim Mousavi-Ardebili, then head of the Judiciary (later founder of Mofid University in Qum). She also contacted Ayatullah Jannati, who wrote to Khomeini. She went to Khomeini, still dressed in male habit. He issued a fatwa, a document that she could use if challenged in activities of daily life, that changing sex with a doctor's approval is not prohibited. Khomeini's womenfolk thereupon cut her a chador.

Najmabadi points out that other activists contest Mulk-ara's account, suggesting that they themselves were the prime mover in the story. It is the structure of connections and lobbying that is important here more than who gets credit. But the telling of the story constitutes a critical moment in Mulk-ara's personal transition narrative and in the charter narrative for transsexuals to legally live trans lives before sexual reassignment surgery. Born male, Mulk-ara lost her job in the 1970s at Iran's National Radio and Television when she began to cross-dress. She consulted Ayatullah Behbehani, who opened the Qur'an. It fell open to the sureh of Maryam. Behbehani told her to contact Khomeini in Najaf. Khomeini confirmed that sex change was permitted, and Mulk-ara began to plan for a sex-change operation in Thailand.

The revolution intervened, and she had to wait nineteen years, until 2002, living as a *muhajijibah* (woman in hijab). Passport control wouldn't let her leave the country for the sex-change operation unless she appeared in male habit because her passport was still in her male name, despite having documents approving the sex change and instructing authorities to change her name once the sex-reassignment surgery was completed (Najmabadi 2013: 8).

Two points emerge from this conversation between philosophy and anthropology, Qum and Paris: (1) moral local worlds are constructed out of ethical pragmatics, the face and call and need expressed in the interchange between the vulnerable other and the self; (2) international politics, be it human rights or feminist discourses, and media circuits (telekommeiny cassettes, television, cinema, headline journalism, documentary editing, globalatinization, cartooning and poster graphics, Internet and social media) can become disempowering for those they attempt to aid, and thus require the kind of feedback that ethnography can provide and an openness to rethinking international verities and pieties.

I think of Derrida reading against the grain of ontologies in search of friendship, metabolizing texts back into living commentary and conversation; of Corbin searching for live spiritual inspiration in Persian and Islamic illuminationst philosophies (Suhravardi, Mulla Sadra), discovering ancient Zoroastrian wisdom and neo-Platonic translations; of Tabataba'i and his circle attempting to bring to life an ossified religious institution, plumbing both traditional philosophy and Jungian psychiatry for a "return to self" of self-confidence in a modern world; of Moinzadeh doing the same in California; of Najmabadi ethnographically tracking the pragmatics of living in Iran; and of Mulk-ara wanting to live with room to maneuver.

3. HANNAH ARENDT, MUHAMMAD SANATI, AND ORKIDEH BEHROUZAN

CATACOUSTICS IN TEHRAN

> The human condition in its plurality.
> —Hannah Arendt

Reading Hannah Arendt in Tehran, 2007

Why Hannah Arendt in 2007? (She died in 1975.) Why in Tehran? Was the interest in Arendt in Tehran confirmation of Danny Postel's *Reading Legitimation Crisis in Tehran* (2006)? Postel argued that Tehran intellectuals were no longer interested in revolutionary political philosophy but rather in liberalism. Habermas, Rorty, Rawls, and Arendt were all subjects of much interest, and the first two had recently been invited to Tehran (by Ramin Jahanbeglu). Suspicious of efforts at a "velvet revolution," the Iranian government pursued a series of campaigns against intellectuals, jailing Ramin Jahanbeglu, Haleh Esfandiari, and Kain Tajbash, to be followed by many others, including two of the physician architects of Iran's national program for control of HIV/AIDS, which had won a World Health Organization designation as "Best Practices."

Derrida would not have been surprised by this autoimmune frenzy of position taking vis-à-vis the global circuits, or that the Salman Rushdie affair of the 1990s would be followed a decade later by the Muhammad cartoon affair, each a testing of the circuits of a new global postal system of telekommeiny and cartoonery. Cartoonery can get out of control if the circuits aren't checked. Between the Danish cartoons and the retaliatory Iranian-hosted Holocaust cartoon controversies, there was a domestic cartoon ruckus in which a government-affiliated Tehran newspaper ill-advisedly published a nine-cartoon attack about fear of the United States stirring up ethnic conflict using the metaphor of stirring up Turkish-speaking cockroaches. The mischievous Holocaust cartoon competition mobilized a transnational network of cartoonists who recirculated old Nazi tropes against Jews now refitted to U.S.-backed Israelis oppressing Palestinians, headlined by President Ahmadinejad's recirculating of Khomeini's line that the Zionist state would eventually be wiped off the pages of time. That was the day that Ahmadinejad was chased off the Amir Kabir University campus by student hecklers.

So now imagine yourself (say, in a story in the style of Saadat Hasan Manto) in these circumstances as a member of the Tehran Jewish community. Asserting love of country and the long, pre-Islamic roots of Jews in Iran, the leadership of the community wrote an open letter to President Ahmadinejad protesting his insinuations that the Holocaust might not have happened, or if it did wasn't really so bad. The letter was posted on the Internet, and many Iranian intellectuals signed in support. Government reaction was not slow: the letter was taken down, the leadership of the Jewish community was removed, and its community magazine was closed. A Potemkin visit was hastily organized for the diplomatic corps to show how well the Jewish community is treated and what pride Iran takes in having the largest Jewish community in the Muslim world (some 25,000 left from over 100,000 in 1979). Leaders of the Jewish community were told to stay home so as not to mar the diplomats' impressions.

In Iran as elsewhere, however, things are never as simple as they seem. The former council president, a fairly well-known movie producer, was given funds to produce two new film projects. A prominent figure in the community, he had been a student activist in the early 1960s and had met Khomeini in those days. When Khomeini returned, he led a delegation to meet the ayatullah and persuaded him to publicly protect the Jews as long as they disavowed Zionism. The opportunistic slippage back and forth between Iranian officials' use of "Jews" and "Zionists" remains a powerful disciplining tactic, given its built-in deniability. "Did I say Jews? I meant Zionists." It is not surprising that this film producer's reaction should also have been nuanced and multiple. On the one hand, "It is not a serious matter," he said. "I've been through these things for forty years now." On the other hand, he delivered a lecture on Arendt to the Jewish community in their community center in Sheikh Hadi neighborhood, once a cosmopolitan neighborhood of Jewish and Muslim business partners, Armenians and Zoroastrians, where Jews no longer live, and the landmark Armenian Andre's Café has been shuttered.

■ Arendt is, of course, a very interesting choice for a Jewish Iranian to select, and it appeared that this was no spur-of-the-moment selection, for she had been a favorite philosopher of the film producer for many years. He was delighted that in the audience was someone who had listened to Arendt as a student at the University of Chicago in the 1960s. The talk was very good, beginning with Arendt's biography, her distinction between just living (as animals do, including migration, seasonal changes, house building, even tool use) and living the life of thought and intentionality. There were passages on the importance of politics and the role of Rosa Luxemburg, Heidegger and the Nazis, Arendt's time in France and the United States, her relations with Israel and her exchange with Gershom Scholem, and a longer passage on the Adolf Eichmann controversy, the point of which was that Nazism, not the miserable functionary, should be on trial.

Only in the question period did he respond directly to her legacy for today, first by nodding, as it were, to the pact with Khomeini, noting that were Arendt alive today she would be talking about the holocaust of Iraqis just as she opposed the Vietnam War, that she rejected defense of Jews alone, that holocausts have happened throughout history to the Jews and others. But then he spoke also to what was on the audience's mind: what was important about the Holocaust issue was that when attacked, one not remain silent but defend oneself and not just allow well-meaning others to say everything would be okay. One needs to answer words with words: *harf be harf zadan*. Not remain silent. There was applause, and as he stepped down from the stage, the female head of a Jewish hospital stood and gave an emotional tribute to his teaching and leadership over the past three decades. Her emotional tones clearly reflected her shock at having been prevented, as one of the Jewish community's leaders, from going to her hospital during the staged visit of the foreign ambassadors. More applause.

The tribulations of the Jewish community in Tehran might be a hieroglyph of conditions more generally in the Islamic Republic, one explored on a psychiatric level by Orkideh Behrouzan in her 2010 dissertation and in a paper we have co-authored for Devon and Alex Hinton's edited volume on nightmares and traumas in today's world. At issue are (a) a major sensibility shift in the past two decades from philosophical and poetic indirection to relatively direct public discourse about interpersonal troubles, anxieties, mental illness, and acting out; (b) Café Ruzbeh, a multidisciplinary experimental space for psychiatric residents that flourished briefly in the 1990s, and the shifts in Iranian psychiatry; and (c) the use of the blogosphere for creating an affective space for self-recognition of a generational voice.

The reading of Arendt (concerned with the stateless) against that of Behrouzan (concerned with stuckness) contains cross-generational issues and civil rights issues that come together in the struggles over the future of the Iranian soul.

The 1360s (1980s) Generation, Scattered around the World

> We are the *daheh shasti*, the sixties generation [1360s/1980s]. We are scattered around the world. We wear colorful clothes, but our insides are all black, dark and depressed. We want to extract this bitterness from life and show it to you. . . . We are the most screwed-up generation. We are the *khamushi* generation, born and raised under those periods of *khamushi* [lights off, silenced, asphyxiated]. We have no voice. We want to have a voice.
> —Radio Khamushi podcast, Tehran, 2008

Writing the intimate history of several generations raised in Iran since the 1979 revolution no longer can be done only in Iran but must perforce follow the migration of many of "the best and brightest," and others, to Europe, the United States, and Australia. The history of medicine and psychiatry in Iran can be done in Iran for the first half of the twentieth century, as Cyrus Schayeghi's (2004) dissertation initiates, but that of the second half and particularly of those born since 1981 increasingly must also be accessed through the careers and insights on their experiences of those who have left. Behrouzan—trained at the University of Tehran Medical School and having experienced psychiatry rounds and research in oncology in the teaching hospitals of Tehran—begins to assemble materials for a multistrand ethnographic and oral history of Iranian psychiatry, of generational emotional sensibilities, and of public health efforts in such arenas as mental health, addiction, and HIV/AIDS.

Behrouzan first collects what one can of pharmaceutical statistics and suicides and suicide attempts for Iran since the revolution of 1979. Often all one can get are hospital-based numbers. The account of the limitations is itself an account of the infrastructural problems. A remarkable datum is the January 2009 acknowledgment by the Ministry of Health of a problem of suicides and dysphoria (a culture of sadness) and the announcement of a program to "engineer happiness." Overmedication of children for attention-deficit hyperactivity disorder, doctors suspect, is correlated with the generational anxiety and stress dysfunctions of one generation transferred onto their children.

A second methodological effort is to chart generational psychological experiences through changes in children's television programming, styles of mandated dress, what could and could not be talked about, slogans chanted in school, and songs that catacoustically mark and date at least four generations: those young during the revolution, those born during the eight-year Iran-Iraq War, and those who came into awareness during the two postwar reconstruction periods (first focused on the economy under Rafsinjani, and then on civil liberties under Khatami). In June 2009 an explosion of rage brought together parental (adolescents or young adults during the revolution) and younger generations, exposing deep rifts previously repressed.

Third, over the past two decades there has been the rise of what Behrouzan calls the "psychiatric self." More remarkable than the struggles with depression (clinical or cultural) is the change in how Iranians talk about their interpersonal relations and psychological feelings, the rise of both psychiatric and self-help psychological talk. "Suddenly" Iranians have begun to use psychological talk in a new and more open way that is not always routed through the indirection of traditional philosophical-literary tropes of the sort analyzed by Walter Benjamin and analogously found in the constellation of passion plays (*taziyehs, shabi*), young men's rhythmic flagellation groups (*dasteh*), *rowzehs, khotbehs*, visual imagery (paintings, posters, flags, banners), music and chanting (e.g., the beat of the *zurkhaneh* and chants about Imam Ali) that make up the Karbala Paradigm (Fischer 1980).

Mehdi Abedi and I followed out some of the psychological patterns of grief among émigrés to the United States in the 1980s and the feelings of a limbo or purgatory of stuckness (*avareh*; Fischer and Abedi 1990). Byron Good and Mary Jo Good, with the psychiatrist R. Moradi (who also served on Moinzadeh's [2004] dissertation), worked on depression among Iranians in California in the same period, and Mazyar Lotfalian did a number of case histories on distraught Iranians in California publicly acting out in dramatic ways that made it into the newspapers also in the early years after the revolution (Good, Good, and Moradi 1985; Lotfalian 1996).

But in the past few years in California and Tehran, popular talk shows have encouraged people to talk about their problems in psychological terms. In the 1980s, when Lotfalian interviewed psychiatrists in the San Francisco Bay Area, there were topics about which they said patients could not speak in Persian; if at all, it had to be in English, either because of the taboos involved or because the semantics did not exist or work sufficiently in Persian. This is no longer the case, nor is it just California talk disseminated by satellite radio and TV. Behrouzan provides a history of the PANA movement in Tehran and the shifting trends within psychiatry itself in Iran, from late Qajar asylums to neuropsychiatry from France in the 1930s and 1940s, translations of Freud in the 1950s, a Jungian fascination via Corbin and illuminationist philosophy in the 1960s and 1970s, and struggles since between psychopharmacology and talk therapies as in the United States but intensified by the lack of psychiatric social workers and other trained referring infrastructures.

Behrouzan points to the blogosphere as providing an affective arena for the post-1979 generations. Many had felt isolated, as if theirs were individual, deep experiences of repressed family conflict, only in 2009 fully able to reconcile the anger at a repressive parental generation that denied them the freedoms of childhood and adolescence and the sense of hope and future that the parents had experienced before the revolution. In the explosions of 2009 suddenly the liberatory language of the parents from 1979 and 2009 came together. But the blogosphere was where the self-identified "asphyxiated generation" or the "1360s (1980s) generation" was able to identify itself as a culturally distinctive formation.

Former medical students use the blogosphere to recall Café Ruzbeh, a space in their psychiatric residencies created by Dr. Muhummad Sanati for multidisciplinary discussions about psychiatry, literature, history, and symbolic forms. Sanati has written on Sadegh Hedayat, the symbolic figurations in the Shahnameh, and other cultural forms as a way of opening up thinking about anxiety structures and psychological patterns. In that spirit, Behrouzan facilitates efforts to think through state mental health policy, the contested role of media, generational experiences, and exacerbated stresses in almost every Iranian family.

The struggle for the soul of Behrouzan's generation, of those who preceded and those who now are coming afterward, is far from over.

■ I think of Arendt in her sixties (listening to her) lecturing at the University of Chicago or amid other émigrés at the New School for Social Research in New York writing in the aftermath of Hitler, Stalin, and the devastations of World War II, events that left so many stateless or moved into new polities (starting conditions for her political philosophy and repeatedly of the world's since then). I think of her and wonder at her position as a beacon, still, for political philosophy in Tehran three decades after her death.

Where new social contracts are forged, "where word and deed have not parted company, where words are not empty and deeds not brutal, where words are not used to veil intentions but to disclose realities, and deeds are not used to violate and destroy but to establish relations and create new realities" (Arendt [1958] 1998: 200)—there is the political, the polis, the capacity of human beings for action, for the unexpected, the new, forged from capacities for forgiving and promising, retrospection, and forward looking. Derrida will call it "democracy to come." Only in what Kant calls an "enlarged mentality" (of the expanding geographical and anthropological knowledge of the world) is there the ability to think in the place of everybody else, to deal with particulars in their particularity without subsuming them under pregiven universals, instead seeking the universal out of the particular, to have judgment.

Harf be harf zadan

I think of the warm *Tischgesellschaft*, dinners and conversations, with Drs. Muhammad Sanati and Mahdiyeh Moin in Tehran, a Persian miniature of Kantian and Arendtian opinion and judgment formation about today's youth, about group therapies and medications, and about the psychology of Iranian symbolic forms. Through the work and conversation with their student and mine, Dr. Orkideh Behrouzan, I am drawn into their reminiscences of Café Ruzbeh as now one of several spaces, including the blogosphere, for reflecting back upon the psychosocial purposes of psychiatry and the historical shifts of psychiatry's various forms and contexts in Iran. I revel in the cross-ties of accounts of the Tehran Psychiatric Institute's complex histories in the work of both Najmabadi and Behrouzan, and the work in California of Dr. Robert Moradi in the work of Byron and Mary-Jo Good and that of Hassan-Ali Moinzadeh. The cross-ties, in their complementarities, confirmations, and differences, help create an ethnographic archive from which anthropology and philosophy both might be created in conversation for "living in a topsy-turvy world, a world where we cannot find our way by abiding by the rules of what once was common sense" (Arendt [1958] 1998: 383).

The Jewish community in Tehran and the 1360s generation in Iran and in the diaspora just want to live their actual lives in a world of equal Arendtian citizenship, grounded in the plurality of the human condition, where everyone is the same in being human, and no one is interchangeable with anyone else, because each human being is particular, different, uniquely capable of the unexpected and new.

4. EXIT INTERVIEW

ANTHROPOLOGIA AND PHILOSOPHIA

These days, when an Iranian academic, anthropologist or philosopher, goes abroad to a conference, he or she may be grilled before being allowed to leave: Why are you going? Who is paying for your trip? What do they want you to say about Iran? (Why else would they pay for your trip?) We know you may not agree with us but we want to make sure you at least have a sensibility of solidarity with us. It is a performance one must undergo, just as one must undergo ideological vetting before getting into a university. Similarly when seeking asylum, one must learn to perform the correct profile that immigration officers can recognize as "authentic." We are in a world beyond the jargon of authenticity, where modalities of access are beyond those of master-slave (power-resistance) and where the conditions of possibility for Arendtian politics, Habermasian public spheres, Rawlsian procedural justice, or Derridean democracy are at best yet to come.

Philosophy (for the Greeks, the Hindus, and the Jews) arises in dialogue. Dialogue beats with (gendered) questions (Jabes 1976). Questions beget debate; debate begets logic, rhetoric, poetics, and drama. Drama, epic, parable, and ritual address family, friends, neighbors, and others. Anthropology arises (in Herodotus, the Chinese traveler Fa Hsien, the Muslim geographer al-Biruni, the Jewish physician and collector of materia medica in Kerala da Orta) in the traffic between and across communities of discourse, in trade, translation, and curiosity. Traces of signatures and contexts remain in writing, to be reconstructed, redeemed, and reoriented (Benjamin, Derrida). Pasts and futures are redeveloped in forgiveness and promises (Arendt).

For Kant, Durkheim, Freud in his work on group psychology, Wittgenstein and Lyotard on language games and meaning determined by use, Lacan grappling with the social nature of language as a symbolic arena knotted together with the imaginary and the real, for Arendt in postwar repair, Benjamin and the surrealists contemplating the rise of mass politics and coercive authoritarian subjectivation, for Derrida collecting the cinders and ashes for a European democracy to come, for Modarressi savoring Persian accents and Naficy's Washington Persians, for Najmabadi's and Osanloo's transsexuals and divorce-seeking wives negotiating with psychiatrists, bureaucrats, and Islamic courts—for all these modern authors, individuation, personhood, relative autonomy, character occur only in groups, in increasingly differentiated social structures.

According to Cornelius Castoriadis (1999 [2007]) two opposed meanings of *anthropos* were held in tension for the Greeks of the fifth century BCE. For Aeschylus in *Prometheus Bound* (ca. 460 BCE), *anthropos* stands between animals and gods (*therion e theos*), between the bestial and the divine. Aeschylus thus works with a "structuralist" anthropogony or genesis of *anthropos*. Before Prometheus's gifts to mankind—of fire and the arts of culture, of memory and foresight of death, of discerning the potentials of action and creation (*prattein, poiein*)—men and women were like zombies. They saw without seeing, heard without hearing, lived in sunless caves unable to distinguish the seasons, and were without discernment (*ater gnomes*). Men and women were, in other words, placeholders in the structural scheme between gods and beasts and were transmuted into human beings, alchemically or by mutation as it were, by Prometheus's gifts.

By contrast, for Sophocles in *Antigone* (ca. 442 BCE), *anthropos* is a drive, a compulsion of self-fashioning that weaves together the laws of the polis and the equally strong passions of political life. *Anthropos* in this account is self-educating (*edidaxato*). *Edidaxato* is self-reflexive, an example of the grammatical middle voice in which agent and object of agency are indistinguishable. Of *anthropos*, Sophocles says, "numerous are the terrors and wonders (*deina*) but nothing is more wondrous and terrifying (*deinon*) than man (*polla ta deina kouden anthropou deinoteron pelei*)." The gods (like comic book characters) are fixed in their qualities, but man is self-creating, self-modifying, and challenged to weave together (*pareiron*) the bonds of polities. *Antigone* is a play about the need to weave together loyalty to ancestral tradition (the Burkean republicanism of incremental conservatism) with loyalty to the self-legislating rule of law (the Jeffersonian republicanism of new constitutions every twenty years). The tragedy comes from the *hubris* of Antigone and Creon, each loyal to one principle, neither able to weave the two together (*pareiron*) into the passionate embrace of the work and working of the polis (*astuonomous orgas*, whence also orgasm, explosive passion).

The Greeks, as Miriam Leonard (2005) shows, once again become important in post–World War II French philosophical thinking about democracy, ethics, and reconstruction, often in direct contrast to earlier German readings of *die Griechen* (especially those of Hegel, Nietzsche, and Heidegger). While the dialectic of French-German dialogue is constitutive of modern European philosophy, often it is by way of diversion through the remains of dialogues between the Persians and Greeks or indeed the Hindus and the Greeks.

The oldest of these Greek remains is *The Persians*, the play by Aeschylus (472 BCE), one in a series of Greek meditations on the civilizational dialectic between two kinds of states (continental empire, maritime city-state alliances), and more philosophically between hubris and prudence at various segmentary levels of governance and political action.

As in a series of chess games, the place of Persia is sometimes black, sometimes white; Sparta and Athens play a similar chess game of contrasts and moves. In Herodotus, Stewart Flory argues (1987), the Persians and the several Greek city-states are staged as counters in a cyclical structural reversal between rich and poor, corrupt and noble, brave and coward, ignorant and sophisticated (corrupted by deceit and luxury, as ibn Khaldun would again articulate in the fourteenth century). Sparta is a society in Plato to which the Athenian Stranger counterposes the virtues of education through play and dialectical debate, with the added pleasures of testing, and keeping one's head, while drinking wine as a superior pedagogy to the Spartan nondrinking asceticism and unison chanting to instill feelings of unquestioning solidarity and unity and hardening for sacred defense of the homeland (much as Khomeinist Iran has adopted). Philosophically the chess game continued in the mid-twentieth century with Karl Popper's casting of the open society against the authoritarianism of the philosopher-kings of the Republic, a position taken up by his student Sorush against the Khomeinists, who in turn fear the spirit of criticism, debate, and play as a "velvet revolution" certain to topple their efforts to control the state, the polity, and the youth.

Western philosophy too has its parallel internal dialectic, with the language game of symbolic logic and desire for univocal linguistics modeled on Frege or Russell in Anglo-American philosophy dismissing the language games of Wittgenstein, the intersubjective and language-mediated phenomenology of Dilthey and Cassirer, or the social worlding of anthropology (Veena Das's poisonous knowledge, Arthur Kleinman's local moral worlds, Byron and Mary-Jo Good's postcolonial disorders) or that of today's Iranian ethnographic philosophers of the everyday (Modarressi, Naficy, Najmabadi, Moinzadeh, Behrouzan). The rationales for Anglo-American philosophical language games in machine translation and for the pleasure of the language games are not objectionable as long as they are not used to bar philosophies of greater range for the tasks of actual living in the world amid all its conflicts and plurality.

NOTES

1. Friendship has been thematized recently again by a number of philosophers, notably by Derrida (1994) taking up Emmanuel Levinas's ethics as first philosophy, and reading it together with Aristotle's division of friendship into three forms, involving problematics of love, politics, and gender. I play along with the importance of Greek terms (e.g., *philia*) in philo-sophical discussion, but with Levinas and Derrida (and Wittgenstein, John Dewey, William James, and others), I try to metabolize texts back into situated living commentaries, dialogues, and conversations, while also expanding the cultural frames of reference. In the oral performance at Harvard (and in October 2012 at the Department of Anthropology, Stockholm University, at the invitation of Shahram Khosravi) I

opened by trying to acknowledge in small but telling, even catacoustic details mutually informing histories, interactions, projects, and ever-expanding conversations, often of long standing, with every participant in the symposium as precisely exemplifying both the anthropological and the philosophical enterprises of learning along with others.

2. See Fischer (2009b).

3. I take the term *catacoustics* from a brilliant essay by the philosopher Philippe Lacoue-Labarthe, "The Echo of the Subject" in *Typography* (1989), and have used it in several essays, especially one several years ago on trauma and depression in Iran (Behrouzan and Fischer, forthcoming) and on musicality and rhythm in the aesthetics of politics in Iran in 2009 (Fischer 2010b). It refers to the "phenomenon of a 'tune in one's head' that 'keeps coming back'" (Lacoue-Labarthe 1989: 150).

4. Compare the play of gazes in the shifts of sexual positionalities in Persian paintings over the course of the Qajar period (1785–1925; Najmabadi 2005). In poetry and painting, young beardless males with just a hint of mustache as objects of beauty and desire almost indistinguishable from female beauty are replaced by women as the signifier of beauty, partly in response to the European gaze and the experience of travels and travelogues in Europe. The outward gaze of a woman looking into a mirror not at herself but at the viewer, or young males with averted gaze conscious of being gazed at once established a triangular play of gazes. Thus scenes of Yusef and the street women called by Zulaikha to witness to her beloved's beauty allow the male viewer as well to gaze upon this icon of eternal paradisiacal desire. So too amorous couples with cups of wine signify the menservants (*ghilman*) and female beauties (*hur*) of paradise in the Qur'an, the wine of intoxication. Over time the positions of *amrad* (adolescent male), *mukhannah* (young adult male wishing to be the object of other males' desires), and *ghilman* become increasingly veiled, and female figures of desire begin to be shown with bare breasts or breasts emphasized by transparent clothing as the signifier of desire. The separation of sexual inclination from the obligations of marriage also becomes veiled. Najmabadi argues that contemporary ideologies of feminism and gay and lesbian rights not only obscure such historical patterns but interfere with the abilities especially of transgenders, but also gays and lesbians, to negotiate their legal and other ways in today's world (see section 2).

5. On the contrast between a UN-style debate at the School for International Studies of the Ministry of Foreign Affairs of the Islamic Republic of Iran and a debate at Mofid University in Qum, see Fischer (2004b). On Qur'anic debates, see chapter 2, "Qur'anic Dialogics," in Fischer and Abedi (1990). On media debates, see Fischer (1983).

6. See Fischer and Abedi (1990: chapter 5).

7. In Zoroastrian purity rituals, the *pavi* (a channel of water) is used to separate sacred and pure spaces from profane ones.

8. On *sigheh* or *muta'* marriage, see Shahla Haeri (2002).

9. On the beginnings of the efforts to modernize the madrasseh system in the 1970s, see Fischer (1980), especially chapter 3. Ayatullah Abdul-Karim Mousavi-Ardebili served as chief justice of Iran in 1981–89 and briefly for two months as acting president in 1981 after the removal of Abdul-Hassan Banisadr. When Khomeini died in 1989, he resigned from the Supreme Court, returned to Qum, and founded Mofid University.

10. Defenders of the mystical tradition might sharply argue that what exists in Afghanistan is perversion insofar as money and power are the drivers. And it is precisely that division between the dominance dynamics and homosocial affection that is the subject of much casual male joking in Iran; to be caught on the wrong side of this is a matter of consequence. The most recent of a number of investigative journalist accounts on *bacce bazi* in Afghanistan is the documentary by Najibullah Quraishi and Jamie Doran, *The Dancing Boys of Afghanistan*, a Clover Films production for WGBH/Frontline, that aired on April 20, 2010, http://www.pbs.org/wgbh/pages/frontline/dancingboys/etc/credits.html.

11. Najmabadi notes also that a double negative in Khomeini's *Tahrir al-wasilah* (*Clarification of Questions*, or in Persian, *Towzih al-Masa'el*, that ayatullahs issue, largely copied from one another) also provides considerable legal wiggle room. On this book, see Abedi and Fischer (1985).

CHAPTER 9

Ritual Disjunctions:

Ghosts, Philosophy, and Anthropology

Michael Puett

■ Allow me to begin with a ritual as described in the *Records of Rites* (*Liji* 禮記), one of the ritual classics from early China.[1] To set the scene, let us suppose that a ruler passes away. The ruler's son becomes the new ruler, who then performs sacrifices to his deceased father. In these sacrifices, an impersonator would play the ritual part of the deceased, receiving sacrifices from the living. In the example at hand, the living ruler's son would play the impersonator role for the ghost of his grandfather (the ruler's deceased father): "Now, according to the way of sacrificing, the grandson acted as the impersonator of the king's father. He who was made to act as the impersonator was the son of he who made the sacrifice. The father faced north and served him. By means of this, he made clear the way of a son serving his father. This is the relation of father and son" (ICS 131/26/14).[2]

The stated goal of the ritual is to inculcate in each performer the proper dispositions that should hold in the relationship between father and son. But the ritual did not involve these participants simply coming in and acting in their ritually proper roles, with the father acting as a proper father and the son acting as a proper son. On the contrary, the entire ritual operated precisely through a series of role reversals: the ruler would have to behave as a proper son to his own son, who would in turn have to behave as a proper father to his own father.

The disjunction between these ritual roles and the behavior that would exist outside the ritual is underlined repeatedly: "The ruler met the victim but did not meet the impersonator. This avoided impropriety. When the impersonator was outside the gates of the temple, then he was seen as a subject; when he was inside the temple, then he was fully the ruler. When the ruler was outside the gates of the temple, he was seen as the ruler; when he entered the gates of the temple, he was fully the son. Therefore by not going outside, he made clear the propriety of ruler and subject" (ICS 131/26/13).

Both of these passages conclude with the same point: the proper relationship between father and son, as well as that between ruler and subject, is defined precisely by the demarcations of the ritual space. For these demarcations to work, the participants must relate to each other according to their ritual roles. Indeed the ability of the ruler to approach his son (who would be playing the role of the ruler's father) with proper filial dispositions is given as a definition of proper sacrificial action: "Only the sage is able to sacrifice to the High God, and only the filial son is able to sacrifice to his parents. 'Sacrifice' [xiang] is to face toward [xiang]. One faces toward it, and only then can one sacrifice to it. Therefore, the filial son approaches the impersonator and does not blush" (ICS 126/25.6/7).

If the ruler so succeeds in developing these filial dispositions, then the sons and grandsons throughout the realm will be moved by the ruler's filiality as well, and he will come to be seen as the father and mother of the people: "Therefore, if his power is flourishing, his intent will be deep. If his intent is deep, his propriety will be displayed. If his propriety is displayed, his sacrifices will be reverent. If his sacrifices are reverent, then none of the sons and grandsons within the borders will dare be irreverent. . . . If his power is slight, his intent light, and he has doubts about his propriety, then, when seeking to sacrifice, he will not be able to be reverent when it is necessary to be so. If he is not reverent when sacrificing, how can he be taken as the father and mother of the people?" (ICS 133/26/22).

The overall goal of the ritual is becoming clear. Following the death of the ruler, the deceased father must be made into a supportive ancestor, the ruler must be a proper descendant to this ancestor, and the ruler's son must learn to be a proper son to his father, the new ruler. Moreover the ruler must train himself to treat the people as his family, and the people must come to act toward the new ruler as if he were their father and mother.

Hopefully all of this is accomplished in the ancestral sacrifice. The result of the ritual is that the ruler, by playing the part of the son to his own son, learns to become a proper descendant to his deceased father, who is impersonated by his son, just as his son, by playing the part of the proper father, learns to become a proper son to his father. Implicit in the ritual is the hope that the deceased father, by occupying the grandson playing the role of the father, will be trained to become a proper ancestor, and the populace, seeing the ruler properly playing the role of son to his deceased father, will in turn be moved to play the role of son to the ruler—just as the ruler comes to play the role of father and mother of the people.

As explicated elsewhere in the text, the same logic plays out in relation to the sacrifices to Heaven, through which, as one could at this point predict, the ruler becomes the Son of Heaven and Heaven comes to see the ruler as his son (Puett 2005).

Thus, through these sets of rituals, an array of potentially antagonistic forces—Heaven, the ghost of a recently deceased ruler, the new ruler, his son, and the populace—come to have filial dispositions toward each other. As a result, the entire realm becomes, ritually speaking, a single family, linked through familial dispositions. Instead of interactions being dominated by dispositions like anger, jealousy, and resentment, the interactions within rituals are defined by the proper dispositions associated with the relations between particular roles in a patriarchal hierarchy: ancestor, father, son. Ritually speaking again, the world—including Heaven, ghosts, and living humans—comes to function as a perfect patriarchal lineage built up through father-son dyads.

But, of course, this is not the way the world really operated. And the very nature of the ritual and the reason the ritual would (hopefully) be effective were predicated on underlining such a disjunction between the ritual and what existed outside of it. The father and son would not enter the ritual space and be required to behave as a proper father and son to each other. On the contrary, the working of the ritual demanded that the ritual roles be clearly separated from the world outside of the ritual, with the father playing the role of the son and the son playing the role of the father.

This might seem like an odd place to begin an essay on anthropology and philosophy. And all the more so because the text I have been quoting from is not an ethnographic description of a ritual but rather a work of ritual theory from classical China. My reason for quoting it at such length is because I would like to argue that the ritual theory glimpsed here opens up some interesting possibilities for anthropological theory in general, and more particularly some interesting issues for ways to bring together anthropological theory with philosophy.

To help lay out the argument, allow me to begin by reflecting a bit on how material like that just discussed has already played a role in the development of anthropological theory and (to a much lesser extent) philosophy. I do so in order to argue that the material has been appropriated and domesticated in ways that perhaps limit its potential interest.

To begin with ancestors, premodern China has long been posited as one of the world's clearest examples of a culture predicated on ancestral worship. Indeed one of the most influential studies of premodern Chinese culture described the Chinese as having "lived under the ancestors' shadow" (Hsu 1967). In such a vision, the Chinese purportedly lived in a world in which they would be expected to follow the path laid out by their ancestors, to whom they would be offering constant sacrifices as acts of obeisance. One of the major breaks between premodern and modern China is thus often presented precisely as a shift from living under the ancestors' shadow to living in one's own (see, e.g., Xin 2000).

Formulations of Chinese cosmology follow similar lines. If ancestral sacrifice has come to play a canonical role in anthropological discussions of premodern social practices, premodern Chinese visions of the world have played a comparable role in studies of cosmology.[3] Premodern Chinese cosmology is often described as one of harmonious monism, wherein the entire cosmos was linked by the same lines of continuity as found among human families. Here again the breakdown of this traditional cosmology is often posited as one of the key issues in the formation of a modern China.

As should already be clear, however, such descriptions of premodern Chinese culture have arisen in part by taking the ideal results of ritual action and presenting them instead as founding assumptions. These views find strong confirmation in the material discussed earlier, but they are presented not as assumptions but as the world normatively created within a ritual space—a ritual space that is explicitly contrasted with what exists outside.

But one can generalize the point. There was a recurrent tendency in nineteenth- and twentieth-century theory to emphasize the degree to which so-called traditional societies assumed themselves to be living in a cyclical, harmonious cosmos. Around such views an entire framework developed focused on the shift from a harmonious to a fragmentary cosmology, from a continuous to a discontinuous world, from traditional worldviews to modern. Mircea Eliade (1954) is but one highly influential example among many that could be mentioned. It is notable, however, the degree to which such narratives—Eliade's very much included—rested for their evidence on so-called traditional cosmologies from rituals.

This tendency to read ritual statements as cosmological assumptions has been noted by Maurice Bloch (1977) as well, with a particular focus on the issue of time. Bloch offers as an example Clifford Geertz's famous interpretation of Balinese views of cyclical time, as contrasted with the predominantly linear visions of time purportedly dominating in the modern West. Bloch notes correctly that Geertz's arguments rest primarily on evidence drawn from rituals. He argues that instead of presenting a dichotomy between cyclical and linear views of time in terms of cultural assumptions (in this case, traditional Bali on the one hand and the modern West on the other), the distinction should instead be between ritual constructions of time and lived experience. The former, Bloch argues, are often cyclical, while the latter are universally linear.

Discussing the difference between cyclical and linear visions of time in terms of ritual versus nonritual forms of experience is certainly an improvement over the attempt to place such a distinction into a tradition/modernity narrative. However, Bloch's solution has its dangers as well. What lies outside ritual for Bloch is still essentially what we experience, the "we" now being read as universal humans as opposed to modern humans. Culture (however understood) is thus largely taken out of the discussion of our lived experience. But there is a danger that the work of ritual is being misunderstood as well, as it simply comes to occupy the same distancing place in our theoretical frameworks that "traditional cosmologies" did in an earlier generation.

Let me explain what I mean by *distancing*. It is not just that, because of these frameworks (be they "tradition/modernity," or "ritual/universal lived experience"), we are in danger of systematically misreading huge amounts of ritual materials and the cultures that produced them—a serious danger in itself. It is that, by placing these materials and cultures within the frameworks we do, we guarantee that they can be nothing but the objects of our theoretical discussions and philosophical projects. Unless, for example, we really want to believe we live in a harmonious, cyclical cosmos, or—in another framework—to enter a ritual space that constructs such an experience, then any material drawn from such a culture could never be something we would allow ourselves to think through or learn from. A ritual text, read in such a way, could be nothing other than an interesting document from another world—one about which we could perhaps have great nostalgia but one that never really threatens our theoretical models or makes us think anew.

But what if we were to do the opposite? What would happen if we were to develop our philosophical and theoretical orientations using indigenous theories as well, allowing those theories to challenge the models within which we have become so used to thinking? Invaluable work has been undertaken in demonstrating the degree to which our theoretical models are dependent on specific—primarily Protestant—religious traditions (see, e.g., Asad 1993; Sahlins 1996). So perhaps now we are in a position to start building theoretical models from other traditions as well.[4] As with any theory, such approaches will mask as much as they reveal, but by building from numerous different theoretical orientations coming from different traditions, we may be more likely to see the workings and implications of these masks and revelations.

Let us return to the issues of ritual and lived experience in classical China in order to get a better sense of some of these workings in practice. And let me start by saying a few more words about early Chinese religious practice. I will focus on those practices dominant in the Warring States and Han (ca. fifth through first centuries BCE), the period during which our ritual text mentioned earlier was written.

The world in classical China was composed of numerous different energies and powers in constant interaction with each other. These interactions were usually conflictual and potentially highly dangerous. In terms of interactions between humans, the energies of what we would call negative emotions—anger, jealousy, resentment—could erupt at any moment, and often for seemingly minor and mundane moments. Hence the possibility at any moment of the emergence of fights, conflicts, and violence. This was equally true of the energies within the human body. The interactions of these energies with each other and with energies outside the body could often be quite destructive, resulting in sickness and death. Then things would get worse: after death, the energies of anger and resentment would harden and become focused explicitly on those still alive. The resulting energies would haunt the living, bringing about yet more sicknesses and yet more deaths. And these are just the energies associated with humans. There are other energies and beings throughout the cosmos that suddenly emerge for reasons unclear to us. Our interactions with them as well are often equally dangerous.

Given such a world, attempts were made to name these energies, to map them, to chart their common patterns of interactions so that they could be understood and altered. The various energies in the human body, for example, were mapped, with constant effort to see what forms of exercises and dietetics could alter the ways the energies interacted both within the body and with energies outside the body. One of the more famous ways of doing this was to classify some of the energies as *yin* and others as *yang*, and then to seek exercises and dietetics to bring these different energies into greater balance and harmony and thus avoid sickness. Another was to classify the different energies into different phases that would then be harmonized with similarly classified energies in the environment. But it is important to emphasize that these classifications and mappings were not ontological descriptions of the human body or the larger cosmos; they were mappings of various patterns of interaction with the goal of altering those interactions in favorable ways.

This was equally true of the energies that would be classified as nonhuman. The dangerous energies that would be released after death, for example, were called *gui*. When referring to them as deceased humans, the term is best translated as "ghost." But not all gui are necessarily dead humans. The term can also be used to map those highly dangerous creatures that exist in the larger world. We usually do not know the origins of such creatures; they may or may not be deceased humans. In such cases, the term *gui* is perhaps best translated as "demon." Either way, a gui is an extraordinarily dangerous creature whose interactions with living humans are dominated by energies of anger, resentment, and viciousness.

As with the energies within the human body, the goal was to identify the forms of work that could be undertaken to alter the nature of the interactions between humans and these gui. When the gui were deceased humans, the goal was to transform the highly dangerous interactions between ghosts and living humans into one between ancestors and descendants. Here again, these terms must be understood relationally. It is not that the substance of something called a ghost would be transformed in an ontological sense into something radically different that could be called an ancestor. Rather the relations between the living humans and the creature would be altered such that different and (from the perspective of the human) better patterns of interaction would be created.

If the gui was not clearly related to a group of living humans who could then relate to it as an ancestor, then the goal would be to make it into a god or goddess—again in a relational sense. It would be treated as a god or goddess, given a place in the pantheon, and provided with sacrificial offerings on a defined schedule—the key, again, being to alter the forms of interaction between humans and the gui, shifting it to one of mutual support rather than antagonism and conflict.

These same points would hold for the interaction of humans with the natural environment. Many of these interactions would be dangerous and highly conflictual: animals attacking and killing humans, humans eating poisonous plants and dying, cold temperatures developing in which humans freeze to death, rains and droughts occurring that lead to floods and lack of adequate water. Here too the goal would be to alter and transform these relations. In this case, such a transformation was accomplished initially through domestication: by domesticating the animals and plants and creating an agricultural world in which the domesticated plant would be harvested according to the shifts in temperature and rains, what had been a highly dangerous set of interactions becomes a harmonious one, in which the interactions are on the contrary productive for humans. The result is a harmonious world based upon cyclical time.

But, again, it is not that the cosmos itself has been fully transformed. In all of these cases, we are dealing with human attempts to alter sets of relationships. The energies in one's body are never fully harmonized; the world is never fully domesticated; the gui are never fully transformed into ancestors or into gods and goddesses. The world of our experience is thus one not of harmony but of constant ruptures of dangerous energies that must yet again be contained, altered, and transformed. This is true at the level of our bodies and the constant dangers of illnesses; it is true at the level of our interactions with other humans, which can at any moment be overtaken with energies of anger and resentment and even shift into violence; it is true of our dealings with the ancestors and gods, who at any point can and often do revert to being dangerous ghosts; it is true of our work with the larger cosmos, from which we receive endless disasters that are highly destructive of human flourishing. Not only is harmony not an assumption nor a pregiven state; it is, on the contrary, something one is constantly working to achieve and never succeeding in accomplishing for any length of time.

In short, there was no assumption in early China of a harmonious, monistic cosmos. The problem was precisely that it was, in our experience, fragmented or, perhaps more accurately, pluralistic—pluralistic not in the political sense but rather in the literal sense of the word. The world consists at every level of ever-changing beings and energies in constant (and often conflictual) interaction—a world thus filled with, among other things, highly dangerous and capricious ghosts. The goal was then to develop a set of practices to transform that world into something that was, for brief periods of time, slightly more harmonious, in the sense of having better relationships and better forms of interaction.

As is probably becoming clear, the reason that these practices from classical China could be so misread is that the materials explicitly say all of the things that are commonly attributed to Chinese culture in general. But these are not descriptions of beliefs but rather attempts to map and transform a world that is seen as not operating this way.

A couple of examples will help to make the point. The text I quoted from earlier is the *Records of Rites* (*Liji*, 禮記). In another chapter of the work ("Li yun"), the development of the ritual system is explicitly compared to the development of agriculture. Both worked to produce a harmonious system through domestication—in the one case domesticating aspects of the natural world such that, in their transformed state, those elements would allow for higher levels of human flourishing, and in the other case domesticating human dispositions such that they allow for the same. In both cases of agriculture and ritual, all under Heaven comes to be taken as a "single family" (ICS 9.22/62/5).[5] But, of course, the world is not really a single family; it is simply domesticated at both the cosmic and societal levels to operate as such to whatever degree possible.

Another chapter of the same text (the "Jifa") presents the pantheon of gods as a humanly constructed one, organized according to the hierarchies and patterns advantageous to human growth (ICS 123/24/9). The resulting pantheon is a perfectly ordered hierarchy—but, at the same time, of course it is not.

Simply put, humans are not living under the ancestors' shadow. The deceased are ghosts who have been domesticated into relationships defined to benefit the living. And these domesticated relationships are never enduring. The ancestors are constructed, ordered, and arranged into a lineage by and for the benefit of the living, at the same time that they haunt and attack the living (Puett 2010a).

Those who would present classical Chinese culture as having assumed a harmonious cosmos with which humans should try to accord, and of assuming a world of ancestral models to whose wills the living should try to conform, have taken the results of such ritual actions and presented them as foundational assumptions. But this completely misses the point of what animates and motivates the endless constructions of such claims. These constructions work precisely because, in a sense, they do not work. Or, more precisely, they work only as a constant process, in which these highly dangerous interactions are endlessly being worked on, mapped, classified, and transformed—endless because these transformations never work for any lengthy period of time. Underlying the endless (and often contradictory) mappings, the endless ritual work, and the endless sacrifices is the knowledge that these practices are always doomed to ultimate failure. The ancestors, to give one prominent example, always revert to being ghosts.

And, of course, even calling them ghosts is already using a mapping to describe the phenomenon. They are best thought of as ruptures, as emergences of dangerous energies that will then be named (as ghosts) and worked upon through ritual activity.

■ It is this endless work, and the tensions that underlie the ritual calls for cosmic harmony, that we have missed and domesticated in our models of this material. One of the best examples of a text from classical China that asserts a model of a harmonious, monistic cosmos can be found in several chapters of the *Baihu tong*, in which the authors work out seemingly endless chains of interactions of phenomena according to various correlated cosmological phases. But instead of reading this as the sign of an assumption of a monistic cosmos, we need to see the agony underlying the writing of such a text, the agony of knowing that of course the mapping does not really work—and hence the felt need to continue the mapping in such compulsive detail.

This might seem at one level like a pessimistic vision. And at one level it certainly is. It helps to explain the strong emphasis in the songs and poetry of China on loss—loss of an earlier moment when relationships with friends or family were robust and deep. But the flip side of this is a strong commitment to the importance of those moments when the relationships, for an inevitably brief period of time, actually do work. Emphasizing the fragility of robust relationships also deepens their power.

But it is also not pessimistic for another reason: it is simply not the case that the participants would necessarily want the ordering, mappings, and rituals to always work perfectly. And perhaps this is a good moment to return to the ritual with which we began.

The background behind the ritual should now be clear. When the ruler dies, the danger is that he will become a highly dangerous ghost, that the father will fail to be a good ruler or a good father, that the son will fail to live up to his duties as an heir apparent, and that the populace will fail to support the new ruler. The goal of the ritual is to create a harmonious, hierarchical relationship between them of ancestor-father-son. Underlying the ritual, of course, is the clear knowledge that this is not the way the world operates.

Along these same lines: notable for its absence in the ritual is a female figure. The ritual works by removing the females who not only gave birth to the males in question but who (we know from other documents about the lived reality of the time) played a crucial role in running the court. The result is a perfect, patriarchal line moving from ancestor to son. Moreover, ritually speaking, the ruler serves as both father and mother of the people. The entire realm is thus organized in such a patriarchal form, with Heaven above and the ruler below as Son of Heaven and parent to the populace.

But it is not simply that the participants know that the world does not operate this way. The ritual itself works precisely by underlining the fact that the world does not operate this way. Hence the role reversals that animate the ritual. Perhaps there might be a danger that the father would foolishly believe that, outside the ritual, he really does live up to his role as a father. But he certainly knows that he is not the son of his own son. The key to the ritual is that each participant is not only called upon to perform his respective role properly; each participant is also called upon to perform a role that by definition he is not playing outside of the ritual. One trains one's disposition to interact properly precisely by being forced to act out the disjunction of such interactions from the nonritual space.

What animates the ritual, then, is the set of negative interactions that operate outside the ritual space—a son, for example, acting as a proper father to a father with whom he just had a vicious argument. But the opposite is true as well. It is not just that the interactions within the ritual space do not exist outside the ritual space; it is that the participants would not fully wish such a ritual world to be eternal and fully successful anyway. In the example at hand—a walk into the ritual space after a vicious fight—the ritual space would presumably be tempting. But a purely male-based patriarchal order—if such a thing were somehow possible—would hardly have appealed to all of the participants. Or rather it in part might have appealed and in part would not have appealed, and in that tension lies the work of the ritual.

Allow me to expand the point with reference to the claim mentioned earlier, that in early China people lived their lives under the ancestors' shadow. As is now becoming clear, the characterization is wrong in not just one but in several senses. To begin with, it is the father, not the deceased ghost being transformed into an ancestor, who is empowered by the sacrifice. In the perfect world constructed by the ritual, the father becomes the fulcrum of all the relationships, connecting Heaven, the ancestors, and the populace, with himself at the center. Of course, the ruler is also called upon in his ritual role to play the part of father (to his son and the populace) and son (to his father and Heaven) properly, so hopefully he is being transformed through the ritual as well. Nonetheless, if successful, the sacrifice dramatically empowers the father in this constructed patrilineal cosmos, whereas everyone else (including the ghost-cum-ancestor) is defined by him.

Such an outcome may well have appealed to the ruler, but it could hardly have seemed fully appealing to the rest of the participants. In our hypothetical example of the son who enters the ritual space having just endured a vicious argument with his father, the ritual moment of having his father subservient to him may seem desirable, but the son also knows that the result of the ritual will be an empowerment of his father and will indeed quite probably play to his father's worst desires for even more power. Thus in the ritual role of playing the father, the son is haunted not only by the anger and resentment from just before entering the ritual space but also by the knowledge that the implication of the ritual moment of subservience is ultimately an enhancement of the power of the father and probably an enhancement of the father's drive for power. But any consolation that could be gained by the knowledge that the empowerment effects of the ritual will in fact never fully work is also belied by the fact that the failure of the ritual also means a return to the negative emotions of anger and resentment that can often pervade the relationship outside of the ritual space—or, in the example at hand, the relations that led to the vicious argument.

So it is not just that humans do not live under their ancestors' shadows, and it is not just that the ancestor always reverts to being a ghost. It is that the ritual enactment is haunted at every level by the implications of the role-playing, wherein all of the various transformations are both non-enduring and highly ambivalent.

It is indeed a ritual that operates precisely through these hauntings. At each level the enactment is haunted by the emotions and dispositions of the other levels. Even the perfect ritual moment is haunted by the facts that it is so clearly marked as discontinuous from the world of our experience, that ruptures will inevitably occur in the enacted relationships, and that the perfect ritual relationships are in fact not only not fully desirable but, from the point of view of many of the participants, extremely chilling. And the power of the ritual depends precisely on these hauntings, and hence the emphasis on disjunction.

The same holds true for our cosmological text mentioned earlier. Would the authors really have wanted to live in a seamless, perfect world of flawlessly harmonious correlations? Probably in part yes and in part no, and hence the chilling tensions underlying the production of such a compulsively detailed text.

But let us return to the rituals and ask a very basic question: Why would such rituals be productive? Instead of thinking about ethics in terms of moral judgments, the material under discussion focuses on embodiment, with the participants being called upon to play particular roles and to inculcate the proper dispositions associated with those roles. But it is a curious type of embodiment that actually works to heighten the anxieties that such role-playing entails. The ritual roles are to be embodied, and the proper dispositions associated with those roles are to be inculcated, but the embodiment is clearly presented as impossible to achieve fully, and not even something that one would necessarily want to achieve fully. The ritual, and the ethics of the ritual, thus play in the tensions between the world of ritual and the world of experience, and the discontinuity between the two defines the efficacy of the ritual itself.

I suspect the reason such a ritual works is precisely because it heightens the tensions of our different layerings of emotions and dispositions. All of our interactions and relations are based on complex emotions and conflicting role expectations. There is always a danger that these interactions will become violent and dangerous, but there is never an easy solution to how these relations can be improved. And the rituals in question work precisely by underlining that complexity. Rituals help us refine our dispositions and transform our more dangerous emotions into ones that allow us to relate better to those around us. But these perceived better relations are not only not complete; they have their own dangers as well. Hence the emphasis on disjunction and reversed-role-playing, all of which work to highlight the ambivalences, complexities, and dangers not only of one's dispositions toward others but also of the refined dispositions associated with the rituals. By so highlighting these ambivalences, complexities, and dangers in the very acts of embodiment, the actors hopefully will become ever better at working at these conflicting dispositions in their daily life as well.

Here too one can generalize the point. Once the actions involved in what an earlier anthropology described as ritual and cosmology are taken out of the frameworks that read them as representative of a traditional worldview emphasizing harmony and continuity, one can glimpse a set of practices that we have perhaps been misreading rather systematically. Far from representing a world of harmony and continuity, they often, to quote from Robert Orsi's (2005: 170) outstanding study of the workings of Catholic rituals, operate in "the register of the tragic."

Let us return to our theoretical models. As should be clear by now, the ritual theory from the *Records of Rites* under discussion—and, for that matter, the cosmological theories as well—are not theory in the way we usually tend to use the word. These are not theories that attempt to describe the nature of ritual or the nature of the world. They instead work precisely like the rituals themselves, but at a metalevel. They describe a world of perfectly harmonious interactions that are neither enduring nor even enduringly desirable, and describe them in a way that underlines the tensions that make them work. Hence their fascinating strength, once taken out of our models that have so successfully domesticated them and stripped them of their complexity. All theories mask and reveal, but the ones under discussion allow that play of masking and revealing to be part of their power.

So what would it mean if we were to take these materials seriously as a philosophical position, as theory in this new sense?[6] And what would it mean if we were to think of an anthropology that would be inspired by it? To begin with, it would focus our attention on the complexity and tense layerings of emotions that underlie our activities. It would provide an extraordinarily rich language to talk about the degree to which such activities are worked around the fear and hopes of constant emergences and ruptures, and the degree to which those emergences and ruptures are then actively worked upon in turn. It would help us to envisage an anthropology that focuses on the common, the mundane, and the everyday, that emphasizes the extraordinary potentials for the eruptions of violence in the common and mundane, that underlines the forms of activity utilized to transform such eruptions, and that highlights the dangers of those forms themselves.[7]

It would also help us to envision an ethics that would be based on embodiment, not simply in the sense of embodying a particular role and set of values but, more important, by doing so with the full understanding that such an embodiment is by definition impossible to achieve fully. The same point would hold for our theoretical work, which would be seen less as producing models to explain behavior and more as productive but always limited frames for working with the complexities of endlessly conflicting relationships. Both ethics and theory therefore would be seen to operate, to refer again to Orsi, in the register of the tragic.

It might also help us to develop a critical vocabulary to rethink many of the comparative categories that underlie our nineteenth- and twentieth-century theoretical models—categories like ritual and cosmology. Many of these categories have been abandoned recently, precisely because they are so connected with the types of frameworks mentioned earlier by figures like Eliade. But perhaps our goal on the contrary should be to revitalize these categories by taking indigenous theories about them seriously and exploring the phenomena and practices associated with them accordingly.

In short, using these indigenous theories might help us to break down some of our own assumptions about how theory operates and to develop new ways of thinking with and through frameworks that are more deliberate in their transformative work. The goal should not be just to deconstruct twentieth-century theoretical categories but to utilize indigenous visions to rethink our categories and the nature of categories altogether. Such an approach could be, one hopes, a move toward a truly philosophical anthropology and a truly anthropological philosophy.

NOTES

I am deeply grateful to Veena Das for her invaluable comments on an earlier draft of this chapter. My thanks as well to Das, Michael Jackson, Arthur Kleinman, and Bhrigupati Singh, both for inviting me to the "Anthropology and Philosophy" workshop and for their own groundbreaking work in pulling together the fields of anthropology and philosophy. All four have been strong influences on the ideas and approach attempted in this essay.

1. *The Records of Rites* (*Liji*, 禮記) is one of the most influential texts on ritual in East Asia. The chapters were written over the course of the fourth, third, and second centuries BCE and were compiled into a single text by the first century BCE. The text was thereafter defined as one of the "Five Classics" and became part of the standard educational curriculum throughout East Asia for much of the subsequent two millennia.

2. References to the text of *Liji* are cited as ICS. My translations here and throughout have been aided greatly by those of James Legge (1885).

3. Perhaps the most influential such presentations are Granet's (1934) and Weber's (1951).

4. I have been tremendously inspired in this effort by the work of Veena Das, whose explorations of indigenous theories have opened up new ways of thinking about violence and everyday life. See, most recently, her outstanding "Violence and Nonviolence at the Heart of Hindu Ethics" (2012b).

5. For a fuller discussion of the chapter, see Puett (2010b).

6. For preliminary attempts to do this, see Puett (2010a); Puett et al. (2008), particularly 18–42.

7. I have been deeply influenced by Veena Das's work in this regard, both for her focus on the ethics of ordinary life, including the forms of violence that appear in the everyday and the types of ethical work that can be undertaken therein, as well as for her commitment to exploring these issues in terms of the indigenous theories of the cultures in question. See, for example, Das (2007, 2012a).

CHAPTER 10

Henri Bergson in Highland Yemen

Steven C. Caton [1]

■ In grappling with the question of time or temporality more broadly since my book, *Yemen Chronicle*, I have inevitably come to grips with the philosophy of Henri Bergson, especially his notion of duration, which I hold to be most important for my analysis of tribal violence and mediation in highland Yemen. As philosophers go, especially one who was as long-lived as he, the oeuvre is not large, but the texts are dauntingly difficult. First enunciated in his *Essay on the Immediate Data of Consciousness*, the idea of duration was further developed in a series of publications spanning a period of forty-five years, most notably in *Matter and Memory*, *Duration and Simultaneity*, and *Creative Evolution*. It was never enunciated in quite the same way in each work and requires close examination through the series of his works, the duration of the concept of duration in Bergson's oeuvre. In this essay, however, there is space only to deal with the concept as it was developed in the *Essay* and *Matter and Memory*.[1]

In this essay I revisit the event as described and analyzed in *Yemen Chronicle* in light of Bergson's concept of duration. In particular I suggest that an understanding of conflict resolution in tribal Yemen, which I have argued depends on a dialectic of violence and mediation, might be greatly enhanced by it. Having, I hope, convinced the reader of this claim, I go on to rewrite a portion of my book, an experimental ethnography-cum-memoir. I argue that this rewriting better captures the temporality of the dispute mediation.

The key chapter in *Essai sur les donnés immédiates de la conscience* ([1989] 1927) is the second, "De la multiplicité des états de conscience, l'idee du durée." It follows a discussion in which Bergson puts forward his first and possibly his most famous maxim: that time must not be thought of in terms of space because it has its own sui generis quality, which Bergson intuits as duration. He says at one point in the *Essai* that the reason time is conceptualized in terms of space is that it allows one to categorize and compare, but that this does not correspond to its consciousness. What, then, does Bergson claim *time* to be?

Chapter 2 begins with a rehashing of the arguments in chapter 1 about space, though now in terms of numbers, and concludes with the claim that numbers are thought of as the juxtaposition of units in space. The argument is also more complexly developed through a distinction between the "actual" and the "virtual" or the "objective" versus the "subjective": "We must distinguish between the unity which we think of and the unity which we set up as an object after having thought of it" (Bergson [1989]1927: 83). Counting a multiplicity of things in the world that are not merely in the mind is "actual"; counting things that are merely in the counter's consciousness (e.g., counting before one goes to sleep) is "virtual," even though the numbers may have correlates in the outer world (e.g., sheep). Virtual counting in the end also depends on symbolic representation, which in turn entails a spatialization or objectification just as much as actual counting does. But, asks Bergson, does this representation correspond to the consciousness of duration, or does it correspond to something else?

We do not get to Bergson's definition of duration until more than halfway through the chapter, but when it finally appears, the passage is stunning:

> Pure duration is the form which the succession of our conscious states assumes when our ego lets itself *live*, when it refrains from separating its present state from its former states. For this purpose it need not be entirely absorbed in the passing sensation or idea; for then, on the contrary, it would no longer *endure*. Nor need it forget its former states: it is enough that, in recalling these states, it does not set them alongside its actual state as one point alongside another, but forms both the past and the present states into an organic whole, as happens when we recall the notes of a tune, melting, so to speak, into one another. (100)

It is interesting that the analogies Bergson draws on to clarify the concept of duration almost always come from the sensory realm of sound—and in particular, music—whereas in *Matter and Memory* the analogies shift to visual media: photography and film ([1908] 1991: 38), mirage (37), kaleidoscope (25), the focusing of a camera (134), the lightning flash (189), searchlights (198). In the same passage of the *Essai* he goes on to elaborate the musical analogy:

> Might it not be said that, even if these notes succeed one another, yet we perceive them in one another, and their totality may be compared to a living being whose parts, although distinct, permeate one another just because they are so closely connected? The proof is that, if we interrupt the rhythm by dwelling longer than is right on one note of the tune, it is not its exaggerated length, as length, which will warn us of our mistake, but the qualitative change thereby caused in the whole of the musical phrase. We can thus conceive of succession without distinction, and think of it as a mutual penetration, an interconnexion and organization of elements, each one of which represents the whole, and cannot be distinguished or isolated from it except by abstract thought. Such is the account of duration which would be given by a being who was ever the same and ever changing, and who had no idea of space. But, familiar with the latter idea and indeed beset by it, we introduce it unwittingly into our feeling of pure succession; we set our states of consciousness side by side in such a way as to perceive them simultaneously, no longer in one another, but alongside one another; in a word, we project time into space, we express duration in terms of extensity, and succession thus takes the form of a continuous line or a chain, the parts of which touch without penetrating one another. Note that the mental image thus shaped implies the perception, no longer successive, but simultaneous, of a before and after, and that it would be a contradiction to suppose a succession which was only a succession, and which nevertheless was contained in one and the same instant. (100–101)

While for Bergson duration cannot be perceived as a simple succession or extension—simple in the sense that each instant of time follows another instant from which it is differentiated like numbers in a sequence—neither is duration a matter of perceiving the present moment only, for duration is also a matter of recollection. That is, in perceiving a "now" we are simultaneously recollecting a "before"; to put it differently, the recollection is virtual in the now that is actual. Once again Bergson draws on a musical analogy to make this clear. "[It is] like a musical phrase which is constantly on the point of ending and constantly altered in its totality by the addition of some new note" ([1908] 1991: 106). Take, for example, the Westminster chime that is heard when bells ring out to mark the time: each successive note is heard with the preceding notes in mind, the product being what Bergson calls an organic whole. That very example also reminds us that an "after" or some expectation or anticipation is as much a part of duration as the "before" or the recollection; when we hear only a quarter of the melody, we know that a quarter of an hour has passed, but we now anticipate something more, the rest of the melody—and hence the hour—to come. There is succession, to be sure, but not in the sense of homogeneous things, for it is cointensive with two other kinds of time: the past and the future. This simultaneity makes duration dependent on the consciousness of heterogeneous states. *Consciousness* is the operative word here. Duration, according to Bergson, is a quality that is subjectively felt and is part of our deepest psychic life. He calls this "the deep-seated self which ponders and decides, which heats and blazes up . . . a self whose states and changes permeate one another and undergo a deep alteration as soon as we separate them from one another in order to set them out in space" (125). This "deep-seated self" coexists with what he calls the "superficial ego," saying of them that "the two seem to *endure* in the same way" (125).

Bergson admits that it is difficult to think of duration in these ways, though he insists that it is nevertheless actualized in such examples as the musical phrase or, more compellingly yet, in dreams. In fact he says that consciousness of duration is relatively rare, "social life in general and language in particular" preferring instead the externalizing, homogenizing and objectifying modes that we associate with our perception of space ([1908] 1991: 128). He does not explain why society or language "prefers" objectification (as opposed to objectification's being the preferred mode in only one of the many ways in which a speaker may be "oriented" in the social world); in any case, to recover the consciousness of duration requires a kind of introspective depth analysis. (And this is before Freud, though one can see some similarities to the latter's method of retrieving matter from the unconscious.) There is certainly a sense in Bergson that social life and language overlay a self that is supposedly more "authentic" and "real," one steeped in the consciousness of duration.

But this begs a larger question: Is duration a useful concept for anthropology?

In *Tristes Tropiques* Lévi-Strauss ([1973] 1992: 56) does not have very kind words for Bergson's *Essai*:

> Beyond the rational there exists a more important and valid category— that of the meaningful, which is the highest mode of being rational, but which our teachers never so much as mentioned, no doubt because they were more intent on Bergson's *Essai sur les donnes immediates de la conscience* than on F. de Saussure's *Cours de linguistique generale*. . . . Rejecting the Bergsonian acts of faith and circular arguments which reduced beings and things to a state of mush the better to bring out their ineffability, I came to the conclusion that beings and things could retain their separate values without losing the clarity of outline which defines them in relationship to each other and gives an intelligible structure to each. Knowledge is based neither on renunciation nor on barter: it consists rather in selecting *true* aspects, that is, those coinciding with the properties of my thought. (emphasis in original)

In light of what I have just said about Bergson, this passage from Lévi-Strauss is doubly ironic, first because Bergson would have agreed with Lévi-Strauss that society and language could not be based on consciousness such as duration (but rather on objectification), and second, because he would have agreed that knowledge is based on selecting what is "true," though for Bergson, of course, the deeper or more authentic consciousness is not the structure of logical thought but the consciousness of duration. According to him, social thought distorts or refracts such consciousness. But the question that Lévi-Strauss poses, if only implicitly, is still valid: For anthropologists who are interested in time as a social phenomenon, are Bergson's insights useful?

In her book *Life and Words: Violence and the Descent into the Ordinary* (2007), the anthropologist Veena Das goes back to Bergson to explore questions of subjectivity and temporality for victims of violence in the 1946–47 Partition between India and Pakistan. It is less the *Essai* from which she draws inspiration than Bergson's *Matter and Memory* ([1908] 1991), and partly as discussed by the philosopher Gilles Deleuze. It is especially the section of that book in which Bergson talks about memory as entailing two *simultaneous* movements, one of *translation* (by which it confronts experience with its own image-movement), the other of *rotation* upon itself, where memory selects from the remembered past an image that is useful for action in the present world, that is attractive to Das. The key idea here is that, for Bergson, though the whole of the past is contained within memory (which I will try to explain below), it is nevertheless contracted to a certain area or "point" in memory to meet the present situation; it then rotates or orients itself to that situation in such a way as to be most resonant or useful for action in it. (I hope what is meant by action will be clearer below.) Suppose something in the present situation evokes a flood of memories from our childhood (this is my example, not Das's); then memories of that childhood rotate upon themselves in such a way that some aspect of them seems most apt or pertinent. Das (2007: 100) goes on to extract two points about Bergson's ideas about memory: "The first is that the past is not remembered as a succession of 'nows'—rather, it is because the whole of the past is in some ways given all at once that it can be actualized in a contracted form. Second, although the process of actualization might involve translation that appeals to the present, there is also the process of rotation in which, independent of my will, certain regions of the past are actualized and come to define the affective qualities of the present moment. In my fieldwork I experienced the latter in the regions of humor in which the past was present as a whole—contracted in response to appeals of a collective kind." Her analysis is subtle and profound, and it is at the core of what Das is trying to capture by memories of violence and destruction. In fact she argues that "duration . . . is not simply one of the aspects of subjectivity—it is the very condition of subjectivity" (98).

How is *Matter and Memory* different from the *Essai* concerning the concept of duration? In *Matter and Memory* Bergson developed his philosophy to the point where action had become the key concept, that is, that the point of being in the world is not representation or knowledge in the ideational sense (as arguably was the view in the *Essai*) but action (or movement) connected to a being's own interests. Bergson was trying to grapple with his time's scientific literature on the brain, and of evolutionary biology, in order to ground his discussion of memory and matter within it. The brain, according to him, is not about representing the world (this is rather like saying that everything in the world is already a sign that we can call an image); it is about receiving images and relaying them to the appropriate parts of the body so that the latter can move or act. Perception, in this view, is defined neither in an idealist nor a realist or determinist frame. Though it operates from the point of a view of a perceiving subject, that does not make it idealist in Bergson's view. (The images *already* exist before the perceiving subject attends to them.) Nor is it determined by outside stimuli, because the perceiving subject would become overwhelmed by the images impinging upon it. By what Bergson calls *discernment* the subject selects some and not other images-stimuli to attend to.

Bergson goes on to distinguish between pure (or virtual) perception (as far as I can tell, an abstraction that does not exist) and lived perception. I don't claim to fully understand what he means by pure perception but here's an attempt. Though perception is always in the perspective of a particular subject, pure perception is the sum total of all possible perceptions or images graspable by all subjects in the world; yet at the same time he seems to speak of it as the sum of all the perceptions *possible* to one subject only (possible but not, I take him to mean, always actual). Lived or actual perception, on the other hand, has to do with all the images one takes in at any particular moment or discerns in order to act in the world.

Memory too is distinguished between pure or virtual and lived or bodily memory; pure memory does exist in the unconscious mind—it is more than an abstraction—and consists of *all* memories the subject has ever had (this is what is meant by a memory of the total past), whereas bodily memory is those memories retrieved from the unconscious for the subject's discernment and eventual action in the world now. It is with regard to the latter problem of discernment, if I understand Bergson correctly, that the image-movements of translation and rotation become pertinent.

But where, exactly, does duration come into this description of memory in Bergson's philosophy? It would appear to be at the point of contact S in Bergson's famous cone in *Matter and Memory* ([1908] 1991: 152, figure 4), the point of *action* which is also the quasi-instantaneous bodily memory. The point S is in actuality not a point in a spatial sense, though we might speak of it in such terms; it is not a terminus of duration, but duration itself. The one passage in *Matter and Memory* with the lengthiest discussion of duration is the following: "The duration wherein we see ourselves acting, *and in which it is useful that we should see ourselves*, is a duration whose elements are disassociated and juxtaposed. *The duration wherein we act* is a duration wherein our states melt into each other" (152, my emphasis). There appear to be two kinds of duration, just as there are two kinds of memory: one is of our reflexively "seeing ourselves" acting or imagining ourselves acting; the other is the duration of the act in the world. What we might call the structure of duration is different in each instance: in the former, that of reflection, the elements of duration are "disassociated" and "juxtaposed"; in the latter, that of action, the elements meld into each. As such, the entire analysis of the *Essai* is folded into image-perception and action in the world that are of fundamental concern in *Matter and Memory*, and the notion of duration is modified as a result.

I agree with Das's insight that duration, especially as understood by Bergson, is the very condition of subjectivity, and I turn now to a study of violence and mediation—to be sure a very different case from the one she examines in her book—to see how our developing understanding of Bergson's duration might prove fruitful.

CONFLICT MEDIATION IN YEMEN

When I did fieldwork in highland Yemen in 1980 on tribal poetry, an "event" of abduction occurred in which a young man, a *sayyid* (a descendant of the Prophet Muhammad) from a *hijrah* or sanctuary inhabited mostly by his kinsmen, was accused of absconding with two young women from a neighboring tribal village.

A lengthy mediation process ensued. It began when the father of the oldest of the kidnapped girls stormed into the hijrah to announce his accusations and to challenge the kinsmen of the accused, whom he held responsible for his action. He demanded they answer his charges by taking his dagger (*jambiyyah*) from its scabbard, which he held aloft for an instant, and then declared, "I challenge you!" He then handed his dagger to a person who happened to be standing next to him, thought to be a neutral party in the case, a low-status servant of the village by the name of Hussein, and by doing so designated him as the mediator. Hussein could not refuse; it is a moral obligation to try to resolve disputes peacefully even if one doesn't want to; there is no way to escape such a responsibility. The sheikh's accusers in the hijrah declared they were honorable men and would listen and respond to his charges. Their moral obligation to accept the mediation was as great as it was Hussein's to facilitate it. And so the mediation began. The whole process would not be over (if in fact these things are never "over") for another six months.

Hussein managed to secure a truce for twenty-four hours, until the sheikhs of the region (known as Khawlan) could come and take over from him. Meanwhile the sheikh's tribal followers positioned themselves with their rifles on the mountaintops surrounding the hijrah, threatening to attack if the young man accused of the crime were not found along with the two young women he had abducted. The truce was extended for another two days in order to give the search parties extra time to apprehend the missing. When they came back empty-handed, a round of violence began. The tribesmen surrounding the hijrah fired upon it, and the marksmen of the hijrah responded in kind. I was living in the hijrah at the time and was frightened, to say the least, at this turn of events but was assured by my friends that the tribesmen "did not mean it" and that this violence was merely a "game." I interpreted this to be a staged violence, a theatrical display of force, to signal the seriousness with which the accusers held the hijrah responsible for a terrible crime committed by one of their own, and that the dispute had better be resolved justly or the situation would become more serious. Indeed a new truce was declared, guaranteed by the defendant's holding two hijrah males hostage while the mediation continued.

This consisted of several rounds of talks, some in the hijrah, some in the plaintiff's village, presided over by leading regional sheikhs who tried to gather evidence, evaluate it, and then declare judgments of punishment and compensation in accordance with tribal law. Poetry was composed by the various parties in the mediation, attempting to analyze the case and deliver moral judgments about it. At first this poetry exhorted everyone to do the right thing and agree to a speedy resolution, but as the mediation dragged on (for reasons explained below) the poetry became more critical either of the plaintiff or the defendant, depending on how the poet saw the case, and this led to a polarization of views that in a sense made the situation more tense. Meanwhile it did not help matters that the search parties found the young man but not the two young women (or so it was assumed at the time), and under physical duress he confessed to having taken them out of the region and leaving them in a hotel in a southern city, where their trail then went cold. Fears of what happened to them worsened, the disgrace on their tribe deepened, and the sheikh would not agree to settle unless and until the women were found.

The weeks dragged on and their whereabouts remained a mystery, and so the mediators advised the aggrieved sheikh to accept the fact that they would never be found and that it would be best if he agreed to a final settlement. As often happens in the more significant disputes, the mediation became embroiled in larger political issues of the time (a power struggle between local sheikhs; a disagreement with the central government over its intentions of uniting with southern Yemen, the People's Democratic Republic of Yemen; and the meddling of Saudi Arabia in Yemen's internal affairs), with its goals held hostage to diverse political motives. Indeed one interpretation is that the plaintiff was persuaded by his supporters, a powerful tribe in eastern Yemen, to attack the hijrah on grounds that had to do with the tribe's larger political agenda rather than his own grievance over the disappearance of the women. Whatever the reasons, and they remain convoluted and obscure to this day, the hijrah was attacked and overrun three months after the initial event of abduction, leaving seven people dead (killed on the spot or expiring from their wounds later), though none, miraculously, were from the sanctuary.

Once again a truce was negotiated, and once again mediators were called in, this time at the highest level of the tribal system (in other words, the head sheikhs of the major tribal confederations in Yemen). Once again evidence was weighed and poetry declaimed, exhorting the two sides to come to a final resolution. And once again the process ran afoul of political machinations of various kinds. Words became more acrimonious and the situation devolved into armed violence again, this time with the plaintiff's village overrun by supporters of the hijrah. But this turned out to be the end of the matter. The two sides agreed to a final settlement, costing the hijrah dearly in fines and goods, with the young man handed over to the government for a protracted prison term. The two women were declared "lost." It had been six months since the initial salvo, when the sheikh stormed into the hijrah to make his denunciations.

Before going on to the question of temporality in the dispute mediation, one last point needs to be made. Violence does not have the same form throughout the dispute. At the beginning, it has the appearance of a "game" or a "staging" of violence, signaling that honor has been besmirched and requires restitution, but then there is a shift into violence of another sort, which we might call "brute force" or coercion, where blood might be shed. The first form declares that the defendant is still part of the moral community but needs to make amends if he is to remain within it; the second says that the defendant has forfeited the right to remain within the moral community. While it is possible analytically to distinguish these two kinds of violence, it has to be borne in mind that there is no abrupt or clear transition from one to the other in the *course* of the dispute itself. Whether one is in a moment of one form of violence or the other can in actuality be quite ambiguous, and I contend that this is necessarily so, for it is this ambiguity that allows room for maneuvering and pressure by all the parties in the dispute. The other point to bear in mind is that violence is not, as one might suppose, in contradiction with the concept of mediation but an essential part of it. Violence and mediation are in a dialectical relationship to each other throughout. It is easy to see why violence would call for mediation, though not so obvious, perhaps, why mediation would call for violence. Evans-Pritchard in his analysis of political behavior among the Nuer already understood this point: the possibility of violence—indeed its actuality—pressures disputants to resolve their differences in the end.

Yemen Chronicle

Among other things, my book grapples with questions of temporality in the dispute, though understood mainly in terms of an "event analysis" that had preoccupied a number of anthropologists and historians (Sahlins, Dening, Das, and Caton) at the time of its writing. My focus on the event was also influenced by the way my friends in the hijrah spoke about what had happened; they referred to it as the *hadith* (the happening), and later, as the event sprouted more and more complications for reasons I adumbrated earlier, they referred to it in the plural, as the *ahdath* (the events). In other words, an analytical focus, sharpened by theoretical concerns in anthropology, was congruent with a folk theory that tried to make sense of the world in seemingly similar terms.

Memory figured importantly in the event, in two senses. The first had to do with the memory of the subjects in the event who remembered past violence in the recently concluded Yemeni Civil War (1962–74) that inflected their feelings toward one or the other party in the dispute. It also figured importantly for me, an eyewitness to the event, because I narrated it twice—once in my diaries and field notes that were close in time to the actual event (and therefore also filled with lacunae and other problems that are inevitable in "eyewitness" accounts), and again in my book written more than twenty years later. In the course of that writing (or more accurately a palimpsest of writing, for I decided to include many of the texts of the first writing in the text of the second writing), I began to remember things about the event that I never wrote in my notes, diaries, or letters, though I was convinced they had occurred nonetheless—and in spite of the fact that they were recollected twenty years later. To put it differently, I wrestled with two memories of the event: the memory of what had just happened or what people told me had happened (a typical problem of memory in fieldwork) and the memory of what had happened years before. I believe it was Halbwachs who distinguished between similar acts of memories which he held to be distinct: the act of recollecting something (the willful construction of an account of what happened) and the act of involuntary memory that floods into consciousness.

This posed an epistemological challenge for me: Should I discredit the later memories because their contents were never inscribed in the initial act of recollection (on the grounds that field notes are the only legitimate basis of ethnography)? Or should I include the involuntary memories, in effect asking the reader to believe me when I said that the things the memories refer to existed or actually happened? Ethnographers always ask readers to believe in them as reliable narrators, as literary critics might say, because they rarely, if ever, get to see the ethnographer's field notes; why not, then, also ask readers to believe in them as reliable memory-agents? Indeed I claimed (though this cannot be tested) that most ethnographies are based on a combination of written notes and remembered materials, though the distinction is never made clear in the actual texts, nor is the epistemological challenges such a distinction might raise for the work in question adequately broached.

My purpose now in looking back on *Yemen Chronicle*'s analysis is certainly not to recant it but to consider how other facets or dimensions of temporality, namely duration, might, first of all, push the analysis further and, second, offer a provocation to rewrite *Yemen Chronicle*.

Before I begin that analysis, let me say a few things about how the book was written. *Yemen Chronicle* is a reflexive ethnographic account of the event just described, which occurred while I was in the field. I kept a diary of the event, and like most diaries, I broke up the entries into separate days of the month. It is a chronicle of the event, consisting of entries in which I try, as best as I could figure them out, to delineate the succession of "nows" that occurred (in the simple sense of "now this happened, now that" and so forth). When I was later arrested by national security police on suspicion of having been a foreign agent who was fomenting local unrest through the event, my notes were impounded and the villagers eventually learned of the diary and facetiously called me the historian (*mu'arrikh*) of the events (*ahdath*). In other words, they thought of me as their chronicler (hence one meaning of the word in the book's title, the other being a chronicle of field-work that was entangled in the event).

Like a diary, a chronicle breaks up time into discrete units, such as days of the week or months of the year, that are homogeneous in the sense that every day is like every other day and they follow each other in succession, waiting, as it were, to be filled by some "event" or other. Recalling Bergson, this is a notion of time on the analogy of extension in space, where each day is like a bounded, self-contained object, these "objects" stretching out in succession like books on a shelf.

But there are problems with this way of knowing the event, both for the anthropologist and for the indigenous actors in the event. To illustrate some of these problems, many of which I mention in the book, let us consider the kidnapping of the young women: at first I thought of it as a discrete moment, when a young man talked two tribal women into getting into his car, which he then drove out of the area, and I marked it as such by saying that it occurred on such-and-such a day of the chronicle. But how discrete is this event in fact? The kidnapping, an actual event, had a "before" and it certainly had an "after," and in representing this heinous act to themselves the villagers recollected other events that seemed to have endured (to use a Bergsonian term) in it. The kidnapping also anticipates other events (such as armed violence) that were entailed by it (these being virtual at the time of the kidnapping). By a "before," I do not mean a causal event necessarily (e.g., the possibility that the young man had fallen in love with one of the women), but more like a state or condition of relationship between the social group of the sayyids of the young man and the tribal group from which the women hailed that had endured in the act of kidnapping (let us call it a disposition of resentment and even mistrust); similarly for the "after," which might be a further rupture or continuation of that relationship.[2] Thus rather than a succession of discrete events, one has a duration of a state or states that interpenetrate. If a chronicle is not the best trope to capture this, what is? Do we even have a word for such a genre?

AN ANALYSIS OF DURATION IN THE EVENT

Let us now see how a Bergsonian notion of duration might be helpful for understanding the dispute's temporalities of violence and mediation. When the sheikh stormed into the hijrah to accuse the young sayyid man of abducting the women, the abduction was cast as the act of violence that provoked his response, or that his challenge was tragically a duration of it, albeit in a symbolic form of staged violence. Tragedy is precisely a sense that evil events have temporalities beyond their specific "nows," despite all that we might do to limit or contain them in those "nows"; the difference is that I am not speaking of a causal link of "nows" that one senses in tragedy (what is sometimes spoken of as its inevitableness) as much as an inexplicable confluence or convergence of them. It is difficult to make this clear, even if I am convinced of the distinction, but let me go on to describe the duration of violence. The sheikh's challenge prefigured or imagined the duration of the violence in an attack on the hijrah. This is to say that in the moment of his taking out his dagger and uttering his accusation, the past (in the form of the deed of abduction), the present (in the form of staged violence), and the future (in the form of premonition of an armed attack on the hijrah) were not aligned as so many causes or effects but were melded, as Bergson would have it, into a confluence of moments. How can this be? For those in the hijrah who knew about tribal disputes, and certainly for the tribesmen whose mediation process it was, after all, there was, upon reflection, an awareness of the distinct phases and forms of violence that could play themselves out (what Bergson would call their heterogeneity) but that in the actual act of the sheikh's challenge, they were melded together—or to borrow from another realm of analogy, oceans, these currents conjoined to form a powerful undertow whose frightening depth and pull threatened to catch us and send us into a vortex. And this was not to be the end of the consciousness of this abduction's violence and its duration, for it was always remembered as being virtual in the actual forms of violence that subsequently played themselves out in the dispute, the attack on the hijrah and then the attack on the plaintiff's village.

It would be a mistake to limit the analysis of duration to the problem of violence, however, for mediation too has a temporality essential to it. Once Hussein secured a truce and the sheikhs from Khawlan came to listen to the stories of the tribal village and the hijrah, the parties in the dispute were in a moment of mediation, one that was crucial to endure for a successful conclusion of hostilities. When the mediation broke down, as it did several times during the course of the six months that the dispute lasted, sheikhs at higher and higher levels of the regional and national tribal systems intervened and took over from the lower-level sheikhs whose efforts had come to naught, and they now had to persuade the disputants to remain *in* the moment of mediation rather than in the moment of coercive violence. Even this way of putting it is not precise enough, for it suggests that these temporalities of violence and mediation interrupt each other rather than having the dialectical relation I wish to claim for them. That is, it is not true that violence begins and mediation stops or vice versa (which is, as Bergson would say, a spatializing way of understanding temporality) but rather that they co-endure, though with one having more intensity or salience than the other at different moments in the dispute. Perhaps, following Bergson, we might resort to a musical analogy. Think of the temporalities of violence and mediation like voices in a fugue that not only are played simultaneously but intricately mingle and interact with each other, each urging the other on, each tempering the other.

Having learned from Bergson a rich and complex concept of duration, and having applied it to the analysis of the dispute mediation between a hijrah and a tribal village in Khawlan al-Tiyal in 1980, I now perform an experiment to see how such understandings might inspire a rewriting of *Yemen Chronicle*. I choose to rewrite the scene that opens chapter 2, "Anger Be Now Thy Song," that begins with the rumor that is spreading in the sanctuary about an abduction of two tribal women and is immediately followed by the entrance of the enraged sheikh who accuses a sayyid man from the hijrah of the abduction and then delivers his challenge and ultimatum. The original was a diary entry written on January 19, 1980, the day of the abduction, and was reproduced unchanged at the beginning of chapter 2.

> There is a rumor making the rounds of the stores. Two young tribal women from the neighboring hamlet, Sarkhan, were supposed to have been abducted by a man from another tribe.
>
> "See, Seif, how unruly and uncivilized the tribes are. Such a dreadful thing could never happen here, a place of piety and civilization. We are peace-loving and law-abiding."
>
> My friends in the sanctuary never tire of telling me that tribal Khawlan al-Tiyal is nothing but confusion and chaos, in which their little village is a haven of tranquility. Fawdha, a word akin to anarchy, is how they describe the region.
>
> Suddenly there is an uproar, every bit as shattering as an explosion. The sheikh from the village of Sarkhan has stormed into the marketplace alone, unarmed, and furious. He announces that two females, aged ten and fourteen, are missing from his village, and accuses a nephew of one of the sanctuary sada of abducting them.
>
> "It must be a terrible mistake or misunderstanding," one man exclaims. His comrades concur, for it is unthinkable to them that one of their own should have committed such a terrible deed.
>
> "There's no mistake," the sheikh avers grimly. "Summon to me the man responsible for the boy."

When the latter—who happens to be the uncle, not the father—arrives, the sheikh from Sarkhan performs the ritual I have seen on other, less serious occasions of public disagreement or protest. He removes his dagger—the beautiful curved silver blade with the gazelle-horn handle known through Yemen as the jamiyya—from its sheath and, for an instant holding it aloft, where it catches the glint of afternoon sun, pronounces the words "I challenge you!" He hands the dagger to a third party who happens to be standing nearby. He is Hussein the Servant. For the time being, this man is to be the mediator of the dispute, until the more important sheikhs can be summoned to resolve it. The uncle ruefully utters the conventional response, "And I am respectful," passing his thumb across his forehead, a gesture familiar to me from other occasions when I saw this ritual performed, and signaling the defendant's readiness to listen to the charges. He, too, then hands his dagger to the mediator.

In vain Hussein tries to soothe the sheikh's anger. Not only does he accuse the boy, and his uncle who is responsible for him, of the most heinous crime imaginable, but he holds the entire sanctuary accountable. He renews his challenge, only this time broadening its scope:

"If the girls and the boy are not found and returned to Sarkhan before sundown, the sanctuary will be plunged into war."

He then departs as quickly as he has come. Hussein the Servant scurries after him. The rest of the men in the marketplace close ranks around the uncle, reassuring him that there must be some grotesque misunderstanding, which will be cleared up momentarily—yet I can see that they are unnerved.

Here is the rewritten scene:

How could it be, he kept asking himself, that what the little shepherd boy had said was true, and the young man they called Abdullah, the same who had been hanging around the village in the past few days, had made off with his own daughter and niece in his white Toyota. He grieved for her, his beautiful, intelligent, strong-willed daughter, the favorite of his children, the one he had slated for marriage to the son of the great Sheikh al-Dailami in the east. True, she had opposed the idea, but in time she would accept the great honor such a match would bestow upon her and her tribe. A twinge of suspicion about her came over him, but he repressed it. In any case, she was lost to the sheikh's son now, not to speak of being lost to her own father, who had loved her more dearly than anyone else in this world. He began to burn with shame. People would say that he had been careless, allowing Abdullah to hang around his children when he did not know him personally or question his intentions, and that he brought this dishonor on himself and his family through his own lack of vigilance. But Abdullah was a sayyid and a son of the hijrah, so he had of course trusted him. He realized now what a fool he had been. Anger like bile rose in his throat, choking him, as he thought of this betrayal. How could the hijrah, which his tribe had protected during countless conflicts in the past, including the Civil War, have raised such a boy to act so monstrously toward their neighbors and friends? Fear was mingled with these emotions, fear of what would happen after he had confronted them with his accusation, fear of the war that would erupt if they could not come up with the Culprit Abdullah, his daughter, and his niece. He had been called in to mediate many disputes and knew what would be in store in this one, the difference being that now he was the plaintiff in the case. He hoped this terrible mess would end after he and his men made a show of force by ringing the hijrah with his guns and maybe firing upon it, wounding one of sayyids perhaps as a way of getting back some of his honor. But if Abdullah and the girls were not found, he could not see a good outcome to this. There would be no way of making amends.

He entered the sanctuary and stood in the middle of the souq. He said nothing at first, just stood there, with a terrible look on his face, a look of someone struggling to contain his emotions enough so that he could carry out the ritual he knew he had to perform, a ritual he had performed countless times before but never on such a momentous occasion. The people in the market began to notice him, began to notice the expression on his face, and they grew quiet as they meekly assembled before him. They were filled with bewilderment and dread, for they knew he would not stand in the way he did, like a statue, without greeting them, without saying a friendly word, unless he was upset, something for which they were to blame.

"Summon to me the man responsible for the boy, Abdullah." And then it occurred to them, as if they had been struck by a lightning bolt, that the rumor that had been making the rounds was true, that one of their own stood accused of having abducted the two tribal girls. How was this possible? They were genuinely incredulous. One of their own did this? Impossible. This was some horrible mistake. The sheikh grimly shook his head, signaling that there was no mistake.

Suddenly the uncle of Abdullah appeared, confused and afraid. It was explained to the sheikh that the father was away, in Sana'a. The sheikh turned to face this man and then performed the ritual. He took out his jambiyyah from its scabbard, held it aloft, where it glinted for a split second with the reflection of the sun, and pronounced the dread formula, "I challenge you [I hold you to account]!" Everyone witnessing the act had the same terrible and sinking feeling, that something awful had flowered into this poisonous bloom, one that would sow a field of unwanted weeds they would struggle to extirpate for months, even years to come. "If the boy and the girls are not found and returned to Sarkhan before sundown, the sanctuary will be plunged into war."

Let me say at the outset that I do not claim to know what was going through the sheikh's mind the moment he confronted the hijrah with his accusations. For all I know it could have been that he wanted to strike everyone in sight, so furious was he at the hijrah. What I am attempting is a representation of a consciousness that is the foundation of a particular subjectivity (as Das would say), positioned in a certain way in the social system (as father, tribal leader, a one-time supporter of the descendants of the Prophet, a plaintiff in a case, a tactician in a mediation process in which he had participated numerous times before and therefore knew well, and so forth), and what content and form such a representation might take. This is a different understanding of consciousness in a psychological sense: it is a construct or an imagined interiority. It might help to know that every thought attributed to him in my passage was at one time or another attributed to him either by his followers, the mediators, or the inhabitants of the hijrah, attempting to "explain" his position in the dispute by asking me to put myself empathetically in his place. For example, when I asked why the sheikh persisted in "dragging out" the dispute, I was told to put myself in his position—or, as I might say now, to understand the consciousness of someone in his position—and then I would realize that a father would not easily give up on finding his own child even if success seems less and less likely. In a similar vein I attribute thoughts to people in the hijrah that were actually attributed by those same people days if not weeks after the event; for all I know in the actual scene of confrontation with the sheikh they were thinking about the safety of themselves and their loved ones. The point is not to get into anyone's head but to construct or imagine a consciousness focusing on the perception of duration from a certain subject position and within a particular event.

The passage is structured in two parts, the first capturing some of the sheikh's interior thoughts and emotions, in which time is heterogeneous and juxtaposed (the various "nows" of the abduction, the time of the Civil War, the anticipated time of troubles ahead, etc., being turned around and examined in the sheikh's head), the second part being duration in the *act* of his challenge delivered to the people of the sanctuary in which these times are melded and made continuous with each other. I have done this in response to Bergson's reworking of the concept of duration in *Matter and Memory* discussed earlier. Another thing to note is that I struggled with how to represent this idea of duration and chose certain metaphors for this purpose (just as Bergson struggled with metaphors from music and visual media of his day for the same purpose). Thus the metaphor of the weed (admittedly stolen from Shakespeare) is meant to convey something that sprouts from a seed and continues to grow and endure through time.

Here it is rewritten as something else, as the subjective consciousness or interiority of the sheikh, the father whose daughter and niece had been abducted. Obviously it is something I have imagined, for this passage was not reconstructed from anything the sheikh or the people of the sanctuary had said to me at the time. Had I chosen to rewrite a different passage in which I speak of my *own* consciousness of temporality as duration, I might have avoided having to bracket it as imagined, as opposed to, say, recollected, because it is someone else's interiority being represented. But this illustrates the challenge of attempting to capture this kind of temporality ethnographically. Unless one asks the right sort of questions of the informant or friend, it is difficult to access this sort of interiority and have anything very specific or detailed to say about it. Because I focused on the question of the event at the time of the initial fieldwork—how it was represented in public discourse, especially in poetry, and how people attempted to make sense of it (or failed to do so)—the question of duration, which one might say subsumes the event within itself, was, if not exactly lost, then certainly obscured. I could not, then, rewrite *Yemen Chronicle* from this angle, only passages that might qualify as imagined or even purely fictive. This does raise the larger question of whether it would be interesting and even possible to do fieldwork with a focus on duration per se and then write an ethnography that would capture this subjective consciousness of duration throughout the work rather than merely periodically. I know of no such work, but perhaps there ought to be one.

NOTES

1. Among the commentators on Bergson's philosophy, certainly the most famous is Gilles Deleuze in his book *Le Bergsonisme* (1968) and two essays that appeared in a collection, *L'Ile deserte et autres texts* (2007), in particular the essay "La conception de la différence chez Bergson." I am mindful, of course, of the way Deleuze draws on Bergson's thoughts on visual perception from *Matter and Memory* in his own volumes on cinema, but this is too complex a matter for this essay. Besides Deleuze, it is worth bearing in mind that there are at least two other magisterial commentaries on Bergson. One is *Henri Bergson* (1959) by Vladimir Jankélévitch, a book-length study that very patiently explicates Bergson's ideas and places them within the history of philosophy (something Deleuze does not do); the other, a series of essays by Merleau-Ponty, "Eloge de la philosophie" (1960b) and "Bergson se faisant" (1960a). (By the way, William James in both *Pragmatism* [1907] and *A Pluralistic Universe* [1909] had insightful things to say about Bergson. The two corresponded with each other and read each other's work deeply. It has been argued, in fact, that it was James's *Principles of Psychology* [1890] more than any other psychological work of the time that influenced Bergson's way of thinking about action and thought in his *Matter and Memory*.)

2. Where this Bergsonian analysis may break down is that while in this philosopher's view duration is a matter of quality and thus of consciousness, a consciousness that is deeply embedded in the self—a self that is moreover socially constructed—the analysis does not necessarily help us understand how the consciousness of duration might be different for differently positioned individuals within the social system. Could one even ask in this perspective whether the consciousness of duration is intersubjectively constituted?

CHAPTER 11

Must We Be Bad Epistemologists?:
Illusions of Transparency, the Opaque
Other, and Interpretive Foibles

Vincent Crapanzano

■ In the early 1960s, I was asked to translate and transcribe an exchange, if it can be called that, between an American Air Force pilot and a Soviet pilot whose plane had entered West German airspace. It was the height of the cold war. I had been drafted and taught Russian and served in various capacities as a translator.[1] In this case, I was probably confirming a translation that had been made several times by various intelligence agencies. The exchange was unforgettable—just words repeated over and over again. It ran something like this:

> American pilot (in a slow, steady voice, entirely unemotional): Please identify yourself. You have entered West German airspace. You have sixty seconds [or two minutes—I don't remember exactly how long] to exit.
> Russian pilot (in a younger, panicked voice): *Ya ne ponimajo.* I don't understand. I don't know where I am. Please. My instruments have failed. I don't speak English. Please. Speak Russian.
> American pilot (in the same monotone): You have entered West German airspace. If you don't exit in sixty seconds [?] I will fire.

As the exchange was repeated, the Russian pilot's terror grew, and the American's voice tightened in frustration. "I will have to fire. Get out! Get out!" he cried. "I am about to fire." There followed the briefest, longest silence, the ratata of gunshots, a scream, the whining of a crashing plane, and a laughter I had never heard before and hope never to hear again. The American pilot was laughing uncontrollably. It was an empty laughter, devoid of all meaning, all understanding, primordial, surging, or so it seemed to me, from the depths of his being, an expression of horror from an unwilling perpetrator. It marked an absolute break in a contact—phatic, personal, intimate—between two men trapped in an inevitability that ought never to have been.

The pilots' encounter was far more complex than it might at first appear. It was not simply a failure of communication that occurred because neither pilot understood the language of the other or because, as enemies, they could not trust each other. The circumstances were fraught with danger. Lesser occasions have been *causae belli* in circumstances far less tense than those of the cold war. The pilots had been prompted by the seriousness of their mission. But, in their desperation, these concerns were lost to an immediate danger. Two enemies, alone, in midair, engaged in the most intimate fashion possible with each other. There could be no trust between them, but trust, bathed even in mistrust, was demanded. No, they did not understand each other.

Yes, they understood each other: their mutual terror, their helplessness, the impotence of their words, eventually their pleas, and their anticipation, their certainty, of the inevitable.

They were connected in an un-understanding that was embedded in the deepest understanding—one that was conveyed by sounds, yes, words, empty of meaning, incarnating significance. They knew. Opacity had surrendered to transparency in that briefest, longest moment. That I knew absolutely, as I listened again and again to those words, those sounds. Such was their power.

But did I know? Did they know? Could I know? Could they know? I knew nothing about them—that is, in any normal sense of who they were. They knew nothing about each other. And yet . . .

■ I begin with this memory, for it evokes several of the themes I discuss in this chapter. I am concerned with those moments of un-understanding, of the haunting possibility of the total or near-total absence of understanding, and with how those moments, that possibility, figures (if only through denial) in human relationships. I am, in other words, concerned with the opacity of the other and, by extension, with the threat of solipsism, the existence and knowledge of other minds, phatic (bodily) connection, empathetic capacity, projective manipulation and responsibility—in short, with what it means to know someone.

Philosophers have been concerned with these questions at least since Hegel elevated the *other* to a category of philosophical inquiry.[2] Anglo-American and Continental philosophers have taken different, at times radically different approaches to them, but they generally share in their claims to universalism an uncritical ethnocentrism.[3]

Whatever their position, they rest their arguments on examples that, for the most part, they seem to invent without due regard to the social and cultural contexts in which they advance them and their supporting examples or to the diegetic contexts of the examples they use. I suggest that some of the confusion that surrounds the knowledge of the other, the existence of other minds, and solipsism, rests on most philosophers' failure to use as the generative basis for their arguments actual, richly contextualized examples. My position is clearly that of an ethnographer.

In what follows I look at how events, taken for the most part from my fieldwork, determine the parameters of—and evidence for—our knowledge and understanding of the other. Although my focus is primarily on interlocution and, in consequence, on linguistic and communicative conventions,[4] I also consider the experiential background of these engagements (or non-engagements), as I have tried to in my discussion of the pilots' encounter and my encounter with their encounter. I am concerned in particular with the constitutive effect of communicative conventions (e.g., speech genres), interpersonal etiquette (e.g., appropriate ways of being with someone) and their transgression (e.g., eroticizing a manifestly nonerotic meeting), and the confusion of speech genres on modes of knowing, interpreting, and manipulating (what transpires in the mind of) the other. I am equally interested in what I take to be the experiential *Anlage* (e.g., loneliness, isolation) of philosophical concepts like solipsism, but given the scope of my discussion, I can make only implicit reference to their linkage. My essay is meant to be suggestive and not conclusive. I will be asking many more questions than I can answer or even that are answerable. I make no claim to philosophical rigor, though I hope the philosophical and ethnological implications of what I have to say will create the disquiet that I take to be one of the primary missions of both disciplines.

■ Given a prevailing epistemology—one to which I am not immune—that worries about other minds, about the opacity of the other, and about the threat, or rather the reality, of solipsism, I am forced into an ill-fitting skepticism.[5] As social actors, we are obliged by the standards of that epistemology to be bad epistemologists. Social engagement requires knowledge of the other: of what that other is thinking, planning, and expecting. Interpretation is pushed beyond its limits. This is particularly true in those societies, like the Euro-American, where interiority is the locus of assurance: the metaphorical ground for certainty. We can never know the mind of the other, and yet we must act as if we do. The interiority of the other becomes a locus of projection, hypothesis, and speculation, all of which we tend to ignore, at least in ordinary social transactions. In facilitating social engagement, convention, etiquette, and habituation mask the hypothetical quality of the assumptions we make about the other. But I suggest that lurking behind what comfort that masking offers is the terror—the governance—of the opacity of the other and at times oneself.[6]

But are there other epistemologies—those of the heart, for example—that do not focus on an unknown other? Do their adherents find assurance in interiority? Or do they look to the external—the body—for assurance (Duranti 1988)? Does the exterior offer sufficient indices of engagement, commitment, and prediction? Does the moral override the epistemological? Can the two be separated? To what extent are these epistemological concerns symptoms of the fragmentation and alienation that have accompanied the rise of modernity?

I raise these questions, in part, to call attention to the play of different epistemological assumptions in social exchanges. They are particularly important in the progression and evaluation of anthropological research, especially when the anthropologist is working with "exotic" peoples. Then epistemological differences or their effect on interpersonal relations and styles of communication are particularly salient. They are, under normal circumstances, far less obvious when researchers are working in their own society or in one that has become so familiar that the differences are taken for granted. This is one of the dangers inherent in fieldwork in one's own society, above all when the researcher has had little or no cross-cultural experience. True, the ethnographic stance demands a certain distancing from—an exoticizing of—the people under observation, but that perceptual artifice, that *Verfremdungeffekt*, to use Brecht's term, is still rooted in one's own culture without any cross-cultural corrective.

■ I am confronted with the Other—others in all their complexity, their opacity, the responsibility they demand of us, the morality they source, their presumed desire for recognition, to be known and yet preserve a secret, a mystery, the wholly personal, that preserves identity despite inner and outer contextual pressures.

I think of my first encounters with the people I have studied. I am the object of their gaze—their curiosity, their fear, their friendliness, their caring, their suspicion, and their self-interest. Despite what empathy, what intuitive capacity, I have, I can never fully know what they are experiencing. Their gaze may draw me in, welcomingly, lovingly, or penetrate me with such terrifying aggression that, overcome with the fear of being fully known, without a secret, judged, I freeze, become an object to myself—their creation.

Note the contradiction! It's important: *I cannot know the other, but the other can know me.*

In a defensive gesture, supported by my anthropology, I turn my gaze on them. I objectify them. Their bodies, faces, eyes become objects of a desperate hermeneutics. I turn them into informants.

But I want them to be more than informants. I want them to be friends. I want them to know me, as I would like to be known. I want to be as open as possible. I want us to live, despite its perils, in the solicitude of the intersubjective. How else can we converse? Come to know each other? Cooperate in my research?

Most anthropological accounts of first meetings emphasize, anecdotally, the opacity of the other and the relief the anthropologist feels when that opacity gives way to something—some thought, some attitude, some emotion—that he or she recognizes. Far less attention is paid to how anthropologists reveal themselves, in terms not only of their explanations of why they are there but of their affective responses, their gestures, tones of voice, expressions of interest and concern. Do they smile? Do they laugh? Do they push? Do they settle back and relax? We assume that they do not know the conventions of getting to know someone that are prevalent in the society they are entering—that they find themselves in an extremely perplexing situation and, under the circumstances, can have little perspective on themselves. They are, I suggest, particularly insensitive to the paralexical messages they send out. They often, as has happened to me, focus on only one of those potential clues—blushing, for example, or a tightened voice, or sweating, or wringing of hands.

■ It was a Sunday afternoon. I entered the house of the *moqaddem* (the leader) of a team of exorcists, the Hamadsha, in a shantytown in Meknes

(Crapanzano 1973). I had come to Morocco to study the Hamadsha's curing practices. I had met the moqaddem and several of his musicians the previous Friday after a public ceremony they perform every week, the object of which, at the time, seemed to me to be simply mercenary. I told him I was so impressed by the ceremony that I would like to discuss it with him in private. The moqaddem led me into a room, which, to my surprise, was packed with men and women. They eyed me. I was taken aback, speechless. I had no idea who they were, what they were thinking. With the help of my field assistant, who was not from Meknes and who did not know any of them, I explained my intentions. They listened attentively, without expression—at least that is how I saw them. No one said a word. Their silence was as unbearable as their scrutinizing. I went on talking, nervously repeating myself, as I tried to elicit a response from them. I was sure that they would never agree to work with me. Then, when I had nothing more to say, I fell silent, as did my assistant, who, I learned later, had felt as I did. He had been particularly upset by the fact that they had not even offered us tea—an egregious breach of Moroccan hospitality.

The silence seemed endless. I wanted to flee. And then Dawia, the wife of the moqaddem, broke the silence by asking me whether I had had any dreams before coming to Meknes. I had had one that seemed relevant, but since I had no idea how it would be interpreted, I hesitated to tell it. All eyes were on me, expectant. That expectation left me no choice. I had to tell them my dream, no matter how they would understand it. *I am lying on the floor of a* qobba *(one of the little white shrines that dot the Moroccan countryside in which, it is believed, a saint was buried or, as the Moroccans say, lived). The hennaed and bejeweled hand of a woman reaches in through a narrow slit window and pulls me out. I am amazed. How could I have passed through such a narrow slit? I wake up.* Upon hearing my dream, everyone in the room began talking excitedly, nodding, saying, "Yes, yes," and looking at me with open curiosity. Finally, Dawia said, "Aïsha, Lalla Aïsha, has sent for you. Welcome." Her welcome was repeated by all of the moqqadem's guests. Tea was served. Though I didn't know what Dawia meant, my relief was enormous. I was bombarded with questions about where I had come from, how long I was going to stay, where I was living. Was I married? Did I have a family? Was my wife in Meknes? Would I take photographs? Would I write my book in French, Arabic, or English?

Dawia was referring to Aïsha Qandisha, the principal *jinniyya*, or she-demon, with whom the Hamadsha have dealings. At the time, I thought that her appearance in my dream had simply authenticated me. It certainly did that, since the Hamadsha became the most open and cooperative, indeed friendly people with whom I have ever worked. But now I realize that her visitation was more than an authorization. For the men and women in the room, it was a way of knowing me. I had revealed through the dream and, presumably, through the way I told it a significant dimension of myself. What I didn't know then was that Dawia had taken an enormous risk, for she, like all Moroccans of her milieu, believed that in telling a dream you convey to your interlocutor its blessing if it is a good dream or its evil if it is a bad one. I also did not know that often, when a stranger—I, for example—entered a village in the nearby Gharb plains, where many of the Hamadsha came from, the women he first met, less often the men, would tell him that they had dreamed of his coming, even though they had never met or even heard of him before. It was a mode of greeting, but also a sign of recognition.

The dream not only initiates a relationship but gives it an oneiric dimension and, in consequence, an ontological status and interpretive privilege that overrides the ordinary. It gives access to—for lack of a better term—the person, but insofar as the dream mediates a relationship, it is impossible, I believe, to separate the dreamer from the dreamed, as Yeats might have put it, or the dream narrator from his or her interlocutor. In other words, the dream has power. The knowledge of the dreamer, if knowledge it is, is, I believe, attitudinal and, at a remove, morally evaluative rather than conceptual.

The Moroccans speak of knowledge of the heart (*qalb*), and I believe they would refer to this attitudinal knowledge in terms of the heart.[7] It is an unfolding, a hovering, as it were, between the actual and the potential. This is not to say that Moroccans are incapable of discussing people and relationships in conceptual terms. They are keen, often skeptical observers who, in my experience, are concerned with intentions and masked intentions. Despite their emphasis on knowledge of the heart, their skepticism extends to their knowledge of the other.

It is often expressed in dismissive terms, especially when whoever they are referring to has acted badly. "What can I know?" they ask. "Only God knows." The seeming contradiction between these two attitudes toward knowing the other is less salient when understood not in epistemological terms but in moral-evaluative ones. There are people whose immoral stature precludes knowledge of the heart, though the heart may "alert" you to their untrustworthiness, their evil. They must be treated, if treated at all, with great caution.

I cannot, of course, vouch for the accuracy of my depiction of Moroccan modes of knowing the other, especially since it was not central to my research. My point, however, is that knowing the other, the other's thoughts, is subject to social conventions that are deeply rooted in the epistemological and moral assumptions of a people.

▓ What in fact do we mean when we say we know another person? What do we mean when we say we know what someone is thinking? What are we referring to when we speak of other minds? Are we referring to whatever we mean by subjectivity? Consciousness? Its locus, if in fact it has a locus? Thought? Perception? Emotion? Sensation? Imagination? Or intuition?

Saul Kripke (1982: 126), discussing Wittgenstein on other minds, asks if we have any idea of what a mind is. Can we ever experience the world as the other does? Can we experience the pain of the other—as the other experiences it? (Why is pain so frequently used as an example in the speculations about other minds?) Can we accept what the other says he or she is thinking, feeling, or imagining as evidence of (what he or she is) thinking, feeling, sensing, or imagining? Wittgenstein ([1958] 1973: 90, 256) asks, "Now, what about the language which describes my inner experiences [*Erlebniße*] and which only I myself can understand? How do I use words to stand for sensations?—As we ordinarily do? Then are my words for sensations tied up with my natural expressions of sensation? In that case my language is not a 'private' one. Someone else might understand it as well as I.—But suppose I didn't have any natural expression [?] for the sensation, but only had the sensation? And now I simply associate names with sensations and use these names in descriptions."

Are we required to take a skeptical stance whenever anyone reports what he or she is thinking, feeling, sensing, or imagining? Indeed that he or she is thinking, feeling, sensing, or imagining? We cannot separate these reports from the contexts in which they occur. They serve rhetorical purposes. They have illocutionary and perlocutionary force. They are understood in accordance with prevailing communicative conventions. Some of these conventions are rooted directly in the grammar of language. I am thinking specifically of those languages, Estonian, Pomo, Quechua, and Tanana (an Arawak language), that require evidential and/or epistemic particles that indicate the source of—and the degree of confidence speakers have in—the information they are conveying (Aikhenvald 2004: 1–11).

That speakers use expressions that manifestly report inner experiences—thoughts, feelings, or dreams—does not mean that they have in fact had these experiences. They may simply be exploiting the rhetorical force of inner experience to convince their interlocutors of what they are saying. This *manniera de communicarse* was certainly true of the Alumbrados and other Spanish baroque mystics (de Certeau 1992: 156). Do we have any evidence, for that matter, that Saint Augustine actually experienced his conversion as he describes it in his *Confessions*? Or was it an elaboration designed to facilitate the conversion of his readers? Did the Fundamentalist preacher actually *feel* he had reached rock bottom? Or had he actually lost all hope until Jesus spoke to him? Does the libertine really feel the love he claims? Did the women in Gharb who greeted me with a dream really have the dream?

Reports of inner experience have to be evaluated in terms of the evidentiary force a people give to inner experience. As I have argued in *Imaginative Horizons* (Crapanzano 2004: 1003–120), we cannot accept such reports at face value, as many phenomenologically oriented anthropologists (including me, at times) have done, unless we take into consideration the epistemological weight given to inner experience and the moral commitment to mimetic accuracy. Those ethnographies that, like Godfrey Lienhardt's (1987) *Divinity and Experience: The Religion of the Dinka* or, for that matter, my own early work on the Hamadsha, attempted to reconstruct the intentional or motivational structure of subjective experience of peoples who articulate their intentions, as *patiens*, in terms of spirits, failed to give due consideration to the metaphorical, indeed the ontological weight given to the spirits.

My late friend, the Moroccan artist Ahmed el Yacoubi, showed me an extraordinarily powerful picture of a woman's face emerging indistinctly, mysteriously from a cloudy background, which he had painted the previous week. He looked at it in wonderment and fear, as if it had been painted by someone else. "I was made to paint her. I saw her. She gave me no choice. She moved my hands, my brushes, my colors." "She?" I asked. Ahmed answered indirectly, with a turn of phrase that indicated a jinniyya, possibly Lalla Aïsha, as he pointed nervously at the face in the picture. I said it reminded me of Laurel, the woman he had been living with and with whom he had just broken up. "Yes, it was she. She came to me through that door, at night." I did not press Ahmed. I knew him well enough (!) to know that "she" referred at once to Laurel and to the jinniyya.

Muses can be dangerous. Even when they are simply rhetorical, they always represent more than we (want to) assume they do. They emerge, we say, from the depths of the psyche, from that mysterious no-place we call the unconscious, in which alien identities coalesce and familiar ones are sundered. But need we place this no-place in the psyche? Did the Hamadsha? Would the Dinka? Would Saint Teresa? Milarepa? Homer? No-place can perhaps be any-place. How can we know? Must we assume a common place to communicate? To know each other?

But how do we know we are communicating? Isn't that as problematic as knowing the other? Can we dismiss the problem on pragmatic grounds? And in so doing, do we lose something? Gain something? The freedom or the isolation—the infinite solitude—of the hypothetical?

The philosopher Alec Hyslop (2009: 4–5) notes that there are three principal grounds on which philosophers justify our beliefs about other minds: (1) the best-example one, that is, the assumption that others have an inner life is the best indicator of their conduct; (2) the analogical one, that is, that as others behave as I do they must be endowed with a mind like mine; and (3) the criterial one, in which behavior is simply regarded as a criterion for the existence of their minds. Inference is sidestepped.[8] It is, of course, one thing to justify a belief and another to hold it—to believe.

Do we ever doubt, that is, experientially, the existence of other minds? Why has the existence of other minds become a philosophical preoccupation? Does it relate to a singular epistemology in which abstraction is severed from experience—the experience that founds it? In which, as Walter Benjamin (1968b: 155–57) argued, experience (*Erlebnis*) has been diminished with the rise of modernity? In which belief, the conceptualization of belief, is cut off from believing? Does solipsism preclude the belief in other minds? It is not as strange a question as it might first appear to be. Solipsistically I can believe in other minds as entities within my mind's close. Do I then treat solipsism ironically? Does solipsism preclude an ironic stance? Can I separate arguments for solipsism from solipsistic experience? From feelings of isolation, loneliness, *Angst*, and absolute solitude? From an inward turn in which the world—the other—fades away? Or, in an opposite, centripetal move, in which the world—the other—is drawn in? Do the two moves constitute the same experience? The same abstraction of that experience? Ought we to distinguish two (perhaps more) concepts of solipsism?

■ The threat that we are not communicating, that we are not understood, that we can never know if we have been understood, produces an anxiety that governs our relations and mode of communication with our interlocutors. We repeat. We rephrase. We plead. We manipulate. We gesticulate. We look. We touch. And we reflect, responsively.

Obviously, though largely ignored, every exchange is accompanied by what I have called shadow dialogues—the silent mentation, the self-conversation, that accompanies all exchanges and is in response, at least tangentially, to those exchanges (Crapanzano 1992: 213–15). They affect the course of the exchanges they shadow both dramatically and in terms of content. Put simply: What is my interlocutor really thinking about? What and why am I saying or doing what I am saying or doing? What is he getting at? Who does she think I am? We can never really know what these conversations are in our interlocutors and, strictly speaking, in ourselves, insofar as they are recollected and therefore subject minimally to what transpired in the interim between the thought and its recall.

There are two characteristics of shadow dialogues that are pertinent to the dynamics of interlocution that require mention here. Both concern the interlocutor. (1) Is the interlocutor an objectification of an "I," a "me"? Or is the interlocutor the person with whom one is dialogically engaged? Or is the interlocutor "impure," a blurring of the two interlocutors: the "me" and the dialogical partner. We might want to understand this blurring of identities in psychological terms, but it also deserves grammatical consideration. (2) Unlike the primary dialogue in which the interlocutor is always a "you" (a second-person indexical pronoun), in the shadow dialogues the interlocutor may be either a "you" or a "he" or a "she"—a referential pronoun. "I wonder what on earth you mean by that." "I wonder what on earth he means by that."[9] We may understand the use of the third person here as a distancing objectification of the "you." How these two characteristics relate to one another has yet to be worked out. It would appear, though, that the complex grammar of the other (as "you" and/or "he" or "she") suggests that the other (at least as it is interpolated) is never simply a static objectification of the referential pronoun ("he" or "she") but subject as a "you" to the indexical progress of an exchange—to the shifts in identity that occur during the conversation. The other is as such inconstant. This pronominal shifting furthers an ambivalent relationship with that other. As a "you," it draws one in or repels. It is, in any case, dynamically personal, engaging. As a "he" or "she," it is distanced, subject to judgment and criticism, and tends toward the static, depersonalized, and observable.[10]

My concern is less with the content of such shadowing than with its effect on our exchanges, including the shadow dialogues themselves. How are our exchanges affected by our reluctant acknowledgment of them? What are the consequences of the immediately unknown, the unknowable, on our exchanges? Do the unknown and the unknowable open a space of assumption, projection, and empathy? Must we perceive the shadow dialogues as necessarily evaluative? Judgmental? The gaze, by the way, is never simply a look; it too is evaluative.[11] Evaluation is, of course, not necessarily negative.

Do the constraints—the focalization—of rational discourse, as Habermas would insist, or of communicative and moral conventions, override the effect of shadow dialogues on the progress of our personal engagements? They too may be subject to the same constraints.

◼ Our awareness of and the elaboration of these shadow dialogues in our interlocutors and in ourselves vary with the intensity of the exchange. I imagine they were minimal and sporadic for the two pilots engaged in a life-and-death struggle. For me, listening to a recording of their words, knowing that the Soviet plane had been shot down but not knowing whether the pilot had survived, my silent reflections were maximal as I struggled to make sense of what they were saying and reconstruct what had happened. On a more mundane level, shadowing is probably minimal in the heat of lovemaking but not in seduction. In other situations, such as negotiating a contract or deposing a witness, shadow dialogues can be quite complex and may in fact play a rhetorical role, as, for example, when interlocutors pause, knit their brows, or otherwise indicate that they are thinking to themselves but are not revealing what they are thinking.

Shadowing is cultivated in professional encounters, such as anthropological fieldwork and psychotherapy. Although psychotherapists and psychoanalysts have reflected on the methodological and interpretive implications of free association, anthropologists have given little attention to the role of mentation that accompanies their exchanges in the field on the progress of their research, the nature and quality of their findings, and the interpretation of those findings. They certainly played a significant role in my research on whites living in apartheid South Africa in the early 1980s. They were, I am sure (!), always asking themselves what I was really thinking as they talked to me, just as I was asking myself whether they really meant what they were saying or were saying what they thought would make an appropriate impression on me. My questions and comments were often designed to discover their "true" thoughts, opinions, and feelings, and many of them seemed to know exactly what I was doing. For some, our exchanges became an irresponsible duel, and if those exchanges departed too far from whatever my informants thought was too serious, too fundamental, too dangerous for such play, they would begin to argue heatedly with me (often without knowing, only imagining, what I thought) or they would sink into uncooperative sulks. (Note that my descriptions of these encounters requires a "knowing" what they were thinking.)

Om Piet and his cousin Max, two of the most conservative Afrikaners I met, received me with conventional hospitality, tempered by suspicion and curiosity, on Om Piet's farm in the village I have called Wyndal in the Cape province where I conducted most of my research. From the start they sparred with me, laughing, pulling my leg, and teasing me with stereotypes of the "Yanks," but when I asked them about why the schools for blacks received so little funding compared with those for whites, they grew angry. Om Piet said I had not been in South Africa long enough to understand the situation. "Kafirs are slow learners. We want to educate them, but it takes time. Look, it took three hundred years to get them to wear pants and shirts. Three hundred years! You and your President Carter and your Waldheim—he's the worst of the lot, running that communist organization filled with Kafirs—want to rush us. But they don't know the Kafirs." Max added, "It's easy for you Americans to talk. You killed off your Red Indians. We never did that to our blacks. What right have you to tell us . . ." Om Piet interrupted him and, by asking me if I wanted to see the apple and pear orchids, ended the interview. I was thankful that they had not given me time to respond, since I wasn't at all sure I could maintain my ethnographic perspective.

■ What are true thoughts, opinions, and feelings? What does "true" mean? What are the criteria that determine the true?

Of the multitude of answers that have been given to this question by philosophers and psychologists, I would stress the role of genre—speech, literary, and behavioral genres—on the construction and evaluation of the thoughts, opinions, and feelings that lie behind our ethnographic exchanges. I am particularly interested in the way such constructions and evaluations precipitate the sense of an elusive person—self or mind-self—when eliciting or simply listening to testimonies.

Mohammed, one of the first Harkis I met, was a well-connected activist. Before I could finish explaining that I wanted to write a book about the

Harkis—those Algerians who had fought as auxiliary troops for the French during Algeria's war of independence—Mohammed interrupted me impatiently, saying he would provide me with list of *témoins* who would tell me how they had been abandoned and betrayed by the French. And he did, calling Harkis all over France, explaining my project before I had time to finish my explanation. The mention of a book, particularly one in English, was all he really needed to know.

At the time I did not pay attention to Mohammed's use of *témoin*, or witness, but its importance soon became clear. The Harkis and their children all referred to my interviews as giving testimony (*témoignage*). They hoped I would publicize their mistreatment in the English-speaking world. Mostly illiterate peasants, they had joined the French less for political reasons than for survival in a war-torn country. Considered *collaborators* by most Algerians, seventy thousand (some say as many as 150,000) out of approximately 250,000 were slaughtered at the end of the war, in 1962. Despite warnings of an imminent bloodbath by French officers under whom they served, the Gaullist government refused the Harkis and their families entry into France. Finally, under public pressure, de Gaulle offered sanctuary to the survivors. Once in France, they were settled in camps and forestry hamlets, some for as long as sixteen years.[12] Many of them and especially their children, like Mohammed, have been campaigning for the recognition of the sacrifices they made for France, compensation for the losses they sustained, and an apology from France. Though they have received some recognition and compensation, they have never received—and expect never to receive—an apology. They are realists, they say, "France's conscience."[13]

It became immediately clear that the Harkis wanted me to be their advocate, a position, I explained, I could not accept. I promised to tell their story as objectively as I could. Let the facts speak for themselves, I said. Though they accepted my position, they never abandoned the hope that I would become their advocate, and this hope governed the course of many of our encounters. Their témoignages often resembled legal briefs. Their two goals—to convince me of what they had suffered and to convince me to become their advocate—were often at odds with each other and with my own research interests. This led us to monitor carefully what we said to each other. They were asking themselves, I am sure, what I was thinking, just as I was asking myself what they were thinking. I looked for clues in the progression of our exchanges, turns of phrases, their use of figurative language, changes in emotional register, facial expressions, pauses, interruptions, and modes of being silent as well as clues in my own reactions to what they were saying. Were they telling the truth? Exaggerating? Skipping over important points that might interfere with their goals? My goals? Was I losing perspective? The most disturbing question I found myself asking was whether their frequent tears were sincere or designed to produce an effect in me. None of these thoughts (with the possible exception of my questioning their crying) was exceptional. What was noteworthy, if not exceptional, was the way their testimonies, as manifestly personal as they were, produced in me a sense that behind their words was an elusive mind—a mind-self—that I could not reach. I understood this at the time in psychological terms. Their mistrust, generated by feelings of being betrayed and abandoned impeded my reaching their "true selves," of "really" knowing them.[14] But did it? Had I come to really know them? Or was I caught in an epistemology of suspicion in which what lies under the surface—what has to be mined—is somehow more real, truer, more authentic than what lies on the surface? How deep must we go before we believe we know someone? How does the depth metaphor relate to our preoccupation with solipsism?

■ Surface and depth, like outer and inner, are metaphors that give spatial expression to (or, some would argue, ground) our evaluative epistemologies. If not explicitly then implicitly, the body figures in many of the philosophical discussions of solipsism. After 1911, when Husserl refocused his attention on the "natural world," which he had hitherto bracketed, he could no longer avoid problems of intersubjectivity, knowledge of the mind of the other, and solipsism. In the *Cartesian Meditations* he rephrases the problem by asking not how the ego understands the other but how the other is constituted for the ego. His argument is far too complicated to treat here. Suffice it to say that, unlike the direct experience of the body—that is, in Husserl's terms, *originalter*—the experience of the (animated) other can never be fully grasped by the ego. It does, however, offer verifiable indications of its mental life. As we experience our bodies primordially, so we experience the other's body and thereby his or her perspective on a shared perceptual field. (Analogy seems to slip in here.) Husserl likens the experience of the other to that of a memory, which is lived through secondarily. The other, he suggests, modifies phenomenologically ego's experience but is nonetheless comprehended by the ego's primordial sense of "my owness." Ultimately, then, the intersubjective can never escape the grasp of the singular consciousness.

As we can conceive (metaphorically) of bodily expression as a language, at times intended and at times unintended, we have to ask why we take it to provide an exceptional mode of entry into the mind of the other—an entry that we do not grant, or uneasily grant, speech. Wittgenstein ([1958] 1973: 222) says, "I can know what someone else is thinking, not what I am thinking. It is correct to say 'I know what you are thinking,' and wrong to say 'I know what I am thinking.' (A whole cloud of philosophy condensed into a drop of grammar.)" But, as with the body, so with speech; we hypothesize what the gesture or phrase tells us about what is going on in the mind of the other. Only a naïf would accept at face value what his or her interlocutor is saying he or she is thinking. Do we place greater credence in body than in spoken language because we assume the body gives unmediated expression to what is transpiring in the other's mind? There is always a gap—*différance*—between what one thinks and what one says. But can't the body dissemble? Are there epistemologies that ignore the gap between thought and speech? However we answer these questions, we have to situate our answers in a cultural moment in which the "body"/body has come to serve rhetorically as an escape from seemingly irresolvable epistemological conundra (Crapanzano 2004: 69–70). We have also to recognize a paradox in the role we attribute to the body as at once surface (exteriority) and yet revealing depth (interiority).

▓ In his reversal of the priority Husserl gave to consciousness over existence, Heidegger simply argues that one of the ontological givens of *Dasein* is being-with: *Mitsein, Mitdasein.* Heidegger (1962: 161) summarizes his position:

> Being-with is such that the disclosedness of the Dasein-with of Others belongs to it; this means that because Dasein's Being is Being-with, its understanding of Being already implies the understanding of Others. This understanding, like any understanding, is not an acquaintance [*Kenntnis*] derived from knowledge [*Erkennen*] about them, but a primordial [*urspringlich*] existential kind of Being, which, more than anything else, makes such knowledge and acquaintance possible. Knowing oneself [*Sichkennen*] is grounded in Being-with, which understands primordially. It operates proximally in accordance with the kind of Being which is closest to us—Being-in the world as Being-with; and it does so by acquaintance with that which Dasein, along with Others, comes across in its environmental circumspection and concerns itself with—an acquaintance in which Dasein understands. Solicitous

concern is understood in terms of what we are concerned with, and along with our understanding of it. Thus in concernful solicitude the Other is proximally disclosed.

Heidegger sidesteps the question of the subjectivity of the other. His is a sort of ontologically grounded etiquette of knowing engagement with the other, which is far closer to the commonsense view than his language leads us to believe. Working beside someone is getting to know him or her. Heidegger's (1962: 153–63) position is in fact more complex, since he distinguishes between Being-with, a rather romantic notion of an authentic relationship, from Being-with-one-another (*Miteinandersein*), in which the intimacy, the authenticity of Being-with is lost, giving way to the neutered, impersonal, leveling, public They—*das Man*—an inevitable precipitate of social life.

There are, of course, modes of knowing the other that come from being and working with the other. We become attuned to others, attentive to their needs, sensitive to their feelings, so habituated to them that we can anticipate their reactions in some situations. But is being-familiar-with the same as knowing someone or even knowing about someone?

■ Can we not think of the mind of the other without thinking of its malleability—our manipulation?

I came to Barbara Endicott's home to continue an interview I had had with her a week earlier. Barbara had been living for less than a year in Wyndal. Her husband, an engineer, was working on an enormous irrigation project. Barbara was young, attractive, articulate, and quite seductive. She was a charismatic Christian and, since her arrival in Wyndal, had been active in an evangelical renewal that began at about the time she arrived. I was particularly interested in her views on the role that the renewal played in the lives of the villagers. She expressed interest in my project and saw her Christianity as a way, perhaps the only way, to overcome South Africa's virulent racism. She was, in her own way, an activist.

I began the interview by asking Barbara to qualify some of the things she had told me at our previous meeting, but before I could introduce a new subject, she interrupted me. "Vincent, you asked me a lot of questions last time. I have only one question to ask you. Have you received the baptism of the Spirit?" I felt trapped. "No," I answered, and Barbara began to witness to me. She jumped unpredictably from doctrinal statements to personal reminiscences, to descriptions of how Jesus had changed her life, to how He would change mine, to asking me about my childhood, my life, my family, my work, my disappointments, inspiring guilt, shame, sadness, and loss wherever she could, expressing seductively God's care for me, her—His—love, His infinite mercy, the promise of salvation, and the inexpressible joy I would feel. Interspersed in this rapid-fire, vertiginous barrage of words were requests—commands really—which I refused as long as I could, that we pray together. She took my hand, leading me, trying to lead me, to kneel before her and pray. No matter how I protested, asserting my disbelief, attempting to change the subject, explaining, rather pathetically, that I was late for an appointment, Barbara insisted. Finally, I gave in. I allowed her to pray over me. She pressed her hand on my head. I mumbled the words after her, but said—to her disappointment, I imagine—nothing spontaneously. Evangelicals are mistrustful of formal prayers. You are supposed to have a personal relationship with Jesus, your pal. However moved I was by Barbara's concern, dizzied by her words, aroused by her eroticism, drained by her emotion, and exhausted by her indomitable perseverance, I was never moved by the Holy Spirit. I left, feeling maliciously victorious but saddened by her evident disappointment.

With the possible exception of its seductive tone, Barbara's proselytizing was quite conventional. Her disappointment might even be seen as rhetorical, but I don't think it was. (Was she disappointed in herself, in me, in—might I say—Jesus?) On the other hand, once I grasped her intention, I had no thought, no interest, in what was going on in her mind. Her intention domineered. I simply wanted to flee but was trapped because I didn't want to offend her and, more practically, to lose what rapport I had with her and, in all likelihood, with other villagers. Conversely, she was emotionally (she would probably say "spiritually") driven to bring about a fundamental change in me. In my mind-set. She may have wondered what I was thinking and feeling as she began to work on me; she may have looked for signs of my spiritual condition as her witnessing continued. In fact, at strategic times she asked me how I could deny myself the promise of salvation. How could I live without hope? The witnessing lasted well over three hours. But as it reached a heightened pitch, any interest she had in what I was thinking and feeling was, I believe, supplanted by what I *must* feel and think. We were not conversing. She was inducing, and I was resisting. There was no time for evaluation. We were caught, in our respective ways, in each other's desire. Opacity had given way to determination, the power of which is no doubt attested to by the length of this entry.

■ I have stressed rational approaches, edging at times on the irrational, to overcoming the threat of solipsism or penetrating the opacity of the other. Ought we to consider the effect of different practices as a response to the possibility or the "reality" of solipsism: moments of ritual exaltation, the entanglements of self and other in loving and lovemaking, in friendliness and being friendly, indeed in hating, mourning, melancholia, and jubilation arising from communal activities such as praying together, dancing, and singing? I have not considered less rational (as we understand "rational") attempts to know and manipulate what the other is thinking, feeling, sensing, and imagining: mind-reading, telepathy, the cultivation of intersubjective sensitivity, intense empathetic identification, and altered states of consciousness deemed to transcend the boundaries of the self and enter those of another, and other magical practices.[15] Marcus Course (2009) has recently argued that there is a class of Mapuche songs (*ül*) whose features—the use of the first-person pronoun, intextualization, and musicality—so encapsulate the *singular* composer's subjectivity that the singer comes to "inhabit" that subjectivity. Course suggests that the inhabiting of another's subjectivity through song "resonates and responds to a problem of epistemological solipsism grounded in Mapuche ideas about the singularity of the human person" (295). I am not doing justice to his complex argument. I do want to note that the stress on the notion of the person, which coordinates with our self-centered psychological understanding, blinds us to the reciprocal effects of the relations between self and other from within a solipsistic frame.

■ Lest I be accused of ethnocentrism, inevitable as it is, I will now strategically reverse my culturally sanctioned stress on the negative consequences of opacity and solipsism. I want to suggest that they may also have a positive effect by exposing the unknown, the unknowable—the mysterious. Given (to use the jargon) the rational instrumentalism that prevails today, we have focused far more attention on solving mysteries—on conquering the unknown—than on the mystery, the unknown, and the unknowable in and of themselves. It seems to me that social life relies on mystery, the creative, the imaginative possibilities that the mysterious opens up, as much as it relies on the constraints of convention, tradition, and habituation. It is mystery that charms us, inspires us, and even binds us together as individuals and collectivities.

How often are we attracted to or fascinated by someone we find mysterious?[16] Is it a quality of the unknown—its "unknownness"—that attracts us? Or is it the desire to know—to understand? The two probably cannot be separated, but they may be given different weight. Of course, we can also cultivate mystery for our own purposes. It figures in seduction. It can be empowering. Think of the shaman. Of Rasputin. Of the aura of mystery, however banal, that surrounds political leadership. It can be as protective as anonymity.

The mysterious is associated with the esoteric, the occult, the obscure, the secret, the abstruse, the enigmatic, and the inscrutable. All of these suggest something behind the surface—the surface meaning—that is not immediately evident and may seem to have deeper, symbolic, or mystical significance. The focus is on the mysterious object: the other. It is noteworthy that *mystery* is derived through the Greek *mysterion* (secret rites), *mustês* (an initiate in a secret cult), and *mueîn* (to initiate) from *muein* (to close the eyes or mouth; to keep a secret, as in religious initiation). This derivation suggests that the mysterious lies in both the quality of its object and an attitude—the blindness and muteness—of its beholder. Can we then say that the mysterious quality of the other lies not only in that other's opacity but also in the perceiver's (willed or habituated) blindness? Muteness?[17] The mysterious would have to be understood intersubjectively, as mutually generated by ego and other. Solipsism would weigh on the side of ego at the expense of the other's contribution; opacity, on the side of the other at the expense of ego's contribution. Each would distort the dynamics of intersubjectivity, interlocution, and, in other terms, the capaciousness of the *we*. But is this reduction of the epistemological to the psychological justified? Or is it simply playing into a culturally sanctioned avoidance of the recognition of the unknowable and the un-understandable? Are we destined to such a shrinkage of purview?

█ As I noted earlier in discussing shadow dialogues, the other—the dialogical partner—is, I can now rephrase it, riven by the interpellation of the "you" and the distancing of the "he" or "she." As a *you*, interpellated, the other loosens its mask as it engages as an *I* with its *you*, but that mask is pulled tight again when it is pinioned as a *he* or a *she*, losing thereby the magic, as momentary as it may be, of the *we* of dialogical engagement. We might say, as a *he* or *she*, it is subjugated by the look of the other. Does the paralyzing look of the other, but not necessarily the tender look, transform the *you* into a *he* or a *she*? The French novelist and literary-philosophical critic Maurice Blanchot (1955: 337–40) says that it is the transformation of the *I* into the *he* that produces the literary, a space that, as he sees it, rests on absence, timelessness, and inconsequential freedom. But we might ask at this concluding juncture: What is produced in ordinary life when the *you* is transformed into a *he* or *she*? Blanchot might well answer *death* or its figurative equivalent, but we, less courageous, would settle for presence, stasis, and effectual constraint, and hope for the transformation of the *he* or *she* into a *you*. For—shadow dialogues aside—it is the *you* engaged with the *I* that produces the possibility, *but only the possibility*, of the *we*. It is within the confines of the *we* that the mystery of consociation manifests itself, as, at the same time, like Heidegger's *they*, it moves entropically toward dissolution in the banality of the habitual, the conventional, and the taken-for-granted.[18]

EPILOGUE

Arizona. The mid-1960s. A Navajo reservation. The first day of my first fieldwork. I remember the mixture of excitement and apprehension I felt when I was introduced to Forster Bennett, the Navajo in whose camp I was to live for the next several months. It was dusk. I could barely see Forster's face or those of his children, which were cast in shadows by the flickering light of the kerosene lantern in the kitchen. We were standing outside, in front of the window. As I had been told that it was impolite to look Navajos in the eye, I avoided any eye contact with Forster. Having settled on the terms of my living arrangements, he led me to the hogan where I was to sleep. He and his children lived in a cinderblock house a few yards away. I lay on top of my sleeping bag, which I had laid out on the bedsprings of an old cot. Feeling very lonely and hungry, as I had had no dinner, I thought about what we—the twelve students—had been told about Navajo etiquette in an orientation week that had been arranged by the summer field-training program in which I was enrolled. Aside from avoiding eye contact, we had been instructed to approach a Navajo camp slowly, not to expect the Navajo to greet us effusively, not to shake hands hardily, to be patient in our questioning, and to respect the Navajos' silence.

The Navajo are laconic, we were told. We were given no explanation for any of these "rules." They were the Navajo way. As I lay there, I realized that within a week the orientation had not only furnished us with the kinds of stereotypes anthropologists are supposed to correct but had infantilized us and exoticized the Indian. The orientation had stressed the psychological effect of Navajo etiquette on us. (Culture shock was in vogue at the time.) Little attention had been given to our effect on the Navajo. Unlike the other students in the program, I had lived and traveled abroad extensively, and yet even I was apprehensive. The Navajo had been rendered opaque.

In the weeks that followed I had to unlearn most of what I had been told. It was not that the "rules" were wrong; it was that they were cast as rules, at best as practices. It is true that, as on that first night, I did experience a loss of self-assurance, an inner absence, a loneliness that was rather more ontological than psychological, that stemmed, I supposed, from Navajo modes of affirmation. But I soon adjusted to them. Indeed I became comfortable with them, particularly the way Navajos approached one another. If they came to a camp, they would park their pickup a few hundred yards away, wait in it for several minutes, and then slowly walk up to the camp, stand beside the door for a while before knocking, and when they entered, they would remain silent for what seemed to me at first an inordinate amount of time before stating their purpose.

I had been told that the Navajo were careful not to intrude into each other's life-space. No doubt this is true and seems to coordinate with their silences, their laconic interventions, and their avoidance of eye contact. But it also coordinates with their view of the cosmos, whose harmony is to be preserved at all levels of engagement. Interpersonal relations are, in this view, more than personal. They have, if I am not being too romantic, greater extension—providing the surround in which the *diné*, the people, as the Navajo refer to themselves, engage with one another. How do self and other figure in this surround—which, I should add, stresses flows of energy and movement? How do opacity, other minds, one's own mind, and the sense of isolation that may provide the ground for solipsistic speculation figure? How, at least metaphorically, are the "I", "you," "we," and the third-person personal pronouns configured? Experienced? Who are we in fact addressing when we address the other? The singular individual? A representative of a community? The community? An occupant embedded in the world?

These are, of course, rhetorical questions that are meant to evoke a corrective dimension to what I have been probing in this chapter.

NOTES

1. Given the political tensions of the time, I was, in fact, pressured into enlisting and could thereby attend the Army Language School.

2. Anglo-American philosophy has been far more concerned than Continental philosophy with the problem of other minds. It became a philosophical problem in the nineteenth century with John Stuart Mill, though Thomas Reid had already noted it in the eighteenth century (Hyslop 2009).

3. There are, of course, philosophers who have recognized the limitations on their outlook by their ethnocentrism, though often, as in the case of Lucien Lévy-Bruhl, they dismiss the challenges posed by "philosophical" assumptions of other cultures by declaring those cultures inferior or by overriding them metalinguistically. Or, like Husserl, they acknowledge them and then ignore them. In a letter to Lévy-Bruhl on March 11, 1935, Husserl—to be sure toward the end of his life—acknowledges, according to Merleau-Ponty's (1964: 107–8) paraphrase, that the phenomenologist does not have access to universal reflection without the anthropologist's experience and cannot depend on imaginary variations on his own experience. Husserl goes so far as to write, "On the path of the already largely developed intentional analysis, historical relativism is incontestably justified as an anthropological fact."

4. I use *convention* to refer not to a static prescriptive form but to a dynamic vector that has limited directionality.

5. I am arguing not that a solipsistic episteme is the only one current among philosophers but that many of their stances, such as Heidegger's characterization of *Dasein* as "being-with" or Wittgenstein's language-game approach to the problem, which appear to avoid solipsism, are in fact responses to it. In making this observation, I am assuming an ethnographic perspective that is concerned not with the validity of philosophical arguments but with the importance of solipsism in philosophical discourse (Kripke 1982: 125, 141–43). For example, JSTOR has 7,663 entries on *solipsism*. It would seem that it is of particular significance in the anthropologist's engagement with—for lack of a better term—exotic others who, like most of us most of the time, may not worry about solipsism.

6. For lack of space, I do not address the problem of self-opacity. It is for another essay.

7. Pandolfo (2009: 88) describes a Moroccan imam's understanding of the heart: "The heart is at once the center of feeling and the faculty of the imagination (*tasawwur, takhayyul*), the metaphysical place of faith and connectedness with the divine and the organ that oversees the circulation of blood in the body.

Affects first experienced, induced and imaged by the *nafs* [roughly the soul], the desiring soul, are transmitted to the heart. The heart receives those images and visions (*suwarân*) and their 'impression' or engraving sets the spiritual-existential tone in the person, which in turn produces bodily effects by impacting the circulation of blood and the organs."

8. Hyslop (2009: 4–5) in fact distinguishes two interrelated approaches to the problem of other minds: the epistemological, which I described earlier, and the conceptual, which asks on what grounds we can form a concept of the mental states of others. Solutions to the conceptual problem generally rely on similar arguments to the epistemological.

9. There are, of course, occasions when the other is incorporated in the "we," as, for example, in "I wonder where we'll end up."

10. I am using English personal pronouns here, metaphorically, in full recognition of the fact that the pronominal structure of languages differs in significant ways (e.g., presence or absence of dual forms, exclusive and inclusive first-person plurals). Although there are, for example, first- and second-person personal pronouns in Sanskrit, there are, strictly speaking, no third-person ones. The demonstratives (n., *tat, etat, idam,* and *adas*), without being attached to a substantive, are used instead. They indicate proximity to the speaker: *etat* and *idam* have greater proximity than *tat*; *adas* is more distant than *tat*. The distinction between the pronouns and the demonstratives parallel, in more marked fashion, the distinction between indexical pronouns (i.e., first- and second-person personal pronouns, *I* and *you*) and referential ones (i.e., *he, she, it*) that are anaphoric or cataphoric. I am indebted to Veena Das for alerting me to Sanskrit usage but note that she bears no responsibility for my discussion of them.

11. Evaluation plays an essential role in Hegel's master and slave allegory. It is not simply recognition.

12. The Harkis, as French citizens, had the right to leave the camps whenever they could. Illiterate, speaking little French, shocked by what had happened to them, and disoriented by their transfer to an alien and unwelcoming country, many were unable to adjust to their new environment and had, in any case, few opportunities to find work outside the camps.

13. For details and extensive bibliography, see Crapanzano (2011).

14. It was only in informal conversations, when the Harkis' goals had relaxed, that I began, so I felt, to know them—their thoughts and feelings. Conversation is, of course, a communicative genre or constellation of communicative genres.

15. All of these practices have been topics of ethnographic concern but rarely if ever understood in the epistemological terms that I have suggested in this essay.

16. It should be clear that I am focusing here on only the mysterious dimension of human encounters, and not on those encounters with "natural" phenomena— with what Whitehead called "the vast darkness of the subject" in his thanking Bertrand Russell for his exposition of quantum theory at Harvard (Bateson 1958:

280). Bateson himself, noting the inability to predict from a system of complexity C what it would be like if it had complexity C+1, ends his 1958 epilogue to *Naven* with this observation: "Certain mysteries are for formal reasons impenetrable, and here is the vast darkness of the subject." We are, of course, in no position to assume even that there are formal reasons for not being able to penetrate the mysteries inherent in consociation.

17. Freud would refer to unconscious factors and relate mystery to the uncanny, but unless we take a Lacanian position, which recognizes the consequential role of the other—the other's voice—in the (formation of the) unconscious, the psychoanalytic position, focused on the individual, fails to account for the intersubjective nature of the uncanny: the mysterious (Lacan 1966).

18. On a number of occasions (Crapanzano 1992, 2000, 2004, etc.), I have postulated the role of the Third, a metapragmatic function that, among other things, determines communicative conventions, genre, style, and so on. It would seem that the "strength" of that determination (however measured) would effect the tension between mystery and banality. But, at this point, this is only speculation.

CHAPTER 12

Action, Expression, and Everyday Life:
Recounting Household Events

Veena Das

■ In my ethnographic work in Delhi, mostly with low-income urban families over the past ten years, I have witnessed immense struggles over housing, water, and electricity. One could ask: What could ever be of philosophical interest in the trivial details of the insecurities of everyday life here? Yet as I sit in dark rooms without windows or in the shadow and smells of heaps of waste collected from the neighborhood hospitals or factories, and listen to stories about what it took to get an official document or the extent of effort made to carry, perched on the back of a bicycle, gallons of water from a tube well or a water tanker, I hear the protests of a Beckett character: "You're on earth, you're on earth, there's no cure for that." I feel that if a conversation between anthropology and philosophy is to have any meaning at all for me, philosophy must learn to respond to the pressure of questions that I encounter in these settings. Instead of the sovereign subject whose utterances carry force because they are authoritative (I promise, I declare, as in Austin's [1962] examples of illocutionary force), I am interested in the fragility of the subject and of the context as mutually constitutive of the work of inhabitation.[1]

A DIFFERENT REGION OF PHILOSOPHY

Which regions of philosophy might be compelling to such an inquiry? In my earlier work, on the ways violence folds into the everyday, I had turned to Stanley Cavell's philosophy as expressing a desire or even a craving for the ordinary (see Das 2007). Yet Cavell's picture of the everyday is inflected with dark shades in which doubts arise unbidden within, say, quotidian kinship, as a man wonders if this child is really his (Cavell 1988) or if his wife might not after all be a witch (Das 1998, 2007). For me, Cavell's thought became important because it spoke to the kind of experiences I encountered in my fieldwork. Even more, Cavell himself searches for how the desire for philosophy might be expressed in the low, the ordinary, and the humble, as in his turning to Hollywood melodrama as that which inherits the skeptical problematic in American popular culture.

I wish to go back to another instance in which a fleeting contact is made between a philosophical thought and an anthropological insight. Commenting on my book *Life and Words*, Cavell (2007: xiv) had this to say: "The further insight of Das's that I refer to is her recognition that in the gender-determined division of the work of mourning the results of violence, the role of women is to attend, in a torn world, to the details of everyday life that allow a household to function, collecting supplies, cooking, washing, and straightening up, seeing to children, and so on, that allow life to knit itself back into some viable rhythm, pair by pair. Part of her task is to make us ponder how it is that such evidently small things . . . are a match for the consequences of unspeakable horror, for which other necessaries are not substitutes." He goes on to add, "In the background of my sense of these matters a remark from Wittgenstein's *Journals* . . . plays a role that I know I still imperfectly, or only intermittently, understand but that I feel sure is illuminated by this nearly inconceivable mismatch of harm and healing. 'The whole planet can suffer no greater torment than a single soul.' We are touching here on matters that will seem to take moral philosophy, with its assessments of goods and its exhortations to duty and to contracts, quite beyond its accustomed paths" (xiv). I take this remark as an invocation and a blessing that in agreeing to acknowledge those aspects that we understand only imperfectly or intermittently, we are willing to be open to a future together.

In the rest of this chapter I propose to take one strand from Cavell's philosophy and trace the notions of action and expression through his commentaries on Austin. I then ask how events in my fieldwork among the urban poor further provide moments of connection through which mutual illumination can occur. I am making a move here that is the opposite of moves made by many anthropologists who look to philosophy as providing the theory and to anthropology to give evidence from empirical work to say how things really are (see, e.g., Robbins 2010). For me, it is the concrete events of my fieldwork that clarify the ideas I find in Austin and Cavell and reassure me that the philosophical puzzles they bring up can and do arise in the concrete relations and weaves of life we inhabit. I found myself attracted to Cavell's work because his philosophy is able to respond to the pressures from my ethnography. I take seriously his declaration that "in Derrida's heritage we cannot truly escape *from* the traditions of philosophy; in mine we cannot truly escape *to* philosophy" (Cavell 1988: 19, emphasis in original).

Cavell's ideas on the everyday and its relation to action and expression do not develop in a linear fashion; he himself has described his thinking as reticular. So the best I can do is to present salient points within the network of concepts that account for the double character of the everyday as both the source of annihilating doubts and a cure against them. I then identify the point at which Cavell comes to think of skepticism as a *gendered* doubt. Finally, I consider how Cavell's notion of language offers a serious amendment to Austin's notion of performative utterances by reorienting us to think of the relative weight we assign to action and expression. While the order of normativity captured by Austin in the discussion on illocutionary force remains intact in Cavell's amendment, the side of perlocutionary force is considerably modified by bringing into play simultaneously the disorders, improvisations, and passions that are laced with these orders of normativity.

THE SCANDAL OF THE EVERYDAY

In his Tanner Lecture on the uncanniness of the ordinary, Cavell (1988: 176) lays out what he calls the topography of the ordinary in the following manner: "It stands to reason that if some image of human intimacy, call it marriage, or domestication, is the fictional equivalent of what the philosophers of ordinary language understand as the ordinary, call this the image of the everyday as domestic, then the threat to the ordinary that philosophy names skepticism should show up in fiction's favorite threats to forms of marriage, viz. in forms of melodrama and tragedy." I note two important points for my purposes: first, that the threat to the ordinary does not come from an image of isolated and specialized examples, as in Descartes's piece of wax, but rather from the homeliness and familiarity with such genres as that of melodrama in Hollywood films; second, there is the imperative to find and name what image the everyday takes as well as how doubts that might annihilate that everyday arise within a particular formation, be it literature or film or autobiography. Thus the threat to the ordinary appears within the weave of everyday life, and it is the task of the analyst to recognize it. An example Cavell offers is the declaration in the beginning of Poe's "The Black Cat," the famous tale of horror, that what Poe is placing before the world sincerely and without comment is "a series of mere household events." But such mere household events, like the purloined letter in another Poe story, might go without comment just because they are before our eyes.

This is one picture of the relation between the uneventful repetitions of the everyday and the threats contained in it—conceptualized through the image of the domestic, of the common, of the low and the familiar.

Another example is Cavell's analysis of Max Ophüls's 1948 film *Letter from an Unknown Woman*, in which he takes us through a journey, the guiding question of which is, How do the banal images of everyday interactions become death-dealing images for the man who has simply failed to "see" the significance they held for the woman? These images are now evoked in the words of the woman, who declares herself to be speaking from a beyond—"By the time you read this letter, I would be dead"—thus making the words themselves ghostly. The question then becomes, How might we create within the repetitions of the everyday a present carved from or out of the past? In what manner might we make the past yield a present that is not ghostwritten?

A further issue is expressed in Cavell's perplexity as to why both psychoanalysis and cinema have been formed by their address to the suffering of women. His coming to a realization that what goes on in the name of skepticism in philosophy has a gendered dimension is not simply one argument among others; it is a traumatic discovery: "It [*The Winter's Tale*] has raised unforgettably for me, I might say traumatically, the possibility that philosophical skepticism as inflected, if not altogether determined by gender, by whether one sets oneself aside as masculine or feminine. And if philosophical skepticism is thus inflected then, according to me, philosophy as such will be" (Cavell 1997, 100–101).[2]

THE FRAGILITY OF ACTION AND THE FRAGILITY OF EXPRESSION

A fundamental insight of Austin's (1962) theory of performative utterances is that such utterances take action and speech to be aspects of each other; in other words, action does not follow or precede speech but rather *is* the speech act itself. Austin's great achievement was to have displaced the centrality of the proposition in philosophical discussions of language by showing that there was a region of language for which it was not the truth and falsity of utterances that mattered but rather their felicity or infelicity. Most anthropological works have found the notion of illocutionary force extremely productive for the analysis of public performances such as ritual—contexts in which convention is secure. I propose, however, that the other side of Austin's work is the fragility of human action; he isolates two poles of this failure: when action misfires because the world has a say in it and when it is abused because the utterance was insincere. In the former case, I shot the wrong donkey because my hands trembled; in the second case, I intended to shoot your donkey, though I told you that I was going to shoot mine.

In his marvelous essay on excuses, Austin (1969a) offers us a way to think of the fragility of human action related to two linked aspects of our being: that of our embodied character and that of our existence as beings with language. We might say that the first lies on the action side of performative utterances and the second on the side of expression. Yet there is something not quite satisfactory in Austin's account of performative utterances or speech acts; they work very well when the action is public and the conventions are in place but not so well when conventions are themselves insecure.

I acknowledge Austin's achievements in showing that speech acts might be validated only in part by an associated utterance: there must be other conditions in place without which the utterance leads to misfires. Austin's analysis reveals that beyond conventions of speech, there is another layer of conventions in the absence of which we can make propositional statements but cannot make language do the work of accomplishing many social acts of a public nature, especially ritual and ceremonial acts. But does Austin's theory work when conventions are not in place or the context of stable actions disappears? Austin was quite aware of these lurking dangers, as shown by his exclusion of the literary from his understanding of the ordinary. "A performative utterance," he says, "will be in a peculiar way hollow or void, if said by an actor on stage, or if introduced in a poem or a soliloquy" (Austin 1962: 3). The exclusion of the literary, however, does not ward off the dangers that he sensed, for if performative utterances could appear hollow when the context was wrong, then constative utterances too could act as performative ones if the context was right. This led Austin to suggest that we give up the constative/performative distinction altogether and start again, since any and every utterance could work as a performative. Cavell (2005b) detects in this gesture the timidity of philosophy to deal with emotion or passion. Why is this the end of the story, he asks, and not its beginning?

In his recent work on passionate utterances Cavell asks us to reconsider how our pictures of the stability of conventions and orderliness of speech acts might constrain the way we think of language and passion. For Austin, a significant difference between illocutionary force and perlocutionary force of performative utterances was that in the former case we do something *in* saying something, while in the latter case we do something *by* saying something. Cavell offers the case of passionate utterances as a subtype of performative utterances and places them in symmetrical opposition to speech acts that have illocutionary force. Thus passionate statements such as "I love you" cannot rely upon convention but must stake a claim to be unique to that speaker and that addressee. Further, such utterances single out the addressee—the second person to whom the words are addressed and not the first person who commits herself to, say, a promise or a marriage. While someone naming the ship *Queen Elizabeth* relies on the authority that he wields to make the public utterance effective or felicitous, the one who utters a passionate statement declaring his love, for instance, makes himself vulnerable. If we were less focused on the action aspect of speech acts and more on expression, says Cavell, we would see that perlocutionary force is not external to the speech act, as Austin had argued, but is the internal possibility of the expression itself. Now performative utterances and passionate utterances appear to Cavell not as two types of utterances but as two possibilities of the speech act—the first opening up the possibility of participation in the order of law (as reflected in the orderliness of speech and its ritual or formal character) and the second as the improvisation stemming from disorders of desire in which the speech act renders the speaker vulnerable to risks. Cavell (2005b: 185) is proposing not a balance between orderly ritualized speech and improvisations in speech but rather the realization that the double nature of the everyday finds expression in the double nature of speech acts themselves: "From the roots of speech, in each utterance of revelation and confrontation two paths spring: that to responsibility of implication and that of the rights of desire. The paths will not reliably coincide—but to have them both open is what I want of philosophy."

A final point I want to make comes from Cavell's earliest work; it relates to the intuitions about words and their meanings that come not from shared opinions but from sensibilities that have been forged by participation in forms of life. A classic passage from his essay "The Availability of Wittgenstein's Later Philosophy" (1962: 52) gives us a picture of how we learn to project words in new contexts while retaining the sense of their internal consistency:

> We learn and teach words in certain contexts, and then we are expected, and expect others, to be able to project them into further contexts. Nothing insures that this projection will take place (in particular, not the grasping of universals nor the grasping of books of rules) just as nothing insures that we will make, and understand, the same projections. That on the whole we do is a matter of our sharing routes of interest and feeling, modes of response, senses of humor and of significance of fulfillment, of what is outrageous, of what is similar to what else, what a rebuke, what forgiveness, of what an utterance, of when an utterance is an assertion, when an appeal, when an explanation—all the whirl of organism Wittgenstein calls "forms of life."

Our ability to project words—Cavell's examples of feeding the lion, feeding the meter, and feeding your pride—are all ways in which our relation to particular objects in the world, how it is inhabited by lions and machines and emotions, is disclosed in our ability to project and our confidence that our words will be received. For example, the fact that I can say "feed your pride" but not "feed your happiness" might tell me that pride is the kind of emotion that might grow with flattery but that happiness cannot be increased by flattery. It also shows that words cannot be projected in a solipsistic way since there is an inner constancy to them. For Cavell, this inner constancy cannot be derived from a book of rules, but I think, in addition, there is an idea of the natural that is at play here.[3] The natural cannot be equated with the "given" since different languages will bring out different ways in which ideas of pride are constructed, but the natural cannot be completely equated with the constructed either. Let us say, for now, that it is almost as if our constructions are necessary to show how a particular history of the natural might be disclosed within a particular form of life in this particular corner of humanity, as distinct from another one.

With these thoughts in mind, let me briefly recapitulate the main points I will mobilize in the following sections. First, I want to reiterate that the everyday is the site for both routines, habits, and conventions as well as disorders, doubts, and despair. Cavell expresses this double character of the everyday as the shadowing of the everyday by skeptical doubts expressed in idioms of kinship or the domestic, and sees in the tendency of philosophy to reduce skepticism to an intellectual puzzle or riddle, a denial of the threat that skepticism poses to ordinary life. Second, our life as embodied creatures and as beings with language reveals the everyday as an invitation to participate in the orders of law and simultaneously expresses the disorders or improvisations with desire. Finally, in Cavell's understanding, belonging does not mean that we give allegiance to our culture *as it stands*, but the form that the labor of criticism takes, as well as the effort to bring about the eventual everyday growth from within the disappointments of the actual everyday. What it is to inhabit the everyday within the scene of disappointment is an abiding theme of Cavell's work. All these issues, I contend, are necessary to the picture of the everyday that Cavell's work discloses. They invite the participation of anthropology to the project of making the everyday count but also make philosophy itself count as a mode of thinking in the everyday.

MAKING A WORLD INHABITABLE

Sanjeev Gupta lives in Punjabi Basti, a neighborhood in Delhi that, in official parlance, is known as an "unauthorized colony." Inhabitants of such places are not officially entitled to sanitary services or water or electricity connections since they live in places that are not recognized by the city as authorized residential areas, but of course residents arrive at different kinds of arrangements to secure access to these goods. Though the law defines the status of the unplanned settlements and the various types of administrative regulations to which they are subject to create the impression of an orderly legal process through which these places are administered, the boundaries between the legal and the illegal are not at all clear. Thus there are different administrative acts that govern these unplanned settlements on such matters as provisions of public services, restrictions over eviction, and claims for alternative housing; however, smuggled into these official documents is the uncomfortable realization that the government is dealing with many of these issues after the fact—that different kinds of urban settlements have grown by "illegal" occupation of government-owned land often right under the noses of the authorities and that acts of enumeration and classification are running to catch up with this kind of growth from the ground up. Gupta explained the process as follows: "It is not as if there is an existing map on the basis of which a colony is developed. Rather, a map is forcibly put on spaces that have come into being haphazardly, and which continue to grow and change as new opportunities and needs arise for the poor." If the poor learn to dwell in these spaces, it is by learning what it is to be "thrown" into a political and legal landscape that cannot be deciphered, except through their engagement and action on their environment.

I will not go into the detailed history of Punjabi Basti except to indicate two features essential for understanding the story that follows. The first is that the families of the earliest settlers that we could locate all indicated that they had moved from different parts of Delhi soon after 1976, when a National Emergency was declared and the infamous forced sterilization and beautification drive in Delhi was implemented (Tarlo 2003). However, Punjabi Basti did not come about as a resettlement colony—a term that designates areas to which the poor were forcibly relocated during the beautification drive. Rather many of these families voluntarily moved here because they saw the opportunity to claim empty land. Second, Punjabi Basti is spread over a hilly terrain, with makes different streets stretch over different levels. Each small segment of this locality can be said to have a slightly different history: part landfill, part rocky terrain from which large slabs were extracted, part forest. The process of settling the area has thus required different kinds of labor, such as clearing the forested part, filling out craters created by extraction of large slabs by builders, and leveling the ground to make roads negotiable. There was a strong sense of the legitimacy that residents claimed for their actions. As one woman said to me, "Sister, everyone lives over occupied land. All these rich owners of bungalows [kothiwale]—did they come to earth owning land? Did they have to put in the kind of labor that we did to make this uninhabitable place into a dwelling?"

As the locality became more settled, a market in housing developed by which early encroachments were converted into "plots" and sold to new buyers. Though such plots and ownership are not recorded in the revenue registers with a khasra [plot] number, the rights to buy and sell are recognized within the local worlds. Those living in recognized slums are protected from eviction by legal acts such as the Slum Areas Act of 1956, but the majority of the people living in unplanned settlements have very limited legal protection. An interesting question is, How have areas such as Punjabi Basti been able to protect their dwellings? I will relate one segment of this complex story to shed some light on the character of everyday life through Sanjeev Gupta's role in the successful electrification of the colony. I will then reflect on the question of what kind of ethical voice we can locate within these projects of dwelling and building.

I was walking with my research collaborators, Simi and Purshottam, up the steep street on which Sanjeev Gupta lives in December 2011. On the corner of the street there were placards announcing the office of an NGO that Gupta has founded, and close to it another one with some information about the West Delhi Congress Youth Committee on which his name appeared prominently along with other, better-known political leaders. I had heard many times that the street on which we were standing was once much below the level of other streets, and water used to gush downward and often enter the houses during the monsoon. Gupta, on his own initiative, had brought truckloads of loose soil, plastic, and other material and had it laid on the road to raise its level. Because of the narrow lanes, cars and trucks could not reach that spot, so he hired donkeys to carry the load (a practice still prevalent). For many residents, the event that marked Gupta as a leader was when he saw that a donkey was not able to climb up the street as it became steeper, so he put his shoulder against its back and putting his weight behind it, he pushed the donkey to help it move. This joining of his own body with the body of the donkey became emblematic of the labor that settled this colony.

I start with this story to give a sense of Gupta's commitment to action. Yet as we shall see, there is no given grid on which his actions move; he has to improvise all the time. The vulnerability of his actions, the risks of failure—all alert us to the fact that outside of conventional ritualized action there is also a different way of stitching action and expression together that should be considered for any theory of performative utterances and the force they carry. While Cavell seems to have placed action on the side of illocutionary force of speech acts and expression on the side of perlocutionary force, the story that will unfold tells us about improvisation, disorder, and vulnerability on the side of both action and expression.

Now to the question of what makes electricity flow. Walking in Punjabi Basti, one is struck by the presence of seven large transformers with high-tension wires installed on bits of land at the street corners, in the bits of greenery that pass for parks, and in one case on the side of a temple. There are no empty stretches of land on which these transformers could be installed, so the electricity company and the residents have done the best they could despite the risks of placing these transformers in crowded spots.

The story of the electrification of this neighborhood begins with the privatization of electricity in Delhi between 2000 and 2002. When power reforms began in 2002 in Delhi in light of the heavy losses incurred by the state-owned Delhi Vidyut Board, the Board was unbundled into three privately owned companies. Gupta and many others told us about the terrible harassments that residents faced when electricity officials lodged complaints with the police about theft of electricity. As in most such neighborhoods, people had earlier drawn electricity illegally from street poles to lines to their homes, shops, or *karkhanas* (workshops) to power domestic or commercial appliances. The networks of private contractors and low-level officials of the Municipal Corporation who were routinely bribed had assured the residents that they did not face criminal charges for theft of electricity. Now, with privatization, residents were finding that the game plans had completely changed. Gupta used his position as the president of the Zonal Congress Committee to arrange a meeting (sometime in 2005) between the representatives of the locality and the officer in charge from the zonal division of the company (BSES) to discuss the issue of electricity theft and harassment. Here is the description of what transpired; I juxtapose fragments of the account given by Gupta (in Hindi) over several informal discussions with an account of the issues involved in electrification as given by one of the officers (Vidyut Sir) of the private company who granted me an interview (mostly in English).[4] The fragments come from different moments; it is also the case that Gupta was often relating the story in the presence of objects that materialized the story, while Vidyut Sir was sitting in a small conference room of a posh private bank, which he had since joined.

> Sanjeev Gupta: After electricity was privatized, there was this big move to install meters. Now as you know, in colonies like these there were no regular meters. There were local contractors who used to supply electricity for payment by drawing lines from the high-tension wires, or else many people drew the lines themselves and there were regular payments extracted by the local linesmen and the policemen. We said to Vidyut Sir, "Sir, we have been demanding a regular supply of electricity but you do not sanction meters for us. On top of it, you file complaints and the police treat us like criminals. What kind of justice is this?" Vidyut Sir replied that their records showed how much electricity had been consumed in this locality and what was the recovery of money against it. He said vehemently, "I say on that basis, I say that I have proof, I say that people are stealing—they are thieves." We said, "Sir ji, how can you call us

thieves? If you don't give us electricity on the grounds that we are not an authorized colony, and people naturally need electricity—a man wants to run a fan, his little children are burning in the heat, he will get electricity with whatever means—then why call him a thief?"

Vidyut Sir: My boss and I were both very struck by Sanjeev Gupta's argument. We thought ethically how could we accuse them of theft when we have not responded to their needs? There was a lot of discussion within the management. From the business angle, there was a market here, but could we manage it? There were huge problems of how to identify houses correctly. The addresses were all haphazard; there were no numbers or names of streets. It was a maze.

Sanjeev: I was truly stung by the accusation of theft [*Ye baat mujhe bahut lag gayi*—this utterance struck me]. We said, Sir ji, we will remove this stigma that we are a colony of thieves. Vidyut Sir guided us— so did another officer. The big issue was that houses did not have addresses in sequential order, streets did not have names or numbers. Sometimes if a linesman was expected to deliver a bill, the client would simply rip apart his meter and say, "My house is not C4. That house is in another street."

Vidyut: We advised them that they had to get a proper map of the area with house numbers in order. They had to submit a list of names of households with proper addresses. Without such a list we could not install regular meters.

Gupta and some other leaders then organized meetings in the area and persuaded most households to contribute Rs. 200 per household for a map of the area. After many difficulties because of the topography of the area and because houses were not on one level, a private firm of architects finally made a map. After an exchange of many letters, petitions, and pressure from the chief minister's office, the town planner of the Municipal Corporation finally approved the map. This enabled the BSES to prepare a list of consumers and to install meters in the houses after augmenting electricity supply by installing seven transformers in the area. In the process each house was given a new number, but Gupta managed to get the electricity company to agree to write both the old number and the new number on the bills, so that now in all official correspondence the address appears to be a composite of the two numbers.

I do not want to give the impression that all this—the map making, the assigning of new numbers, the installation of the transformers—was achieved by agreements arrived through rational deliberative discourse. Accusations have been made in the locality that all the money that was collected was not properly accounted for. There were fights over the exact location of the transformers, but the gravest threats to Gupta came not openly but in many covert ways from the network of "entrepreneurs" who had earlier supplied electricity illegally and whose business was adversely affected.

One day, when Gupta was relating the efforts they had to make to complete the project, he suddenly choked up, and I saw that his eyes were tearing. He said, "I was even attacked one night when I was coming home." "What happened? How? Did you get hurt?" "No but they showed me a revolver and told me to stop these activities" "Who were they?" "Oh, the ones who do this *dukandari* [market transactions but carrying a tone of illicit transactions here], whose *dhandha* [illicit work] would have stopped." "Did you report it to the police?" "No, the local police are always on their side." "So what did you do? How do you know you are safe?" "I told you, I was not a diehard Congress man. I am in the party because I cannot do without it. So those above were informed, and they must have talked to them—after all, the ones who were intimidating me are also part of the same setup."

Gupta's shifting moods, his feelings of being powerful and vulnerable at the same time, were clear in most stories he told. The moment that he recalled with great pride was that of the inauguration of the transformers, the most significant aspect of which was that no ceremony was performed to mark the occasion. "There was much discussion. Should we get a Brahmin to tell us the *muhurat* [auspicious moment] for the inauguration? Who should we invite? Should we invite Lalotia [the local Member of the Legislative Assembly]? But then there are others, like Krishna Teerath, the MP. She is also from this area and has done a lot for us. Should it be the electricity officials? They are the ones who guided us to overcome every obstacle. Then I decided: no muhurat, no inauguration, no leader. When the transformers started functioning and the whole area was electrified, the politicians, the ones who sit above, were amazed."

Relating a scene in which Gupta enacts an imaginary conversation that Gupta is having with the political leaders who consider themselves as patrons of the local leaders:

E1. Oh, how did *this* happen?
H1. *Arre, ye kaise hua.*
E2. Transformers were put in.
H2. *Transformer lag gaye.*

E3. The whole area got electrified.

H4. Pura area electrify ho gaya.

E5. And we were not called to inaugurate?

H5. Aur hamen mahurat pe bulaya bhi nahin gaya?

E6. Oh Sahib, who are you anyway?

H6. Aji sahib, aap hote kaun hain?

E7. You are our representatives—we chose you.

H7. Aap to hamare numaynde hain—hamne aap ko chuna.

E8. It is due to us that you sit above.

H8. Hamari vajah se aap aaj unchi jagah baithe hain.

E9. Otherwise who were you?

H9. Nahin to aap the kaun?

E10. You should have asked after us when we suffered.

H10. Aap ko to hamse puchna chaahiye tha jab ham takleef mein the.

E11. Why should we call you for this occasion?

H11. Ham aap ko kyon bulayen is mauke par?

E12. Did you spill blood and sweat as we did?

H12. Aapne hamari tarah khun paseena bahaya hai?

I will comment on the distribution of voices that Gupta enacts in this imaginary dialogue a little later. Let me first switch to another moment on another day when Gupta was relating the same story as we waited under a makeshift arrangement of chairs in the street where we were to be addressed by a representative of the Civil Defense Department on disaster preparedness. With a sadness in his voice as we looked at the narrow winding lanes and the new construction on shaky foundations, making it apparent that no relief could be physically rushed here if an earthquake were to hit Delhi, Gupta said, "That day, when the transformers began to function—only we knew from which personage to which other we had to run, who are the people before whom we had to rub our foreheads on the ground [*kis kis ke peeche-bhage, kis kis ke samne matha ragda*]." The reference to a gesture that signifies utter abjection may not have literally taken place, but the language conveys the embodied sense of humiliation.

Commentary

Sanjeev Gupta is not known in the neighborhood for his rhetorical skills. Yet I am impressed that his and others' stories are woven around objects in a manner that illuminates the interpenetration of persons and things specific to the lifeworlds from which they emanate. In his reflections on the decline of aura, Benjamin (1968a, 2008) wrote that stories told about objects of use belong to their aura. He traced the decline of storytelling to the fact that commodities become obsolete so quickly that they do not have time to collect stories about them.[5] In listening to Gupta and others I found that public objects—a transformer here, a tube well there, a tile with the picture of a god placed on a rock at the corner of two roads—gathered stories around themselves that gave experiences of the place a lively quality. Eli Friedlander (2012: 147) comments on Benjamin's notion of aura to suggest that the significance Benjamin associates with a work of art or with experience more generally is the sense that there is more to the object than meets the eye: "The figure of an aura of light emanating from an object and surrounding it, making it slightly more than it is, suggests that there is a space of meaning that comes with the object and allows us to relate to it significantly. This is possible insofar as the object is embedded in tradition."

The storytelling around objects in this case was not about being embedded in tradition, nor about our memories of objects from our childhood, but rather about how objects are embedded in the future that Gupta imagines for his neighborhood and for his own place in it. I want to focus on three specific episodes and their related expressions for a closer reading. These are (1) the open declaration in a public meeting by Vidyut Sir that the neighborhood in which Gupta lives is a colony of "thieves" and the entanglement of expressions and actions that follow from that declaration; (2) Gupta's confession that there is indeed not much difference in the moral standing of those who threaten him and those who protect him; and (3) his remarkable performance of the voicing though which he brings the absent figures of the politicians within his discourse through the mode of irony.

It is tempting to analyze these three episodes that make up the narrative tension in his account by using techniques of linguistic analysis or metapragmatics (Benveniste 1971; Silverstein and Urban 1996), but much would be lost if we remained at that level of analysis. I turn instead to the issues I raised in the earlier sections on how action and expression are stitched together as utterances and move between illocutionary force and perlocutionary force, the orders of law and normativity, and the improvisations introduced by desire, emotion, and passion.

Consider the first episode, when Vidyut Sir declares that they cannot supply electricity to a neighborhood of *thieves*. The utterance has an element of performance in it, and since the declaration is made by someone whose words carry the imprint of the laws of the state, we might say that though the utterance does not in itself make the residents into thieves, neither is the statement hollow or void.[6] In fact it is because the residents have already been treated as thieves and are being harassed by the police for complaints of theft of electricity that the statement has illocutionary force. Instead of treating it as an indicative statement to which we could attach values of truth or falsity, Gupta turns it into a language game of challenge and counterchallenge. "Sir, we will wipe out this stigma," he declares. This is one point at which we could stop, as McDowell (1998: 4) in his powerful analysis of performative utterances implies we could: "Speech acts are publications of intentions: the primary aim of a speech act is to produce an object—the speech act itself—that is perceptible publicly and in particular to the audience, embodying an intention whose content is precisely a recognizable performance of that very speech act. Recognition by an audience that such an intention has been made public in this way leaves nothing further needing to happen for the intention to be fulfilled."

Put differently, we might say that McDowell's analysis would separate the aspect of performance from the aspect of action. Performative utterances would be completely on the side of expression, albeit expression in the public sphere. This theoretical move knits together the inside and outside, intention and action, primarily through the communicative acts in public between one who has expressed an intention and another who has received it. Although McDowell is offering a general theory of speech acts, the action under consideration seems to me to be primarily a description of ritualized action appropriate to such contexts as those of religion and law, in which we draw artificial boundaries, separating the action that takes place within these boundaries from its ramifications outside (see also Lee 1997). However, once we see ritual action as contiguous to other actions, we see that the punctuation marks we placed around segments of action do not really work. This is why it is interesting to see how the transformation of a simple commercial transaction—a seller supplying a product to a consumer—becomes an ethical action for both Vidyut Sir and Gupta. This brings me to the second point: Gupta's confession that there is no difference in the moral standing of those who threatened him and those who protect him.

I think it is important to realize that from the dramatic contesting statements about theft, two paths open up for ethical action. On the part of the electricity official Vidyut Sir, there is an amazing shift of perspective as he reflects on what it is to be denied elemental needs in the urban context and whether an ethics of commercial action would require him to create the conditions of possibility in which the residents of the neighborhood could construct themselves as "responsible consumers" and not thieves. For Gupta, the ethical action is to wipe out the stigma of being thieves. The materiality of electricity then enfolds in itself questions of what it is to be doing things in a legitimate way. Yet Gupta is aware that in order to remain alive he must accept the protection of those he considers corrupt, those who intimidate others, who use threats of violence and yet have both good and bad points. Ethical paths for him are strewn with the general conditions of life in which no one can claim moral purity. If the relation between the orders of normativity embodied in the illocutionary force of utterances and the disorders of life embedded in perlocutionary force are so woven together, Gupta and Vidyut Sir's actions make it clear that the securing of everyday life as a space of ethical action is at best a striving toward a different everyday. I circle back to Gupta's opening statement that our friendship should be with the earth.

Finally, let us consider how the moment of the inauguration of the new transformers, or rather the significant gesture of *not* inaugurating them, tells us about the political subjectivities in question. After telling me that he decided to ignore the powerful political leaders who have represented the area, Gupta creates an imaginary dialogue in which he distributes his narration between the voice of an imaginary politician and the "we" that represents the neighborhood. This dialogue brings the imaginary figure of the politician into our presence; in Goffman's (1974) sense these are figures that have been brought forth by the speaker's acts of narration. Gupta is not a neutral narrator here; rather the effect of irony is achieved by such phrases as "Aji sahib, aap hote kaun hain?" (H6), in which the respectful address of *sahib* (meaning a white man, an officer) and *aap* (honorific second person) is juxtaposed with *aji*, a term of address that can make suspect the respectful phrases that follow. In short, we have an enactment whereby the politician is put in his or her place. The flight into imagination as witnessed in the imaginary dialogue enacted here and the expression of power with which the voter in a democratic society is endowed in Gupta's speech (lines E6/H6 to E10/H10) is, however, fleeting, as Gupta later recalls, outside the frame of this imaginary dialogue the actual humiliating events of supplication about which only he and they, his political patrons, know.

It is thus that Gupta and some of his neighbors gave me the necessary clues for interpreting Cavell's statement that I cited earlier: "From the roots of speech, in each utterance of revelation and confrontation two paths spring: that to responsibility of implication and that of the rights of desire. The paths will not reliably coincide—but to have them both open is what I want of philosophy."

WHEN WORDS ARE LIKE WILD HORSES

Speech, however, is a slippery companion. In the next case, written as a short interlude before I discuss the question of inexpressibility, I describe the case of Prem Singh, who lives in Bhagwanpur Kheda, a similar low-income neighborhood. Walking in the street in Bhagwanpur Kheda one cold day in 2003, I found, snuggling among various posters and graffiti on the walls of houses, a computer-generated poster in Hindi:

Insaan ke roop mein kutte
Unke bhaunkne ka
Na koi samay hota hai
Na koi Seema

Dogs in the form of Humans
Of their Barking
Neither is there any specific time
Nor any limit

Led by a vague curiosity, I asked some young boys who had gathered around, seeing me read that notice, "Who has put it up?" There were sniggering comments: "Some madman. We don't know, ask the others." As I stood staring at the poster, Prem Singh opened the door of his house just enough to peep out. He then signaled for my research collaborator Purshottam and me to come inside.

The story of this poster emerged in one burst; it seemed that Singh had been waiting for an opportunity to pour out his version of events. I give a brief indication of the setting: Delhi in those days was in the grip of dengue fever. Public health messages about cleanliness were everywhere. In the better-off localities the municipal workers were routinely checking on flowerpots and coolers to see that water was not collecting. In the poorer localities, where sanitation and cleaning of drains were completely absent, these messages were treated as just words.

Singh felt that something needed to be done about the garbage and the dirt; the rains had made the stink from open drains overwhelming. He started pouring buckets of water mixed with a cleaning agent into the street to clean it. However, since there was no proper drainage the water ended up in dirty puddles. His immediate neighbor objected because his six-year-old son slipped and fell in these puddles. The verbal exchange of insults and bickering threatened to become a bigger dispute as neighbors started taking sides and people joined in to watch what was going on for sheer entertainment. Singh described this moment: "The fights began to accelerate—at one time I thought this would become a *danga* [riot]. So I withdrew. Then I thought, 'Man has only the right over his *karma* [action]. If my good action does not bear fruit, that is not my fault. Look at where I live—how can good acts prosper here?'"

Yet Singh was still seething with rage. "I am not a sage," he said. "I wanted people to know that my neighbor was just a useless man [*bekar admi*]. That is when I thought of these words. He is like a dog, and just as when a dog barks in the middle of the night other dogs join in, the neighbors had joined in this chorus of dogs. As I said, there is no time or limit to their barks. The people here, they are just *chuda chamars* [pejorative reference to scavenging]. The government does not care—it is a hell made of garbage, dirt, and disgusting, filthy insects. I thought at least some people who read it, even if they do not want to come out in the open against my neighbor, will understand and the feelings will gather and he will be shamed."

Despite his hopes, though, Singh did not get any encouraging responses from his neighbors. He even made a trip to the High Court in Delhi to put up this poster on the walls, hoping that some spirited lawyer would take notice and file a petition on his behalf. The courts have been known to entertain public interest litigation cases on similar matters, but his actions elicited no response.

But then, Singh said, as his cause was a righteous one, God opened a path. He had been listening to various accounts in Hindi of "Liberation Iraq," led by the American and European "coalition of the willing." He then realized that George Bush was not only the president of America (*Amrica* in Hindi) but was also the leader of the whole world. These different fragments of news made him feel that he had been shown a path. When God closes one way, he opens another, he said.

So he drafted a letter in Hindi to President Bush, got it translated and printed on nice paper, and posted it to "White House, Washington, USA." The letter, written in the style in which government applications are made, said, "Respected Sri Bush, Respectfully, I wish to submit that I have heard that you have vowed to clean the world of terrorists and to bring democracy to the whole world. I want to report that my neighbors are spreading dirt in our streets and objecting to my efforts to keep the streets clean. As you are the great leader of the world I hope you will take action in this matter. Your humble servant, Prem Singh [Address]."

As it happened, Singh received a reply from the White House that expressed appreciation for his support of President Bush. He showed the letter to his neighbors as a sign of the rightness of his cause, but many of them considered it a sign of his craziness: "He expects the American president to come here and have our streets cleaned?" To which Singh replied, "I have always done my duty. As Lord Krishna said, one should do one's karma without any hope that it will bear fruit." For his neighbors, this karma is turning into a constant irritation, as he floods various government departments with letters and petitions that sometimes go unnoticed and at other times seem to lead to troubling consequences. In one case he complained to the Delhi Development Authority about an unauthorized extension of the house that a neighbor was undertaking, resulting in the neighbor's having to pay a huge bribe to the housing inspector who showed up. One can detect a shift in the way the neighborhood has come to regard him, from a somewhat laughable crank to one who could harm them because of his stubborn character and his seeming lack of care for the consequences his actions generate.

Commentary

There are three different segments of this story that I want to select for further comment: (1) the reference to his neighbors as chudas and chamars, pejorative terms for previously untouchable castes; (2) the animal metaphor; and (3) the letter to President Bush and the circulation of petitions. Each of these segments leads us to think of the allegorical import of this story and the dangers of words that come not from grand events but from within the nooks and crannies of the everyday.

Prem Singh's reference to his neighbors as chudas and chamars, as scavengers, is less a use of a caste slur to insult another than a commentary on the neighborhood itself. After all, Singh belongs to the Jatav (chamar) caste, as do many others in the neighborhood, so these derogatory terms simply would not carry the same force as they would if deployed by an upper-caste man. Yet given the political sensitivities around caste terms such as chamar in the political culture, such words cannot be allowed to pass from the private to the public realm. The use of the animal metaphor allows the expression of a public insult and challenge, while simultaneously expressing the squalor and dirt of the neighborhood of which Singh himself is a part.

It is useful at this point to take up a suggestive moment in Cavell's (2005b) work where he writes that passionate utterances might be thought of as one among other modes of discourse characterized by different perlocutionary objectives. Say that in declaring my love for you, I deny that I need to consider the question of my standing with you and instead claim authority to speak for a particular institution (say, assuming that you must marry me because I stand in the right institutional relation to you), "then my passionate declaration becomes something else." Cavell suggests that this "something else" might be an instance of moralism. Similarly instead of demanding a response, I speak to stifle your speech; then my speaking might approach hate speech and I might use my words to brand you (182). Singh's statements do not quite amount to hate speech in the way slogans against lower castes emerge during caste riots or fragments of speech against another religious group in sectarian riots brand the other group as cowardly or impotent (see Mehta 2010). Yet they have the makings of something that could spin out of control.

Singh's letter to Bush might seem at first like a harmless absurdity produced by the global circulation of news, yet the letter was not conjured out of nothing. In fact, like some others in the neighborhood, Singh was used to writing "petitions" to particular gods, such as Hanuman Ji, in one of the temples that receive them. The form of the petition (*arji*) is usually in the nature of a request followed by a pledge: *If I succeed in such-and-such task, I will give you such-and-such offering*, with the name and address of the person seeking the god's intervention and the name of a witness appended to the petition (see Malik 2010; Taneja 2010). Thus it seems to me that there is an act of projection through which President Bush is brought within the local world. As Cavell explains, when we project words from one context to another, the criteria for determining what is similar to what, what is outrageous, what is funny, what serious, grow out of our forms of life and not from any universal givens or from any book of rules. In the case of Prem Singh there is a sequence of actions with continuous shifts in the way these actions are tied to different perlocutionary objectives. One might say that unlike the classic case of illocutionary force in which "I do" might be seen to accomplish the act (if the conditions of felicity are present), in the case of actions with perlocutionary effect there is a continuing possibility that acts might morph from one into another that could lead to a stitching together of different contexts in unpredictable ways or could lead to the erosion of the fragile threads that allow social life by keeping contexts apart. This is one way I understand how the dangers that Cavell gathers under the sign of skepticism grow within the everyday.

INEXPRESSIBILITY, OR THE WITHDRAWING OF ONE'S WORDS

In the two cases discussed earlier, we found speech acts that were pronounced publicly and hence had an element of performance. The third case I want to discuss speaks to the theme of confession and the unbearable character of painful knowledge that women sometimes carry and protect others from. I want to loop back to my discussion of Cavell's "traumatic" discovery that philosophy is inflected by the question of gender. As I put it earlier, what on the male side of the gender divide presents itself as an issue about the knowing subject becomes on the side of the female the issue of her knowability or of making herself known. Recall that in the film *Letter from an Unknown Woman* the woman was able to speak, as in having a voice, only from the side of death. The case of Sheela, the woman I present here, complicates the issue by asking: To whom can one make oneself known?

Sheela's family is among the small number of upper-caste families in Punjabi Basti. Upper-caste histories in these neighborhoods often reveal that following some kind of adversity—business failure, disinheritance by the parents, elopement, or, as in this case, displacement after the Partition of India—one branch of the family must move to a low-income neighborhood. In Sheela's case, her natal family had escaped from the riots in Pakistan, but her father died soon after. So she grew up in her maternal uncle's house along with her mother, two sisters, and five older cousins. She was married at an early age to a much older man, who in other circumstances would have been considered below the status of her natal family. In the course of researching other issues in Punjabi Basti, I got to know her well. And although she never narrated in one long story the facts of her sexual abuse as a child, little bits would come out on different occasions when we were together, in such expressions as *"Mere naal vi bure karam hoye* [Bad acts happened with me too]." For instance, once when she was helping her eight-year-old granddaughter to change into a new dress, she became tearful and, putting her hand on her mouth as if to block speech from bursting out, said, "Oh god, this is how little I was when . . ." She did not elaborate, but something in her past had rotated and confronted her at this moment.[7] As a child Sheela was often slapped, sometimes beaten with a cane [*dande padte the*], not by her other relatives but by her mother. This aspect, though, she recalled with a kind of cheerfulness, commenting that her mother had to beat her to signal her own status toward her relatives, who, though not well off, had taken the additional burden of dependent relatives. "What could she do—there was a compulsion [*mazboori thi*]." Elsewhere I have described this as the aesthetics of kinship (Das 2007, 2012a).

Though she let some expressions of her hurt escape in my presence, I never asked and she never said whether she had told the story of her abuse to anyone, including her husband. As I have described elsewhere, in matters of sexual violation, there is an agreement in families displaced by the Partition that one does not ask any explicit questions; instead one allows oneself to be marked by the knowledge that comes one's way. Here the anthropologist's mode of being converges into that of the others in the community. There were two occasions, though, when Sheela did tell me something. The first occurred when I told her that there was a discipline called psychoanalysis in which therapeutic interventions consisted of the "patient" talking every week for an hour with the therapist, saying whatever came to her mind. She said that she wished she could find a guru who would understand her without her having to say anything. Then she went on to say that she could imagine "talking" about those things, but she could not imagine ever saying aloud the name of the person who had violated her. "I cannot even say it aloud to myself. It is like I am holding something in me, tight as a fist, a coiled snake, and if that came out, the world would be thrown into chaos [*duniya utthal putthal ho jayegi*]."

The second occasion arose when we were talking about a death in the neighborhood. Sheela remarked that people give too much credence to the words of a dying person. But who knows what comes to possess them, she said. Her eyes seemed to wander as she said, "My mother said to me on her deathbed, 'You have to forgive me for a lot, no?'" Then Sheela looked at me directly and said, "That was cruel [*Ye zulm tha*]. She asked me such a question—if, I say yes, it confirms that *I* knew that *she* knew. And now with one word, all that will be wiped away? If I say no, then what kind of human being [*banda*] is this who cannot forgive this dying woman?"

Commentary

What is it about a name that holds such powers of destruction? At the first level of reflection we could link Sheela's inability to name her abuser to other taboos on the name in this form of life (see also Das 2007). Thus, for instance, in India people generally avoid using proper names in conversation, instead using kinship terms to address even relative strangers. There is a strong taboo against a married woman uttering the name of her husband; it is said that doing so would shorten the husband's life. Thus the refusal to speak the name of one's husband comes from the desire to protect and honor him. In Sheela's case, however, her abuser did not stand in any normative relation to her, yet she says she feels nauseous, physically ill and in the throes of a panic if she were to pronounce her abuser's name even silently to herself.

There is another register of proper names that might have a greater resonance with the dread that Sheela feels in uttering the name of her abuser. While it is meritorious to recite the name of any god or goddess, it is only the ritual adepts, such as diviners, who can safely get a demon to reveal its name. But I believe that this cultural resonance does not apply to Sheela, who is not talking about someone else, a third person, whether human or demon, but about herself, the first person—and one's relation to oneself is not based on observational knowledge. As Anscombe (1975) argued in her classic essay on the first person, one does not use the word *I* to refer to oneself as one would use other pronouns to refer to a second or third person. Although there might be room for debate on Anscombe's claim that the *I* is nonreferential under all conditions, there is little doubt whom I mean when I use the first person. The self is not one object among others; I do not infer how I am feeling by observing myself (Wittgenstein [1958] 1973). Yet in Sheela's experience, there is a name embedded in her body that destroys the intimacy she has with herself. She cannot let go of this name without making the universe go topsy-turvy. She cannot bear to make that part of herself known in which this name resides as a hostile alien.

Once acknowledgment comes of what happened to her as a child, it comes as a question. Sheela experiences the dying statement by her mother as lethal because it too is not offered to elicit a response but rather to stifle her voice. For Sheela, the labor of letting go is too much to bear. For her, her mother's question was like a snare to put her in a terrible double bind, and she responded to it by not responding at all. What kind of an end is this?

In the case of perlocutionary effects, Cavell (2005b: 184) is most inter-ested in the fact that "in the case of classic performative utterances, fail-ures to identify the correct traditions are characteristically reparable: the purser should not have undertaken to marry us, but here is the captain. . . . Our future is at issue, but the way back, or forward, is not lost." In the case of passionate utterances, Cavell writes that the risks are of a different order. He gives the example of Carmen's "No, you do not love me," sung in response to Don José's protestations of love in his "Flower Song" as a definitive case of perlocutionary sequel or "consequence," in which the end is not conventional or predictable. Also, much more is at stake than misfires of actions; for Car-men, part of her identity (the part that loved Don José) is dead.

Sheela too refused to respond to her mother's fateful utterance, and something of her own identity as the daughter seemed to have ended. No-tice that she referred to herself as a human being (What kind of human being am I who cannot forgive a dying woman?) and not as a daughter. I cannot say if in going about her daily life—cooking, sewing, fetching water—she finds the space where the broken arteries of her childhood can be repaired or if her sense of living in a world that cannot see what is before its eyes, such as the abuse of a child, runs parallel to the performance of these activities. I am not the one who can offer the last word on this subject.

CONCLUDING COMMENTS

How does an understanding of the everyday, as attempted here, stitch to-gether a philosophy of the performative force of utterances and an eth-nography of the striving of the urban poor? I am struck by the fact that in all three cases the subject is brought into being by an act of accusation. This is perhaps clearest in the case of Sanjeev Gupta, for his whole story unfolds in relation to the moment when his neighborhood is called a neighborhood of thieves. It is not as if such accusations always lead to the poor being convicted of wrongdoing, but there is a prevailing sense that their forms of survival make them guilty. It is almost a part of the atmo-sphere in which they live and breathe.

While one might say that at the end of the day all I have reported are mere household events, but, like Poe's recounting of household events, certain forms of lethal possibilities are folded into these narrations. For me, the unfolding of events within the quotidian scenes I described cre-ated the texture of the ordinary that might have been easily missed in a lofty aerial view of these lives. In each of the three commentaries I offered one can see that in securing the everyday, the propensity to exile oneself from life and language was ever-present, as was the effort made by each of the three protagonists to bring about an everyday that could be improved, more attuned to their desires for neighborhoods and families in which lives could be lived better—however different the tracks in which their actions and expressions slipped.

In putting my relation to my interlocutors in my ethnographic work along with my relation to Cavell on the same plane intellectually and emotionally, I am not forgoing criticism (in either direction) but advancing a way in which criticism might engage a work positively. The modern concept of criticism is usually equated with the sensibility of standing either in a court of judgment or in the expression of indignation, but what I found when I tried to interpret Cavell through the lives of my interlocutors, who are also in some ways my teachers, was that his works blossomed and increased in worth. Instead of generalizations I have simply followed the routes opened by the puzzles and perplexities, the improvisations, and the knitting together of expressions and actions, as my best guides to understand the philosophical puzzles that Austin and Cavell give expression to. The labor of making the ordinary appear: I take that to be one way in which anthropology might find a footing in the world. Perhaps it might also offer the lure of the concrete to philosophy.

NOTES

I gratefully acknowledge the participants in my recent graduate seminars, "Performance in Anthropological Theory" and "Anthropology and Philosophy," particularly Andrew Brandel for his comments and his encouragement. I thank the members of ISERDD, who helped in the mapping of the public facilities and in tracking events relating to provision of public goods in the area. The data on public goods were gathered under the auspices of the project entitled "Citizens and the State in Urban India," supported by the Economic and Social Research Council, U.K., grant number RES-167-25-0520, located at the Center for Policy Research in Delhi. I am grateful to Michael Walton for his support, and to all the residents of Punjabi Basti I offer my grateful thanks. I am indebted to Stanley Cavell for all he has given so graciously that has enriched my work and my life.

1. See Berlant (2007) for the concept of nonsovereign agency.

2. Such a gendered division does not imply that the active and the passive, agency and patiency, can simply be mapped on men and women but rather, are to

be seen as aspects of the human being, as well as two poles on which action moves (see Das 2007; Reader 2007, 2010).

3. For instance, in Austin's example, you cannot say "I inadvertently stepped on the baby"; what is at stake is not rules of linguistic grammar but something like Wittgenstein's notion of philosophical grammar that assumes that criteria grow out of the mutual absorption of the natural and the social in any human form of life.

4. All personal names except that of Sanjeev Gupta are pseudonyms. The suffix *sir* simply follows local practice to denote respect.

5. See Hansen (2008) for an excellent account of how the notion of aura was narrowed in time to refer primarily to aesthetic objects, whereas initially it could be the property of all objects.

6. I have in mind the contrast one could make with a statement such as "I name the ship Queen Elizabeth" (Austin 1962: 5).

7. For the notion of rotation, see Bergson ([1908] 1991) and Das (2007).

Abedi, Mehdi, and Michael M. J. Fischer. 1985. "Introduction." In Khomeini, Ruhollah. A *Clarification of Questions: An Unabridged Translation of Resaleh Twozih al-Masa'el*. Boulder, Colo.: Westview Press.

Abimbola, Wande. 1973. The Yoruba Concept of Human Personality. In G. Dieterlen, ed., *La notion de personne en Afrique noire*. Paris: Centre National de la Recherche Scientifique.

Achebe, Chinua. 1975. *Morning Yet on Creation Day: Essays*. London: Heinemann.

Adamson, Tim. 2005. Measure for Measure: The Reliance of Human Knowledge on the Things of the World. *Ethics and the Environment* 10(2): 175–94.

Adorno, Theodor. 1998. *Critical Models: Interventions and Catchwords*. Trans. Henry W. Pickford. New York: Columbia University Press.

Agamben, Giorgio. 1998. *Homo Sacer. Sovereign Power and Bare Life*. Stanford: Stanford University Press.

———. 2009. *The Signature of All Things: On Method*. New York: Zone Books.

Aikhenvald, Alexandra. 2004. *Evidentials*. Oxford: Oxford University Press.

Anscombe, G. E. M. 1975. The First Person. In Samuel Guttenplan, ed., *Mind and Language*. Oxford: Clarendon Press.

Aquinas, Thomas. 2000. *Summa Theologica*. Vol. 22. Trans. Anthony Kenny. Cambridge: Cambridge University Press.

Arendt, Hannah. (1958) 1998. *The Human Condition*. Chicago: University of Chicago Press.

———. 1991. *On Revolution*. London: Penguin.

Aristotle. 1999. *Metaphysics*. Trans. Hugh Lawson-Tancred. New York: Penguin.

Asad, Talal. 1993. *Genealogies of Religion: Discipline and Reasons of Power in Christianity and Islam*. Baltimore: Johns Hopkins University Press.

———. 2004. Afterword. In Veena Das and Deborah Poole, eds., *Anthropology in the Margins of the State*. Santa Fe, NM: School of American Research Press: 279–89.

———. 2007. *On Suicide Bombing*. New York: Columbia University Press.

———. 2011. Thinking about the Secular Body, Pain, and Liberal Politics. *Cultural Anthropology* 26(4): 657–75.

Ashforth, Adam. 2005. *Witchcraft, Violence, and Democracy in South Africa*. Chicago: University of Chicago Press.

Austin, J. L. 1958. Pretending. *Proceedings of the Aristotelian Society Supplementary Volumes* (32): 261–78.

———. 1962. *How to Do Things with Words*. Cambridge: Harvard University Press.

———. 1969a. A Plea for Excuses. In J. O. Urmson and G. J. Warnock, eds., *Philosophical Papers*, 175–204. Oxford: Oxford University Press.

———. 1969b. Pretending. In J. O. Urmson and G. J. Warnock, eds., *Philosophical Papers*. Oxford: Oxford University Press.

Badiou, A. 2000. *Deleuze: The Clamor of Being*. Trans. Louise Burchill. Minneapolis: University of Minnesota Press.

Baker, Lynne Rudder. 2008. On the Very Idea of a Form of Life. *Inquiry: An Interdisciplinary Journal of Philosophy* 27(1–4): 277–89.

Barcia, Roque. 1889. *Diccionario General Etimológico de la Lengua Española*. Madrid: Álvarre Hermanos.

Bateson, Gregory. 1958. *Naven: A Survey of the Problems Suggested by a Composite Picture of the Culture of a New Guinea Tribe Drawn from Three Points of View*. 2nd edition. Stanford: Stanford University Press.

———. 1976. *Steps to an Ecology of Mind*. New York: Ballantine.

Baugh, Bruce. 1992. Transcendental Empiricism: Deleuze's Response to Hegel. *Man and World* 25: 133–48.

Behrouzan, Orkideh. 2010. Prozak Diaries: Post-Rupture Subjectivities and Psychiatric Futures. Ph.D. diss., MIT.

———. 2011. The Significance of History, Gender and Language: An Epidemic of Meanings in the Islamic Republic of Iran. In J. Klot and V. K. Nguyen, eds., *The Fourth Wave: An Assault on Women, Gender, Culture and HIV in the 21st Century*, 319–46. Paris: UNESCO.

Behrouzan, Orkideh, and Michael M. J. Fischer. Forthcoming. "Behaves Like a Rooster and Cries Like a [Four Eyed] Wolf": Nightmares, Depression, Psychiatry, and the Rise of Iranian Psychiatric Selves. In Alex Hinton and Devon Hinton, eds., *Genocide and Mass Violence: Memory, Symptom, and Intervention*.

Benjamin, Walter. 1928a. *Einbahnstrasse*. Berlin: Ernst Rowalt Verlag.

———. 1928b. *Ursprung des deutschen Trauerspiel*. Berlin: Suhrkamp.

———. 1968a. *Illuminations*. Translated by H. Zohn. New York: Schocken Books.

———. 1968b. On Some Motifs in Baudelaire. In *Illuminations*. New York: Schocken.

———. 1977. *The Origin of German Tragic Drama*. Trans. John Osborne. London: NLB.

———. 1979. *One Way Street*. Trans. Edmund Jephcott and Kingsley Shorter. London: NLB.

———. 2008. *The Work of Art in the Age of Mechanical Reproduction*. London: Penguin.

Benoist, Jocelyn. 2003. Structure, causes et raisons: Sur le pouvoir causal de la structure. *Archives de Philosophie* 66(1): 49–72.

———. 2008. Le "dernier pas" du structuralisme: Lévi-Strauss et le dépassement du modèle linguistique. *Philosophie* (98): 54–70.

Benveniste, Emile. 1971. *Problems in General Linguistics*. Miami: University of Miami Press.

Bergson, Henri. (1889) 1927. *Essai sur les donnés immédiates de la conscience*. Paris: Presses Universitaires de France.

———. (1908) 1939. *Matière et mèmoire: Essai sur la relation du corps a l'esprit*. Paris: Quadrige/PUF.

———. (1908) 1991. *Matter and Memory*. Trans. N. M. Paul and W. S. Palmer. New York: Zone Books.

———. 1935. *The Two Sources of Religion and Morality*. London: Macmillan.

———. 1956. *Laughter*. New York: Doubleday.

———. 2001. *Time and Free Will: An Essay on the Immediate Data of Consciousness*. Trans. F. L. Pogson. Mineola, N.Y.: Dover.

Berlant, Lauren. 2007. Slow Death (Sovereignty, Obesity, Lateral Agency). *Critical Inquiry* 33(4): 754–80.

———. 2011. *Cruel Optimism*. Durham: Duke University Press.

Bessire, Lucas, dir. 2006. *From Honey to Ashes*. Watertown, Mass.: Documentary Educational Resources.

———. 2011. Apocalyptic Futures: The Violent Transformation of Moral Human Life among Ayoreo-Speaking People of the Paraguayan Gran Chaco. *American Ethnologist* 38(4): 743–57.

Bhaskar, Roy. 2008. *A Realist Theory of Science*. London: Taylor and Francis.

Biehl, João. 2005. *Vita: Life in a Zone of Social Abandonment*. Berkeley: University of California Press.

———. 2013. The Judicialization of Biopolitics: Claiming the Right to Pharmaceuticals in Brazalian Courts. *American Ethnologist* 40(3): 419–36.

Biehl, João, and Peter Locke. 2010. Deleuze and the Anthropology of Becoming. *Current Anthropology* 51(3): 317–51.

Biehl, João, and Ramah McKay. 2012. Ethnography as a Political Critique. *Anthropological Quarterly* 85(4): 1211–30.

Biehl, João, and Amy Moran-Thomas. 2009. Symptom: Subjectivities, Social Ills, Technologies. *Annual Review of Anthropology* 38: 267–88.

Biehl, João, and Adriana Petryna, eds. 2013. *When People Come First: Critical Studies in Global Health*. Princeton: Princeton University Press.

Blanchot, Maurice. 1955. *L'espace littéraire*. Paris: Gallimard.

Bloch, Maurice. 1977. The Past and the Present in the Present. *Man* 12: 278–92. Reprinted in *Ritual, History and Power: Selected Papers in Anthropology*. London: Athlone Press, 1989.

Boeck, Filip De. 2005. The Apocalyptic Interlude: Revealing Death in Kinshasa. *African Studies Review* 48(2): 11–32.

Bornstein, Erica, and Peter Redfield. 2010. *Forces of Compassion: Humanitarianism between Ethics and Politics.* Santa Fe, N.M.: School for Advanced Research Press.

Bourdieu, Pierre. 1977. *Outline of a Theory of Practice.* Cambridge: Cambridge University Press.

———. (1980) 1990. *The Logic of Practice.* Stanford: Stanford University Press.

———. 1981. Preface to Paul Lazarsfeld, Marie Jahoda, Hans Zeisel, *Les Chomeurs de Marienthal.* Paris: Editions de Minuit.

———. 1984. *Distinction: A Social Critique of the Judgment of Taste.* London: Routledge and Kegan Paul.

———. 1990. *In Other Words: Essays towards a Reflexive Sociology.* Cambridge, U.K.: Polity Press.

———. 1991. *The Political Ontology of Martin Heidegger.* Cambridge, U.K.: Polity Press.

———. 1993. Concluding Remarks: For a Sociogenetic Understanding of Intellectual Works. In C. Calhoun, Edward LiPuma, and Moishe Postune, eds., *Bourdieu: Critical Perspectives.* Chapel Hill: University of North Carolina Press.

———. (1996) 2003. *The Rise of Western Christendom.* 2nd edition. Malden, Mass.: Blackwell.

———. 2000. *Pascalian Meditations.* Cambridge, U.K.: Polity Press.

———. 2005. Remembering the Poor and the Aesthetic of Society. *Journal of Interdisciplinary History* 35(3): 513–22.

Bourdieu, Pierre, with Abdelmalek Sayad. 1964. *Le déracinement: La crise de l'agriculture traditionelle en Algérie.* Paris: Editions de Minuit.

Bourgois, Philippe, and Jeffrey Schonberg. 2009 *Righteous Dopefiend.* Berkeley: University of California Press.

Bradbury, R. E. 1973. *Benin Studies.* Ed. Peter Morton-Williams. London: Oxford University Press.

Brown, Peter. (1996) 2003. *The Rise of Western Christendom: Triumph and Diversity, A.D. 200–1000.* 2nd edition. Malden, Mass.: Blackwell.

———. 2005. Remembering the Poor and the Aesthetics of Society. *The Journal of Interdisciplinary History* 35 (3): 513–22.

Bynum, Caroline Walker. 1995. *The Resurrection of the Body in Western Christianity, 200–1336.* New York: Columbia University Press.

———. 2011. *Christian Materiality: An Essay on Religion in Late Medieval Europe.* New York: Zone Books.

Canguilhem, Georges. 1989. *The Normal and the Pathological.* New York: Zone Books.

———. 1994. Le Concept et la Vie. In *Études d'histoire et de philosophie des sciences concernant les vivants et la vie.* Paris: Librairie Philosophique J. Vrin.

Cannell, Fenella. 2004. The Christianity of Anthropology. *Journal of the Royal Anthropological Institute* 11: 335–56.

Carrithers, M., M. Candea, M. Sykes, M. Holabraad, and S. Venkatesan. 2010. Ontology Is Just Another Word for Culture: Motion Tabled at the 2008 Meeting of the Group for Debates in Anthropological Theory, University of Manchester. *Critique of Anthropology* 30: 152–200.

Castoriadis, Cornelius. (1999) 2007. *Figures of the Thinkable*. Stanford: Stanford University Press.

Caton, Steven C. 2005. *Yemen Chronicle: An Anthropology of War and Mediation.* New York: Hill and Wang.

Cavell, Stanley. 1962. The Availability of Wittgenstein's Later Philosophy. *Philosophical Review* 71(1): 67–93.

———. 1979. *Claim of Reason: Wittgenstein, Skepticism, Morality, and Tragedy.* New York: Oxford University Press.

———. 1987. The Avoidance of Love. In *Disowning Knowledge in Six Plays of Shakespeare.* Cambridge: Cambridge University Press.

———. 1988. The Uncanniness of the Ordinary. In *Quest of the Ordinary: Lines of Skepticism and Romanticism.* Chicago: University of Chicago Press.

———. 1995. *Philosophical Passages: Wittgenstein, Emerson, Austin, Derrida.* Oxford: Wiley Blackwell.

———. 1996. *A Pitch of Philosophy: Autobiographical Exercises.* Cambridge: Harvard University Press.

———. 1997. *Contesting Tears: The Hollywood Melodrama of the Unknown Woman.* Chicago: University of Chicago Press.

———. 2002. *Must We Mean What We Say? A Book of Essays.* Cambridge: Cambridge University Press.

———. 2005a. Henry James Returns to America and to Shakespeare. In *Philosophy the Day after Tomorrow.* Cambridge: Harvard University Press.

———. 2005b. Performative and Passionate Utterance. In *Philosophy the Day after Tomorrow.* Cambridge: Harvard University Press.

———. 2005c. *Philosophy the Day after Tomorrow.* Cambridge: Harvard University Press.

———. 2007. Foreword. In *Life and Words: Violence and the Descent into the Ordinary.* Berkeley: University of California Press.

Chambers, Samuel A., and Terrell Carver, eds. 2008. *William E. Connolly: Democracy, Pluralism and Political Theory.* Abingdon, UK: Routledge.

Clastres, Pierre. 1998. *Chronicle of the Guayaki Indians.* New York: Zone Books.

———. 2007. *Society against the State: Essays in Political Anthropology.* New York: Zone Books.

———. (1980) 2010a. Marxists and Their Anthropology. In *Archeology of Violence.* Los Angeles: Semiotext(e).

———. (1980) 2010b. Savage Ethnography (on Yanoama). In *Archeology of Violence*. Los Angeles: Semiotext(e).

Cohen, Lawrence. 1995. Holi in Banaras and the Mahalund of Modernity. *GLQ: A Journal of Lesbian and Gay Studies* 2(4): 399–424.

Corbin, Henri. 1960. *Terre Celestiel et corps de ressurection de l'Iran mazdeen a l'Iran shi'ite*. Paris: Buchet/Chastel-Correa.

———. 1990. *Spiritual Body and Celestial Earth: From Mazdean Iran to Shi'ite Iran*. Trans. Nancy Pearson. London: Tauris.

Course, Magnus. 2009. Why Mapuche Sing. *Journal of the Royal Anthropological Institute* 15(2): 205–313.

Crapanzano, Vincent. 1973. *The Hamadsha: A Study in Moroccan Ethnopsychiatry*. Berkeley: University of California Press.

———. 1985. *Waiting: The Whites of South Africa*. New York: Random House.

———. 1992. *Hermes' Dilemma and Hamlet's Desire: On the Epistemology of Interpretation*. Cambridge: Harvard University Press.

———. 2000. *Serving the Word: Literalism in America from the Pulpit to the Bench*. New York: New Press.

———. 2004. *Imaginative Horizons: An Essay in Literary-Philosophical Anthropology*. Chicago: University of Chicago Press.

———. 2011. *The Harkis: The Wound That Never Heals*. Chicago: University of Chicago Press.

Das, Veena. 1998. Wittgenstein and Anthropology. *Annual Review of Anthropology* 27: 171–95.

———. 2007. *Life and Words: Violence and the Descent into the Ordinary*. Berkeley: University of California Press.

———. 2010. Engaging the Life of the Other: Love and Everyday Life. In Michael Lambek, ed., *Ordinary Ethics*. New York: Fordham University Press.

———. 2012a. Ordinary Ethics. In Didier Fassin, ed., *A Companion to Moral Anthropology*. West Sussex, U.K.: Wiley.

———. 2012b. Violence and Nonviolence at the Heart of Hindu Ethics. In Mark Juergensmeyer, Margo Kitts, and Michael Jerryson, eds., *The Oxford Handbook of Religion and Violence*. Oxford: Oxford University Press.

Das, Veena, and Deborah Poole. 2004. *Anthropology in the Margins of the State*. Santa Fe, N.M.: School of American Research Press.

Das, Veena, et al. 2000. *Violence and Subjectivity*. Berkeley: University of California Press.

Das, Veena, et al. 2001. *Remaking a World: Violence, Social Suffering, and Recovery*. Berkeley: University of California Press.

de Certeau, Michel. 1992. *The Mystic Fable: The Sixteenth and Seventeenth Centuries*. Chicago: University of Chicago Press.

Deleuze, Gilles. 1959a. Bergson, 1859–1941. In *L'Ile deserte et autres textes: Textes et entretiens 1953–1974*. Paris: Les Éditions de Minuit.

———. 1959b. La conception de la différence chez Bergson. In *L'Île deserte et autres textes: Textes et entretiens 1953–1974*. Paris: Les Éditions de Minuit.

———. 1968. *Le Bergsonisme*. Paris: Presses Universitaires de France.

———. 1983. *Nietzsche and Philosophy*. Trans. Hugh Tomlinson. New York: Columbia University Press.

———. 1990. *The Logic of Sense*. New York: Columbia University Press.

———. 1991. *Bergsonism*. Trans. Hugh Tomlinson and Barbara Habberjam. New York: Zone Books.

———. 1994. *Difference and Repetition*. New York: Columbia University Press.

———. 1995. Control and Becoming. In *Negotiations: 1972–1990*, 169–76. New York: Columbia University Press.

———. 1997a. Appendix: Review of Jean Hyppolite's *Logique et Existence*. In Jean Hyppolite, ed., *Logic and Existence*. Albany: State University of New York Press.

———. 1997b. *Essays Critical and Clinical*. Minneapolis: University of Minnesota Press.

———. 1998. Having an Idea in Cinema. Trans. Eleanor Kaufma. Ed. Eleanor Kaufman and Kevin Jon Heller. In *Deleuze and Guattari: New Mappings in Politics, Philosophy, and Culture*. Minneapolis: University of Minnesota Press.

———. 2001. *Pure Immanence: Essays on a Life*. Trans. Anne Boyman. New York: Zone Books.

———. 2004. *Desert Islands*. Los Angeles: Semiotext(e).

———. 2007. *L'Île deserte et autres texts: Textes et entretiens 1953–1974*. Ed. David Lapujade. Paris: Les Éditions de Minuit.

Deleuze, Gilles, and Félix Guattari. (1972) 1983. *Anti-Oedipus*. Minneapolis: University of Minnesota Press.

———. (1980) 1987. *A Thousand Plateaus: Capitalism and Schizophrenia*. Minneapolis: University of Minnesota Press.

———. 1994. *What Is Philosophy?* New York: Columbia University Press.

Derrida, Jacques. 1980. *La carte postale: De Socrates à Freud et au-delà*. Paris: Flammarion.

———. 1987. *The Post Card: From Socrates to Freud and Beyond*. Trans. Alan Bass. Chicago: University of Chicago Press.

———. 1994. *Politiques de l'amitié*. Paris: Galilée.

———. 1997. *The Politics of Friendship*. Trans. George Collins. New York: Verso.

Derrida, Jacques, and Christie V. McDonald. 1981. Choreographies. *Diacritics* 12(2): 66–76.

Descola, Phillipe. 2006. Beyond Nature and Culture. *Proceedings of the British Academy* 139: 137–55.

Devisch, René. 1999. Sorcery and Fetish. In René Devish and Claude Brodeur, eds., *The Law of the Lifegivers: The Domestication of Desire*. Amsterdam: Harwood.

de Vries, Hent, and Sam Weber, eds. 2001. *Religion and Media*. Palo Alto, Calif.: Stanford University Press.

Dewey, John. 1958. *Experience and Nature*. New York: Dover.

Dreyfus, Hubert, and Paul Rabinow. 1993. Can There Be a Science of Existential Structure and Social Meaning? In C. Calhoun, Edward LiPuma, and Moishe Postune, eds., *Bourdieu: Critical Perspectives*. Chapel Hill: University of North Carolina Press.

Dumézil, G. 1988. *Mitra-Varuna: An Essay on Two Indo-European Representations of Sovereignty*. Trans. Derek Coltman. New York: Zone Books.

Dumont, Louis 1980. *Homo Hierarchicus: The Caste System and Its Implications*. Chicago: University of Chicago Press.

Duranti, Alessandro. 1988. Intentions, Language and Social Action in Samoan Context. *Journal of Pragmatics* 12: 13–33.

Durkheim, Emile. 2001. *The Elementary Forms of Religious Life*. Trans. Carol Cosman. Oxford: Oxford University Press.

Eliade, Mircea. 1954. *The Myth of the Eternal Return, or, Cosmos and History*. Trans. Willard R. Task. Princeton: Princeton University Press.

Elias, Norbert. 1994. *The Civilizing Process: The History of Manners and State Formation and Civilization*. Trans. Edmund Jephcott. Oxford: Blackwell.

Eliot, T. S. 1968. *Four Quartets*. London: Faber and Faber.

Emerson, Ralph Waldo. 1844. Experience. In *Essays: Second Series*. Boston: James Munroe.

Erami, Narges, 2009. The Soul of the Market: Knowledge, Authority and the Making of Expert Merchants in the Persian Rug. Ph.D. diss., Columbia University.

Esposito, Roberto. 2008. *Bio: Biopolitics and Philosophy*. Minneapolis: University of Minnesota Press.

Evans-Pritchard, E. E. 1976. *Witchcraft, Oracles, and Magic among the Azande*. Oxford: Clarendon Press.

Fassin, Didier. 2005a. Compassion and Repression: The Moral Economy of Immigration Policies in France. *Cultural Anthropology* 20(3): 362–87.

———. 2005b. L'Ordre Moral du Monde: Essai d'Anthropologie de l'Intolérable. In Didier Fassin and Patrice Bourdelais eds., *Les Constructions de l'Intolérable*. Paris: Découverte.

———. 2007. *When Bodies Remember: Experience and Politics of AIDS in South Africa*. Berkeley: University of California Press.

———. 2009. Another Politics of Life Is Possible. *Theory, Culture and Society* 26(5): 44–60.

———. 2010. Ethics of Survival: A Democratic Approach to the Politics of Life. *Humanity: International Journal of Human Rights, Humanitarianism and Development* 1(1): 81–95.

———. 2011. *Humanitarian Reason: A Moral History of the Present*. Berkeley: University of California Press.

———. 2012. Introduction: Toward a Critical Moral Anthropology. In Didier Fassin, ed., *Companion to Moral Anthropology*. Oxford: Wiley Blackwell.

Faubion, James D. 2006. On the Semantics of Sacral Action. In Matthew Engelke and Matt Tomlinson, eds., *The Limits of Meaning: Case Studies in the Anthropology of Christianity*. New York: Berghahn.

Ferme, M. 2004. Deterritorialized Citizenship and the Resonances of the Sierra Leonean State. In Veena Das and Deborah Poole, eds., *Anthropology in the Margins of the State*. Santa Fe, N.M.: School of American Research Press.

Fernandez, James. 1982. *Bwiti: An Ethnography of the Religious Imagination in Africa*. Princeton: Princeton University Press.

Fischer, Michael M. J. 1973. Zoroastrian Iran between Myth and Praxis. Ph.D. diss., University of Chicago.

———. 1980. *Iran: From Religious Dispute to Revolution*. Cambridge: Harvard University Press.

———. 1983. Imam Khomeini: Four Ways of Understanding. In John Esposito, ed., *Voices of Resurgent Islam*. New York: Oxford University Press.

———. 2004a. *Mute Dreams, Blind Owls, and Dispersed Knowledges: Persian Poesis in the Transnational Circuitry*. Durham: Duke University Press.

———. 2004b. Persian Miniatures: Two Kinds of Dialogue in Iran. *Middle East Insight* 1(1).

———. 2009a. Body Marks (Beastial/Divine/Natural): An Essay into the Social and Biotechnical Imaginary 1920–2010 and Bodies to Come. In *Anthropological Futures*. Durham: Duke University Press.

———. 2009b. Reading Hannah Arendt in Tehran. In *Anthropological Futures*. Durham: Duke University Press.

———. 2010a. Comment on Biehl, João, and Peter Locke, "Deleuze and the Anthropology of Becoming." *Current Anthropology* 51(3): 337–38.

———. 2010b. The Rhythmic Beat of the Revolution in Iran. *Cultural Anthropology* 25(3): 497–543.

Fischer, M. M. J., and Mehdi Abedi. 1985. Foreword to Ayatollah S. Ruhollah Mousavi Khomeni, *A Clarification of Questions*. Trans. J. Borujerdi. Boulder, Colo.: Westview Press.

———. 1990. *Debating Muslims: Cultural Dialogues in Postmodernity and Tradition*. Madison: University of Wisconsin Press.

Flory, Stewart. 1987. *The Archaic Smile of Herodotus*. Detroit: Wayne State University Press.

Fortes, Meyer. 1983. *Oedipus and Job in West African Religion*. Cambridge: Cambridge University Press.

Fortes, Meyers, and E. E. Evans-Pritchard. Introduction to *African Political Systems*. London: Oxford University Press.

Foucault, Michel. 1977. Theatrum Philosophicum. In *Language, Counter-Memory, Practice*. Ithaca: Cornell University Press.

———. 1980a. *The History of Sexuality*. New York: Vintage.

———. 1980b. Questions of Geography. In Colin Gordon, ed., *Power/Knowledge: Selected Interviews and Other Writings, 1972–1977*. New York: Pantheon.

———. 1989. *The Will to Knowledge: The History of Sexuality, Volume 1*. London: Penguin.

———. 1990. *The Use of Pleasure*. Vol. 2 of *The History of Sexuality*. Trans. Robert Hurley. New York: Vintage.

———. 1997. The Masked Philosopher. In P. Rabinow, ed., *Ethics, Subjectivity and Truth*. New York: New Press.

———. 1999. What Is an Author? In J. Faubion, ed., *Aesthetics, Methods, and Epistemology*. New York: New Press.

———. 2001. *The Hermeneutics of the Subject: Lectures at the College de France, 1981–1982*. London: Palgrave Macmillan.

———. 2008. *The Birth of Biopolitics: Lectures at the College de France, 1978–1979*. Trans. G. Burchell. London: Palgrave Macmillan.

———. N.d. *O que é um autor?* Lisbon: Passagem.

Friedlander, Eli. 2012. *Walter Benjamin: A Philosophical Portrait*. Cambridge: Harvard University Press.

Freud, Sigmund. (1915) 2005. On Transience. In Matthew von Unwerth, ed., *Freud's Requiem*. New York: Riverhead Books.

———. 1957. The Sense of Symptoms. In *The Standard Edition of the Completed Psychological Works of Sigmund Freud*, vol. 16, *1916–1917*. London: Hogarth.

———. 1961. *Civilization and Its Discontents*. Trans. James Strachey. New York: Norton.

Garcia, Angela. 2010. *The Pastoral Clinic: Addiction and Dispossession along the Rio Grande*. Berkeley: University of California Press.

Gbadegesin, Segun. 1991. *African Philosophy: Traditional Yoruba Philosophy and Contemporary African Realities*. New York: Peter Lang.

Geertz, Clifford. 1973. *The Interpretation of Cultures*. New York: Basic Books.

———. 1980. *Negara: The Theatre State in Nineteenth-Century Bali*. Princeton: Princeton University Press.

———. 1983. *Local Knowledge: Further Essays in Interpretive Anthropology*. New York: Basic Books.

———. 1988. *Works and Lives: The Anthropologist as Author*. Palo Alto, Calif.: Stanford University Press.

———. 1995. *After the Fact*. Cambridge: Harvard University Press.

———. 1998. Deep Hanging Out. *New York Review of Books*, October 22.

———. 2000. *Available Light: Anthropological Reflections on Philosophical Topics*. Princeton: Princeton University Press.

Gertner, Jon. 2012. *The Idea Factory: Bell Labs and the Great Age of American Innovation*. New York: Penguin.

Goffman, Erving. 1974. *Frame Analysis: An Essay on the Organization of Experience*. New York: Harper and Row.

Good, Byron, Mary-Jo DelVecchio Good, and Robert Moradi. 1985. The Interpretation of Dysphoric Affect and Depressive Illness in Iranian Culture. In A. Kleinman and B. Good, eds., *Culture and Depression*. Los Angeles: University of California Press.

Goodman, Nelson. 1978. *Ways of Worldmaking*. Indianapolis: Hacket Publishing.

Granet, Marcel. 1934. *La pensée chinoise*. Paris: La Renaissance du Livre.

Greenblatt, Stephen. 2009. All in War with Time for Love of You: Torben Eskerod's Faces. In Torben Eskerod, ed., *Campo Verano*. Heidelberg: Kehrer Verlag.

———. 2012. "Shakespeare and the Shape of a Life: The End of Life Stories" and "Shakespeare and the Shape of a Life: The Uses of Life Stories." Tanner Lectures in Human Values. Princeton University Center for Human Values, March 15 and 16.

Groddeck, Georg. 1977. *The Meaning of Illness: Selected Psychoanalytic Writings*. Ed. Gertrud Mander. London: Hogarth Press.

Guattari, Félix. 2008. In Flux. In *Chaosophy: Texts and Interview 1972–1977*. Los Angeles: Semiotext(e).

Guha, Ramchadra. 1983. Forestry in British and Post-British India: A Historical Analysis. *Economic and Political Weekly* 18(45–46): 1940–47.

Habermas, Jürgen. 1990. *Moral Consciousness and Communicative Action*. Trans. C. Lenhardt and S. W. Nicholsen. Cambridge: MIT Press.

Hadot, Pierre. 1995. *Philosophy as a Way of Life: Spiritual Exercises from Socrates to Foucault*. Trans. Michael Case. Oxford: Blackwell.

Haeri, Shahla. 2002. *Law of Desire: Temporary Marriage in Shi'i Iran*. Syracuse, N.Y.: Syracuse University Press.

Hage, Ghassan. 2003. Comes a Time We Are All Enthusiasm: Understanding Palestinian Suicide Bombers in Times of Exighophobia. *Public Culture* 15(1): 65.

———. 2009. Key Thinkers Public Lecture: Pierre Bourdieu. *Monthly: Australian Politics, Society and Culture*. http://www.themonthly.com.au/key-thinkers-ghassan-hage-pierre-bourdieu-1504.

Halpern, David. 2005. *Social Capital*. Cambridge, U.K.: Polity Press.

Han, Clara. 2011. Symptoms of Another Life: Time, Possibility, and Domestic Relations in Chile's Credit Economy. *Cultural Anthropology* 26(1): 7–32.

———. 2012. *Life and Debt: Times of Care and Violence in Neoliberal Chile*. Berkeley: University of California Press.

Hansen, Miriam B. 2008. Benjamin's Aura. *Critical Inquiry* 14: 336–75.

Hansen, Thomas B., and Finn Stepputat. 2006. Sovereignty Revisited. *Annual Review of Anthropology* 35: 295–315.

Hardiman, David. 1987. *The Coming of the Devi: Adivasi Assertion in Western India*. New Delhi: Oxford University Press.

Hegel, G. W. F. 1952. *The Philosophy of Right*. Oxford: Clarendon Press.

Heidegger, Martin. 1962. *Being and Time*. Trans. Robinson and Macquarrie. New York: Harper and Row.

Heran, François. 1987. La Seconde Nature de L'habitus: Tradition Philosophique et Sens Commun dans le Langage Sociologique. *Revue Francaise de Sociologie* 28: 385–416.

Herzfeld, Michael. 1988. *The Poetics of Manhood: Contest and Identity in a Cretan Mountain Village.* Princeton: Princeton University Press.

———. 1992. *The Social Production of Indifference.* Chicago: University of Chicago Press.

———. 1997. *Portrait of a Greek Imagination: An Ethnographic Biography of Andreas Nenedakis.* Chicago: University of Chicago Press.

Hess, Linda. 1987. Kabir Rough Rhetoric. In Karine Schomer and W. H. McLeod, eds., *The Sants: Studies in a Devotional Tradition of India.* Berkeley: University of California Press.

Horton, Robin. 1961. Destiny and the Unconscious in West Africa. *Africa* 31(2): 110–16.

Hsu, Francis L. K. 1967. *Under the Ancestors' Shadow: Kinship, Personality, and Social Mobility in China.* Stanford: Stanford University Press.

Huang, Kwang Kuo. 2011. *Foundations of Chinese Psychology: Confucian Social Relations.* New York: Springer.

Husserl, Edmund. 1970. The Vienna Lecture (Appendix). In *The Crisis of European Sciences and Transcendental Phenomenology.* Evanston, Ill.: Northwestern University Press.

Hyslop, Alec. 2009. Other Minds. *Stanford Encyclopedia of Philosophy.* Accessed November 23, http://plato.stanford.edu/entries/other-minds/.

Idowu, E. B. 1962. *Oludumare: God in Yoruba Belief.* London: Longmans.

Illanes, María Angélica. 2007. *Cuerpo y sangre de la política: La construcción histórica de las Visitadores Sociales (1887–1940).* Santiago: LOM Ediciones.

Imbert, Claude. 2008. *Lévi-Strauss, le passage du Nord-Ouest: Précède d'un texte de Claude Lévi-Strauss, Indian Cosmetics.* Paris: L'Herne.

———. 2009. On Anthropological Knowledge. In Boris Wiseman, ed., *The Cambridge Companion to Levi-Strauss.* Cambridge: Cambridge University Press.

Jabes, Edmond. 1963. *Le Livre des Questiones.* Paris: Gallimard.

———. 1976. *The Book of Questions.* Trans. Rosemarie Waldrop. Middletown, Conn.: Wesleyan University Press.

Jackson, Michael D. 1998. *Minima Ethnographica: Intersubjectivity and the Anthropological Project.* Chicago: University of Chicago Press.

———. 2004. *In Sierra Leone.* Durham: Duke University Press.

———. 2005. *Existential Anthropology: Events, Exigencies and Effects.* New York: Berghahn Books.

———. 2009. An Anthropological Critique of the Project of Philosophy. *Anthropological Theory* 9(3): 235–51.

James, Henry. 1902. Preface to *The Wings of the Dove.* New York: Charles Scribner's Sons.

James, William. 1890. *The Principles of Psychology.* Vols. 1 and 2, *Advanced Course.* New York: H. Holt.

———. 1896. *The Will to Believe and Other Essays in Popular Philosophy.* New York: Longmans, Green.

———. 1899. *Talks to Teachers on Psychology and to Students on Some of Life's Ideals.* New York: H. Holt.

———. 1902. *The Varieties of Religious Experience: A Study in Human Nature; being the Gifford Lectures on Natural Religion Delivered in Edinburgh in 1901–1902.* London: Longmans Green.

———. 1903. The Ph.D. Octopus. *Harvard Monthly,* March 1.

———. 1907. *Pragmatism: A New Name for Some Old Ways of Thinking.* Indianapolis: Hackett.

———. 1909. *A Pluralistic Universe.* Lincoln: University of Nebraska Press.

———. 1977. *The Writings of William James: A Comprehensive Edition, Including an Annotated Bibliography Updated through 1977.* Edited with introduction by John J. McDermott. Chicago: University of Chicago Press.

———. 1978. *Pragmatism and the Meaning of Truth.* Cambridge: Harvard University Press.

Jameson, Fredric. 2009. *Valences of the Dialectic.* Verso: London.

Jankélévitch, Vladimir. 1959. *Henri Bergson.* Paris: Presses Universitaires de France.

Jensen, Casper Bruun, and Kjetil Rödje. 2012. *Deleuzian Intersections: Science, Technology, Anthropology.* New York: Berghahn Books.

Johnson, Galen. 1993. Phenomenology and Painting: "Cézanne's Doubt." In Reader G. Johnson, ed., *The Merleau-Ponty Aesthetics.* Evanston, Ill.: Northwestern University Press.

Keane, Webb. 2010. Minds, Surfaces, and Reasons in the Anthropology of Ethics. In M. Lambek, ed., *Ordinary Ethics: Anthropology, Language, and Action.* New York: Fordham University Press.

Kertzer, David. 1988. *Rituals, Politics and Power.* New Haven: Yale University Press.

Khan, Naveeda. 2006. Of Children and *Jinn*: An Inquiry into an Unexpected Friendship During Uncertain Times. *Cultural Anthropology* 21(2): 234–65.

Khera, Reetika. 2006. Political Economy of State Response to Drought in Rajasthan, 2000–03, *Economic and Political Weekly* 41(50): 5163–72.

Khosrovi, Shahram. 2007. *Young and Defiant in Tehran.* Philadelphia: University of Pennsylvania Press.

Kleinman, Arthur. 1973a. The Background and Development of Public Health in China: An Exploratory Essay. In M. E. Wegman, T. Y. Lin, and E. F. Purcell, eds., *Public Health in the People's Republic of China.* New York: Josiah Macy, Jr. Foundation.

———. 1973b. Medicine's Symbolic Reality: A Central Problem in the Philosophy of Medicine. *Inquiry* 16: 206–13.

———. 1973c. Some Issues for a Comparative Study of Medical Healing. *International Journal of Social Psychiatry* 19: 159–65.

———. 1973d. Toward a Comparative Study of Medical Systems. *Science, Medicine and Man* 1: 55–65.

———. 1978. *Culture and Healing in Asian Societies: Anthropological, Psychiatric and Public Health Studies.* Cambridge, Mass.: Schenkman.

———. 1980. *Patients and Healers in the Context of Culture: An Exploration of the Borderland between Anthropology, Medicine, and Psychiatry.* Vol. 3. Berkeley: University of California Press.

———. 1986. *Social Origins of Distress and Disease: Depression, Neurasthenia, and Pain in Modern China.* New Haven: Yale University Press.

———. 1988a. *The Illness Narratives: Suffering, Healing, and the Human Condition.* New York: Basic Books.

———. 1988b. *Rethinking Psychiatry: From Cultural Category to Personal Experience.* New York: Free Press, Collier Macmillan.

———. 1995. *Writing at the Margin: Discourse between Anthropology and Medicine.* Berkeley: University of California Press.

———. 1999. *Experience and Its Moral Modes: Culture, Human Conditions, Disorder.* The Tanner Lectures on Human Values, vol. 20, 357–420. Salt Lake City: University of Utah Press.

———. 2006. *What Really Matters: Living a Moral Life amidst Uncertainty and Danger.* Oxford: Oxford University Press.

———. 2011. A Search for Wisdom. *Lancet* 378(9803): 1621–22.

Kleinman, Arthur, et al., eds. 1997. *Social Suffering.* Berkeley: University of California Press.

Kleinman, Arthur, et al., eds. 2011. *Deep China: The Moral Life of the Person. What Anthropology and Psychiatry Tell Us about China Today.* Berkeley: University of California Press.

Koestler, Arthur. 1975. *The Act of Creation.* London: Pan Books.

Koo, Jo Jo. 2007. The Possibility of Philosophical Anthropology. In G. W. Bertram et al., eds., *Socialté et reconnaissance: Grammaires de l'Human.* Paris: L'Harmatten.

Kripke, Saul. 1982. *Wittgenstein on Rules and Private Language: An Elementary Exposition.* Oxford: Blackwell.

Kristeva, Julia. 1977. *Le Sujet en Procès: Polylogue.* Paris: Seuil.

Lacan, Jacques. 1966. *Ecrits.* Paris: Seuil.

———. 1989. Science and Truth. *Newsletter of the Freudian Field* 3: 4–29.

Lacoue-Labarthe, Philippe. 1989. The Echo of the Subject. In Christopher Fynsk, ed., *Typography: Mimesis, Philosophy, Politics.* Cambridge: Harvard University Press.

Laidlaw, James. 2002. For an Anthropology of Ethics and Freedom. *Journal of the Royal Anthropological Institute* 8(2): 331.

Lambek, Michael. 2010. Towards an Ethics of the Act. In Michael Lambek, ed., *Ordinary Ethics: Anthropology, Language, and Action*. New York: Fordham University Press.

———. 2011. Kinship as Gift and Theft: Acts of Succession in Mayotte and Ancient Israel. *American Ethnologist* 38(1): 2–16.

Latour, Bruno. 2012. *Enquête sur les modes d'existence: Une anthropologie des Modernes*. Paris: La Découverte.

Laugier, Sandra. 2001. Wittgenstein and Cavell: Anthropology, Skepticism, and Politics. In Andrew Norris, ed., *The Claim to Community: Essays on Stanley Cavell and Political Philosophy*. Stanford: Stanford University Press.

Laugier, Sandra, 2011. Introduction to the French edition of *Must We Mean What We Say? Critical Inquiry* 37(4): 627–51.

Lee, Benjamin. 1997. *Talking Heads: Language, Metalanguage and the Semiotics of Subjectivity*. Durham: Duke University Press.

Legge, James. 1885. *Li Chi: Book of Rites*. Oxford: Oxford University Press.

Leonard, Miriam. 2005. *Athens in Paris: Ancient Greece and the Political in Post-war French Thought*. Oxford: Oxford University Press.

———. 2011. Introduction to the French edition of *Must We Mean What We Say? Critical Inquiry* 37(4): 627–51.

Lescourret, M., ed. 2009. *Pierre Bourdieu: Un philosophe en sociologue*. Paris: Presses Universitaires de France.

Levinas, Emmanuel. 1987. *Time and the Other*. Trans. Richard A. Cohen. Pittsburgh: Duquesne University Press.

———. 2001. Is It Righteous to Be? Interviews with Emmanuel Levinas. Ed. Joel Robbins. Stanford: Stanford University Press.

Lévi-Strauss, Claude. 1966. *The Savage Mind*. London: Weidenfeld and Nicolson.

———. 1967. *Structural Anthropology*. Garden City, N.J.: Anchor Books.

———. 1969. *Elementary Structures of Kinship*. New York: Beacon Press.

———. 1971. *Mythologiques*. Paris: Plon.

———. (1955) 1992. *Tristes Tropiques*. New York: Penguin.

———. 1981. *The Naked Man: Mythologiques*. Vol. 4. Chicago: University of Chicago Press.

———. 1985. *The View from Afar*. Chicago: University of Chicago Press.

———. 1988. *The Ways of the Masks*. Seattle: University of Washington Press.

———. 1995. *Saudades do Brasil: A Photographic Memoir*. Seattle: University of Washington Press.

Lévy-Bruhl, Lucien. (1923) 1985. *How Natives Think*. Princeton: Princeton University Press.

Lewis, Philip. 1985. The Measure of Translation Effects. In Joseph Graham, ed., *Difference in Translation*. Ithaca: Cornell University Press.

Lienhardt, Godfrey. 1987. *Divinity and Experience: The Religion of the Dinka*. Oxford: Clarendon Press.

Liji. N.d. Chinese University of Hong Kong, Institute of Chinese Studies, Ancient Chinese Text Concordance Series.

Lotfalian, Mazyar. 1996. Working through Psychological Understandings of the Diasporic Condition. *Ethos* 24(1): 36–70.

Malik, Aditya. 2010. In the Divine Court of Appeals. In Timothy Lubin, Donald Davis, and Jayanth Krishnan, eds., *Hinduism and the Law: An Introduction*. Cambridge: Cambridge University Press.

Malinowski, Bronislaw. 1927. *Sex and Repression in Savage Society*. London: Routledge.

Marcus, George. 2008. The End(s) of Ethnography: Social/Cultural Anthropology's Signature Form of Producing Knowledge in Transition. *Cultural Anthropology* 23(1): 1–14.

———. 2012. The Legacies of "Writing Culture" and the Near Future of the Ethnographic Form: A Sketch. *Cultural Anthropology* 27(3): 427–45.

Marcuse, Herbert. 1966. *Eros and Civilization: A Philosophical Inquiry into Freud*. Boston: Beacon Press.

———. 1968. *Negations: Essays in Critical Theory*. Trans. Jeremy J. Shapiro. London: Allen Lane.

Marriott, McKim. 1966. The Feast of Love. In Milton Singer ed., *Krishna: Myths, Rites, Attitudes*. Hawaii: East-West Center Press.

Mauss, Marcel. 1990. *The Gift: The Form and Reason for Exchange in Archaic Societies*. Trans. W. D. Halls. New York: W.W. Norton.

May, Rollo. 1958. The Origins and Significance of the Existential Movement in Psychology. In R. May, E. Angel, and H. F. Ellenberger, eds., *Existence: A New Dimension in Psychiatry*. New York: Basic Books.

McDowell, John Henry. 1994. *Mind and World*. Cambridge: Harvard University Press.

———. 1998. *Meaning, Knowledge and Reality*. Cambridge: Harvard University Press.

McFarland, Ian A. 2001. Who Is My Neighbor? The Good Samaritan as a Source for Theological Anthropology. *Modern Theology* 17(1): 57–66.

Mehta, Deepak. 2010. Words That Wound: Archiving Hate in the Making of Hindu-Indian and Muslim-Pakistan in Bombay. In N. Khan, ed., *Beyond Crisis: Re-evaluating Pakistan*. Delhi: Routledge.

Merleau-Ponty, Maurice. 1960a. Bergson se faisant. In *Signes*. Paris: Gallimard.

———. 1960b. Eloge de la philosophie. In *Eloge de la philosophie et autre essais*. Paris: Gallimard.

———. 1962. *The Phenomenology of Perception*. Trans. Colin Smith. London: Routledge and Kegan Paul.

———. 1964. *Signs*. Evanston, Ill.: Northwestern University Press.

———. 1965. *The Structure of Behaviour*. Trans. Alden L. Fisher. London: Methuen.

———. 1973. *The Prose of the World*. Evanston, Ill.: Northwestern University Press.

Merleau-Ponty, Maurice, and Galen Johnson, eds. 1993. *The Merleau-Ponty Aesthetics Reader: Philosophy and Painting*. Evanston, Ill.: Northwestern University Press.

Merleau-Ponty, Maurice, and Claude Lefort. 1968. *The Visible and the Invisible: Followed by Working Notes*. Evanston, Ill.: Northwestern University Press.

Meyer, Michel, ed. 2002. Pierre Bourdieu et la Philosophie. *Revue Internationale de Philosophie* (2).

Miller, D., M. Rowlands, and C. Tilley. 1995. *Domination and Resistance*. London: Routledge

Modarressi, Taghi. 1985. *The Book of Absent People*. Garden City, N.Y.: Doubleday.

Moinzadeh, Hassan Ali. 2004. Secret of Gay Being: Embodying Homosexual Libido in the Iranian Imagination. Ph.D. diss., Pacifica Graduate Institute.

Montaigne, Michel de. 2004. *The Essays: A Selection*. Trans. M. A. Screech. Harmondsworth, U.K.: Penguin.

Moody-Adams, Michele. 1997. *Fieldwork in Familiar Places*. Cambridge: Harvard University Press.

————. 2004. *Epistemology and Practice: Durkheim's The Elementary Forms of Religious Life*. Cambridge: Cambridge University Press.

Morris, Rosalind. 2010. *Can the Subaltern Speak? Reflections on the History of an Idea*. New York: Columbia University Press.

Moyn, Samuel. 2004. Of Savagery and Civil Society: Pierre Clastres and the Transformation. *Of French Political Thought. Modern Intellectual History* 1(1): 55–80.

Naficy, Hamid. 2001. *An Accented Cinema: Exilic and Diasporic Filmmaking*. Princeton: Princeton University Press.

Naficy, Nahal. 2007. Persian Miniature Writing: An Ethnography of Iranian Organizations in Washington, D.C. Ph.D. diss., Rice University.

Nafisi, Azar. 2003. *Reading Lolita in Tehran*. New York: Random House.

Najmabadi, Afsaneh. 2005. *Women with Mustaches and Men without Beards: Gender and Sexual Anxieties of Iranian Modernity*. Berkeley: University of California Press.

————. 2013. *Sex-in-Change: Configurations of Gender and Sexuality in Contemporary Iran*. Durham: Duke University Press.

Nesbitt, Nick. 2005. The Expulsion of the Negative: Deleuze, Adorno, and the Ethics of Internal Difference. *SubStance* 107, 34(2): 75–97.

Nietzsche, Friedrich. 1955. *The Use and Abuse of History*. New York: Macmillan.

————. 1969. *Ecce Homo*. New York: Vintage Books.

————. 1990. *Twilight of the Idols*. Trans. R. J. Hollingdale. New York: Penguin Classics.

————. 2003. *Beyond Good and Evil*. London: Penguin.

————. 2006. *On the Genealogy of Morality*. Trans. Carol Diethe. Cambridge: Cambridge University Press.

————. 2007. *On the Genealogy of Morals*. Trans. K. Ansel-Pearson. Cambridge: Cambridge University Press.

Ong, Aihwa, and Stephen Collier. 2005. *Global Assemblages: Technology, Politics and Ethics as Anthropological Problems*. Oxford: Blackwell.

Orsi, Robert A. 2005. *Between Heaven and Earth: The Religious Worlds People Make and the Scholars Who Study Them*. Princeton: Princeton University Press.

Osanloo, Arzoo. 2009. *The Politics of Women's Rights in Iran*. Princeton: Princeton University Press.

Pandolfo, Stefania 2005. Nibtidi Mnin il-hikaya [Where do we start the tale?]: Violence, Intimacy and Recollection. *Social Science Information* 45: 349–71.

————. 2009. Soul-Choking: Maladies of the Soul, Islam, and the Ethics of Psychoanalysis. Islam, special issue of *Umbri(a): A Journal of the Unconscious* 71–103.

Parry, Jonathan. 1985. *The Gift*, the Indian Gift, and the "Indian Gift." *Man* 21: 453–73.

Peabody, Norbert. 2003. *Hindu Kinghip and Polity in Precolonial India*. Cambridge: Cambridge University Press.

Phillips, Adam, and Barbara Taylor. 2009. *On Kindness*. New York: Picador.

Pinto, Louis. 1998. *Pierre Bourdieu et la Théorie du Monde Social*. Paris: Albin Michel.

Postel, Danny. 2006. *Reading Legitimation Crisis in Tehran: Iran and the Future of Liberalism*. Chicago: Prickley Paradigm Press.

Puett, Michael. 2005. The Offering of Food and the Creation of Order: The Practice of Sacrifice in Early China. In Roel Sterckx, ed., *Of Tripod and Palate: Food, Politics, and Religion in Traditional China*. New York: Palgrave Macmillan.

————. 2010a. The Haunted World of Humanity: Ritual Theory from Early China. In J. Michelle Molina and Donald K. Swearer, eds., *Rethinking the Human*. Cambridge, Mass.: Center for the Study of World Religions.

————. 2010b. Ritualization as Domestication: Ritual Theory from Classical China. In Axel Michaels, Anand Mishra, Lucia Dolce, Gil Raz, and Katja Triplett, eds., *Ritual Dynamics and the Science of Ritual*, Vol. 1: *Grammars and Morphologies of Ritual Practice in Asia*. Wiesbaden: Harrassowitz Verlag.

Puett, Michael, Adam Seligman, Robert Weller, and Bennett Simon. 2008. *Ritual and Its Consequences: An Essay on the Limits of Sincerity*. Oxford: Oxford University Press.

Putnam, Robert. 1993. *Making Democracy Work: Civic Traditions in Modern Italy*. Princeton: Princeton University Press.

Rabinow, Paul. 2003. *Anthropos Today: Reflections on Modern Equipment*. Princeton: Princeton University Press.

————. 2007. *Reflections on Fieldwork in Morocco*. 2nd edition. Berkeley: University of California Press.

———. 2011. *The Accompaniment: Assembling the Contemporary.* Chicago: University of Chicago Press.

Rabinow, Paul, and George Marcus, with James Faubion and Tobias Rees. 2008. *Designs for an Anthropology of the Contemporary.* Durham: Duke University Press.

Rabinow, Paul, and Nikolas Rose. 2006. Biopower Today. *Biosocieties* 1(2): 195–217.

Radcliffe-Brown, A. R. 1940. Preface to M. Fortes and E. E. Evans-Pritchard, eds., *African Political Systems.* London: Oxford University Press.

Rahimi, Nasrin. 2011. Translating Taghi Modarressi's Writing with an Accent. In Mohammad Ghanoonparvar, ed., *Festschrift for Gernot Windfuhr.*

Ravaisson, Felix. 2009. *Of Habit.* Trans. Clare Carlisle and Mark Sinclairs. New York: Continuum.

Reader, Soran. 2007. The Other Side of Agency. *Philosophy* 82(4): 579–604.

———. 2010. Agency, Patiency, and Personhood. In *A Companion to Philosophy of Action.* Oxford: Wiley-Blackwell.

Redfield, Peter, and Erica Bornstein. 2011. *Forces of Compassion: Humanitarianism Between Ethics and Politics.* Sante Fe, N.M.: SAR Press.

Richardson, Robert D. 2006. *William James: In the Maelstrom of American Modernism. A Biography.* Boston: Houghton Mifflin.

Robbins, Joel. 2010. Anthropology, Pentecostalism and the New Paul: Conversion, Event and Social Transformation. *South Atlantic Quarterly* 109(4): 633–52.

Rohani, Talieh. 2009. Nostalgia without Memory: Iranian-Americans, Cultural Programming and Internet Television. Master's thesis, MIT.

Róheim, Géza. 1971. *The Origin and Function of Culture.* New York: Doubleday.

Roseberry, William. 1997. Marx and Anthropology. *Annual Review of Anthropology* 26: 25–46.

Rouch, Jean. 2003. *Ciné-Ethnography.* Ed. and trans. Steven Feld. Minneapolis: University of Minnesota Press.

Sahlins, Marshall. 1996. The Sadness of Sweetness: or, The Native Anthropology of Western Cosmology. *Current Anthropology* 37(3): 395–428.

Sartre, Jean-Paul. 1940. *L'Imaginaire: Psychologie-Phénoménologique de l'Imagination.* Paris: Gallimard.

———. (1961) 2004. On Violence. Preface to Franz Fanon. In *The Wretched of the Earth.* New York: Grove Press.

———. 1983. *Between Existentialism and Marxism.* Trans. John Matthews. London: Verso.

———. 1987. *The Family Idiot: Gustave Flaubert 1821–1857.* Trans. Carol Cosman. Chicago: University of Chicago Press.

———. 2004. *The Imaginary: A Phenomenological Psychology of the Imagination.* Trans. Jonathan Webber and Arlette Elkaïm. London: Routledge.

Schayeghi, Cyrus. 2004. Science, Medicine and Class in the Formation of Semi-Colonial Iran, 1900s–1940s. Ph.D. diss. Columbia University.

Scheper-Hughes, Nancy. 2001. *Saints, Scholars, and Schizophrenics: Mental Illness in Rural Ireland*. 20th anniversary edition. Berkeley: University of California Press.

Schmitt, Carl. 1985. *Political Theology: Four Chapters on the Concept of Sovereignty*. Trans. George Schwab. Cambridge: MIT Press.

Schore, Allan N. 2003. *Affect Regulation and the Repair of the Self*. New York: Norton.

Scott, Joan. 1990. *Domination and the Arts of Resistance: Hidden Transcripts*. New Haven: Yale University Press.

———. 2011. *The Fantasy of Feminist Theory*. Durham: Duke University Press.

Serrano, Sol. 2008. *¿Qué hacer con Dios en la República? Política y secularización en Chile (1845–1885)*. Santiago: Fondo de Cultura Económica.

Shakespeare, William. 2008. Sonnet 15. In *The Oxford Shakespeare: The Complete Sonnets and Poems*. Ed. Colin Burrow. Oxford: Oxford University Press.

Silverman, Kaja. 2009. *Flesh of My Flesh*. Stanford: Stanford University Press.

Silverstein, Michael, and Greg Urban. 1996. The Natural History of Discourse. In *Natural Histories of Discourse*. Chicago: University of Chicago Press.

Simmel, Georg. 2004. *The Philosophy of Money*. Trans. Tom Bottomore and David Frisby. London: Routledge.

Singh, Bhrigupati. 2006. Re-inhabiting Civil Disobedience. In Hent de Vries and Lawrence Sullivan, eds., *Political Theologies*. New York: Fordham University Press.

———. 2011. Agonistic Intimacy and Moral Aspiration in Popular Hinduism: A Study in the Political Theology of the Neighbor. *American Ethnologist* 38(3): 430–50.

———. 2012. The Headless Horseman of Central India: Sovereignty at Varying Thresholds of Life. *Cultural Anthropology* 27(2): 383–407.

Slatman, Jenny. 2009. Phenomenology of the Icon. In B. Flynn, W. J. Froman, and R. Vallier, eds., *Merleau-Ponty and the Possibilities of Philosophy*. Albany: State University of New York Press.

Smith, Daniel W. 2003. Deleuze and Derrida, Immanence and Transcendence: Two Directions in Recent French Thought. In Paul Patton and John Protevi, eds., *Between Deleuze and Derrida*. New York: Continuum.

Srinivas, M. N. 1969. *Social Change in Modern India*. Berkeley: University of California Press.

Stern, Daniel. 1985. *The Interpersonal World of the Infant: A View from Psychoanalysis and Developmental Psychology*. New York: Basic Books.

Stewart, Kathleen. 2007. *Ordinary Affects*. Durham: Duke University Press.

———. 2011. Precarity's Form. Supervalent Thought. http://supervalentthought.com/sensing-precarity-allison-stewart-garcia-berlant-mclean-biehl/.

Strathern, Marilyn. 1981. *Kinship at the Core: An Anthropology of Elmdon, a Village in North-west Essex in the Nineteen Sixties*. Cambridge: Cambridge University Press.

Taneja, Anand. 2010. This Is How One Pictures the Jinn of History. Unpublished manuscript.

Tarlo, Emma. 2003. *Unsettling Memories: Narratives of the Emergency in Delhi.* Berkeley: University of California Press.

Taussig, Michael. 1997. *The Magic of the State.* New York: Routledge.

Ticktin, Miriam. 2011. *Casualties of Care: Immigration and the Politics of Humanitarianism in France.* Berkeley: University of California Press.

TRI. 2004. Baseline Socio-economic Survey of Sahariya—A Primitive Tribal Group of Rajasthan. Udaipur, Rajasthan: M. L. Verma Tribal Research and Training Institute.

Tronick, Edward. 2003. Dyadically Expanded States of Consciousness and the Process of Therapeutic Change. *Infant Mental Health Journal* 19(3): 290–99.

———. 2007. *The Neurobehavioral and Social-Emotional Development of Infants and Children.* New York: W.W. Norton.

Tronto, Joan C. 1993. *Moral Boundaries: A Political Argument for an Ethic of Care.* New York: Routledge.

Vaudeville, C. (1975) 1987. Sant Mat: Santism as the Universal Path to Sanctity. In Karine Schomer and W. H. McLeod, eds., *The Sants: Studies in a Devotional Tradition of India.* New Delhi: Motilal Banarsidass.

Viveiros de Castro, Eduardo. 2009. *Métaphysiques Cannibales.* Paris: PUF.

———. 2010. The Untimely, Again. In Pierre Clastres, ed., *Archaeology of Violence.* Los Angeles: Semiotext(e).

Weber, Max. 1951. *The Religion of China.* Trans. H. Gerth. New York: Free Press.

Wittgenstein, Ludwig. (1958) 1973. *Philosophical Investigations.* Trans. G. E. M. Anscombe. 2nd edition. Oxford: Blackwell.

———. 1978. *Remarks on Color.* Trans. G. E. M. Anscombe. Berkeley: University of California Press.

Worms, Frederic, and Camille Riquier. 2011. *Lire Bergson.* Paris: Presses Universitaires de France.

Xin Liu. 2000. *In One's Own Shadow: An Ethnographic Account of the Condition of Post-reform Rural China.* Berkeley: University of California Press.

Zeydabid-Nejad, Saeed. 2009. *The Politics of Iranian Cinema.* London: Routledge.

Žižek, Slavoj. 2004. *Organs without Bodies: On Deleuze and Consequences.* New York: Routledge.

JOÃO BIEHL is Susan Dod Brown Professor of Anthropology at Princeton University. He is the author of *Vita: Life in a Zone of Social Abandonment* (2006), and *Will to Live: AIDS Therapies and the Politics of Survival* (2007). He is currently writing a history of the Mucker War, a religious war that took place among German immigrants in nineteenth-century Brazil.

STEVEN C. CATON is a professor of contemporary Arab studies and anthropology at Harvard University. He is the author of *Yemen Chronicle* (2005), *Lawrence of Arbia: A Film's Anthropology* (1999), and *Peaks of Yemen I Summon* (1999). He is currently continuing to research and teach on the topic of water sustainability and is working on a book project on Abu-Ghraib through the lense of Frankfurt School critical theory.

VINCENT CRAPANZANO is Distinguished Professor of Anthropology and Comparative Literature at the Graduate Center of the City University of New York. He is the author of *The Fifth World of Foster Bennet: A Portrait of a Navaho* (1972), *The Hamadsha: A Study in Moroccan Ethnopsychiatry* (1973), *Tuhami: A Portrait of a Moroccan* (1980), *Waiting: The Whites of South Africa* (1985), *Hermes' Dilemma and Hamlet's Desire: On the Epistemology of Interpretation* (1992), *Serving the Word: Literalism from the Pulpit to the Bench* (2000), *Imaginitive Horizons: An Essay in Literary-Philosophical Anthropology* (2004), and *The Harkis: The Wound That Never Heals* (2011).

VEENA DAS is Krieger-Eisenhower Professor of Anthropology at The Johns Hopkins University.She is the author of *Structure and Cognition: Aspects of Hindu Caste and Ritual* (1977, 2012), *Critical Events: An Anthropological Perspective on Contemporary India* (1995), *Life and Words: Violence and the Descent into the Ordinary* (2007), and a forthcoming manuscript, *Affliction: Health, Disease,*

Poverty (2014). She is completing a book with Michael Walton on forms of citizenship among the urban poor and is continuing with her long-term interest in understanding philosophical texts in Sanskrit that bear on anthropological issues.

DIDIER FASSIN is James D. Wolfensohn Professor of Social Science at the Institute for Advanced Study. His books include *When Bodies Remember: Experience and Politics of AIDS in South Africa* (2007), *The Empire of Trauma: An Inquiry into the Condition of Victimhood* (with Richard Rechtman, 2010), *Humanitarian Reason: A Moral History of the Present* (2011), and *Enforcing Order: An Ethnography of Urban Policing* (2013). His most recent project explores how immigrants, refugees, and minorities are treated in France.

MICHAEL M. J. FISCHER is Andrew W. Mellon Professor in the Humanities, Anthropology, and Science and Technology Studies at Massachusetts Institute of Technology. He is the author of *Iran: From Religious Dispute to Revolution* (1979), *Anthropology as Cultural Critique* (with George Marcus, 1999), *Debating Muslims: Cultural Dialogues in Postmodernity and Tradition* (with Mehdi Abedi, 1990), *Emergent Forms of Life and the Anthropological Voice* (2003), *Mute Dreams, Blind Owls, and Dispersed Knowledges: Persian Poesis in the Transnational Circuitry* (2004), and *Anthropological Futures* (2009). Most recently he has been teaching and doing fieldwork on biopolis and the life sciences initiative in Singapore.

GHASSAN HAGE is Future Generation Professor of Anthropology and Social Theory at the University of Melbourne. His books include *White Nationa: Fantasies of White Surpemacy in a Multicultural Society* (1998), *Against Paranoid Nationalism: Searching for Hope in a Shrinking Society* (2003), and *Arab-Australians Today: Citizenship and Belonging* (2002). His current projects include a study of the experience and circulation of political emotions concerning the Arab-Israeli conflict among Muslim immigrants in the Western world and a reconception of inter-cultural relations.

CLARA HAN is an assistant professor in the Department of Anthropology at The Johns Hopkins University. Her research has explored issues of urban poverty, health, and violence in low-income neighborhoods in Santiago, Chile. Her publications include *Life in Debt: Times of Care and Violence in Neoliberal Chile* (2012), and a forthcoming handbook entitled *An Anthropology of Living and Dying in the Contemporary World*, co-edited with Veena Das.

MICHAEL JACKSON is Distinguished Visiting Professor of World Religions at Harvard Divinity School. His books includes *Allegories of the Wilderness: Ethics and Ambiguity in Kuranko Narratives* (1982), *At Home in the World* (1995), *In Sierra Leone* (2004), *Excursions* (2007), *The Palm at the End of the Mind* (2010), *Life within Limits: Well-being in a World of Want* (2011), *Road Markins: An Anthropologist in the Antipodes* (2012), *Between One and Another* (2012), *Lifeworlds: Essays in Existential Anthropology* (2013), *The Other Shore: Essays on Writers and Writing* (2013), and *The Wherewithal of Life: Ethics, Migration, and the Question of Well-Being* (2013). His is also the author of three novels, a memoir, and seven volumes of poetry.

ARTHUR KLEINMAN is the Esther and Sidney Rabb Professor of Anthropology at Harvard University. He is the author of *Patients and Healears in the Context of Culture: An Exploration of the Borderland Between Anthropology, Medicine and Psychiatry* (1980), *Social Origins of Distress and Disease: Depression and Neurasthenia in Modern China* (1986), *The Illness Narratives: Suffering, Healing and the Human Condition* (1988), *Rethinking Psychiatry: From Cultural Category to Personal Experience* (1988), *Writing at the Margin: Discourse Between Anthropology and Medicine* (1995), and *What Really Matters: Living a Moral Life Amidst Uncertainty and Danger* (2007).

MICHAEL PUETT received his Ph.D. from the Department of Anthropology at the University of Chicago and is currently the Walter C. Klein Professor of Chinese History at Harvard University. He is the author of *To Become a God: Cosmology, Sacrifice, and Self-Divinization in Early China* (2004) and co-author, with Adam Seligman, Robert Weller, and Bennett Simon, of *Ritual and its Consequences: An Essay on the Limits of Sincerity* (2008).

BHRIGUPATI SINGH is an Assistant Professor in the Department of Anthropology, Brown University. He has recently completed a book manuscript titled "Poverty and the Quest for Life: Spiritual and Material Striving in Contemporary Rural India" (forthcoming 2014). He is currently beginning a new set of projects: a book of essays with the working title "What Comes After Postcolonial Theory?" and an ethnographic research project on religious and secular forms of healing for psychic tensions and disorders in urban north India, specifically focusing on anxiety disorders as a window into contemporary India.

nature of, 284, 285; electrification and, 287–92; eventual, 286; philosophy of performative utterances and, 303; repetitions of, 282; securing of, 304; space of, 295; words and, 298, 299

evidence, of others' experiences, 261

evil, 260

examples, as basis for arguments, 256

exchange: ethnographic, 266–67; shadow dialogues and, 263–66; social, 257

excuses, Austin on, 283

existentialism, 42, 48n1

experience: cross-cultural, 257; ego and, 268; structure of, 262–63

expression: action and, 281, 288, 293, 304; in first meetings, 258; fragility of, 282–86, 300; of inner experiences, 262; in public sphere, 294; spatial, 268. *See also* inexpressibility

exterior, exteriority, 257, 269

Fa Hsien, 213

Faizieh Seminary, 197

Falsafi, Sheikh Muhammad-Taghi, 196–97

Fanon, Frantz, *The Wretched of the Earth*, 67

Fassin, Didier, 7, 16–17, 72, 167

fathers: ritual role reversal of, 228–30; role of in early China, 218–20, 227

fear, of being known, 258

felicity and infelicity, of performative utterances, 282–83, 299

feminism, feminists, 201, 202

Fernandez, James, on occult, 38

fieldwork, 12, 245, 257, 280; hierarchy of, 103; philosophy and, 30, 107; theory and, 27

film, films, 198, 281, 282

Fischer, Michael M. J., 6; on anthropology, 21–22, 115; *Debating Muslims*, 202

Flory, Stewart, 215

flux, concept of, 108

force: politics and, 10; violence as, 243

forgiveness, 301

Fortes, Meyers: *African Political Systems*, 8–10; on Tallensi, 39, 41

Foucault, Michel: biology and, 16; biopolitics and, 54–59, 65, 69, 70; Dumézil and, 168; lexicon of, 53; as philosopher, 1, 159; regimes of power and, 95; on subjects, 104; "Theatrum Philosophicum," 162; "What Is an Author?" 99–100; *Will to Knowledge*, 55

France, 1, 67, 167, 193, 210; French Revolution and, 56, 92n2

freedom, 7–8; in communication, 263; as concept, 3; determinism and, 39; Lévi-Strauss on, 14

Freud, Sigmund, 49n5, 210, 213; on desire, 46; on mystery, 278n17; on transience, 94–95

Friedlander, Eli, on Benjamin's notion of aura, 293

friendship, friends, 78–79, 85, 215n1, 258

future, duration and, 237, 247

gay, as term, 199

Gaza Massacre, 64

Gaza Strip, Israeli invasion of, 64

gaze, object of, 258

Geertz, Clifford, 14, 27, 94, 109, 111; on anthropology, 50; on Balinese view of time, 221–22

gender, 280, 281, 300, 304n2

genealogies of thought, 160, 162

generativity, as concept, 13
genre, role of, 266
Germany, 191
gestures, 258
Gharb, 260
ghosts, 220, 224–29
globalization, anthropology and, 4
gods, goddesses, 224–26
Goffman, Erving, on imaginary figures, 295
Good, Byron, 210, 212, 215
Good, Mary Jo, 210, 212, 215
Goodman, Nelson, on plurality of worlds, 5–6
gossip, 79–81, 191
governance, 257
grammar, philosophical, 269, 305n3
Greeks, philosophy and politics of, 57, 180–81, 213–14
Greenblatt, Stephen, on artists, 102–3
Groddeck, Georg, on "it," 49n7
Guattari, Félix, 97, 108–13, 159–61, 180–81; *Anti-Oedipus*, 163; ethnography and, 104; on philosophy, 50, 51; on schizophrenia, 166–67; *A Thousand Plateaus*, 163, 186n5
Guayaki, 108–10
gui, 224, 225
Gupta, Sanjeev, 293–95, 303, 305n4; electrification of Punjabi Basti and, 287–92

Habermas, Jürgen, 206, 265
habit, 7–8, 20, 143
habituation, 257
habitus, 17, 143; Bourdieu and, 8, 142–46, 150–54; dispositionality and, 148–49; eavesdropping as, 139; *illusio* and, 155; reality and, 150–52

hadith, 199
Hafez, 199, 200
Hage, Ghassan, 7–8, 17, 67; on anthropology, 23
Halbwachs, 57–58, 244–45
Hamadsha, 258, 259, 262–63
Han, Clara, on biology, 18
Hansen, Miriam B., 305n5
Hardiman, David, *The Coming of the Devi*, 176
Harkis, 266–67, 277n12
heart: epistemologies of, 257; knowledge of, 260; Moroccan understanding of, 276n7
Hedayat, Sadegh, 211
Hegel, G. W. F., 162, 174, 214, 277n11
Heidegger, Martin, 200, 205; on being-with, 269–70; Bourdieu on, 141; on *Dasein*, 276n5; *die Griechen* and, 214; habitus and, 153; Iranian philosophers and, 201; Kleinman on, 15; on others, 21, 274; philosophical anthropology and, 25n1
Heraclitus, 92n7
Heran, François, on habitus, 143
hermaphroditism, 203
Herodotus, 213, 214
Herzfeld, Michael, ethnographic biography and, 33
hexis, as Aristotelian notion, 144, 146, 150
hijrah (sanctuary), 241
Hinduism, 298, 299, 302; Holi, 177; mythology of, 186; philosophy and, 213 politics and, 179; Sanskritization and, 176; spirits in, 172; Thakur Baba and, 173
Hinton, Alex, 208
Hinton, Devon, 208
HIV/AIDS: in Iran, 206, 209; in South Africa, 58

insults, public, 299

intensities: concept of, 23, 160, 183

intention, intentionality, 5, 259, 260, 262, 294

interiority, 257, 269

interlocution, interlocutor, 256, 260, 264, 269, 273

interpretation, modes of, 256, 257

intersubjective, intersubjectivity, 114, 258, 268, 273

interviews, 289–90

intimacy, 78, 83, 270, 281

intuition, 258, 261, 284

Iran: cultural politics of, 200; HIV/AIDS control in, 206, 209; homosexuality in, 199; Jews in, 206–7, 212; melancholia of, 191–92; revolution of (1977–79), 190, 195, 196, 205, 208, 209; philosophers of, 201, 215; psychiatry in, 209–10; refugees from, 189–90; return of Khomeini to, 197; transformation moments of, 194–95; transsexuals in, 201, 203–5

Iran-Iraq War, 193, 209

Iraq, U.S. invasion of, 68

irony, 295

Islam: charity and, 75; in China, 131; debate in, 202; Hinduism and, 179; humanism and, 198; thought embodied in, 4

isolation, 263

Israel, 206; in *Precious Life*, 60–61, 64–68, 70

Jackson, Michael, 15, 20, 22; *In Sierra Leone*, 102

Jahanbeglu, Ramin, 206

James, Henry, 14; *The Wings of the Dove*, 26n7

James, William, 17, 125, 134, 215n1; on divided self, 127; human condition and, 136n1; Kleinman and, 119, 127–29, 136n4; "The Ph.D. Octopus," 137n6; *A Pluralistic Universe*, 253n1; *Pragmatism*, 253n1; *Principles of Psychology*, 128, 132, 253n1; psychology taught by, 120; on religion, 129–31; *Talks to Teachers*, 128; on truth, 32; *The Varieties of Religious Experience*, 128–32; *The Will to Believe*, 128

Jami, 199

Jankélévitch, Vladimir, *Henri Bergson*, 253n1

Jannati, Ahmad, Ayatullah, 204

Jinn, 172, 175

Johnson, Galen, 92n7

Judaism, Jews: charity and, 75; in Iran, 206–8, 212; philosophy and, 213

Jung, Carl, 200

Kabbah, Tejan, 33

Kafka, Franz, 195

Kalabari Ijo, 41

Kant, Immanuel, 15, 25n1, 141, 211, 213

Karimi-nia, Hojjat ul-Islam Muhammad Mahdi, 204

karma (action), 297, 298

Khatami, Muhammad, 196, 209

Khawlan, 241, 248

Khomeini, Ruhollah Mostafavi Musavi, Ayatullah, 197, 201, 203–4, 206–7, 217n, 217n119

kindness, 71, 79, 83–84, 89–90; Christianity and, 81–82

kinship, 10, 29, 32, 77, 285, 301

Kiraads, 164, 177

Kleinman, Arthur, 15, 215; biological norms and, 17; *Deep China*, 131; divided self and, 18; on theory, 22

Kleinman, Joan, 15, 121–26, 129

Wittgenstein, Ludwig, 20, 21, 69, 213, 215, 215n1; anthropology and, 25; Cavell on, 284–85; on ethnographic fieldwork, 27; Kleinman on, 15, 123; on moral philosophy, 280; noncritical differences and, 4; on other minds, 261, 269; on philosophical grammar, 305n3; *Philosophical Investigations*, 69; on rules, 7; solipsism and, 276n5
women, 300–303; as candidates for office, 198; as caregivers, 127; in family courts, 203; in films, 282; functioning of household and, 280; gossip and, 79; in La Pincoya, 77; poverty programs and, 91; power of, 43; suffering of, 282
words, 298, 299, 300–303
work, Kuranko on, 30–31

World Health Organization, 206
World Social Forum, 172
World War I, 193
World War II, 211
worlds, 4–6, 22, 261, 263

Yacoubi, Ahmed el, 262
Yaka, ethnography of, 47
Yazd, Iran, 188, 191, 192–95, 197
Yeats, William Butler, 260
Yemen, tribal conflict in, 234, 241–43
Yemeni Civil War, 244
Yoruba, 39–40

Zerstreuung, 192
Zeydabdi-Nejad, Saeed, 198
Zionism, 206–7
Zoroastrianism, 200, 205, 216n7